T0328819

ECONOMIC PRINCIPLES OF LAW

Economic Principles of Law applies economics to the doctrines, rules and remedies of the common law. In plain English and using non-technical analysis, it offers an introduction and exposition of the 'economic approach' to law – one of the most exciting and vibrant fields of legal scholarship and applied economics. Beginning with a brief history of the field, it sets out the basic economic concepts useful to lawyers and applies these to assess the core areas of the common law – property, contract, tort and crime – with particular emphasis on their doctrinal structure and remedies. This is done using leading cases drawn from the birthplace of the common law (England and Wales) and other common law jurisdictions. The book serves as a primer to the wider use of economics which has become increasingly important for law students, lawyers, legislators, regulators and those concerned with our legal system generally.

CENTO VELJANOVSKI is Managing Partner of Case Associates; IEA Fellow in Law and Economics; Associate Research Fellow, Institute of Advanced Legal Studies, University of London; Visiting Fellow, Law and Economics Centre, Australian National University; and Affiliate, Interdisciplinary Centre for Competition Law and Policy, Queen Mary College, University of London. Dr Veljanovski was the first economist appointed to a lectureship in a law department at a British university and has written many books and articles on industrial economics, economic reform, and law and economics. He also serves on the editorial boards of several journals, including the *UK Competition Law Reports* and the *Journal of Network Industries*.

ECONOMIC PRINCIPLES
OF LAW

CENTO G. VELJANOVSKI

Case Associates

iea

The mission of the Institute of Economic Affairs is to improve understanding of the
fundamental institutions of a free society by analysing and expounding the role of markets
in solving economic and social problems. It pursues its mission through publications of
monographs, books and a journal, Economic Affairs; and through seminars and
conferences. Much of the IEA's output is available free of charge on www.iea.org.uk

CAMBRIDGE
UNIVERSITY PRESS

CAMBRIDGE UNIVERSITY PRESS
Cambridge, New York, Melbourne, Madrid, Cape Town,
Singapore, São Paulo, Delhi, Tokyo, Mexico City

Cambridge University Press
The Edinburgh Building, Cambridge CB2 8RU, UK

Published in the United States of America by
Cambridge University Press, New York

www.cambridge.org
Information on this title: www.cambridge.org/9780521695466

First published 2007

A catalogue record for this publication is available from the British Library

ISBN 978-0-521-87374-1 Hardback
ISBN 978-0-521-69546-6 Paperback

To Annabel, Liddy and Tom

Contents

Figures

Tables

Preface

The economics of law is an exciting enterprise and a permanent feature of legal scholarship and economics. But it has made limited inroads in Europe especially if one removes the areas of economic regulation and competition law. One of the reasons for this is the unavailability of texts that cover the subject in a non-technical way and without a focus on North American law. *Economic Principles of Law* has been written to redress this imbalance, and to show that the economics of law has equal applicability to the more than fifty common law jurisdictions outside North America, in this case that of England and Wales.

This book is an introduction to the economics of law for the law student and non-economist. It is neither a legal nor economics text. It is a sampler of the way that economics has been used to examine law generally, and in particular the core areas of the common law – property, contract, tort and crime. The economics used rarely goes beyond the first several chapters of an undergraduate economics text covering basic supply and demand analysis. The discussion is deliberately non-technical except for the odd lapses into diagrams (reflecting the author's professional self-indulgence) which are relegated to boxes separated from the main text which may be skipped without destroying the discussion or sowing seeds of doubt in the readers' mind. At the suggestion of one reviewer I have added an economics glossary to assist the lawyer further in dealing with any jargon.

The decision to write this book was sparked by a casual comment by Richard Epstein of the University of Chicago during a visit to London several years ago. The decision did not fully take into account the effort required to read and digest the mountain of literature on the subject, nor the effort required. As Winston Churchill remarked 'writing a book is an adventure. To begin with it is a toy and an amusement. Then it becomes a mistress, then it becomes a master, then it becomes a tyrant. The last phase is that just as you are about to be reconciled to your servitude, you kill the monster and fling him to the public.' I couldn't agree more

Early drafts of various chapters benefited from the valuable and critical comments of Hugh Beale, Peter Cane, Stephen Copp, Roger Halson, Gary Sturgess, three anonymous referees selected by the Institute of Economic Affairs, and four by Cambridge University Press. My thanks to all of them. I also received encouragement from Philip Booth, the Editorial Director of the Institute of Economic Affairs and Chris Harrison, Commissioning Editor for Cambridge University Press. Last but by no means not least my warm appreciation goes to Rebecca Sarker and Annabel Veljanovski for their editorial assistance.

London,   CENTO VELJANOVSKI
September 2006

Table of cases

CHAPTER I

Introduction

> courts in their function of declaring, clarifying and extending legal
> principle must take seriously the economic consequences of what they
> are doing.[1]
>
> Hon. Mr Justice Kirby, 1998

The common law is the core of the British legal system and that of over
fifty other countries originally under British rule. It is one of the great legal
systems, and one whose basic principles provide the core of today's open
and free societies (table 1.1). Yet the common law is also an enigma – seen as
an engine of wealth maximisation and economic freedom but at the same
time opaque and shrouded in ambiguity. It is in the eyes, even of many
lawyers, incoherent, irrational and frequently 'unfair'. In this, some say, it
shares many of the attributes of the marketplace.

This book applies economics to the common law. It has two objectives –
to show how economics has and can be used to study law; and to undertake
specific analyses of the common law of property, contract, tort and crime.
It is an example of the general field known as 'the economic approach to
law', or simply 'law and economics'. This is the application of economic
theory and quantitative techniques to analyse the rules and remedies of the
law.

The economic approach to law is not confined to areas of law which have
economic objectives but to all areas of the common law and beyond to family, crime and procedural law and institutions, where the economic content
is not apparent. In essence, the economic approach uses 'the principle of
economic efficiency as an explanatory tool by which existing legal rules and
decisions may be rationalised or comprehended'.[2] Clearly, the economic

---

[1] M. D. Kirby, 'Comparativism, Realism and the Economic Factor – Fleming's Legacies', in N. J.
Mullany and A. M. Linden (eds.), *Torts Tomorrow: A Tribute to John Fleming*, North Ryde, NSW:
LBC Information Services, 1998.

[2] J. L. Coleman, 'Efficiency, Exchange and Auction: Philosophical Aspects of the Economic Approach
to Law', 68 *California Law Review*, 221–249 (1980) 221.

Table 1.1 *Common law countries*

Africa	Asia	Pacific rim	Caribbean	Europe	North America	South America
Botswana	Bangladesh	Australia	Anguilla	Cyprus	Canada	Falkland Islands
Ethiopia	Hong Kong	Fiji	Bahamas	Ireland	United States	Guyana
Ghana	India	New Zealand	Barbados	England		
Kenya	(Iran)	Papua New Guinea	Belize	Wales		
Lesotho	Israel	Samoa	Bermuda			
Malawi	Malaysia	Solomon Islands	British Virgin Islands			
Namibia	(Nepal)		Cayman Islands			
Nigeria	Pakistan		Dominica			
Sierra Leone	(Saudi Arabia)		Grenada			
South Africa	Singapore		Jamaica			
Tanzania	Sri Lanka		Montserrat			
Tonga	Thailand		St Kitts & Nevis			
Uganda	(United Arab Emirates)		St Vincent & Grenadines			
Zambia	(Yemen)		Trinidad & Tobago			
(Zimbabwe)			Turks & Caicos Islands			

Note: Countries in brackets have mixed legal origins which include elements of the common law. In addition there are a number of smaller jurisdictions which have mixed legal systems with a strong common law element such as Jersey, and Guernsey (Norman/common law), Isle of Man and others

Source: World Bank, *Doing Business in 2004 – Understanding Regulation*, New York: Oxford University Press, 2004; T. H. Reynolds and A. A. Flores (eds.), *Foreign Law Current Sources and Legislation in Jurisdictions of the World*, Fred B. Rothman & Co., 1991.

approach will not be admissible in court, nor is it used or referred to by judges. However, it can assist in understanding and critically assessing the law. Instead of relying on judicial analysis and reasoning it offers the legal scholar an external framework which cuts through judges' linguistic formulations. Concepts such as choice, tradeoffs, incentive effects, **marginal analysis**, externalities, the **cheapest cost avoider** and others form the basis for each discussion of the law. It treats different areas of law in terms of the same functional categories, such as distinctions between care and activity levels, alternative and joint care, accidents between strangers and those occurring in situations where the parties have a pre-existing 'exchange' relationship. It provides a treatment of the common law which holds out the prospects of the unification of its disparate areas.

A SHORT HISTORY OF LAW AND ECONOMICS

Over the last four decades the economics of law has penetrated mainstream legal[3] and economics scholarship and has grown in scale, scope and depth. In the USA, where the subject was first developed, law and economics is now well established in most universities, and has recently spread across Europe and to civil law countries.[4]

The 'birth' of the modern law and economics movement can be dated around the early 1960s with the founding of the *Journal of Law and Economics* under the editorship of Aaron Director and then Ronald Coase.[5] Two articles during this period stand out as establishing the foundations of the economic approach to law – Ronald Coase's 'The Problem of Social Costs'[6] (hereafter, 'Social Costs'), and Guido Calabresi's 'Some Thoughts on Risk Distribution and the Law of Torts'.[7]

'Social Costs' is both the most cited and most misunderstood article in law and economics.[8] This is because it develops a number of themes.

---

[3] In the UK, see H. G. Beale, W. D. Bishop and M. P. Furmston, *Casebook on Contract*, 4th edn., London: Butterworths, 2001; B. A. Hepple and M. H. Matthews, *Casebook on Tort*, 3rd edn., London: Butterworths, 1985; D. Harris, D. Campbell and R. Halson, *Remedies in Contract and Tort*, 2nd edn., London: Butterworths, 2002; A. Clarke and P. Kohler, *Property Law – Commentary and Materials*, Cambridge: Cambridge University Press, 2005.

[4] Such as the Masters Programme in Law and Economics, involving participating universities of Bologna, Hamburg, Rotterdam Ghent, Hamburg, Aix-en-Provence, Haifa, Linköping/Stockholm, Madrid, Manchester and Vienna, see www.frg.eur.nl/rile/emle/universities/index.html. R. van den Bergh, 'The Growth of Law and Economics in Europe', 40 *European Economic Review*, 969–977 (1996).

[5] E. Kitch (ed.), 'The Fire of Truth: A Remembrance of Law and Economics at Chicago, 1932–1970', 26 *Journal of Law & Economics*, 163–234 (1983).

[6] 3 *Journal of Law & Economics*, 1–55 (1960).   [7] 70 *Yale Law Journal*, 499–553 (1967).

[8] Coase's paper is the most cited paper in US law journals, outstripping the next most cited article by two to one. F. R. Shapiro, 'The Most-cited Law Review Articles Revisited', 71 *Chicago Kent Law Review*, 751–779 (1996).

To the economist, 'Social Costs' was an attack on **market failure** as a framework for policy analysis. Economists habitually then used, and still now use, the 'perfectly competitive market' as a benchmark to evaluate economic performance. Market failure was declared if there was any departure from the perfectly competitive market outcome, and the economist would, as almost a reflex action, recommend corrective government intervention. The problem was that this assumed that governments operated costlessly to promote a more efficient outcome. The absence in the economists' world of government failure clearly biased the analysis in favour of state intervention. To paraphrase one wag, only economists could be so naïve as to believe, let alone make practical policy recommendations based on the assumption that politicians and public servants were efficient. 'Social costs' stated that one had to take into account the costs, distortions and inefficiencies of laws and government before any policy conclusions could be drawn.

Coase's criticisms were, however, more profound. He noted that there was an implicit assumption at the heart of the textbook model of perfect competition – that of zero **transactions costs**. Under this assumption, markets simply could not fail – and, further, neither could capitalism, central planning, socialism and regulation. All were equally efficient. The economists' model provided no basis for selecting laws, or an economic system, or even to explain why firms exist or why capital hires labour and not the other way around.

Coase's conclusion was even stranger. He went on to show that irrespective of the legal position regarding harmful activities (more technically called external costs or effects) – such as pollution and road accidents – the law did not affect the efficient solution or market operation. This became known as the '**Coase Theorem**'. It states that in a world of zero transactions costs – where the costs of using the marketplace are negligible – the initial assignment of property rights does not affect the efficient allocation of resources. Thus whether or not the law holds a polluter liable for the harm, the efficient outcome would be generated by the gains from trade available to the parties, not the legal position. That is, market failure was not possible under conditions of perfect competition.

The Coase Theorem generated considerable controversy,[9] striking some as implausible, others as a tautology and many as irrelevant. But its central

[9] Stigler describes the initial reception to the Coase Theorem by twenty Chicago economists at a drinks party at Aaron Director's home: 'We strongly objected to this heresy ... In the course of two hours of argument the vote went from twenty against and one for Coase to twenty–one for Coase. What an exhilarating event!' G. S. Stigler, *Memoirs of an Unregulated Economist*, New York: Basic Books, 1988.

message was initially misunderstood. It was not that law was irrelevant but that it was relevant to an economist because of the existence of positive transactions costs: a factor that economists had hitherto ignored. Coase went on to advocate the study of the world of positive transactions costs, not as many of his critics seemed to believe a perfect frictionless model. Coase's emphasis on transactions costs, a theme he had developed nearly three decades earlier in his analysis of the firm,[10] spawned a variety of economic approaches to institutional analysis such as the New Institutional Economics (NIE),[11] and related work on **principal–agent problems**, and incentive analysis.

Coase's 'Social costs' also attracted the interest of lawyers because it used the English and US laws of trespass and nuisance to illustrate the effects of legal rules when transactions costs were negligible, and when they were prohibitively high. To many, Coase appeared to argue that common law judges had a better grasp of economic theory (and reality) than most economists. The legal notion of reasonableness which runs through the common law was, suggested Coase, possibly a closet version of the economists' concept of **(Kaldor–Hicks) efficiency**. Thus at one level the Coase Theorem was interpreted as a market manifesto; at another that the common law had an underlying economic logic, a theme that would be picked up by later scholars. That Coase did not actually say nor mean either mattered little to the debate which subsequently raged.

In 1967 Guido Calabresi's article 'Some Thoughts on Risk Distribution and the Law of Torts'[12] was the first systematic attempt by a lawyer to examine the law of torts (essentially, accident law) from an economic perspective.[13] Calabresi, a professor at Yale Law School but who had economics training, argued that the goal of accident law should be to 'minimise the sum of the costs of accidents and the costs of preventing accidents'.

Calabresi refined this axiom into a normative theory of legal liability (tort) and public policy for accident losses: the costs of accidents could be minimised if the party who could avoid the accident at least cost was made liable for the loss – i.e. pay compensation. This Calabresi called

---

[10] R. H. Coase, 'The Theory of the Firm', 4 *Economica*, NS 386–405 (1937), reprinted in R. H. Coase, *The Firm, The Market, and The Law*, Chicago: University of Chicago Press, 1988.

[11] O. E. Williamson, 'The New Institutional Economics: Taking Stock, Looking Forward', 38 *Journal of Economic Literature*, 595–613 (2000); O. E. Williamson, *The Economic Institutions of Capitalism*, New York: Free Press, 1985; International Society for New Institutional Economics, www.isnie.org.

[12] 70 *Yale Law Journal*, 499–553 (1967).

[13] Mention should be made of P. S. Atiyah's *Accidents, Compensation and the Law*, London: Weidenfeld & Nicolson, 1970, which introduced the British law teacher and student to Calabresi's economics and was the first serious work by a British lawyer placing law in its wider social and economic context.

the 'cheapest cost avoider'.[14] His idea was simple, and easily illustrated. A careless driver collides with a pedestrian, inflicting expected damages totalling £200. It is discovered that the accident resulted from the driver's failure to fit new brakes costing £50. Clearly, road users and society as a whole would be better off by £150 if the driver had fitted new brakes: a sum equal to the avoided loss of £200 minus the cost of the new brakes, £50. If the driver is made legally liable for the loss – that is, she is required to pay the victim compensation of £200 should an accident occur – then she would have a strong incentive to fit the new brakes. A liability rule which shifted the loss whenever it encouraged careless drivers to fit new brakes would make the efficient solution the cheapest for the negligent motorist. The distinctive quality of Calabresi's work was to show the power of simple economic principles to rationalise a whole body of law, and to develop a coherent basis for its reform.

The fuse lit by Coase and fanned by Calabresi, ignited in US law schools with the work and views of Richard Posner in the 1970s. Beginning with his paper, 'A Theory of Negligence',[15] and refined in later articles and books, a new branch of the economic analysis of law was ushered in, one that the lawyer could use to analyse and rationalise the hotchpotch of doctrines which made up the common law. Posner's approach differed from Calabresi's normative analysis; his was a positive theory designed to 'explain' the common law. Posner advanced the radical and highly controversial thesis that the fundamental logic of the common law was economic; that its doctrines and remedies could be understood 'as if' judges decided cases to encourage a more efficient allocation of resources. If true, this would be a finding of great legal and empirical significance. The idea that economics could unlock the logic of the common law raised its profile among legal scholars, who were either attracted or repelled by the proposition.

Posner had shrewdly tapped into the primary reasons for the failure of economics to make inroads into legal scholarship – or, indeed, impress lawyers. It simply did not address the everyday questions that lawyers and law teachers dealt with. The question – Does tort deter accidents? – is of no importance to the law teacher, if the object is to explain and organise the court's decisions and reasoning. Put crudely, the lawyer and law teacher were apt to argue that if judges did not give economic reasons for their decisions, economic analysis of those decisions was not useful. It was

---

[14] G. Calabresi, *The Costs of Accidents: A Legal and Economic Analysis*, New Haven: Yale University Press, 1970.

[15] R. A. Posner, 'A Theory of Negligence', 1 *Journal of Legal Studies*, 28–96 (1972); W. M. Landes and R. A. Posner, *The Economic Structure of Tort Law*, Cambridge, MA: Harvard University Press, 1988.

clear that to introduce economics to law and lawyers it was necessary to show that it would help in understanding both legal doctrines and the law itself.

Posner not only brought the legal camels to water, but made them drink. His main contribution was to show that simple economic concepts could be used to analyse the law in the way that lawyers traditionally looked at their subject – that is to, 'explain' the rules and remedies of contract, property, criminal, family, commercial, constitutional, administrative and procedural laws. His text *Economic Analysis of Law*, first published in 1973 and now in its sixth edition, was and remains a *tour d'horizon* of the economics to law.[16] The view, which (now) Chief Judge Posner still firmly holds, is that:

> One of the major contributions of economic analysis to law has been simplification, enabling enhanced understanding. Economics is complex and difficult but it is less complicated than legal doctrine and it can serve to unify different areas of law. We shall demonstrate how economics brings out the deep commonality, as well as significant differences, among the various fields of . . . law . . . Economics can reduce a mind-boggling complex of statutes, amendments, and judicial decisions to coherence. By cutting away the dense underbrush of legal technicalities, economic analysis can also bring into sharp definition issues of policy that technicalities may conceal.[17]

Others were, and remain, unconvinced.

The 1970s and 1980s were the growth decades of the law and economics movement, at least in the USA.[18] Increasingly, North American legal scholars began to use economics to rationalise and appraise the law and by the 1980s the movement had firmly established itself as a respectable, albeit controversial, component of legal studies. In the USA many prominent scholars in the field (Bork, Breyer, Calabresi, Easterbrook, Posner and Scalia) were appointed judges, and economics – especially supply-side economics – was thrust to the forefront of the political agenda by reforming governments in both West and East.[19]

---

[16] R. A. Posner, *Economic Analysis of Law*, Boston: Little Brown, 1973; 6th edn., Gaithersburg, MD: Aspen Publishers, 2003.

[17] W. Landes and R. A. Posner *The Economic Structure of Intellectual Property Law*, Cambridge, MA: Harvard University Press, 2003, 10.

[18] W. M. Landes and R. A. Posner, 'The Influence of Economics of Law: A Quantitative Study', 36 *Journal of Law & Economics*, 385–424 (1993). This study finds that the influence of economics on US law was growing through the 1980s but that the rate of growth slowed after 1985.

[19] In March 1993 the *Journal of Economic Literature* published by the American Economics Association introduced 'Law and Economics' as a separate classification, formally recognising the field among economists.

LEGAL VS ECONOMIC REASONING

It will not surprise the reader to learn that lawyers and economists think in different ways. These differences explain both the resistance often encountered to the economics of law, and the contributions the latter can make.

The central difference between legal and economic reasoning is that lawyers look at the past, economists the future. This can be portrayed as a difference between the *ex post* analysis of lawyers concerned with rights, corrective justice and adjudicating disputes, and the *ex ante* or incentive analysis of economists. This distinction needs some explanation.

The lawyer typically begins with a dispute and a loss which has to be resolved. The approach is case by case and focuses on the distributive issue of how to (re)-allocate a given loss between the two or more parties to the dispute. Given this focus, and the professional skills that lawyers have to acquire, law tends to be seen through a narrow lens. There is no necessity to develop either a theory of law or a broad view of its social and/or economic effects. These are simply irrelevant to applying and to understanding the law. Moreover, the wider effects are not likely to be part of the lawyer's experience. If the law is successful in deterring wrongdoing, accidents or crime, it means that a legal dispute has been avoided. In short, successful laws mean less business for lawyers!

The economic approach differs from this practical process of applying law to cases. For the economist, the past is a 'sunk' cost. The economist does not view law as a set of rights and remedies but a system of incentives and constraints affecting future actions. As a consequence, the economists' primary focus is on the wider repercussions of the law on all potential litigants and individuals likely to find themselves in similar circumstances. To use Bruce Ackerman's description, the economic approach requires the lawyer to 'reconstruct the facts' to an earlier period before the dispute when the parties could have reorganised their activities.[20]

As an example, consider a careless driver who has knocked down and injured a pedestrian. The issue confronting the court involves a past event and a loss. This loss cannot, obviously, now be avoided, it can only be shifted by the judge. But the judicial shifting of losses has effects on future victims and injurers, either by altering their behaviour or their post-injury decision whether to litigate or settle the case out of court. Thus, while the lawyer will focus on the actions of the parties to an accident to allocate 'fault', the economist will examine the way that the court's decisions affect

[20] B. Ackerman, *Reconstructing American Law*, Cambridge, MA: Harvard University Press, 1984.

the accident rate, accident costs and the court's case-load. The economist is concerned with the effect that rules have on behaviour *before* the mishap.

THE COMMON LAW

It will strike the lawyer as odd, if not implausible, that economics can and indeed should be used to interpret law. This is particularly so since judges and the law rarely use economics or economic reasoning. It is almost unknown for an English judge today to draw on economics, although this was not unusual in cases in the nineteenth century.

One can understand that it may be useful to know as a policy matter what the effects, costs and benefits of different laws are and their alternatives, but not to interpret the law. The reason why this is possible and plausible lies in the nature of the common law – and, indeed, law itself.

Structure of the common law

Let us begin by describing the main features of common law adjudication.

First, it relies on private enforcement: that is, the parties to an accident or dispute must litigate their claims and fund the costs of litigation and out of court settlements.

Second, disputes are adjudicated by an independent judiciary in adversarial proceedings. The parties – known as the plaintiff but now called the claimant under recent reforms in England and Wales, and the defendant – must present their claim and defence, respectively, to the court. The burden of proof is placed on the claimant to establish that the alleged harm is on the balance of probabilities a legal wrong and it is for the defendant to counter these allegations. The proceedings are said to be adversarial, involving a legal 'contest' before a judge and contrast with most other European civil legal systems where the judge elicits the facts and questions the parties (known as an inquisitorial system).

Third, the common law offers a limited range of remedies which are confined to enforcing the parties' rights or compensating them for their losses. The typical remedy is compensatory damages, which aim to restore the claimant to the position he or she would have been in had the wrong not occurred. In more limited circumstances, the courts may offer an injunction to prohibit or force a party to do something or, in contract disputes, specific performance requiring the party to honour the contract. Courts cannot impose more general penal sanctions such as fines or imprisonment, and can only rarely impose damages in excess of a genuine pre-estimate of the claimant's losses (except in contempt of court).

Fourth, the common law often denies those harmed a remedy. It is generally based on a fault liability or other judgmental standard governed by the conduct of both parties. The law also often provides the defendant with a number of defences or excuses which allow him or her to avoid paying compensation. This means that the common law does not operate as a general (universal) compensation or insurance scheme.

Finally, because of the costs and uncertainty of litigation, an overwhelming proportion of legal disputes and potential cases are settled out of court or abandoned. The proportion of cases coming to court that are meritorious probably numbers a few per cent. That is, litigation is a last resort – or, as is now often said, the common law encourages 'bargaining in the shadow of the law'.[21]

To the above features must be added the way law evolves in common law legal systems. Common law is often described as judge-made law. This is something judges would dispute since they regard themselves as discovering already existing law which they apply to new fact situations. Nonetheless, the common law has evolved over centuries through the decisions of judges in individual cases. These cases – or, rather, the legal precedents they set – create a body of law which must be distilled from the written decisions of judges and, when distilled, must be applied to new cases with different facts. It is, to use a contemporary term, 'bottom-up law' created in an evolutionary and practical way to resolve disputes. This contrasts again with the civil law systems of the rest of Europe, which are based on legal codes devised by governments.

It is also the case that common law judges rarely state general principles of law. Common law has been described as a system of law which places a particular value on dissension, obscurity and the tentative character of judicial utterances so 'that uniquely authentic statements of the rule . . . cannot be made'.[22] The linguistic formulations used by judges such as 'duty of care', 'reasonable foreseeability', 'proximity', and 'reasonable care' have a chameleon-like quality. They are frequently used interchangeably, confusing lawyer and judges alike. The result is that the general principles of English common law are open-ended. '[T]he conceptual

---

[21] The expression is from R. Mnookin and M. Kornhauser, 'Bargaining in the Shadow of the Law', 88 *Yale Law Journal*, 950–997 (1979).

[22] B. Simpson, 'The Common Law and Legal Theory', in W. Twining (ed.), *Legal Theory and Common Law*, London: Blackwell, 1986, 17.

structure of tort law' declared Patrick Atiyah, 'is a disorganised and ramshackle affair'.[23]

Further, there is no general agreement as to the objectives of the common law, and its specific branches. Among lawyers the common law is seen as having three often conflicting objectives – corrective justice, distributive justice (compensation) and deterrence. At a formalistic level there can be little dispute that the common law appears for the most part to be concerned with corrective justice – i.e. 'rendering to each person whatever redress is required because of the violation of his rights by others'.[24] But corrective justice is an empty shell since it lacks a definition of rights or wrongs, although it does stress that much of the common law is concerned with reinstating those wronged to their original position. Few would claim the common law seeks to redistribute wealth in society. Nonetheless, many legal scholars and reformers have sought to assess the law in terms of its ability to compensate accident victims and those 'wronged'. The view that the goal of the common law is compensation is a half-truth. While the routine remedy at common law is compensatory damages these are provided only when there has been a violation of an individual's rights. Thus, like corrective justice this begs the question of how the rights and wrongs are determined. Finally, deterrence is often discussed as a goal of the common law. This sees the law's primary function as influencing conduct and deterring avoidable accidents, interference with property, crimes and other harms. Most legal texts mention this objective only to dismiss it as unsupported in law, and unlikely in practice.

By now enough should have been said to establish the central point and basis of the economic approach. The 'murkiness' of the common law means that the objectives of various legal doctrines and remedies, and their application, must be distilled and interpreted from a myriad of decisions and judicial formulations which lack an overarching structure or a stated justification. It is this that has allowed economics to be used both to interpret and explain the law, and as an aid of organising material to teach it.[25]

This still leaves the question how the forward-looking incentive analysis of economics can be married with that of legal reasoning. The answer lies in

---

[23] P. S. Atiyah, *Accidents, Compensation, and the Law*, 3rd edn., London: Weidenfeld & Nicolson, 1980, 35–36.

[24] R. A. Epstein, 'Nuisance Law: Corrective Justice and its Utilitarian Constraints', 8 *Journal of Legal Studies*, 49–102 (1979) 50.

[25] Benson takes issue with this claim, arguing that the common law differs from customary law as a result of intervention of the King who set up a subsidised court system and forced dispute resolution into the Royal Courts. B. L. Benson, *The Enterprise of Law: Justice Without the State*, San Francisco, CA: Pacific Research Institute, 1990.

one of the accepted objectives of the common law – deterrence. Deterrence is essentially incentive analysis: it treats the law as deterring undesirable activities and encouraging beneficial activities. The only way this can occur is if law generates incentives for individuals, firms, lawyers and others which alter their behaviour.

In many areas, this model of law is plausible. Take one of the core concepts of the common law – fault liability. This is not treated in law as indicating moral culpability but as an objective standard of conduct based on the actions of the parties. One is 'at fault' if the care exercised falls below that regarded by the court as objectively required in the circumstances. That is, liability is tied to actions. In other areas where there is strict liability the link between actions and legal outcomes seems absent. But as will be shown, it is often consistent with the view that the law can be explained, as if it seeks to influence actions to promote more efficient outcome.

It is accepted that deterrence as a legal theory or even objective of law has fallen out of favour among lawyers and policy-makers. The general view is that laws do not deter. Admittedly the evidence is scant, and not enough research has been done to support a deterrence theory, with the exception of crime (see chapter 6). However, the positive theory of law has a somewhat more modest objective. It seeks to explain the law and doctrines, and uses those laws as the data and evidence. Whether these same laws actually deter torts, nuisances and inefficient contract breaches is a separate though closely related matter. This is why the literature often draws a distinction between descriptive and effects versions of the positive theory of law. The former attempts to show that the law does have a plausible efficiency rationale, the latter that law has the predicted deterrent effects which can be empirically identified and quantified.

Why would the common law be efficient?

Other questions quick off the lips of sceptics are: 'Why would the common law be efficient?' and 'What is the evidence?'

'Economic' views of the common law are not new or novel. Historians and legal scholars have claimed in different ways that the common law has been influenced by economic interests and power. Changes to the common law during the industrial revolution from strict to fault liability are claimed to have been driven by the need to protect a nascent industry from a crushing liability from claims from an army of injured workers and a public choking on the fumes and smoke belching from iron foundries. This is sometimes attributed to England's class structure or pressures from a powerful capitalist elite influencing the law and opinions of judges. Others see the development of the common law in nineteen-century England as shaped by an intellectual elite influenced by the ideas of Scottish political philosophers and economists, such as Adam Smith and David Hume, who extolled the virtues of laissez faire and freedom of contract. The judgments, extra-judicial views of judges and the historical record provide strong support for this view in some areas of the common law.[26]

The modern law and economics literature offers several other, admittedly less than satisfactory, explanations why the common law might have an 'economic logic'.[27]

Richard Posner focuses on judges. He claims that common law adjudication (as described above) forces judges to restrict their attention to a narrow range of issues which are correlated with efficiency and wealth maximisation, and make it a poor method for large-scale wealth redistribution. Judges are required to reinstate wronged individuals and firms to their prior position in a process of case-by-case adjudication.[28] This necessarily implies acceptance of the pre-existing distribution of wealth and places a severe constraint on the use of the common law to redistribute wealth. This contrasts with the view of public or statute law which some of Posner's Chicago brethren see as largely focused on redistributing wealth. The central hypothesis of Stigler's 'capture theory'[29] and the economic theory of regulation[30] is that the primary 'product' transacted in the political marketplace is wealth transfers. The demand for legislation comes from cohesive coordinated groups, typically industry or special interest groups; the supply side of legislation is less easy to define given the nature of the political and legislative process. However, the state has a monopoly over one basic resource – the power legitimately to coerce. This leads to the view that because the legislative process is skewed to cohesive groups

---

[26] P. S. Atiyah, *The Rise and Fall of Freedom of Contract*, Oxford: Clarendon Press, 1979; D. Abraham, 'Liberty and Property: Lord Bramwell and the Political Economy of Liberal Jurisprudence – Individualism, Freedom, and Utility', 38 *American Journal of Legal History*, 288–321 (1994). For a sceptical view that the law transformed to redistribute wealth, see R. Epstein, 'The Social Consequences of Common Law Rules', 95 *Harvard Law Review*, 1717–1751 (1982).

[27] For a review of this literature, see P. H. Rubin, 'Why was the Common Law Efficient?', SSRN electronic library (2003).

[28] R. A. Posner, 'What do Judges Maximize?', in R. A. Posner, *Overcoming Law*, Cambridge, MA: Harvard University Press, 1995, chapter 3.

[29] G. J. Stigler, 'The Theory of Economic Regulation', 2 *Bell Journal of Economics & Management Science*, 3–21 (1971).

[30] R. Posner, 'Theories of Economic Regulation', 5 *Bell Journal of Economics & Management Science*, 22–50 (1974); S. Peltzman, 'Toward a More General Theory of Regulation', 19 *Journal of Law & Economics*, 211–240 (1976); G. Becker, 'A Theory of Competition among Pressure Groups for Political Influence', 98 *Quarterly Journal of Economics*, 371–400 (1983).

which can lobby effectively it tends overly to favour special interest groups. Indeed, this gave rise to a pessimistic assessment of the sustainability of a liberal and open society as politics and government became overwhelmed by special interest politics that undermined economic growth and social progress.[31]

Posner's evidence that wealth maximisation underlies the common law is his and others' findings that in a large number of areas common law doctrines can be explained 'as if' they are efficient. Others question the evidence used to establish the efficiency of specific rules.

A more rigorous economic literature has sought to link the development of the common law to the litigation/settlement process and the natural survival of efficient legal precedent. These so-called 'demand-side' models are driven by the motivations of individual litigants for more efficient law. The central hypothesis is that because inefficient laws by definition impose larger losses on the parties, they are litigated more often than efficient laws.[32] Thus even if judges are oblivious to economic efficiency as a legal goal they will have to adjudicate a disproportionate number of cases challenging inefficient laws, and over time the courts will tend to overturn inefficient laws more often than efficient laws. As a result the body of efficient precedent grows, even though at any one time a significant part of the law may be inefficient. That is, the efficiency of law evolves through a myriad of independent individual actions and not by design, as if – to use Adam Smith's metaphor – by some 'hidden hand'.

Subsequent work examining this hypothesis has found that not all roads lead to efficiency.[33] Indeed, the original model was a special case, and private litigation is just as likely to lead to inefficient as efficient law.[34]

Others have employed 'supply-side' models which focus on competition between different courts and other fora for the business of litigants. During the formative period of the common law in England, there was active

---

[31] M. Olson, *The Rise and Decline of Nations*, New Haven: Yale University Press, 1982.

[32] P. H. Rubin, 'Why is the Common Law Efficient?' 6 *Journal of Law & Economics*, 51–67 (1977).

[33] G. Priest, 'The Common Law Process and the Selection of Efficient Rules', 6 *Journal of Legal Studies*, 65–82 (1977); E. L. Priest, 'Selective Characteristics of Litigation', 9 *Journal of Legal Studies*, 399–421 (1980); W. M. Landes and R. A. Posner, 'Adjudication as a Private Good', 8 *Journal of Legal Studies*, 235–284 (1979); J. C. Goodman, 'An Economic Theory of the Evolution of Common Law', 7 *Journal of Legal Studies*, 393–406 (1979); R. Cooter and L. Kornhauser, 'Can Litigation Improve the Law without the Help of Judges?', 9 *Journal of Legal Studies*, 139–163 (1980); T. Eisenberg, 'Testing the Selection Effect: A New Theoretical Framework with Empirical Tests', 19 *Journal of Legal Studies*, 337–358 (1990).

[34] V. Fon and F. Parisi, 'Litigation and the Evolution of Legal Remedies: A Dynamic Model', 166 *Public Choice*, 419–433 (2003); K. Hylton, 'Information, Litigation, and Common Law Evolution', 8 *American Law & Economic Review*, 33–61 (2006).

competition between a large number of courts to attract litigants.[35] This competition occurred between civil and ecclesiastical courts and within civil courts between the Royal (King's Bench, Exchequer and Court of Common Pleas) and feudal, manorial, urban and mercantile law courts. All these vied for the business of litigants and their fees, and were free to adopt the remedies and rules of the others. Adam Smith in the *Wealth of Nations* (Book Five) offers one historical account:

> The fees of court seem originally to have been the principal support of the different courts of justice in England. Each court endeavoured to draw to itself as much business as it could, and was, upon that account willing to take cognisance of many suits which were not originally intended to fall under its jurisdiction. The Court of King's Bench, instituted for the trial of criminal causes only, took cognisance of civil suits; the plaintiff pretending that the defendant, in not doing him justice, had been guilty of some trespass or misdemeanour. The Court of Exchequer, instituted for levying of the king's revenue, and for enforcing the payment of such debts only as were due to the king, took cognisance of all other contract debts: the plaintiff alleging that he could not pay the king because the defendant would not pay him. In consequence of such fictions it came, in many cases, to depend altogether upon the parties before what court they would choose to have their cause tried; and each court endeavoured by superior despatch and impartiality, to draw to itself as many causes as it could. The present admirable constitution of the courts of justice in England was, perhaps, originally in great measure formed by this emulation which anciently took place between the respective judges; each judge endeavouring to give, in his own court, the speediest and most effectual remedy which the law would admit for every sort of injustice.

Zywicki[36] argues this created an incentive for each court to provide unbiased, accurate and quick dispute resolution, and the evolution of efficient law. Indeed, the adoption of the law of merchants (the Law Merchant) into the common law[37] was an important source of efficient law.

Another approach is to determine whether the common law has contributed to greater economic growth and wealth than other legal systems. Two major legal systems vie with each other across the world – the common law and the civil or code-based laws exemplified by France's Code Napoleonic. Hayek, for example, advanced the view that common law contributed to greater economic welfare because it was less interventionist

---

[35] H. Berman, *Law and Revolution: The Formation of the Western Legal Tradition*, Cambridge, MA: Harvard University Press, 1983.

[36] T. Zywicki, 'The Rise and Fall of Efficiency in the Common Law: A Supply-Side Analysis', 97 *Northwestern University Law Review*, 1151–1633 (2003).

[37] B. Benson, 'The Spontaneous Evolution of Commercial Law', 55 *Southern Economic Journal*, 644–661 (1989).

and better able to respond to changes than civil legal systems.[38] Tullock, on the other hand, has argued that the common law method of adjudication is inherently inferior to the continental European civil law system.[39]

Beginning with the work of Barro[40] and Scully[41] there have been a number of empirical studies of the impact of common and civil law (and other) legal systems on economic growth. These have found that, after controlling for other factors, economic growth has been greater in common than in civil law countries.[42] Scully identifies fifty-four countries with common law and ninety-four countries with civil or code-based legal systems.[43] His statistical analysis found that common law countries gave much greater protection of civil liberties than civil law countries, and that in politically open societies real *per capita* income grew at an annual compound rate of 2.5 per cent compared to 1.4 per cent for politically closed societies. According to Scully, 'societies where freedom is restricted are less than half as efficient in converting resources into gross domestic product as free societies. Alternatively, more than twice the standard of living could be obtained with these same resource endowments in these societies, if liberty prevailed.'[44]

Mahoney[45] studied the legal systems of 102 non-socialist countries over the period 1960–92. His empirical research found that economies in countries with common law legal systems grew 0.71 per cent (or one-third) faster, and the standard of living measured by real *per capita* income was 20 per cent greater than countries with civil law legal systems. Mahoney attributes the higher economic performance to a better-quality judiciary, as

---

[38] F. A. Hayek, *Law, Legislation, and Liberty: Rules and Order*, London: Routledge, 1973.

[39] G. Tullock, *Trials on Trial – The Pure Theory of Legal Procedure*, New York: Columbia University Press, 1980; G. Tullock, *The Case against the Common Law*, Durham, NC: Carolina Academic Press, 1997, reprinted in C. K. Rowley (ed.), *Law and Economics – The selected works of Gordon Tullock, Vol. 9*, Indianapolis: Liberty Fund, 2005.

[40] R. Barro, 'Economic Growth in a Cross Section of Countries', 106 *Quarterly Journal of Economics*, 407–443 (1991); R. Barro, *Determinants of Economic Growth: A Cross Country Study*, Cambridge, MA: MIT Press, 1997.

[41] G. Scully, *Constitutional Environments and Economic Growth*. Princeton, NJ: Princeton University Press, 1992. Other important recent contributions include Barro, *Determinants of Economic Growth*; R. Hall and C. Jones, 'Why do Some Countries Produce so Much More Output per Worker than Others?', 114 *Quarterly Journal of Economics*, 83–116 (1999); S. Knack and P. Keefer, 'Does Social Capital have an Economic Payoff? A Cross-Country Investigation', 112 *Quarterly Journal of Economics*, 1251–1288 (1997).

[42] There are other studies which show that property rights, markets and the rule of law contribute to higher economic growth: D. North and R. Thomas, *The Rise of the Western World: A New Economic History*, Cambridge: Cambridge University Press, 1973; N. Rosenberg and L. Birdzell, *How the West Grew Rich: The Economic Transformation of the Western World*, New York: Basic Books, 1986.

[43] Scully, *Constitutional Environments*.   [44] Scully, *Constitutional Environments*, 179.

[45] P. Mahoney, 'The Common Law and Economic Growth: Hayek Might be Right', 30 *Journal of Legal Studies*, 503–523 (2001).

measured by their integrity and efficiency, and greater security of property and contract rights in common law nations.

Other empirical research finds that common law systems are more efficient in governing finance markets,[46] more efficient in settling disputes[47] and have less interventionist laws which promote economic growth.[48] For example Djankov *et al.*'s study of the court procedures required to evict a tenant for non-payment of rent and to collect a bounced cheque in 109 countries found that the procedures were more formal and complex in civil law than in common law countries – judicial decisions took longer, were less consistent, honest and fair and there was more corruption.

This research gives some empirical credence to the view that while the common law may not maximise wealth it produces more wealth (efficiency) than other legal systems.

FURTHER TOPICS AND READING

- For an overview of the economics of law, regulation and competition, see C. G. Veljanovski, *The Economics of Law*, 2nd edn., London: Institute of Economic Affairs, 2006. Other accessible texts written for lawyers and non-economists but with US orientation are R. A. Posner, *Economic Analysis of Law*, 6th edn., Gauthersburg, MD: Aspen Publishers, 2003; D. Friedman, *Law's Order – What Economics Has to do with the Law and Why it Matters*, Princeton: Princeton University Press, 2000. More technical books with wider coverage include R. T. Cooter and T. S. Ulen, *Law and Economics*, 4th edn., New York: Pearson Addison Wesley, 2004; S. Shavell, *Foundations of Economic Analysis of Law*, Cambridge, MA: Harvard University Press, 2005. See also L. Kaplow and S. Shavell, 'Economic Analysis of Law', in A. J. Auerback and M. Feldstein (eds.), *Handbook of Public Economics*, vol. 3, New York: Elsevier, 2002, chapter 25.
- Very useful sources of discussion and reference on specific topics are found in two dictionaries of law and economics: P. Newman (ed.), *The New Palgrave Dictionary of Economics and the Law* (3 vols.), London: Stockton Press, 1998; and B. Bouckaert and G. De Geest (eds.), *Encyclopedia of Law and Economics*, Cheltenham: Edward Elgar, 2000, http://encyclo.findlaw.com/index.html. For an extensive list of texts and other works together with specialist journals, see the Select bibliography at the end of the book. There are also a number of web sites dedicated to law and economics, e.g. http://lawecon.lp.findlaw.com/.
- The first positive theory of the common law was advanced by US Judge Oliver Wendell Holmes, who stated: 'When we study the law we are not studying a

---

[46] R. La Porta, F. López-de-Silanes, A. Shleifer and R. Vishny, 'Law and Finance', 106 *Journal of Political Economy*, 1113–1155 (1998).
[47] S. Djankov, R. La Porta, F. López-de-Silanes and A. Shleifer, 'Courts', 118 *Quarterly Journal of Economics*, 453–513 (2003).
[48] *Doing Business in 2004 – Understanding Regulation*, New York: Oxford University Press, 2004.

mystery . . . the object of our study . . . is prediction.' O. W. Holmes, 'The Path of the Law', 10 *Harvard Law Review*, 457–478 (1897). Atiyah has suggested that English lawyers do not take a similar theoretical and social science approach to US lawyers because England never had a judge like Holmes. P. S. Atiyah, 'The Legacy of Holmes through English Eyes', 63 *Boston University Law Review*, 341–362 (1983). However, the differences are best explained by two other factors – first, in contrast to the USA, it is rare for academic lawyers to be appointed as judges in the UK. Second, law is an undergraduate degree in the UK whereas in the USA, Canada and Australia it is a postgraduate degree. The latter means that most law students have a strong grounding in another discipline such as economics. K. G. Dau-Schmidt and C. L. Brun, 'Lost in Translation: The Economic Analysis of Law in the United States and Europe', 44 *Columbia Journal of Transnational Law*, 602–621 (2006).

- There is a mountain of critical reviews and 'attacks' on the economics of law. One of the most thoughtful and entertaining is A. A. Leff, 'Economic Analysis of Law – Some Realism about Nominalism', 60 *Virginia Law Review*, 451–482 (1974). The main arguments and thrust of the early criticism are discussed in C. G. Veljanovski, 'The Role of Economics in the Common Law', 7 *Research in Law & Economics*, 41–64 (1985) and the less critical C. G. Veljanovski, 'Economic Theorising about Tort', *Current Legal Problems*, 117–140 (1985).

- The economics of law is not confined to the common law. There is a growing literature on and interest in applying economics to the civil law. U. Mattei, *Comparative Law and Economics*, Ann Arbor: University of Michigan Press, 1997; T. Kirat and B. Delfains (eds.), *Law and Economics in Civil Countries*, London: Taylor & Francis, 2003.

- A topic not given separate treatment here is the economics of the legal process and in particular litigation and out-of-court settlement. There is a large theoretical and empirical literature on the effects of legal fees on litigation rates and settlement sums, the way litigation affects legal rules and so on. R. D. Cooter and D. L. Rubinfeld, 'Economic Analysis of Legal Disputes and Their Resolution', 27 *Journal of Economic Literature*, 1067–1097 (1988). For an interesting comparative treatment of common and civil law legal procedures, see G. Tullock, *Trials on Trial – The Pure Theory of Legal Procedure*, New York: Columbia University Press, 1980.

- Does economics reveal the fundamental unity of the common law of contract, tort, property and crime? Some believe that simple economics has done so. Posner, *Economic Analysis of Law*, chapter 24; R. Cooter, 'Unity in Contract, Tort and Property: A Model of Precaution', 73 *California Law Review*, 1–45 (1985); W. D. Bishop, 'The Contract–Tort Boundary and the Economics of Insurance', 12 *Journal of Legal Studies*, 241–266 (1983).

CHAPTER 2

The economic approach

Incentives are the essence of economics.[1]

Edward Lazaar, 1998

The purpose of studying economics is . . . to learn how to avoid being deceived by economists.

Joan Robinson, 1955

Economics, declared John Maynard Keynes over half a century ago, does not offer a body of furnished conclusions, but an approach; a way of thinking about a problem. Its approach centres on choice, trade-offs, consequences, incentive effects, costs and benefits. As such, economics offers a different and external perspective on legal problems which can shed new insights, reveal new relationships and perhaps explain more clearly the law and its effects. The basic economics useful for legal analysis is set out in this chapter.

CHOICE AND SCARCITY

The economic approach to law can be defined as the application of economic theory – mostly price theory and statistical methods – to examine the formation, structure, processes and impact of the law and legal institutions.[2] It employs the same economics used to study the market for beans and steel to analyse law and institutions. This is known as price theory, the study of the interaction and behaviour of individual units in the economy – the firm, the consumer and the worker.

At the heart of price theory are the concepts of scarcity and choice. Without scarcity there would be no need to make choices since in a world of

---

[1] E. P. Lazaar, 'Incentive Contracts', in J. Eatwell, *et al.* (eds.), *The New Palgrave – A Dictionary of Economics, vol. 2*, London: Macmillan, 1998, 744–748.

[2] C. G. Veljanovski, *The New Law-and-Economics – A Research Review*, Oxford: Oxford Centre for Socio-Legal Studies, 1982; C. G. Veljanovski, *The Economics of Law*, 2nd edn., London: Institute of Economic Affairs, 2006.

inexhaustible abundance we would simply take what we wanted. Scarcity, whether in rationing the law or allocating resources, involves choice. Economics is the study of the choices of individuals in their roles as judges, people at risk, litigants and lawyers make in response to harms, to the law and other factors such as costs, income and so on.

Economic rationality

When faced with a choice, individuals and companies must have a basis for selecting between alternatives and how much of each alternative to consume or produce. Economists assume that individuals and organisations do this in a rational way. This is not only a workable assumption but also a necessary one if law is to guide behaviour and actions in a predictable way.[3]

The concept of **economic rationality** has a specific but simple meaning in economics. It means little more than that people prefer more to less and maximise net benefits, whether utility, wealth, or profits, as perceived by them.[4] This theory of rational choice is based on several assumptions – substitutability, marginality and fixed tastes and preferences:

- **Substitutability**   Goods are assumed substitutable for one another (or for money) at the margin. That is, there is a rate of exchange (price) between any pair of goods that will make an individual indifferent between them. This notion of a *trade-off* is central to economic reasoning.
- **Marginality or equi-marginal principle**   Maximising implies equalising marginal values and diminishing marginal returns – i.e. the *equi-marginal principle*. In any activity, to obtain the maximum utility or profit from the available resources they must be allocated so that the marginal benefit from the last unit of a resource devoted to each use is equal to its marginal costs. The maximisation principle thus not only requires that benefits exceed costs for each activity but that the level of each activity be at a point where the marginal costs of expanding the activity are equal to the marginal benefits. To illustrate the importance of marginal analysis consider the debate over whether more migrant workers benefit an economy and what is the optimal number. The debate typically proceeds

---

[3] Recent research suggests that *homo sapiens* displaced Neanderthal man because of their superior economic approach. This suggests that economic rationality may not only be in our genetic makeup but the very reason for our existence. R. D. Horan, E. Bulte and J. F. Shogren, 'How Trade Saved Humanity from Biological Exclusion: An Economic Theory of Neanderthal Extinction', 58 *Journal of Economic Behavior & Organization*, 1–29 (2005).

[4] The choices must also be *consistent or transitive* – i.e. if x is preferred to y, and y to z, then x will be preferred to z.

by claiming that on average migrant workers contribute more than they cost in terms of public services and pressure on a country's infrastructure. However, the correct (marginal) analysis is not to compare average contribution with average costs, as this gives the wrong answer. Suppose the first 100 migrants are bankers and entrepreneurs who each contribute £1 million annually while the last 5,000 migrants are unskilled manual workers contributing only £1,000 annually. If the average cost of supporting migrants is £20,000 annually, then using average figures (which in this case gives £21,000) indicates that migrants are net contributors. However, the truth of the matter is that that they are not because the high earners have distorted the figures and the last 5,000 migrants in fact are causing net losses. The optimal level of migration is not 5,100 migrants annually but only the first 100 migrants. As this shows, the *optimal* level of an activity which yields maximum net benefits is determined by comparing *marginal* costs and benefits, and not average costs and benefits.

- **Fixed tastes and preferences** The tastes and preferences of individuals are assumed to be given and stable. This assumption is related to, and implied by, rational behaviour. If tastes change over time or with past choices, preferences may not be consistent. For positive economics (what is), the assumption of given tastes prevents the economist from rationalising inconsistencies between theory and evidence by ad hoc claims that tastes have changed. For normative economics (what should be), changing tastes would render measures of economic welfare unreliable indicators of changes in individual wellbeing. For example, if tastes are constant one can say that a fall in the price of a good improves the economic welfare of consumers of that good. However, if at the same time consumers' tastes alter so that they come to regard the good as less desirable, it would not be possible to make such a statement.

The assumption of economic rationality is not without its critics. Indeed a whole field of behavioural economics, and behavioural law and economics, has dispensed with the assumption and investigated the implications of the cognitive limits to, and biases of, individual decision-making. This approach is not adopted here for the simple reason that if economic rationality is abandoned then economics loses much of its predictive and explanatory power and can easily collapse into a descriptive approach less likely to produce genuine insights.

The view adopted here is that the economists' assumption of rationality is best regarded not as a description of individual decision-making but as a way of identifying the predictable response of a group of individuals (markets) to changes in the factors which affect choice. As Cooter and Ulen put it, rationality should be viewed 'as an account of behaviour, not as an account of subjective reasoning processes'.[5] In this regard, economic man is 'marginal man' representing the change in a group's response. It thus allows for marked differences in individual responses – and, indeed, may accurately predict behaviour when individuals act irrationally or randomly.[6]

Incentive analysis

Economists believe that groups react in a predictable way to changes in the costs and benefits of the options they face. This incentive analysis is a direct implication of the rationality assumption. As a result prices and laws are primarily viewed as creating incentives which alter behaviour and outcomes.[7]

Incentive analysis is formalised by the economists' 'laws' of demand and supply. These are 'laws' in the sense that they describe observed regularities in behaviour and outcomes. The 'law' of demand states that when the price of a good or service, increases, all other things equal, less is purchased. The proposition that when a good or service becomes more expensive, less of it will be consumed is not a radical one. The 'law' of supply states that as the price increases the quantity supplied increases, holding other factors constant. The interaction of demand and supply creates a *market* and a mechanism by which the plans and actions of those wanting goods and services, and those supplying them are brought into balance at any one time and adjust in a mutually consistent way over time.

The economic approach applies incentive analysis to all economic and non-economic activities. There is no reason not to suppose, and every reason to believe, that incentive analysis has wide application – in drug dealing, prostitution, crime, adoption, sale of body parts, marriage, divorce, illegal immigrants, armies and so on. Economics simply formalises the demand and supply conditions operating in these activities – and, most importantly, works through the implications of how changes in economic and

---

[5] R. Cooter and T. S. Ulen, *Law & Economics*, 4th edn., New York: Pearson Addison Wesley, 2004, 462.

[6] G. S. Becker, 'Irrational Behavior and Economic Theory', 70 *Journal of Political Economy*, (1962) 169–217, reprinted in G. S. Becker, *The Economic Approach to Human Behavior*, Chicago: University of Chicago Press, chapter 8.

[7] For a more detailed discussion of the differecne between legal and economic analysis, see Veljanovski, *The Economics of Law*, chapter 3.

non-economic factors affect the willingness of people to demand and supply the activity under consideration.

The economists' incentive analysis can be illustrated by the law restricting the speed limit. Most people, even those who would regard themselves as law abiding, break the speed limit from time to time. If there is no penalty, people will speed if the benefits they derive at the time exceed the likely costs in terms of the potential likelihood of an accident and its consequences to others and themselves. If a penalty is imposed, the costs of breaking the speed limit rises and, all things equal, we expect that fewer people will speed. Drivers will take into account not only the inherent risks, benefits and costs, but also the potential penalties – the fine, the loss of their licence, potential incarceration and the impact of a conviction on their insurance payments. As the penalties get greater, most people, even non-economists, would agree that less and less speeding will occur. More people will speed if the penalty is £10 than if it is £20,000! This is informal economic modelling.

In looking at the world in this way one is conscious of the fact that the 'price up/quantity demanded down' prediction may not apply to all, or even a large number, of people. If the penalty for speeding (or the price of bread) goes up 5 per cent or 10 per cent many people will simply take it in their stride and not modify their behaviour. If the courts mete out more severe punishment some, maybe many, criminals will simply go on as before. Does this undermine the economists' incentive analysis? Certainly not!

Incentive analysis does not assume that every individual reacts to a curb on his or her actions. Some will react by reducing their participation or cease altogether; others will not. But all that is required for, say, fines, to deter is that a subset of those who previously speed now decide not to, or to do so less frequently. To put it more graphically, criminals at the margin will be deterred by higher penalties; not the psychopath or deranged serial killer.[8] It is the reaction of some that generates the response predicted by the economists' rationality model: clearly, the greater the number sensitive to increases in fines or costs the greater the reaction.

It is often useful to know not only whether an increase in penalties or costs deters or reduces a particular activity, but by how much. A *quantitative measure* of the incentive effects of a change in price, cost or legal sanction is known as its **elasticity**. This measures the proportionate response to a 1 per cent increase/decrease in the price/cost/sanction. An elasticity of minus 1 (–1) would mean that a 1 per cent increase in, say, the penalty imposed

---

[8] For a clear statement of this, see M. Friedman, 'The Methodology of Positive Economics', in Friedman's *Essays in Positive Economics*, Chicago: University of Chicago Press, 1953; see also M. Blaug, *The Methodology of Economics*, Cambridge: Cambridge University Press, 1980.

on criminals leads to a fall (hence the minus) of 1 per cent in the number of crimes. A higher elasticity indicates greater responsiveness. For example, governments have been very skilled at taxing goods which have an inelastic demand (that are unresponsive to price increases) such as cigarettes, alcohol and petrol. This is because they appreciate that the reduction in demand as a result of the price increase will be small – people are either addicted to them (alcohol) or they are an essential input that is very difficult for people to substitute for (petrol).

BENEFITS AND COSTS

Economics uses the measuring rod of money to evaluate economic and legal outcomes. It thus places heavy reliance on assessing the costs and benefits of the law, considerations that will always be relevant when resources are limited. However, the relationship between monetary value, economic efficiency and economic and legal activity is a subtle one, frequently misunderstood. The underpinnings of the efficiency criterion or **cost-benefit criterion** are now set out.

Benefits: willingness to pay (WTP)

The economist is said to know the price of everything but the value of nothing (actually, it's a cynic). This could not be further from the truth – the economist is concerned equally with price and value.

Economic value or benefits are measured by the '**willingness-to-pay**' (**WTP**) of those individuals who are affected. That is, the economist's notion of benefit is similar to the utilitarian notion of happiness (utility) but it is happiness backed by WTP. Mere desire or 'need' is not relevant. WTP provides a quantitative indication of the intensity of individual preferences.

In many markets identical goods frequently sell for the same price to all customers. It follows that individuals with an intense preference for the good – those who would be prepared to pay more – receive a surplus benefit from their purchase which is not measured in the marketplace. This benefit is called the **consumers' surplus** – it is the difference between the maximum WTP and the sum actually paid for a good or service. It is the consumers' equivalent of 'economic profit' to the firm (the difference between revenues and costs plus a competitive return to capital). The concept of consumers' surplus provides a quantitative measure of the economic value of changes in prices and quantities of goods and services. The goal of an efficient economic system is to maximise the joint or total surplus of consumers and manufacturers, not the market price and not money profits (see figure 2.1).

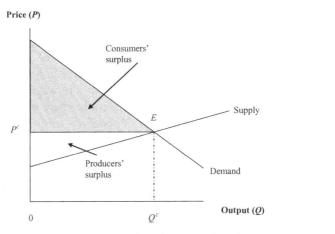

Figure 2.1 Demand, supply and consumers' surplus

The law of supply and demand is depicted in a simple diagram universally used by economists. The demand for a commodity, service or activity is shown as a negatively sloped line (labelled Demand) which shows that a greater quantity is purchased the lower the price. The supply line (labelled Supply) shows the *marginal opportunity cost* of producing an additional unit of the good. Usually the supply schedule is drawn with a positive slope, indicating increasing marginal opportunity costs arising from the growing scarcity of resources. Prices adjust until they 'clear' the market. In a competitive market the market clearing price equals the marginal opportunity costs of production determined by the intersection of supply and demand schedules (E), giving quantity produced and purchased of Q^c sold at price P^c. The market value of the goods sold is the price multiplied by the quantity (given by the rectangle $0 \ Q^C EP$). The consumers' surplus – which is the maximum willingness to pay of all consumers' above the price – is the shaded triangle under the demand schedule. The producers' surplus is the difference between the costs of production including a reasonable profit and the price. It is shown by the unshaded triangle below the consumers' surplus.

Valuing intangibles

It is frequently argued that many aspects of life cannot be reduced to a monetary value – the so-called 'intangibles' of freedom, life, love and the environment. It would be fruitless to deny that these are non-economic in character, and often not traded in a market. But it would be equally foolish to suppose that that point undermines economic analysis. Many intangibles can be valued in monetary terms, and are implicitly done so by individuals and society daily, and are frequently 'traded' in markets.

Take, for example, the choice of a job. It may be claimed that economists assume that people select jobs based on only the wage rate. This is not the case: an individual does not accept a job solely on the basis of its wage or salary but the whole package of benefits – fringe benefits, working conditions, prospects of advancement, security of employment, travel, the reputation of the firm or institution, its location and so on. As a result, people are willing to trade money for more of these attractive factors. Academic lawyers are thus paid substantially less than practising solicitors and presumably remain academics because the total non-monetary benefits exceed the higher salary that they could earn in practice. That is, there is a 'monetary equivalent' of the non-pecuniary employment benefits which, when added to the financial salary, gives us the money value of the total package of benefits received from employment in a particular job. Looked at another way, people are paying for the privilege of consuming these benefits in terms of the forgone salary. This is the way that economists value intangibles.

Take another more extreme example, but highly relevant to tort law – life and death. How can a monetary value be placed on a life? It certainly cannot be done (rationally) by asking the question: 'How much would you pay to stay alive?' Yet the law does this daily in the form of *ex post* damage claims for wrongful injury and death. These payments, viewed prospectively, can be seen as a 'price' for engaging in a hazardous activity – if you negligently injure a pedestrian you must 'pay' compensation that will make the victim whole. While the law may believe that this is possible, the economist does not.

The economist asks the more subtle question: 'How much are those at risk willing to pay to reduce the death rate to save one **statistical life**?' – i.e. a future life of an unknown member of the relevant group. To illustrate, suppose there are 1 million people at risk, each prepared to pay £1 to reduce the risk of death by 1 in 1 million. This means that collectively they would be prepared to pay £1 million to save a statistical life. This valuation of 'life' is derived from the willingness to pay for risk reduction and directly links economic value to the resource allocation issue of how much to spend on risk reduction.

By framing the question in this way the economist is able to adopt a consistent valuation procedure – one which takes into account the preferences of those whose lives are at risk and the society's ability to devote resources to reduce risks – i.e. buy more safety. This simple calculation provides guidance on the vexing question of 'How safe is safe?' or, in a legal context, 'What is reasonable care?' Optimal care is achieved when an additional pound, euro, or dollar spent on reducing risks saves a pound, euro or dollar in *expected* accident losses. 'Optimal' defined in this way means that many accidents are 'justified' – because they would be too costly to avoid. The corollary to this is that just as there can be too little care, there can be excessive care.

Costs as lost opportunities

It is widely believed that economists are obsessed with financial costs to the exclusion of all else. This is not the case. Accountants deal with financial costs and profits, not economists. Economists are concerned with choice and resource allocation and their definition of cost is radically *subjective* and intimately related to individual choices operating within the forces of demand and supply.[9]

It is important that accounting, financial, or historical costs are not confused with economic costs. If a house was bought for £100,000 six years ago and is now valued at £200,000, the **opportunity cost** of the house is £200,000 not the £100,000 initially paid. It is £200,000 because that is what it 'costs' the owner to remain in the house, as it could immediately be exchanged for £200,000, which reflects the house's next best alternative use. The economic cost of a thing is its value in the next best, forgone alternative use, or its opportunity cost.

Economists cost things in this way because they are concerned with the way resources are allocated and want to ensure that resources are allocated to their highest-valued uses.

This also applies to the notion of economic profit. If I produce a good, the costs of production not only reflect my outlay on labour, plant and materials but the profit I sacrifice in not using those resources in their next best use. It follows that the notion of economic costs makes an allowance

---

[9] For an excellent discussion of economic costs, see A. A. Alchian, *Economic Forces at Work*, Indianapolis: Liberty Fund, 1977, chapter 12.

for a 'normal' rate of return on capital or profit (for example, what could be earned by keeping the money in a safe bank account). This is why economists confusingly say that in perfect competition a firm earns 'zero' economic profits.

Costs vs transfers

Economists draw a distinction between a real opportunity cost or loss and a pure wealth transfer. A *real loss* is where there has been a net loss of consumers' and producers' surplus, whereas a *wealth transfer* is where a loss to one entity has been offset by an equivalent gain to another. The most obvious example of the latter is the gains and losses inflicted by competition. Competition maximises wealth in the sense that the losses to those who have been harmed exceed the gains to those who have gained (see discussion of pecuniary externality below). Thus while competition inflicts losses on different producers these offset one another, and are therefore not real or economic losses.

The distinction between a real cost and a wealth transfer can be illustrated by the impact of a Government (*ad valorem*) sales tax on a good. This tax generates revenues for the Government; each time a unit of the good is bought, wealth is transferred from consumers to the Government. This transfer is not a cost since the consumers' loss is the Government's (taxpayers') gain. These losses and gains net out – provided, of course, that the government does not waste the money on activities which generate negative consumers' surplus. However, the increase in the tax-inclusive price causes consumers to buy less of the now more expensive good. This has two effects: society saves the resources that would have otherwise been used to produce the lost output (a gain), but loses the consumers' (and producers') surplus above these (marginal) costs of production. It is this lost economic surplus – which economists refer to as the 'deadweight loss' – that is the real economic cost of the tax: it is the inefficiency generated by the way the tax distorts consumption decisions.

By casting the problem in this way it should be immediately obvious that this 'cost' is not registered in the marketplace as such. The real cost of a tax, law, or any other policy that distorts prices in an economy is given by the value of the output not produced and consumed. Thus the valuation of economic costs and benefits must often proceed on the basis of counterfactual or 'but for' analysis – 'but for' the specific law in question what would have been the costs and benefits? As shown below, and which should be obvious from this example, financial costs – even those based on market prices and objective cost data – do not necessarily measure these economic costs/losses.

Time value of money: discounting and interest

Benefits and costs are often spread over time. It is therefore necessary to adjust future costs and benefits falling in different periods by the *time value of money*, either the interest rate or discount rate. A dollar received or paid in ten years' time is worth less than a dollar in the hand today. This is because humans have a finite life and prefer present consumption to future consumption.

One measure of the time value of money is immediately grasped by most – the future value of money invested today. The interest rate measures the trade-off between present and future deferred consumption in the form of a periodic interest payment. The simple interest rate gives the percentage annual return on a capital sum on the assumption that past interest payments are not reinvested. Compound interest pays a periodic return on both the capital sum and past interest payments accrued in each period – i.e. the latter is interest on interest. The interest rate can be seen as the rate of exchange between present and future consumption.

The discount rate is used to calculate the present value of the early receipt of future income. That is, when one receives an initial sum in lieu of a future stream of income the initial sum must be 'discounted' to reflect its increased value because it has been received early. For example, a person injured by the negligence of a driver may be incapacitated, reducing his or her earning power for the remaining period of their life. If the court awards a lump sum payment it cannot simply tally up the expected future annual income for the remaining years and add them together to arrive at the lump sum figure. The court must take into account that the victim has received the money well before it would have been earned if they had not been injured. The stream of lost income in each period must thus be discounted (reduced) to take account of their receipt before it would otherwise have been earned. For example, if the annual discount rate is 10 per cent, then the value of the dollar to be received at the end of one year is 91 p today. This is because 91 p invested at 10 per cent for one year will return about £1 at the end of the year.[10]

---

[10] This is known as Discounted Cash Flow (DCF) analysis, which gives the sum of money in today's value as the present value. The formula for discounting to a present value figure is $PV = C_t/(1 + r)^n$, where PV = the present value of the cash flow, C_t = the net cash flow in year t, r = the discount rate and n = the number of years over which the cash is received.

Risk and uncertainty

Most decisions take place when the outcome is far from certain. In the face of risk and uncertainty individuals must make choices based on the fact that the outcome, while predictable, is uncertain. In order to do this they must form expectations about the array of future outcomes, assign probability estimates to them and maximise the expected value of these outcomes. In this way individuals are thus able to act rationally in the face of highly imperfect information about the future. Their choices will be *ex ante* efficient based on *ex ante* estimates of the costs and benefits.

Economists use various measures of risk. The most common is the **expected value** or **expected utility** approach. The individual is assumed to take into account the risks and maximise the weighted average returns or utility.

In practice, individuals will have different attitudes to risk. Some are indifferent, most averse and many enjoy risks in some areas of their lives (sport, bungee jumping).

A **risk neutral** person evaluates risk in terms of the *average* or *expected* outcome. Suppose such a person is confronted with a risky venture with the prospect of winning £100 with a 9 in 10 chance and £50 with a 1 in 10 chance, this would be evaluated as a prospect with an expected value of £95 = (0.9 × £100 =)£90 + (0.1 × £50 =)£5. A risk neutral individual maximises his or her expected wealth; this means that they would be indifferent to (treat as the same) a certain sum of £95 and the uncertain prospect with an expected value of £95.

On the other hand, an individual who is risk averse – that is, one who attaches disutility to financial uncertainty – would value the £95 with certainty more than the uncertain prospect with the same expected value of £95. They may regard only an expected value of £90 as the same as the certainty of £95, for the £5 difference represents the risk premium or monetary value of the disutility that the individual attaches to risk.

The trade-off between risk and wealth is a critical aspect of the economics applied to much of the law. It is central to the economics of tort, and to contract and criminal law. For example, one of the central propositions of the economics of law is the concept of a fine or **damage multiplier** that provides the correct *ex ante* incentives when there is uncertainty over the imposition of a fine or damages. To illustrate, assume that a crime inflicts a loss of £100. It may be assumed that a fine or damage payment of £100 would be sufficient to internalise the loss and create the correct incentive to deter the crime. This would confront the injurer with the social costs they impose. However, a fine equal to the loss would be efficient only if it were imposed with certainty. In the real world not all criminals are caught nor law-breakers fined. Thus applying our expected value approach (and assuming that criminals are risk neutral) would mean that the expected fine to which a rational criminal would react would be substantially less than the *ex post* loss. This is because potential offenders will note that there is a substantial probability that they will not have to pay the fine. To illustrate, assume that the conviction rate is only 20 per cent (i.e. a 1 in 5 chance) that the criminal is caught and pays the fine. The average criminal, knowing this, will conclude that he or she has a 20 per cent risk of being penalised and an 80 per cent chance of getting off scot free. The prospective fine is not £100 but the much lower sum of £20 (20 per cent of £100). If the £20 is compared to the harm inflicted of £100 it is clear that the criminal will not be deterred from committing the crime. From an economic perspective there is under-deterrence and an excessive level of crime. To resolve this problem the fine must be increased to take account of the less than complete enforcement. More specifically, the fine should be grossed up or multiplied so that the expected fine equals at least £100. In the example where the conviction rate was 20 per cent, an optimal fine should be five times the loss – or, more generally, $1/c$ times the loss, where c is the conviction rate. Thus one of the lessons of economics is that where detection and conviction are uncertain the optimal fine must be several multiples of the actual loss in order to induce optimal deterrence.

From this approach, several aspects of choice between risky alternatives can be extracted:

- Options are evaluated *ex ante* in the face of imperfect information. Thus the outcome is *ex ante* efficient.
- Risk averse individuals will pay to avoid risk. An individual who has **risk aversion** will regard a lower but certain sum of money as equivalent to a higher expected sum of money. Put differently, the individual is prepared to trade a certain lower sum for the uncertain higher one, the difference representing the *risk premium*.
- For risky options, *ex post* welfare will be different. If the riskless option is selected the individual gets £100. If the risky option with the same expected value is selected the individual may get £100 or, if unlucky, only £50. Thus the individual taking the risky option may be *ex post* worse off.
- Individuals will trade money for risk reduction. If by spending £10 they can increase expected wealth by £20 by lowering the risk they will make such an expenditure (see discussion of a statistical life above).

- In order for laws to be *ex ante* efficient and convey the correct incentive effects they must be multiplied by the inverse of the conviction or litigation rate so that, discounted, they equal the actual losses (see chapter 6 for further analysis).

The above concepts of costs, benefits and risk can now be brought together to define **economic efficiency**. An efficient outcome is where resources, goods and services are allocated to their highest expected valued uses assuming that existing technology is employed in a productively efficient manner.[11]

Economists work with two concepts of economic efficiency – **Pareto efficiency** and **Kaldor–Hicks efficiency**.

A Pareto efficient situation is one in which the welfare of one individual cannot be improved without reducing the welfare of others. This criterion, named after the Swiss–Italian economist Vilfredo Pareto (*Manuel d' Economie Politique*, 1909), is based on three ethical premises or value judgments:

1. That the individual is the best judge of his or her own welfare.
2. That the welfare of society depends on the welfare of the individuals that comprise it.
3. That any change that increases the welfare of at least one individual without diminishing the welfare of any other improves social welfare (the Pareto Criterion).

Pareto efficiency is thus a situation where all parties benefit, or none is harmed, by a reallocation of resources, goods, or assets, or a change in the law.

Pareto efficiency derives its appeal among economists because it is based on the individual and individual choice. The Pareto Criterion is said to be a 'weak' ethical criterion because it should command wide acceptance among those in Western society. At the same time the Pareto Criterion is an extremely restrictive tool for policy analysis. It precludes the economist making interpersonal comparisons of utility: the welfare of one individual cannot be offset or compared to that of another. Since even the most trivial policy change is likely to harm at least one person's interests, the economist will be left with little to say even on matters involving clear net gains.

---

[11] Productive efficiency (or X-(in)efficiency) is achieved when firms produce a given quantity of goods and services at minimum cost.

To circumvent this difficulty the concept of Kaldor–Hicks efficiency – also called potential Pareto improvement, hypothetical compensation test, cost-benefit analysis, wealth maximisation, allocative efficiency, maximisation of joint (producers' and consumers') surplus, or simply efficiency – is used. A policy is Kaldor–Hicks efficient if those that gain can in principle compensate those that have been 'harmed' and still be better off.[12] Or, more simply, the cost-benefit test that the economic gains exceed the losses to whomsoever they accrue. The major difference between Kaldor–Hicks efficiency and Pareto efficiency is that for the former the compensation is only hypothetical. Kaldor–Hicks efficiency thus appears to separate efficiency from the question of wealth distribution, and provides the theoretical underpinning for cost-benefit analysis.

Three qualifications

There are three major qualifications to the proposition that the pursuit of Kaldor–Hicks efficiency maximises wealth.

The second best

The first is the so-called theory of the second best. In economics, two wrongs can sometimes make a right. This arises in an imperfect world where some sectors persistently and irremediably deviate from the conditions required for efficiency. In such cases it is not necessarily correct that the pursuit of Kaldor–Hicks efficiency in one sector will generate a more efficient outcome overall. The constraints imposed by deviant segments of the economy must be taken into account to determine the optimal policy. This is known as the theory of the 'second best'.

Although the theory underlying the second best is complex, its logic is not. Suppose that there is an inefficient industry which prices its goods below marginal social costs because it inflicts uncompensated damage on local residents. Further, assume that for some reason the government cannot impose a corrective policy on the industry. From an economic efficiency point of view this industry's production is over-expanded. Given that this cannot be rectified it will no longer be efficient for all other sectors to price at marginal cost. For example, for products that are highly complementary to those of the inefficient sector it may be efficient to price these above

[12] N. Kaldor, 'Welfare Proposition of Economics and Interpersonal Comparisons of Utility', 49 *Economic Journal*, 549–552 (1939); J. R. Hicks, 'The Valuation of Social Income', 7 *Economica*, 105–124 (1940).

marginal cost so as to discourage their production – and, indirectly, the over-expansion of the inefficient sector.

An example may assist in explaining this concept better. Suppose a group of fishermen get together and organise a cartel to raise the price of fish and their incomes. A cartel is inefficient because it leads to a restriction of output and excessive prices and violates the condition that price equals marginal cost. On the other hand, fishing gives rise to a common property problem. Since no one owns the fish until caught and the oceans are an open access resource the fishing grounds will be over-exploited. This is also bad. Thus, in the normal case a cartel is bad but in this case it moves one closer to the efficient outcome since the cartel in maximising profits effectively asserts *de facto* ownership rights over the fishing resource and restricts fishing and entry. It may be argued that the cartel is not the best solution – fishing quotas or property rights are better – but the practical result is that in the absence of poorly enforced or absent property rights, the cartel achieves a better result even though it violates conditions of efficiency.

The theory of the second best suggests that piecemeal applications of the Kaldor–Hicks efficiency criterion may not maximise the allocative efficiency of the economy. The problem of the second best requires complex calculations and is not easy to determine. Economists often suggest that following first-best efficiency prescriptions is justified because this will increase the likelihood that the deviant sectors will eventually follow suit.

Efficiency–wealth distribution link
Economic efficiency and the distribution of wealth are interlinked. A Pareto efficient outcome implies that all the gains from trade have been exhausted *given the initial wealth and entitlements*. Economic efficiency is therefore a *technocratic principle of unimprovability*: there is no rearrangement of society's productive activity or allocation of goods and services that will improve the economic welfare of society *given the distribution of wealth* upon which market transactions or cost-benefit calculations are based.

It follows that if the wealth in society were redistributed then there would be a different Pareto (and Kaldor–Hicks) efficient allocation of resources. Each different distribution of wealth generates a different pattern of demand, a different set of prices and different production decisions. For example, if wealth is unevenly distributed there will be more Prada handbags and designer goods bought and produced than it if were more evenly spread.[13] From this it should be obvious that an efficient outcome may not be either a good or a just one.

Static vs. dynamic efficiency

Economists also distinguish between **static efficiency** and **dynamic efficiency**. Static efficiency assumes a given level of technology and production techniques. Dynamic efficiency takes account not only of how resources are allocated but the way they are used to expand the production possibilities and capabilities of the economy. This requires that the incentives and factors influencing investment, innovation and research and development (R&D) be taken into account.[14]

Earlier, a sharp distinction was made between the *ex ante* approach of economics and the *ex post* approach of law. This was an exaggeration. Many economic and legal problems arise from the temporal nature of economic activity and require a trade-off between *ex ante* and *ex post* efficiency. Several examples can illustrate this.

The *ex ante/ex post* distinction arises in the design and exploitation of intellectual property rights (IPRs). Strong patent rights may be required to give the appropriate incentives to invest in R&D (dynamic efficiency) but at the potential cost of reducing static efficiency if the legal protection allows the patent holders to charge excessive monopoly prices. Even if the patent does not confer a monopoly right as such, once the invention exists efficiency in consumption from the exploitation of the patented product requires that the price charged for the product be set to the marginal costs of manufacture and distribution, which would not give the inventor/developer any return on his or her R&D expenditure (see chapter 3 for further discussion). Allowing prices above marginal costs would reward investors, but lead to insufficient use of the invention.

Sports leagues provide another example. A sports league imposes restrictions on its clubs/teams, controls the entry of new clubs, restricts player transfers and often cross-subsidises clubs. Some of these restrictions and 'entry barriers' are necessary to create a league sport and to ensure that clubs are more evenly matched so that there is sufficient uncertainty over the outcome to make it attractive to spectators. The creation of a league

---

[13] There is also a technical failing of the Kaldor-Hicks inability to compensate losers. The application of a Kaldor–Hicks test may show that both the original and new situations are efficient when evaluated from the vantage point of the other. The reason for this difficulty is that if an 'efficient' legal reform is enacted and the losers are not compensated then they may be willing to pay the gainers to revert to the original state of affairs given the new price ratio ruling after the change, hence making both new and old situations Kaldor–Hicks efficient.

[14] W. J. Baumol, *The Free Market Innovation Machine*, Princeton: Princeton University Press, 2000.

with these restrictions is *ex ante* efficient. However, these barriers often give a league a monopoly position facing little competition from other leagues. This gives the organisation the 'market power' to impose restrictions that go beyond those necessary for the efficient conduct of the sport and which enable it to overcharge fans and close the league to other clubs.

The tension between static and dynamic efficiency is also found in contract law. This arises particularly when one party is required to make significant contract-specific investment. Take the following example. Assume a number of firms tender to build a railway line from a port to a coal mine. In awarding the contract to build and operate the railway, competitive forces will exist in setting the terms and obligations of both parties. However, after the contract has been awarded and the contractor has committed substantial investment in partially completing the rail line, the mine owner can seek to renegotiate the contract. The situation has been transformed from an *ex ante* competitive one to an *ex post* bilateral 'monopoly' because the contractor is 'locked-in' to the relationship where the actions of either party are not adequately constrained by competitive forces. One party is locked in to the relationship because it has committed capital which has a low alterative value outside the specific contractual relationship.

MARKETS

The concepts of a market and price play key roles in the economic approach. Even in areas where there is not an explicit market the economic approach will often analyse the subject by analogy with the market concepts of supply, demand and price.

A market is a 'place' or 'space' where individuals and firms trade goods, services and other legal claims for mutual gain. It is a decentralised form of social organisation. The centrally planned economy is the polar opposite case.

The principal function of markets is to coordinate the actions and decisions of 'buyers' and 'sellers' through the price mechanism. In a free market the price of, say, oranges clears the market so that there are no queues for oranges or warehouses full of unsold fruit. The market is said to be cleared at this price, or in *equilibrium*. This is due to the 'scissors' of supply and demand. If supply exceeds demand, the price will fall to encourage more purchases and discourage production; if demand exceeds supply, the price will rise to choke off the excess demand and encourage greater production.

The market price provides information to individuals in the economy. In a competitive market the price of a good or service equals the marginal opportunity costs of the resources used to produce it. The competitive price thus tells consumers the sacrifice in the alternative uses of resources that their consumption of an additional unit of the good entails. To know this, all the consumer needs to have is the price. Thus prices economise on information costs and signal to buyers and sellers in situations where both groups are relatively ignorant of the conditions of demand and supply. In this guise a market is a *discovery process* which produces and disseminates relevant information.[15]

Competition based on private property rights and freedom of contract ensures that resources gravitate to their highest-valued uses. It provides constant pressure to force prices down to the (long-run) marginal opportunity cost of production (and distribution). No one seller can raise price above the competitive level without losing sales to its competitors. If a seller seeks to raise the price above the competitive level, the buyer can obtain substitute performance from any one of a number of alternative sellers. Thus the price conveys to buyers and seller the costs that their consumption imposes, as measured by the cost in the next best alternative use, and this ensures that they are not consumed by those who value them at less than the resources that were exhausted in producing the good or service.

To use Adam Smith's metaphor, competition acts as an 'invisible hand' to guide individual self-interest to achieve a collectively desirable result. Where the competitive constraints are weak – as when there is a monopoly (see below) – firms and individuals gain economic power which they can use to manipulate prices to levels which exceed the marginal costs of production, and thereby generate an inefficient outcome.

In summary a competitive market:

- Ensures that individual firms do not have economic power – they are price and contract terms takers, not price and contract terms makers or fixers.
- The competitive price reflects the marginal (social) opportunity costs of production and distribution so that consumers know the real costs to the economy of their consumption decisions.
- Prices convey information in a world where buyers and sellers are relatively ignorant. They can rely on market prices to accurately reflect the opportunity costs of goods and services, without seeking to calculate the myriad steps in producing them.

[15] F. Hayek, 'The Use of Knowledge in Society', 4 *American Economic Review*, 519–530 (1945); T. Sowell, *Knowledge and Decision*, New York: Basic Books, 1980.

Markets can fail, just as government, institutions and the law can fail to achieve efficient and desirable outcomes. Market failure is typically defined as a departure from the efficient outcome of a perfectly competitive market. There are four main types of market failure useful in the economic analysis of law – monopoly, externality, public goods, and imperfect information.

Monopoly

Where firms are powerless the market is competitive; where they have the economic power to raise prices profitably (or impose other onerous terms) above the competitive level then the market is not competitive and does not generate a Pareto efficient allocation of resources. The economist's models seek to capture the absence or presence of 'economic power' of one (monopoly) or several (oligopoly or a cartel) firms. A monopolist charges more and gives less than a competitive industry. As a result, the price it charges exceeds the marginal opportunity costs of production and consumers demand less of the product than is efficient. The social costs of monopoly are the consumers' surplus on the output not produced by the monopolist action of creating artificial scarcity. Monopoly can also adversely affect the other terms of trade (such as product and service quality), reduce innovation, lead to excessive production costs (known as X-inefficiency), and encourage wasteful expenditure to enhance or protect its monopoly position (called **rent-seeking**). On the other hand, it is possible that monopolies are productively efficient because the market will not support more than one enterprise due to economies of scale and high infrastructure costs such as a water pipeline network, and they may be more dynamically efficient because they have a greater incentive to invest in R&D.

Externality

An externality – also referred to as a spillover, third-party effect, external cost/benefit, or divergence between private and social costs – 'arises where one person, in the course of rendering some service, for which payment is made, to a second person . . . , incidentally also renders services or disservices to other persons . . . of such a sort that payment cannot be exacted from the benefited parties or compensation enforced on behalf of the injured parties'.[16]

The concept of an externality has received a rare judicial exposition by Lord Hoffman in *Stovin* v. *Wise*, etc. which declined to hold local authority liable for a failure to take action which resulted in an injury by stating in passing that:

> In economic terms, the efficient allocation of resources usually requires an activity should bear its own costs. If it benefits from being able to impose some of its costs on other people (what economists call 'externalities') the market is distorted because the activity appears cheaper than it really is. So liability to pay compensation for loss caused by negligent conduct acts as a deterrent against increasing the cost of the activity to the community and reduces externalities.[17]

There are two general types of externalities used in legal analysis – **techno-logical externalities** and **pecuniary externalities**.

A technological externality has three essential features: (1) it is inciden-tal to some otherwise legitimate or productive activity; (2) which directly affects the utility or production function of a third party; and (3) is unpriced. Such externalities can either impose losses (such as pollution) or benefits (such as bees pollinating orchards). The presence of external benefits and costs implies that the activity giving rise to them is underexpanded and overexpanded, respectively, relative to the efficient level. This is because the cost structure of the externality-creating industry does not reflect the full social costs/benefits of its activities. It is why an externality is sometimes referred to as a divergence between private costs (which influence individual actions) and social costs (which determine economic efficiency).

Pecuniary externalities are pure **wealth transfers** which result from price changes rather than real, harmful effects reducing the economy's produc-tiveness or individuals' utility. They are a natural consequence of the inter-dependence of market relations. For example, if an individual enters the market for apples and places a large order, his additional demand will raise the price of apples to all other consumers, thus adversely affecting their wel-fare. Such third-party effects, however, do not cause a problem for market efficiency because the loss to existing consumers of apples due to the higher price is exactly counterbalanced by the gain to the producers of apples. The result is Pareto efficient because no side payments (bribes) could be arranged which, if paid to the new consumer, would make him refrain from entering the market for apples.

---

[16] A. C. Pigou, *The Economics of Welfare*, 4th edn., London: Macmillan, 1932, 183.
[17] [1996] 3 All ER 801, 809.

Public good

A public good is one for which consumption of the good by one individual does not detract from that of any other individual – i.e. there is non-rivalrous consumption. The classic example is defence – a standing army provides national defence for all its citizens! Public goods should not be confused with collectively or state provided or produced goods and services. A competitive market may fail to provide an efficient level of a public good because non-payers cannot be excluded, resulting in free riding and preference mis-revelation and the inability to appropriate an adequate return.[18] Because individuals cannot be excluded from consuming a public good, those with high valuations will tend to understate their preferences in the hope of being charged a lower price and others will 'free ride'. Moreover, since a firm cannot exclude non-paying customers these problems may sufficiently impair the ability to extract any payment that no or too little public goods are produced.

Asymmetric information

Imperfect information and ignorance can cause the market to operate imperfectly and consumers and others to make wrong choices and actions. Further, information has public good characteristics so that there may be market failure in its production since it is often difficult for those investing in better and new information to capture the financial returns; hence there is underproduction of useful information. In other cases, the central concern is **asymmetric information**, where one party is better informed than another, and to develop incentives for the revelation of this information to the other. The incentive effects of asymmetric information are of two kinds – **adverse selection** and **moral hazard** (the terms come from the insurance industry). Adverse selection is where one party cannot distinguish between two or more categories of goods, actions, or outcomes which have different costs, benefits, or risks, and therefore makes his or her choice based on the average values of them. As a result, choices are distorted and give rise to perverse incentive effects. In the insurance industry it is assumed that the insurer cannot distinguish good from bad risks and therefore charges both categories a premium based on the average risk of the

---

[18] P. A. Samuelson, 'The Pure Theory of Public Expenditure', 36 *Review of Economics & Statistics*, 387–389 (1954); P. A. Samuelson, 'Diagrammatic Exposition of a Theory of Public Expenditure', 37 *Review of Economics & Statistics*, 350–356 (1955).

pool.[19] As a result bad risks get cheap insurance and good risks get expensive insurance. The losses of the pool then begin to rise as good risks don't insure because of the expense and a disproportionate number of bad risks do because the premiums are cheap. This leads to market failure. Moral hazard is a situation where the availability of insurance or compensation to cover risks and losses, serves to increase the likelihood and magnitude of the losses. This arises because the action of the insured or victim cannot be monitored fully.

It is now possible to recast the economics above into a framework with which to examine the common law.

THE COASE THEOREM

One of the central theoretical propositions of economics is the Coase Theorem. This states, to use Coase's words:

Coase Theorem: '. . . the delimitation of rights is an essential prelude to market transactions; but the ultimate result (which maximizes the value of production) is independent of the legal decision', when transactions costs are zero.[20]

That is in a world where individuals can bargain costlessly, the law does not affect the efficient allocation of resources and, by implication, efficiency cannot be used to select the appropriate law.

The Theorem explained

The Coase Theorem can be illustrated by a factory belching out smoke to the discomfort and ill health of surrounding residents (see figure 2.2). Such pollution is the classic textbook example of a negative externality or external cost. The smoke inflicts uncompensated harm and losses on residents. As a result the polluting firm's profit and loss account does not register the losses to residents and the factory belches out excessive smoke relative to the efficient level. The market fails.

Or does it? Not according to the Coase Theorem. If the law does not protect residents from harm caused by pollution, the residents would have an incentive to negotiate with the polluting firm to secure reductions in the level of pollution. The firm would take into account the losses from pollution through the WTP of residents to reduce the smoke pollution

---

[19] M. Rothschild and J. E. Stiglitz, 'Equilibrium in Competitive Insurance Markets: An Essay on the Economics of Imperfect Information', 90 *Quarterly Journal of Economics*, 629–649 (1976).
[20] 'Social Costs', 27.

(sometimes pejoratively referred to as 'bribes'). If these payments are greater than the profits derived from polluting the firm has a financial incentive to reduce its output of smoke. Thus while all the costs of pollution are not recorded in the firm's profit and loss account, they are nonetheless taken into account and affect the firm's behaviour because reducing pollution further can be turned into revenues!

The Coase Theorem goes further, to state that if the residents have the legal right to block the firm from belching out smoke the firm will negotiate to allow smoke pollution. The polluting firm will seek out the residents and offer them a payment to put up with positive levels of smoke. The residents will be prepared to accept more smoke provided that the payment exceeds their valuation of the discomfort and damage caused by the smoke. For each increment in the level of smoke the parties will compare the firm's offer with the minimum sum the victims will accept until the point where the difference between the two is negligible for further increases in the smoke level – i.e. where there are no further net marginal gains from trade.

The Coase Theorem states that not only will the parties bargain but that the outcome will in both cases be Pareto efficient. The bargaining between the two stops at the efficient level of smoke because at that level of smoke the gains from trade are exhausted. When at the efficient level more or less smoke reduces wealth because the incremental loss to one party is greater than the incremental gain to the other. This is explained in more detail in figure 2.2.

The astute reader will recognise that the logic of the Coase Theorem rides on the rails of the opportunity cost concept – 'that a receipt forgone of a given amount is equivalent to a payment of the same amount'. Where the firm is liable or where it has been prohibited from inflicting further losses, the costs of pollution enter directly into its profit and loss account. In the case where it has no legal responsibility for the residents' losses, the factory still takes account of these at the margin in terms of the forgone payment from the residents to reduce the level of smoke a further unit. Thus regardless of whether the law requires the factory to compensate or does not, at the margin it bears the marginal social costs of the smoke damage.

Endowment effects

Of course, the law affects the distribution of wealth between the parties. If the law favours the factory it gets paid to reduce the level of smoke and does not have to pay the resident for the remaining losses. If the law favours the residents, they not only get fully compensated for their losses but do not

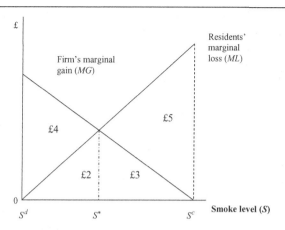

Figure 2.2 Bargaining under the Coase Theorem

The losses and gains from smoke pollution (or any other harm) are depicted by the two schedules.[21] The downward sloping schedule – labelled *MG* – shows the incremental profits to the firm for each additional unit of smoke. This is drawn with a downward slope to indicate that the marginal profit of progressively more smoke diminishes. Read from right to left, it shows the marginal costs (*MC*) to the firm of reducing the level of smoke. The marginal loss (*ML*) line is upward sloping, showing that as the level of smoke increases the incremental loss to residents rises. The efficient level of smoke is S^*, where marginal damage and marginal costs intersect and are equal. This is where a £1 increase in the *MG* to the firm is equal to £1 of damage from increasing the smoke level. This is efficient because it exhausts the gains from trade – higher or lower levels (to the right or left of S^*, respectively) increase the joint loss because one party's incremental gain/loss is higher than the others'. To show why S^* is the Pareto efficient level of smoke that would be negotiated by the parties the gains and losses have been labelled. The numbers represent the economic value of loss and gains of the areas shown – e.g. the upper left-hand triangle represents a gain of £4 to the firm. If the entitlement is assigned to the residents, then bargaining will begin from the far left with no smoke (S^d). The firm will compare its profits from more smoke with the compensation it must pay residents. At smoke level S^*, the residents suffer a loss of £2 and the firm a gain of £6 (=£4 + £2). Thus the firm would be willing to pay up to £6 while the minimum acceptable payment of the residents is £2. There are gains from trade as any sum greater than £2 will be acceptable to the residents. If the law leaves the residents unprotected then the bargaining begins from smoke level S^c. This is the level of smoke at which the firm maximises its profits, ignoring the residents' losses ($MG = 0$ where the MG schedule intersects horizontal axis). This level of smoke is inefficient – the firm's gain is £9 = £4 + £2 + £3 while the loss inflicted on the residents is £10 = £2 + £3 + £5. Thus total (joint) wealth is – £1. Clearly, the residents have an incentive to negotiate to reduce the smoke level-and can make payments to the firm which exceed significantly the profit it earns by being so smoky. Starting negotiations from S^c the residents would be prepared to pay up to £8 to reduce the smoke to the efficient level S^* while the factory would be willing to accept a minimum of £3. Again there are gains from trade to move to the wealth maximising level of smoke. This negotiated solution maximises wealth – net wealth is £2 compared with a net loss of £1. Thus irrespective of the assignment of legal entitlements, the parties will agree the wealth maximising level of harm S^*.

have to pay for reductions in the level of smoke (figure 2.3). However the interrelationship between the law, the distribution of wealth and efficiency is not as straightforward as suggested by the preceding discussion.

First, in situations of zero transactions costs the law will have neither allocative nor distributive effects if the parties are in coterminous exchange or a contractual situation. In such cases, a price already exists between the parties which will adjust to reflect (neutralise) the reallocation of costs/losses brought about by the law.[22] For example, if the neighbours are all employed by the factory then their wage rates can adjust to reflect the harm from smoke and changes in the law will not affect both parties' wealth. If the factory owner is not liable for his workers'/neighbours' losses they will demand a wage premium to reflect the expected losses caused by the smoke. Thus the losses will be reflected in the employer's costs as a higher wage bill. If the law changes so that the factory owner is now liable he will have to pay his workers a resident's compensation if he wishes to continue operating the factory. His profit and loss account now contains an explicit cost in payments or compensation claims for smoke damage. In a perfect Coasean world, the wage bill will fall to offset the larger compensation payments made by the factory owner. Thus while the law alters the wage

[22] H. Demsetz, 'Wealth Ownership and the Ownership of Rights', 1 *Journal of Legal Studies*, 223–232 (1972).

rate it does not alter the costs and wealth of the factory owners and his workers/neighbours. It also does not alter the costs and losses, level of smoke and/or employment levels.

The idea that wage rates will reflect smoke pollution may be thought as implausible. But, as discussed above, wage rates do reflect a number of non-wage factors including the job's location and the local amenities, including the environmental quality. Employers will have to pay more to their workers if the area is unattractive and suffers from pollution. Further, land and house values in polluted areas will be lower, all things considered. While the depressing effect of smoke pollution on land and house prices does not internalise costs on the polluting firm it does act to compensate workers who move into the area when the full extent of the pollution becomes apparent.

In other cases changes in the law may affect both the victims' wealth and the way they value their losses. Following Baker[23] a distinction can be drawn between rights that are valued and traded for commercial reasons because they increase industry profitability (productive rights) and those traded between individuals or neighbours where the harm (or benefit) affects utility levels (which Baker calls 'consumptive rights'). For consumptive rights the willingness to make or accept payments is governed by the impact of the harm on the individual's utility, and this may alter the economic value of the losses and hence the efficient solution.

Specifically, the residents in the above example may place a greater monetary value on their losses when they have the right to a smoke-free environment than when they have to pay the polluting firm to reduce the smoke. In economists' jargon, the residents' WTP will be lower than their willingness to accept (WTA) payment for equivalent reductions in harm. This has been called the wealth effect, ask/offer problem – or, as has been explained in a different way by behavioural economics, as the **endowment effect** or the framing effect.[24] We shall refer to this possibility generally as the endowment effect.

The endowment effect does not undermine the validity of the Coase Theorem (figure 2.3). The outcome of bargaining under zero transactions costs will still be efficient but different under the two legal regimes, because the valuation of losses alters. As stated above, the WTP will be less than the WTA so that the 'loss' will be higher and the efficient level of harm lower when the residents have the entitlement to a smoke-free environment.

[23] C. E. Baker, 'The Ideology of the Economic Analysis of Law', 5 *Philosophy and Public Policy*, 3–48 (1975).

[24] E. J. Mishan, 'Pareto Optimality and the Law', 19 *Oxford Economic Papers*, 247–287 (1967); P. Burrows, 'On External Costs and the Visible Arm of Law', 22 *Oxford Economic Papers*, 39–56 (1970).

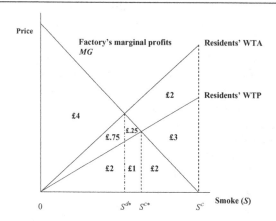

Figure 2.3 The Coase Theorem with endowment effects

Endowment effects give rise to two damage schedules – the willingness to pay for smoke reduction (WTP) (which assumes bargaining from S^c); and the willingness to accept payment to tolerate smoke (WTA) (with bargaining starting from zero smoke). As a result, the law affects the valuation of smoke damage, total wealth and the efficient level of smoke:

• The WTA is higher than the WTP valuation of the smoke.
• As a result, the efficient negotiated level of smoke will be lower when residents have the entitlement to a smoke-free environment than when they do not – i.e. S^{d*} less than S^{c*}.
• Total wealth varies under different laws. When residents have the entitlement to a smoke-free environment, maximum wealth is £4, whereas when the entitlement is assigned to the factory it is £5. These differences do not mean that the latter is preferred or that the former is inefficient. Both are efficient given the initial assignment of property rights because the smoke disamenity is valued differently.
• The distribution of wealth differs considerably under the two entitlement assignments. If the property right favours the factory, the residents not only suffer uncompensated losses of £2.75 (at the efficient level of smoke) but must pay the factory at least £5 to reduce the smoke. If the property right favours the residents, the residents' wealth position is very different. First, they are not out of pocket since they do not pay for the reduction in smoke (which they now value much more at £6.25 vs £3.00) and they are paid at least £2.75 or more given that the factory would be prepared to pay at least £6.75 for them to accept the efficient level of smoke.

However, even though the valuation of losses, the level of wealth and the efficient level of smoke varies with the law, the two outcomes are nonetheless efficient given the initial entitlements. Negotiation between the parties will in both cases continue until the gains from trade are exhausted.

It is not clear in practice how significant endowment effects are. The economists who first identified the technical possibility that consumers' surplus measures could differ regarded this 'a fiddling business not likely to be of much importance'.[25] Some recent research is equivocal[26] and suggests that the differences may be due to faulty survey techniques.[27] Other empirical research suggests that the difference between WTP and WTA may be substantial,[28] and hard to rationalise solely on the basis of wealth differences, the suggestion being that people simply treat real and opportunity costs very differently.

Transactions costs

The Coase Theorem assumes zero transactions costs. The law operates in a world of positive transactions costs so the nature, size and distribution of transactions costs is an important consideration.[29] The concept of transactions costs requires some clarification.

Transactions costs were defined by Coase as the physical costs of search, negotiation and contract formation and monitoring and policing costs. To quote Coase:

In order to carry out a market transaction it is necessary to discover who it is that one wishes to deal with, to inform people that one wishes to deal and on what terms, to conduct negotiations leading up to a bargain, to draw up the contract, to undertake the inspection needed to make sure that the terms of the contract are being observed and so on.[30]

[25] J. R. Hicks, 'The Four Consumer's Surpluses', 11 *Review of Economic Studies*, 31–41 (1943). See also A. M. Henderson, 'Consumers' Surplus and the Compensating Variation', 8 *Review of Economic Studies*, 117–121 (1941).

[26] E. Hoffman and M. L. Spitzer, 'The Coase Theorem: Some Experimental Tests', 25 *Journal of Law & Economics*, 73–98 (1982); E. Hoffman and M. L. Spitzer, 'Experimental Tests of the Coase Theorem with Large Bargaining Groups', 15 *Journal of Legal Studies*, 149–171 (1986).

[27] A. E. Boardman, D. H. Greenberg, A. R. Vining and D. L. Weimer, *Cost-Benefit Analysis – Concepts and Practice*, 2nd edn., Englewood Cliffs, NJ: Prentice Hall, 2001.

[28] J. L. Knetsch, *Property Right and Compensation*, Toronto: Butterworths, 1983, chapter 3.

[29] 'The world of zero transaction costs has often been described as a Coasian world. Nothing could be further from the truth. It is the world of modern economic theory, one which I was hoping to persuade economists to leave.' R. Coase, *The Firm, The Market, and The Law*, Chicago: University of Chicago Press, 1988, 174.

[30] 'Social Costs', 18.

There are two broad types of transactions costs – the physical costs of organising trades and costs arising from strategic behaviour.

Physical transactions costs are easy to define. These are the out-of-pocket and opportunity costs of individuals and firms searching out trades, and of forming, policing and enforcing contracts. These costs will be a function of the number of parties involved and the complexity of the bargaining and trades. They are most likely to be significant in mass-liability and pollution cases. Environmental pollution is often generated by a small number of firms but dispersed over a large number of individuals. Thus even though the aggregate loss is large the loss borne by each individual is relatively small. The physical transactions costs of organising the group and negotiating between them and the victims/injurers may be high and may exceed the individual losses. These will differ between the two sides such that the polluters may have lower physical transactions costs in organising the negotiations and payments. Where there are differential physical transactions costs the locus of legal liability will not have an effect since the cheapest negotiator will be motivated to initiate negotiations as long as there are gains from trade.

A less clearly defined set of costs arises from non-cooperative or strategic behaviour in both large- and smaller-number bargaining settings.[31] These arise from self-interested behaviour which prevents a Pareto efficient outcome even when the parties find it easy to negotiate.

Strategic bargaining problems exist in large-number cases in the form of **free rider** and **holdout problems**. In a mass-pollution case involving a large number of residents a free rider problem may occur. If victims are required to pay a polluting firm to reduce the level of harm they may not be able to agree a payment or schedule of payments which accurately reflects the group's true WTP. Each victim would reason that since any cutback will benefit them irrespective of their individual financial contribution and their refusal to contribute will not have a significant adverse effect on the final outcome, it is personally advantageous to offer a sum substantially below the real loss or refuse to participate at all. If all behave in this way, then the bargaining process does not guarantee an efficient outcome.

---

[31] Economists and other social scientists use game theory to explain behaviour when the parties act strategically in a small number of settings where they recognise that their actions are interdependent. D. G. Baird, R. H. Gertner and R. C. Picker, *Game Theory and the Law*, Cambridge, MA: Harvard University Press, 1994; R. Axelrod, *The Evolution of Cooperation*, New York: Basic Books, 1984. See generally, www.gametheory.net.

Alternatively, if the harm can be inflicted only if victims agree and are paid then a holdout difficulty may arise. Since in large-number cases an agreement must be obtained from all potential victims, each is effectively given a veto over the final agreement. This may cause some individuals to threaten to veto the agreement in order to extract a larger payment which, could, in the limit, preclude the agreement itself. There also may be people who decide that they do not want to allow any pollution or harmful activities

In small-number cases strategic bargaining problems arise when individuals understand that they can directly influence the terms of trade and, to use loose language, are more interested in their share of the pie than its overall size.

The problem is illustrated by the events in *Bradford* v. *Pickles*.[32] Mr Pickles was a farmer who had a spring flowing through his land which supplied water to the town reservoir operated by the Bradford Corporation (the local city authority). He threatened to cut off the water to force the Bradford Corporation to buy his land and make him a rich man. The Bradford Corporation refused to buy Pickles' land because it believed that they had the property rights to the water based on a Private Members' Bill (statutory law). However, the Court disagreed and upheld Mr Pickles' right to do what he wanted with the stream on his property. The law was thereby settled giving the property rights to the stream to Mr Pickles and he could now reasonably assume that the Coase Theorem should now spring into action. Unfortunately, the Bradford Corporation refused to deal with Pickles, treating him as a blackmailer. Pickles then made efforts to divert the stream to make his threats credible which instead sent him bankrupt. He was last seen sailing off to Canada and a new life![33]

As *Bradford* shows, the mere fact that there are only two parties to a potential negotiation does not guarantee that a wealth/utility maximising solution will result. There is a simple explanation why bargaining situations with very low physical transactions costs may not generate a Coasean solution.

The Coase Theorem is usually explained in terms of two or more persons directly negotiating over the level of harm and the terms of a contract. This bargaining process is represented as equivalent to the economist's notion of a market transaction. However, it is not. Markets do not involve bilateral but multilateral trading, where the terms and conditions are the outcome of impersonal market forces. In markets individuals are price (and contract term) takers, and not price makers. That is, they trade on the basis of given terms. In such markets bargaining power and manoeuvres are controlled by the availability of substitute performance. If you don't like the deal, you do one with someone else. In negotiations over 'bads' this is often not the case. If you don't like the prospective deal over reducing your neighbour's noise, you cannot walk down the street and do a deal with some other noisy person. The 'transaction' is involuntary in the sense that the harm creates the necessity to bargain and the victim (and injurer) cannot simply seek an alternative bargain as they could if they were purchasing a normal 'good': that is, there are limited possibilities in some areas for a competitive market in 'bads' (or external goods). Where individuals directly negotiate the terms of trade in bilateral transactions then the terms will be indeterminate (although the limits defined in principle) and they will act strategically. Thus they negotiate not against the basis of established terms but on assumptions about how others will act and vice versa, without there being any reference terms. As a result strategic bargaining problems can arise which may consume significant resources, and may in the limit preclude an agreement.

Ten Coasean tenets

From Coase's analysis ten principles or tenets can be derived relevant to the economics of law:

1. **Law as a factor of production** Law is treated as a factor of production in the sense that it is valued only for its ability to maximise wealth. That is, the economic approach is an instrumental approach which considers law as a means to an end. To many, this will be a controversial if not unacceptable view. Laws are also norms of conduct and reflect ethical and moral precepts. That they have these functions and attributes is not denied, only that for an economist legal rules and remedies have an instrumental function in furthering economic efficiency or other desired goals.

2. **The principle of reciprocity** The typical problem of law and economics is a reciprocal one. Activities clash; interests conflict, and to protect A's interest is to limit B's. 'The problem we face in dealing with actions which have harmful effects', states Coase, 'is not simply one of restraining those responsible for them. What has to be decided is whether the gain from preventing the harm is greater than the loss which would be suffered elsewhere as a result of stopping the action

which produces the harm.'[34] The principle of reciprocality that flows from the recognition of the conflicting demands on scarce resources is central to Coase's analysis.

3. **Causation is irrelevant**   The question 'who caused the harm or accident' is from an economic viewpoint largely irrelevant. Both parties 'caused' the accident in the sense that if one withdrew from the interaction there would have been no harm. Harm is the result of the confluence of two or more activities at a particular point in time. This contrasts with the approach of economists prior to Coase's analysis, who based their policy prescriptions on cost or benefit causation. The so-called Pigouvian approach, named after the English economist Arthur Cecil Pigou,[35] took the view that if A harmed B then the external costs were attributable solely to A – the costs followed the action. This, however, did not take a broader view since the better response may have been to remove B from being a victim. For example, a bridge collapses onto a house. It would seem impossible even to suggest that the victim is responsible or should be held liable for their losses since there is no way that he or she could have prevented the accident. But the issue is not the immediate question of who could have prevented the accident, but whether the losses would have been less had the house not been built so close to the bridge in the first place. This is not to dispute the importance of physical causation or moral precepts surrounding harm, only that from an economic viewpoint causation is not the key factor in determining whether the two incompatible activities should co-locate, and which party should take the avoidance action or bear the losses.

4. **Joint costs**   Since an accident can be viewed as jointly caused, the loss is to be regarded as the *joint cost* of both activities. The implication is that in order for a legal rule or remedy to achieve full efficiency both activities must, either explicitly or as an opportunity cost, bear the full costs of external harmful actions.

5. **Coase Theorem**   The Coase Theorem has already been explained in detail. It states that when transactions costs are negligible and the parties bargain cooperatively the outcome will be efficient. This does not mean that law is irrelevant since the initial legal rights or entitlements need to be set out. But once a legal basis for negotiations has been established, gains from trade will internalise all costs and benefits without laws specifically fashioned for this purpose.

[34] 'Social Costs', 1.
[35] A. C. Pigou, *The Economics of Welfare*, London: Macmillan, 1932, 4th edn.

6. **Cheapest cost avoider need not be the cost bearer**   The party who can most efficiently avoid harm need not be the one who bears the cost of doing so. This falls out of the Coase Theorem, which shows that the efficient outcome occurs irrespective of which party must pay for the reduction in harm. In the pollution example above, the party best able to reduce the level of pollution did so whether required to pay compensation or entitled to be paid to do so. That is, there was an economic symmetry between the polluter pays and victim pays approaches. Real-world examples of the latter abound: governments pay subsidies to industry to abate pollution and bounties to farmers to cut back excessive production. In this sense, economics has no notion of 'harm' and 'benefit', suggesting that these notions really reflect distributional values.

7. **Laws do not have distributive effects in exchange relationship**   Where the parties are in a pre-existing exchange relationship the law will neither affect the efficient outcome nor the relative wealth of the parties. This is because, changes in the law will be offset by adjustment in the price negotiated by the parties for the good or service associated with the harm. Thus laws that make employers liable for injuries to their workers will not increase employers' costs or workers wages because wages will fall to offset damage payments.

8. **Transactions costs are critical**   Markets fail and laws affect efficiency and the allocation of resources when transactions costs are positive. These transactions costs – the physical costs of contracting and the costs of strategic bargaining – are critical to specific assessments of the efficiency of the law. Several implications arise from the discussion of the source of transactions costs above:
   – where they are prohibitive there will be no negotiated solution
   – where they are negligible there will be an efficient solution
   – where the source of the transactions costs is strategic behaviour there may be an efficient outcome or not, even though the process of negotiation is relatively costless; indeed, paradoxically, in small-number cases low physical transactions costs can exacerbate the strategic bargaining problem.

9. **Efficient law requires consideration of the costs of intervention**   The costs of various solutions must be taken into account in determining efficient legal rules. That is, market transactions costs must be balanced against legal process or institutional costs. The latter can be defined as the costs associated with framing, implementing and enforcing non-market responses. The inclusion of these costs has a number of economic implications. First, markets fail only if the legal or regulatory

costs of the proposed solution are less than the market transactions costs which are responsible for the alleged failure.[36] Second, a specific common law rule is efficient if it achieves greater wealth than another or no common law rule. Thus if fault liability increases wealth more than no liability or strict liability then it is an 'efficient' law. Third, the common law will be inefficient if a statutory, administrative, or fiscal device such as no-fault compensation or traffic safety rules can increase wealth more.

10. **Institutions and laws arise to economise on transactions costs**
Another implication of the economic approach is the view that markets, contracts, law and institutions develop to economise on transactions costs, and are often an efficient adaptation to the presence of positive transactions costs.[37] Thus tort law is a cheaper way of internalising accident costs when accident injurers and victims find it too costly to bargain. The firm is seen as an institutional arrangement which substitute internal administrative controls for costly and inefficient arms'-length contracts and so on.

ONE VIEW OF THE COMMON LAW

Perhaps the second most cited article of the law and economics literature is Calabresi and Melamed's[38] framework for looking at a legal system. This provides a useful framework for organising the discussion of the various areas of the common law.

Calabresi and Melamed use three concepts – economic efficiency, **distributive justice** and **corrective justice**:
- economic efficiency has already been defined as maximising the difference between economic gains and costs or loss
- distributive justice is concerned with the fair distribution of wealth and income in society
- corrective justice is 'rendering to each person whatever redress is required because of the violation of his rights by others.'[39]

---

[36] C. Wolf, *Markets or Governments – Choosing between Imperfect Alternatives*, Cambridge, MA: MIT Press, 1988.
[37] R. H. Coase, 'The Theory of the Firm', 4 *Economica*, NS 386–405 (1937), reprinted in R. H. Coase, *The Firm, The Market, and The Law*, Chicago: University of Chicago Press, 1988, O. E. Williamson, *Markets and Hierarchies*, New York: Free Press, 1975.
[38] G. Calabresi and A. D. Melamed, 'Property Rules, Liability Rules and Inalienability: One View of the Cathedral', 85 *Harvard Law Review*, 1089–1128 (1972).
[39] R. A. Epstein, 'Nuisance Law: Corrective Justice and its Utilitarian Constraints', 8 *Journal of Legal Studies*, 49–102 (1979) 50.

Armed with these overarching normative concepts the common law and other legal systems is seen as involving two fundamental choices – how to *define* basic legal rights and how these are to be *protected*.

The first question is to set out a set of basic legal rights, claims and obligations that individuals have and upon which they can base their conduct and economic activity. The decision over entitlements can be based on economic considerations, historical events (war, expropriation, theft), or ethical principles. For example, efficiency considerations would suggest a minimum set of rights for the functioning of a free economy – such as private property, freedom to contract, free mobility of labour, capital, goods and services and a criminal law system. However, there remain wide areas which cannot be decided solely on efficiency grounds. Moreover, the choice of entitlements has a major impact on the wealth of individuals and organisations. For example, if injurers are strictly liable for all losses this will adversely affect their wealth and make victims better off. Calabresi and Melamed see the entitlement decision as essentially one of distributive justice.

Legal rights and entitlements are not self-protecting and may be disputed, violated, or destroyed. They must be protected by the legal system. This is seen as a matter of corrective justice. The common law protects entitlements in one of three ways:

- **Property rule** The entitlement can be traded upon payment to the holder of his asking price in a voluntary transaction prior to the transfer to the purchaser. A property rule provides absolute protection of the entitlement holder's rights and permits only ex *ante* trading through consensual transactions.
- **Liability rule** The entitlement can be involuntarily taken or destroyed upon payment of objective damages determined by the court. That is, the entitlement can be traded in a non-market transaction provided the recipient pays damages after the transaction. Such entitlements can be said to be *ex post* tradeable. Liability rules are a way of facilitating entitlement transfers in situations where accident bargains are precluded by transaction costs. Liability rules are often used for a very practical reason – it is not possible for the parties to negotiate an *ex ante* price. This is most likely to be the case where harms are random or probabilistic, and it is not clear who the victim or injurer is likely to be. Road accidents provide a good example. Road accidents occur between strangers whose identity before an accident is unknown and do not form distinct classes of injurers and victims. It is therefore not feasible for 'victims' and injurers to negotiate a contract before an accident which negotiates a price for exposure

to the risks of an accident, the level of safety/care to be exercised and the compensation to be paid if any. Further, even if such a contract could be negotiated the parties would most likely specify a contract damage rule similar to a liability rule. As Calabresi states, 'liability rules are intensely practical. They enable actions to take place when contractual behaviour, before harm, would not be feasible. Damages after harm replace such unfeasible agreements.'[40]

- **Inalienability rule** The initial entitlement is assigned and its transfer is not permitted.

Legal examples of these three modes of protecting entitlement are easy to provide. Property rules are injunctions in nuisance and specific performance in contract, while the award of compensatory damages protects an entitlement with a liability rule. The inalienability rule tends to be the province of the criminal law and government regulation (e.g. the illegality of slavery).

The common law uses a mix of property and liability rules. The challenge for a positive theory of law is to explain why one rather than the others is used in practice, and for a normative theory to assess the relative efficiency of property and liability rules in the different areas of the law.

FURTHER TOPICS AND READING

- There are a large number of excellent economics textbooks which expand on the economic concepts developed in the chapter, e.g. R. H. Frank, *Microeconomics and Behavior*, 5th edn., New York: McGraw Hill, 2003.
- The discussion in this chapter adheres to the view that economics is the study of choice and incentives. Ronald Coase has disagreed with this definition of the scope of economics. He defines economics as the study of 'the working of the social institutions which bind together the economic system: firms, markets for goods and services, labour markets, capital markets ... and so on.' Paradoxically, Coase is not interested in the application of economics to law, but in improving the ability of economics to explain its traditional subject matter by incorporating the law. For an instructive exchange of views, see R. H. Coase, 'Economics and Contiguous Disciplines', 7 *Journal of Legal Studies*, 201–211 (1978), reprinted in Coase's *Essays on Economics and Economists*, Chicago: University of Chicago Press, 1995; R. A. Posner, 'Nobel Laureate: Ronald Coase and Methodology', 7 *Journal of Economics Perspectives*, 195–210 (1993), R. H. Coase, 'Coase on Posner on Coase', 149 *Journal of Institutional & Theoretical Economics*, 96–98 (1993) and his *Overcoming Law*, Cambridge, MA: Harvard University Press, 1995, chapter 20.

[40] G. Calabresi, 'Torts – The Law of a Mixed Society', 56 *Texas Law Review*, 519–536 (1978) 529.

- Dissatisfaction with the rationality assumption has fostered a new branch of economics – behavioural economics – and its counterpart behavioural law and economics. This seeks to take account of the cognitive limits of individual decision-making under conditions of risk and uncertainty. C. R. Sunstein (ed.), *Behavioral Law and Economics*, Cambridge: Cambridge University Press, 2000; F. Parisi and V. L. Smith (eds.), *The Law and Economics of Irrational Behavior*, Palo Alto, CA: Stanford University Press, 2005. Further, the concept of 'bounded rationality' has been used by the transaction costs or new institutional economics (NIE) approach most associated with the work of Oliver Williamson, e.g. O. E. Williamson, *Markets and Hierarchies: Analysis and Antitrust Implications*, New York: Free Press, 1975, chapter 2. For an exhaustive discussion of the different schools of law and economics, see N. Mercuro and S. G. Medema, *Economics and the Law: From Posner to Post-Modernism and Beyond*, Princeton: Princeton University Press, 1997; 2nd edn., 2006.
- The Coase Theorem rests on a number of assumptions which are spelled out and examined critically in C. G. Veljanovski, 'The Coase Theorem, and the Economic Theory of Markets and Law', 35 *Kyklos*, 53–74 (1982), and R. Cooter, 'The Cost of Coase', 11 *Journal of Legal Studies*, 1–34 (1982). Both these articles stress that bargaining over harms can lead to strategic interactions which block efficient outcomes – i.e. that costless bargaining does not guarantee efficiency.
- Economists have generally assumed rather than established market failure. A classic example often used in economics texts is the bee and the apple. According to the distinguished economist James Meade: bees make honey from and pollinate the apple blossoms. He used this as an example of an external benefit which the market failed to take into account, since the beekeeper and orchardist did not pay for the services they provided one another. Steven Cheung's study of bee keeping showed that this was not the case and that markets could deal with this in the absence of government intervention. In Washington State, there was an active market in nectar and pollination services which was even advertised in the *Yellow Pages* telephone directory. Cheung's study showed a well-developed set of contractual practices which even dealt with other 'externalities' arising from strategic behaviour where apiarists contracted for fewer beehives, taking advantage of the positive benefits of neighbouring orchardists, and the use of pesticide sprays damaging bees. S. N. S Cheung, 'The Fable of the Bees: An Economic Investigation', 16 *Journal of Law and Economics*, 11–33 (1973). For other examples, see D. F. Spulber (ed.), *Famous Fables of Economics – Myths of Market Failure*, Oxford: Blackwells, 2002.
- Some research suggests that people do not view actions in opportunity cost terms as suggested by the Coase Theorem. They regard a financial outlay as different from a forgone opportunity. For example, experimental evidence shows that people who buy ill-fitting shoes are more likely to put up with them than when they are given a free identical pair of shoes. Research on discounts and surcharges for credit cards finds that consumers treat a surcharge for using a credit card as different from a discount for cash, even though they have the

same monetary value. A discount (opportunity cost) for cash is viewed more positively than a surcharge which is perceived as an additional payment. R. Thaler, 'Toward a Positive Theory of Consumer Choice', 1 *Journal of Economic Behavior and Organization*, 39–60 (1980) and the so-called 'prospect theory' has been developed by D. Kahneman and A. Tversky, 'Choices, Values, and Frames', 39 *American Psychologist*, 341–330 (1981). This has been applied to the Coase Theorem in D. Kahneman, J. L. Knetsch and R. Thaler, 'Fairness as a Constraint on Profit Seeking: Entitlements in the Market', 76 *American Economic Review*, 728–741 (1984); R. H. McAdams, 'Experimental Law and Economics', in B. Bouckaert and G. de Geest (eds.), *Encyclopaedia of Law and Economics*, vol. 1, Cheltenham: Edward Elgar, 2000; D. Kahneman, J. L. Knetsch and R. H. Thaler, 'Experimental Tests of the Endowment Effect and the Coase Theorem', 98 *Journal of Political Economy*, 1325–1348 (1990).

• It could be argued that in a world without transactions costs there would be no lawyers. Therefore lawyers and the process of law can be seen, in practice as part of the transactions costs. Indeed, the law in many less developed economies, together with the activities of lawyers, have been seen as a major brake on economic growth. This so incensed some economists in the 1980s that they set out to show that the more lawyers in a country, the lower the *per capita* income and economic growth. A now dated study of fifty-two countries using data for 1960–80 suggested that as the share of lawyers in the labour force increased, the lower a country's economic growth. Lawyers, it seemed were dangerous to a country's wealth. Some lawyers have been offended by this suggestion and subsequent studies have purportedly found little correlation between the number of lawyers and economic growth: G. Hadfield, 'The Price of Law – How the Market for Lawyers Distorts the Justice System', 98 *Michigan Law Review*, 953–1006 (2000).

• The use of efficiency as an ethical theory of law and justice by Posner and others has excited considerable controversy among legal scholars. See the exchange between Posner and Ronald Dworkin – R. A. Posner, 'Utilitarianism, Economics, and Legal Theory', 8 *Journal of Legal Studies*, 103–140 (1979); R. Dworkin, 'Is Wealth a Value?', 9 *Journal of Legal Studies*, 191–226 (1980). The equation of wealth maximisation with justice and even happiness is not made here. For a critical review, see C. G. Veljanovski, 'Wealth Maximisation, Law and Ethics – On the Limits of Economic Efficiency', 1 *International Review of Law and Economics*, 5–28 (1981), reprinted in K. Dau-Schmidt and T. S. Ulen (eds.), *A Law and Economics Anthology 2002*, Cincinnati, OH: Anderson Publishing, 2002.

CHAPTER 3

Property

What is common to the greatest number, gets least amount of care.

Aristotle

Property rights arise because resources are scarce. In a world without scarcity there would be no need to have property rights because there would be abundance. If someone takes your apple, you simply move onto the next apple tree. Where resources are scarce, they have to be allocated between users and uses, and this requires some formal or informal recognition of who owns the resource – and, most importantly, the rights and constraints that attach to ownership. The common law deals with property rights through three branches of the law – property rights are created and defined through the law of property, transferred to higher-value uses through the law of contract (see chapter 5) and protected through the law of torts, particularly trespass, nuisance and crime.

PROPERTY RIGHTS THEORY

Property rights define the nature of political and economic systems, and their economic performance. The economics of property rights tells us why.

The case for property

Consider a world where there was no legally enforceable property and ownership rights. If the ownership of a plot of land or a car was not recognised, anyone could either claim or steal it. The constant threat of theft and the consequent losses would have a number of effects. First, considerable effort and resources would be devoted to asserting claims over others' land and assets, and stealing by individuals and corrupt government officials, and in protecting them from being taken. This would divert effort and resources from productive activity. Second, the fear that one's land and possessions might be 'stolen' would deter people from enhancing their value. They would take a short-term view and not invest in projects which required a large amount of capital with a return over a lengthy period. This would probably mean that capital markets would not develop, as there would be no security for loans. Third, the absence of legal title would make it very difficult to transfer land or an asset to others except within a small circle such as the family or other community/social/ethnic group which recognised individual *de facto* claims. This would mean that apart from local community markets a system for transferring resources to better uses and users would not develop. The economic value of land, capital and assets, and their productivity would therefore not be realised, and used to create further wealth. In short, a society in which there was no recognition of enforceable ownership rights would involve massive economic waste, be inefficient and be stagnant.

The economic waste and inefficiency of a world without property are real and present today. It has been estimated that the poor in the Third World and former communist countries possessed but did not legally own land valued at US $9.3 billion in 1997 prices. This was twice the money in circulation in the USA, twenty times the market capitalisation of listed companies on the stock exchanges of the world's twenty most developed economies and twenty times the total direct investment into all developing and post-communist countries in the decade after 1989. Yet these potentially valuable assets could not be harnessed to create wealth and economic growth:

> Any asset whose economic and social aspects are not fixed in a formal property system is extremely hard to move in the market. How can huge amounts of assets changing hands in a modern market economy be controlled if not through a formal property process? Without such a system, any trade of an asset, say a piece of real estate, requires an enormous effort just to determine the basics of the transaction: does the seller own the real estate and have the right to transfer it? Can he pledge it? Will the new owner be accepted as such by those who enforce property rights? What are the effective means to exclude other claimants?[1]

Enforceable property rights increase wealth by reducing transactions costs and unlocking wealth-creating opportunities. As de Soto concludes: 'By learning to fix the economic potential of their assets through property rights, Westerners created a fast track to explore the most productive aspects of possession.'[2] For example, in the 1990s Peru issued property titles to

---

[1] H. de Soto, *The Mystery of Capital – Why Capitalism Triumphs in the West and Fails Everywhere Else*, London: Black Swan, 2001, 45.
[2] Soto, *The Mystery of Capital*, 50.

1.2 million urban squatters – the result was a 20 per cent increase in the hours worked away from home and a nearly 30 per cent reduction in the incidence of child labour. Thus by creating private property rights parents were enabled to find jobs instead of protecting their homes and having to send their children to work.[3]

The economics of property rights

At its simplest, the economics of property rights[4] claims that the economic value of resources, and the efficiency with which resources and assets are used, are determined by the configuration of property rights in society.

Property rights theorists' stress that the value of goods and services depends on the 'bundle of legal rights' attached to physical and non-physical commodities and assets. Indeed exchange and markets are redefined as trading not in the underlying resources, goods and services but in the different legal claims to them. This is because the bundle of property rights affects economic value. Clearly, the price of a freehold property differs from that of a leasehold or tenancy and these different types of ownership arrangements affect the value of land.

Property rights influence incentives and economic behaviour. Where ownership rights are non-exclusive, or are difficult to define and enforce, a resource will be overexploited if already in existence and underprovided if it must be produced. Individuals and organisations will fail to take account of the economic value of such commonly owned resources and they will be used inefficiently, or a market in otherwise valuable activity may fail to develop.

The economic model has a clear preference for private property rights. Clearly defined private property rights combined with competition are more likely to allocate resources to their most efficient or highest-valued uses. This is because private property concentrates the benefits and costs of an activity or resource on those who make decisions and so their actions are based on a full assessment of cost and benefits. However, the efficiency of any specific property rights arrangement will depend critically on the nature of the bundle of rights which attaches to an asset or resource.

---

[3] World Bank, *Doing Business in 2004 – Understanding Regulation*, New York: Oxford University Press, 2004, 93.

[4] A. A. Alchian, *Some Economics of Property Rights*, Rand Paper 2,316 (1961); *Pricing and Society*, Institute of Economic Affairs (1967); H. Demsetz, 'Some Aspects of Property Rights', 9 *Journal of Law & Economics*, 61–70 (1964); H. Demsetz, 'Toward a Theory of Property Rights', 59 *American Economic Review*, 347–359 (1969).

The approach also identifies market failure with the absence of enforceable property rights, and specifically commonly owned and unowned resources which encourage the overexploitation of the environment, oceans and natural resources. This has led to property rights solutions in place of so-called 'command-and-control intervention' to control overuse and maximise efficiency.

The economics of property rights has a dynamic component: it 'predicts' that the creation and development of property rights is influenced by economic considerations. In a dynamic economy, new cost–price configurations are generated which provide an opportunity for restructuring, and in particular 'privatising' property rights. To quote Harold Demsetz:

> Property rights develop to internalize externalities when the gains of internalization become larger than the cost of internalization. Increased internalization, in the main, results from changes in economic values, changes which stem from the development of new technology and the opening of new markets, changes to which old property rights are poorly attuned ... Given a community's tastes ... [for private vs state ownership], the emergence of new private or state-owned property rights will be in response to changes in technology and relative prices.[5]

Thus, all other things equal, the more valuable the prospective property rights, or the lower the costs of defining and enforcing new rights, the more likely that new rights will be defined. For example, a study by Smith shows that in England land went from privately owned to commons fields (albeit with strict usage rules) back to private use as economic factors changed.[6]

The relationship between efficiency, economic growth and property rights is a two-way street – rights affect economic growth and economic growth alters property rights in an effort to promote greater growth. Indeed, the impact of property rights on economic growth may be more significant than commonly thought. Heitger's empirical study[7] of eighty-four countries over a twenty-year period (1975–95), found that those with secure property rights had higher economic growth, and that higher economic growth led to more secure property rights. A doubling of his 'property rights index' constructed to measure 'security of property' in each country, more than doubled *per capita* income, and was a more important influence on economic growth than capital investment and other standard economic variables!

---

[5] H. Demsetz, 'Toward a Theory of Property Rights', 350.
[6] H. Smith, 'Exclusion versus Governance: Two Strategies for Delineating Property Rights', 31 *Journal of Legal Studies*, S453–S489 (2002).
[7] B. Heitger, 'Property Rights and the Wealth of Nations: A Cross-Country Study', 23 *Cato Journal* 381–402 (2004).

Property as a bundle of rights

The words 'ownership' and 'property' do not have straightforward meanings or legal definitions. Indeed there is a vast legal and philosophical literature on the nature of property and its definition. The economist, for his part, uses the term 'property rights' to embrace any legal, institutional, customary and social constraints on economic activity. For example, Furubotn and Pejovich define property rights as the 'sum of the economic and social relations with respect to scarce resources in which individual members stand in relation to each other'.[8] Barzel draws a distinction between legal and economic property rights, defining the latter as 'the individual's ability, in expected terms, to consume the good (or the service of the asset)'.[9] Alchian and Demsetz, in an early contribution to the economics of property rights, comment:

In common speech, we frequently speak of someone owning the land, that house, or those bonds. This conventional style is undoubtedly economical from the view-point of quick communications, but it masks the variety and complexity of the ownership relationship. What are owned are *rights* to *use* resources, including one's own body and mind, and these rights are always circumscribed, often by prohibition of certain actions. To 'own land' usually means to have the right to till (or not to till) the soil, to mine the soil, to *offer* those rights for sale, etc., but not the right to throw soil at a passer-by, to use it to change the course of a stream, or to force someone to buy it. What are owned are socially recognized rights of action.[10]

The economist's definition of property right is therefore very broad, encompassing law, customs and institutions, and even ethical and societal norms. Here we restrict the term 'property' to that understood by lawyers.

   Where lawyers and economists are agreed is that property is a bundle of rights – or, as it is sometimes said a 'bundle of sticks'. It is not a unitary nor clearly defined concept. For example, a capitalist economy is based on private property, which allows the owner to exclude others and appropriate the residual income from the use of their assets or resources. However, in modern capitalist economies income, goods and services, capital, wealth and property are all taxed, and their use and transfer restricted by laws and

---

[8] E. Furubotn and S. Pejovich (eds.), *The Economics of Property Rights*, Cambridge, MA: Ballinger, 1974, 3. See also E. Furubotn and S. Pejovich 'Property Rights and Economic Theory: A Survey of Recent Literature', 10 *Journal of Economic Literature*, 1137–1161 (1972).

[9] Y. Barzel, *Economic Analysis of Property Rights*, Cambridge: Cambridge University Press, 1989; 2nd edn., 1997, 3.

[10] A. A. Alchian and H. Demsetz, 'The Property Rights Paradigm', 33 *Journal of Economic History*, 17–27 (1973).

governments. Thus while these may still be characterised as 'private property', these legal restrictions affect efficiency, value, the nature of exchange and the actions of their owners and users.

From an economic perspective, the 'bundle of rights' which makes up property has at least four essential features – Exclusivity, Transferability, Appropriability and Divisibility, or what will be called the "ETAD" package. Each of these factors varies along a continuum, and does not operate unrestrained. We shall consider each briefly.

Exclusivity

The most important aspect of property is its exclusivity. Indeed, this attribute is often seen as synonymous with property, and certainly private property. Blackstone defined property as 'that sole and despotic dominion which one man claims and exercises over external things of the world, in total exclusion of the right of any other individual in the universe'.[11]

Exclusive property rights are regarded as efficient because they link costs and benefits to actions and ensure that when individuals and markets move resources they do so taking account of all the costs and benefits. This excludability can vary considerably.

Private property contains the most refined level of excludability, in that the owner is entitled to prevent others from using or acquiring the asset or resource without his prior consent. Even where property is owned by a clearly defined group, or a more nebulous one such as 'the taxpayer' or society, the state has the right and ability to exclude those not authorised from entering onto or using the asset or resource. However, the more diffused the ownership the more likely that individual actions will be taken on the basis of only a proportion of the relevant costs and/or benefits; and that outcome will be inefficient. This is discussed in more detail in the section on common property.

On the other hand, exclusivity even within a private property system cannot be absolute or unrestrained. A monopoly right is perhaps the most exclusive of property rights, but is inefficient because it leads to underexploitation of resources.

Exclusively can also be excessive, leading to what Heller has called the 'anti-commons problem'.[12] This arises where there are a large number of

---

[11] W. Blackstone, *Commentaries on the Laws of England*, 1765/9, book II, chapter 1, 2.
[12] M. A. Heller, 'The Tragedy of the Anticommons: Property in the Transition from Marx to Markets', III *Harvard Law Review*, 622–688 (1998). See also J. M. Buchanan and Y. Yoon, 'Symmetric Tragedies: Commons and Anticommons', 43 *Journal of Law & Economics*, 1–13 (2000).

'owners' who each have the right to exclude, and who must agree to the use or sale of the resource A good example is the fifty or so medieval barons during the fifteenth century who put chains across the Rhine to demand tolls from those travelling along the river. The chains served to 'privatise' the Rhine but slowed commerce and reduced its economic value. Another example is 'patent thickets'. This is where companies seek a large number of patents for related inventions, and then litigate patent infringements against the initial or other patentees in order to extract payment and/or delay or block others from exploiting potentially competitive inventions. Where this occurs the patent system gives multiple parties the right to exclude, which generates wasteful litigation and the underexploitation of inventions.

Transferability

The transferability (or alienability) of property rights in an asset or resource is another key aspect of property. Transferability enables the rights in resources and assets to be traded and exchanged so that they flow to their highest-valued uses. Often the discussion of property, particularly private property, stops at noting that it is an exclusive right. For resources and assets to flow to their most valuable uses, property rights must be transferable. Cheung stresses the importance of transferability to market efficiency:

Competition for and transferability of the ownership right in the marketplace thus perform two main functions for contracting. First, competition conglomerates knowledge from all potential owners – the knowledge of alternative contractual arrangements and the use of resources; and transferability of property rights ensures (via flexible relative prices) that the most valuable are utilized. Second, competition among potential contract participants and a resource owner's ability to transfer the right to use his resources reduce the cost of enforcing the stipulated terms in a contract . . . because competing parties will stand by an offer or accept similar terms.[13]

Private property rights without the ability of owners to sell or buy such rights are not efficient. Take the example of a broadcast frequency allocated to and restricted to use for local television which generates a return of £100. However, if the value of the licence increases to £200 if transferred to another use but this is prohibited, the bandwith will be locked into an inefficient use.

---

[13] S. N. S. Cheung 'The Structure of a Contract and the Theory of a Non-exclusive Resource', 13 *Journal of Law & Economics*, 49–70 (1970).

Appropriability

Assets and resources generate a stream of income, and have a capital value. Economists look principally at the ability to appropriate the *residual income* – revenues minus costs – to determine the impact on economic incentives. A property owner as the **residual income claimant** has a direct interest in ensuring that the economic value of a resource is maximised. The ability and extent of the right to appropriate the residual income from a resource is a key aspect of any property right. Indeed, the value of a bundle of rights will crucially depend on the ability of its owner to appropriate the gains and rewards from his or her exploitation of the resource or asset. Less than complete appropriation of income or rents, unless voluntarily agreed by the owner – say, through a share cropping contract or profit sharing arrangement – will have adverse allocative and incentive effects. The appropriability problem is particularly acute for goods that have public good characteristics (see chapter 2) such as information, intellectual property (see later) and many common property resources.

Divisibility

The owners of valuable assets should be able to partition, re-define and create new property rights in response to changes in economic and market conditions. In particular, they must be able to define new rights which increase the value of the underlying activity or asset. The bundle of rights attached to land or an asset can be extremely complex, defining a myriad of rights to different uses and users – the right of ownership (freehold, tenancy, leasehold, rental and other more sophisticated ownership arrangements through trusts and investment funds), the right of use, the right to cross over, protection against interference through restrictive covenants and actions for nuisance and trespass, the right to shoot animals, the right to take as security for a loan, time share, its securitisation and so on. There will generally be an optimal level of divisibility or standardisation.

COMMON PROPERTY

A resource or asset which is owned by all (society, government, taxpayer, the proletariat, etc.) or unowned is called 'common property', although this is a bit of misnomer. This type of (non-) ownership violates the principle condition of an efficient ETAD package – exclusivity – and, because of this, divisibility, transferability and appropriability. Common property when combined with unrestricted use generates incentives on the part of each individual to use the 'free' resource as intensively and quickly as possible, even though this reduces total wealth, overexploits the resource and, in the case of natural species, may lead to their extinction.

Tragedy of the commons

The scientist Gareth Hardin popularised the inefficiency of common property in his famous article 'The Tragedy of the Commons'.[14] This set out the way that lack of ownership led to overexploitation and eventual degradation of resources which were unowned or commonly owned.

The inefficiency of common property was illustrated by the example of the village commons of feudal England used by villagers to graze their cattle. If each villager is assumed to have unrestricted use of the common land then each will be tempted to graze as many cows as he or she can. Each villager using the village commons treats it as if it is a free resource – i.e. its use and value is priced at zero. Thus for each additional cow he puts on the common land, he appropriates the full benefits but only a fraction of the costs resulting from the overgrazing. It is in the short-term self-interest of each villager to continue adding more cows and to ignore the external costs this inflicts on other villagers. This '**tragedy of the commons**' results in the wasteful and possibly destructive overexploitation of the common land.

This common property problem is applicable to all open access and unowned land and resources. For example, the fish in the sea are unowned and ownership rights can be asserted only by their capture. Again, no single fisherman benefits from conserving the stock of fish. A fisherman, who acts to limit today's catch finds that tomorrow they are someone else's fish![15] The incentive on each fisherman is therefore to catch as many fish as quickly as possible, as this is the only way that he can 'own' the fish. When all act in this way, the economic value of the fishing grounds is dissipated by overcrowding and excessive catches, and possibly the extinction of commercially valuable species (figure 3.1).

This does not mean that fishermen become wealthy. The other consequence of excessive use is that the initially higher return attracts more and more fishermen. This process continues until the average return to fishing is reduced to a level similar to the competitive return to other activities in the

[14] G. Hardin, 'The Tragedy of the Commons', 162 *Science*, 1243–1248 (1968).
[15] H. Scott Gordon, 'The Economic Theory of a Common Property Resource: The Fishery', 62 *Journal of Political Economy*, 124–142 (1954).

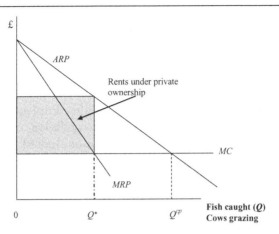

Figure 3.1 Inefficiency of common property

The overexploitation of an unowned or common property resource is shown above. It applies equally to the fishing or village commons examples. The downward sloping schedule labelled *ARP* is the Average Revenue Product to fishing at different levels of catch. The lower downward sloping schedule labelled *MRP* is the Marginal Revenue Product, which shows the marginal return of the next catch. The Marginal Costs (*MC*) to fishermen of catching more fish – in terms of fuel for boats, nets, the amortisation of the boat, crew wages and so on – is assumed to be constant, as shown by the horizontal line. The wealth maximising level of fishing is Q^* where the marginal revenue equals the marginal costs of the last catch of fish – i.e. $MRP = MC$. The economic rents to the sea as a fishing resource are given by the shaded rectangle and are maximised at Q^*. A fishing company which both fished and owned the sea would maximise its wealth and society's by taking only Q^* fish out of the sea. However, if the sea and fish are unowned the only way the rents can be captured is by catching more fish. The positive (unowned) rents at Q^* attract an excessive number of fishermen into the industry. This stops when there are no further rents/profits to be extracted (where $ARP = MC$). Thus competition with no property rights leads to overexploitation (Q^{cp}) with all the rents captured by the fishermen and the stock of fish depleted. In economists' jargon common property leads to **rent dissipation**.

economy after taking into account the costs of fishing and investment in boats and equipment. Thus competition does what it always does – drives down the returns in an industry or activity to its costs. Thus instead of fishermen profiting from the availability of free fish and fishing grounds, they become so overcrowded that none makes more than a reasonable return.

The common property problem is not confined to feudal England, or fish. It is a general phenomenon applicable to pollution, road congestion, oil and mineral exploration, crowding and so on. Indeed, one of the first attempts to link inefficient resource use and property rights by an economist was by Frank Knight in the 1920s, when he analysed road congestion and pricing.[16] Access to the road system is open and unpriced; it is therefore treated as a free resource by motorists and eventually becomes overused and congested. This leads to the call for more road building to alleviate the congestion problem. However, new roads make the time costs of road transport cheaper, calling forth more traffic and the re-emergence of the congestion. The problem is, as for all common property, that each motorist gets the full benefits of the initially faster transport but bears only a fraction of external costs of the increase in congestion his or her use of the road imposes on other motorists. The solution is not the 'build one's way out of congestion' but road pricing, which rations road usage, internalises the costs of congestion on all motorists and helps fund future road building and maintenance which is wealth maximising inclusive of congestion costs.

CREATION OF PROPERTY RIGHTS

The commons problem is seen to apply to all resources, assets and land which are collectively owned and unowned. This, however, is too sweeping a claim and not correct. The 'tragedy of the commons' arises because access is open and use unrestrained. However, those who own resources in common can impose rules or norms which restrict access and use – i.e. governance replaces or substitutes for ownership in managing potential inefficiencies.

Indeed, the tragedy of the commons assumes irrationality on the part of the villagers, who allow a valuable community resource to be squandered to their long-run detriment. If the commons is essential to the livelihood and wealth of the village, would they persist in their destructive course of action? Clearly not, and it comes as no surprise that the feudal commons

---

[16] F. H. Knight, 'Some Fallacies in the Interpretation of Social Cost', 38 *Quarterly Journal of Economics*, 582–606 (1924).

was not a piece of land which all and sundry could use. It was regulated by the villagers, who restricted the number of cows each villager could put on the common land, and the amount of wood they could collect.[17] The villagers established *de facto* use rights in the common property resource backed by sanctions which limited its use. Community norms and controls substituted for property rights in controlling overuse and economic waste.[18]

The practicality of using community norms (*de facto* use rights) as a way of controlling overexploitation varies with the nature of the resource and the numbers involved. The village square tends to be well maintained, whereas Hyde Park after a concert is a rubbish dump. The reason is that in the latter case users are itinerant and bear none of the longer-term consequences of their selfish behaviour – the litter is someone else's problem and there is little voluntary pressure to internalise these costs.

An obvious solution is to privatise the commons and unowned resources. In practice, the absence of exclusive ownership rights may have an economic justification.[19] For some resources it may simply be technologically impossible to work out a titles system, or to define and enforce a property rights system.[20]

The development of property rights will be driven by economic factors, whether based on efficiency or distributive considerations. Above, the optimistic efficiency view of property rights was advanced. This suggested that new property rights evolve when the benefits of privatisation outweigh the costs. Where there is a gross inefficiency in ownership arrangements, it implies significant gains from trade. However, this theory rests on the assumption that individual/group negotiations and political pressure are motivated solely by total gains (efficiency) rather than by their distribution. In reality, the parties are more likely to be concerned by the distribution of prospective gains rather than their total size. That is, rational action results in maximisation of private not necessarily social gains. The driving force for reform will be the expected discounted stream of income (and capital gains) for the different groups. Further, the configuration of transactions costs can lead to strategic behaviour which makes it impossible to move

[17] C. J. Dahlman, *The Open Field System and Beyond: A Property Rights Analysis of an Economic Institution*, Cambridge: Cambridge University Press, 1980.

[18] E. Ostrom, *Governing the Commons: The Evolution of Institutions for Collective Action*, Cambridge: Cambridge University Press, 1990.

[19] H. Demsetz, 'Toward a Theory of Property Rights II: The Competitiveness between Private and Collective Ownership', 31 *Journal of Legal Studies*, S653–S672 (2002).

[20] First proposed by J. Dales, *Pollution, Property and Prices*, Toronto: University of Toronto Press, 1968.

forward. Libecap[21] identifies four factors likely to affect the evolution of property rights:

- size of the aggregate expected gains
- number of and differences among bargaining parties
- information problems
- skewness or concentration of current and proposed shares.

In a nutshell, it is more likely that efficient property rights will evolve where the gains are large, there are few groups with small differences in interest, information is generalised and the gains and losses are not too skewed toward one group.

Alternatively, the Government can directly regulate the number of users, uses and the rate of exploitation of the resource by detailed statutory and administrative requirements (the so-called 'command-and-control approach'). Thus quotas may be imposed, user licences issued and regulation enacted. These statutory responses will be determined by political and bureaucratic procedures, enforced by regulatory bodies and may attract civil and criminal sanctions if infringed. However, regulation is not a perfect solution. In practice, it replaces market failure with non-market or regulatory failure, even though the solution may mark an improvement.

THE ROLE OF PROPERTY LAW

While property rights may evolve in response to economic factors and scarcity, they still need to be legally defined and enforced by some third party, usually the State or the courts. An efficient property rights system would seek to define, enforce and protect property rights, provide a mechanism for the development of new property rights in response to changes in technology, costs and benefits and resolve disputes. More specifically, it would:

1. Define and delineate legally enforceable property rights. This would provide the basis for exchange and production in the economy. The clear definition of property rights plays a major role in protecting expectations, reducing transactions costs and creating incentives for the productive use of resources and assets.

---

[21] G. D. Libecap, *Contracting for Property Rights*, Cambridge: Cambridge University Press, 1989. In an interesting analysis of the development of property right in the USA, Libecap examines the different evolutions of four sets of property rights over mineral rights, timber lands, oil extractions and fishing to explain why in some areas but not in others there has been relatively rapid agreement on new more efficient rights.

2. Provide rules for the transfer of rights between uses and users. This should include rules to establish and enforce legal title, both generally and where there is theft and fraud.
3. Provide a procedure for the creation and recognition of new property rights in response to changes in economic (and social) conditions. In this way, the law can better facilitate economic activity and increase wealth.
4. Resolve disputes over title, and conflicting or incompatible uses. The legal system should protect private property by setting out a system of remedies and penalties.
5. Offer certainty and stability in property rights arrangements so that expectations and returns can be protected.[22] This is related to the exclusivity and appropriability of property. The constant 'fine tuning' of property rights, even if based on economic efficiency, will create uncertainty and risk for investment and economic activity which will diminish the expectation that owners can appropriate the rewards of their efforts, and this will reduce the productiveness and efficiency of the economy. It is arguable that there are long-run benefits to be had from stability, and certainty may often outweigh the gains from more efficient rights based on changing short-run cost-benefit criteria.

INTELLECTUAL PROPERTY RIGHTS

The issues of appropriability, incentives and long- and short-run efficiency are starkly brought to the fore by intellectual property rights (IPRs) such as patents, trade secrets, copyright and trademarks. While this is not an area of common law, the issues that arise have relevance to property law generally.

A patent gives temporary exclusivity to reward inventive and creative activity which is 'novel' and 'non-obvious'. The reason such protection is needed is because intellectual capital such as inventions has public good characteristics which give rise to problems of exclusivity and appropriability. In the absence of a patent, others would copy and use an invention without paying the inventor. Competition between copiers would drive the price of the resulting products to the cost of manufacturing plus copying, offering no return to the original inventor to recoup what might be very high R&D costs. A patent gives its holder legal protection which can

---

[22] As Boulding comments: 'It is not enough to have a good legal concept of property; bundles of rights that constitute property must be secure if economic progress is to take place. For as economic progress always, or almost always, involves the accumulation of physical capital, unless the people who accumulate capital are reasonably secure in its possession and administration, it will not be accumulated.' K. E. Boulding, *Principles of Economic Progress*, London: Staples Press, 1959, 31.

be enforced to compel users to pay, prevent free riding and appropriate the benefits/revenue of his or her exertions.

The patent system has another benefit. The *quid pro quo* of legal protection is public disclosure of the patent to the world at large. Others can acquire information on the patent and its novelty for the cost of a patent application and can build on this to develop other complementary and substitutable devices. The alternative to a patent would be trade secrecy in order to enhance first mover advantages, which arguably would impose a cost on society by reducing the flow of information and retarding the rate of innovation.

These positive effects of patents must be balanced against their negative effects. The first, paradoxically, is that by facilitating appropriability, and hence pricing, a patent leads to an inefficiently low level of consumption of the patented good. This inefficiency arises from the public good nature of inventions. Once an invention has been created, society benefits from its widest distribution and exploitation. The optimal rule for a public good is that no user who places a positive economic value on the patented device should be excluded. Thus efficiency in consumption requires that the price be set at the marginal costs of producing and disseminating the products arising from the invention. However, such marginal cost pricing will not enable the inventor to recover the total fixed costs of the invention plus a return to risk taking and the R&D costs on those inventions which failed. This requires prices in excess of marginal costs and, hence, an inefficiently low consumption of the patented good. Thus, as indicated in chapter 2, there is a tension between static efficiency (assuming a given technology) and dynamic efficiency which requires prices to be higher in order to stimulate innovative activity.[23]

The second source of inefficiency is that a patent may give its owner **market power**. Market power is the ability of the patent owner to charge excessive prices and engage in exclusionary practices to dampen competitive pressures. It should be stressed that an IPR is not a monopoly right *per se* other than in the literal sense of an exclusive right to a particular invention. Nonetheless, it does have the potential to confer market power if the patent is excessively long and/or too broad.

The two guiding principles of patent law developed in Britain in the eighteenth century were that patents should be granted only for new and important discoveries and that the breadth of the patent be proportional

---

[23] The owners of IPRs frequently charge different prices for the same good to different consumers or consumer groups. This price discrimination reduces the misallocative effects of monopoly and the public good distortion of consumption, as would be the case if the same price were charged to all. Price discrimination is good in this area because it leads to greater output.

to the size of the discovery made. Two factors determine the strength of patent protection – a patent's duration and its 'breadth'.

Consider first a patent's life.[24] In theory, the optimal patent life is the number of years in which the marginal social benefits from encouraging inventive activity equals the marginal social costs that excessive pricing and restricted output impose. Assuming that the marginal benefits decline as the number of years of protection increases and the loss due to the misallocative effect rises, then in theory the optimal expiry date is given where the difference between the two, or the net benefits, are maximised. This suggests that an efficient patent system would offer patents of varying durations rather than the present standard (in the UK) twenty-year patent term.

Patent 'breadth' refers to the degree to which patent protection covers similar potential inventions. For example, if a patent system allows the concept of an aircraft to be patented rather than a specific type of aircraft design then the patent system offers broad (horizontal) protection. Greater patent breadth increases the economic losses due to patents because the patent owner faces less competition from close substitutes. In other words, broad patent protection is more likely to confer a monopoly, or at least market power, and thereby impose greater losses on consumers.[25]

The discussion so far has omitted one crucial justification for patent protection – it allegedly encourages invention and innovation.[26] Unfortunately the evidence to date is equivocal. Studies have found that, apart from the chemical and pharmaceutical sectors, patents are rarely the principal means of appropriating the returns from R&D.[27] Indeed, some commentators, most notably the British economist Arnold Plant in the 1930s, argue that the incentive effects of patents and other IPRs are in practice likely to be overwhelmed by the monopoly losses.[28] The first mover advantages of

[24] W. D. Nordhaus, *Invention, Growth and Welfare: A Theoretical Treatment of Technological Change*, Cambridge, MA: MIT Press, 1969.

[25] P. Klemperer, 'How Broad Should the Scope of Patent Protection Be?', 17 *RAND Journal of Economics*, 113–130 (1990).

[26] F. Machlup, *An Economic Review of the Patent System, Study No. 15, Subcommittee on Patents, Trademarks and Copyrights*, 85th Cong., 2d Sess., Senate Committee on the Judiciary, 1958; K. Arrow, 'Economic Welfare and the Allocation of Resources for Inventions', in R. Nelson (ed.), *The Rate and Direction of Inventive Activity*, Princeton, NJ: Princeton University Press, 1962.

[27] The evidence indicates that patents are no more important than the initial advantage an innovator has in exploiting his or her invention before others, and that not much R&D generates profits from patents. W. M. Cohen, R. R. Nelson and J. P. Walsh, 'Protecting Their Intellectual Assets: Appropriability Conditions and Why US Manufacturing Firms Patent (or Not)', Washington, DC: National Bureau of Economic Research, Working Paper 7552 (2000).

[28] A. Plant, 'The Economic Theory Concerning Patents for Inventions', 1 *Economica*, 30–51 (1934); A. Plant, 'The Economic Aspects of Copyright in Books', 1 *Economica*, 167–195 (1934), both reprinted in A. Plant, *Selected Economic Essays and Addresses*, London: Routledge & Kegan Paul, 1974; M. Boldrin and D. K. Levine, 'The Case against Intellectual Property Law', 92 *American Economic Review (Papers & Proceedings)*, 209–212 (2002).

inventors, they argue, are often sufficient to generate an adequate return, and that therefore there is no real risk of underprovision of R&D. If correct, this would undermine the case for patent protection and law. It is for this reason some of the more recent economic literature does not rely on the incentive effects to explain the rationale, structure and effects of intellectual property law.[29]

Patent protection in practice also provides an example of the anticommons problem referred to above.[30] The US patent system has come under severe criticism recently as generating excessive protection and raising transactions costs. Changes to US patent law in the 1980s expanded the scope of patent protection, made it easier to patent by relaxing the novelty and non-obviousness requirements and strengthened the patent owner's rights. This, in turn, led to an explosion in the number of patents, and in patent litigation.[31] As a result, some argue that the US patent system is creating transactions costs and uncertainty which threaten the innovation process. There is growing evidence that patent litigation is being used strategically to foreclose markets and as a rent-seeking device. The patent process can work imperfectly when it grants excessive protection, leading to patent thickets and litigation which give rise to excessive enforcement costs, opportunistic behaviour and potential inhibition and obstacles to the innovation process.

What do we glean from this admittedly brisk discussion of patent law?

- Patent protection enables inventors to appropriate the returns from their efforts.
- The costs and potential inefficiencies of patents are recognised by the law which awards property rights:
  - for only a limited period
  - for novel and non-obvious inventions
  - early in the R&D process to avoid wasteful duplication of inventive activity
  - in return for public disclosure of the invention's details.
- Further, the exclusivity of patents is limited *ex post* through competition/ anti-trust laws which regulate monopoly and anticompetitive abuses.[32]

[29] W. M. Landes and R. A. Posner, *The Economic Structure of Intellectual Property Law*, Cambridge, MA: Harvard University Press, 2003; R. D. Blair and T. F. Cotter, *Intellectual Property – Economics and Legal Dimensions of Rights and Remedies*, Cambridge: Cambridge University Press, 2005; S. Scotchmer, *Innovation and Incentives*, Cambridge, MA: MIT Press, 2004.

[30] A. B. Jaffe and J. Lerner, *Innovation and Its Discontents: How Our Broken Patent System is Endangering Innovation, Progress and What to Do about It*, Princeton: Princeton University Press, 2004, 8.

[31] 'The cost of ideas', *Economist*, 13 November 2004.

[32] I. Rahnasto, *Intellectual Property Rights, External Effects, and Anti-trust Law – Leveraging IPRs in the Communications Industry*, Oxford: Oxford University Press, 2003.

ADVERSE POSSESSION

One peculiar doctrine or rule found in a number of legal systems is that of adverse possession. Adverse possession is where the occupier of land who is not the owner acquires title (ownership) without the consent of or compensation/payment to the 'true' owner. The occupier must hold the property exclusively, continuously, openly and 'notoriously' for a pre-determined period (twelve years in England but this differs from country to country). There have, for example, been a number of high-profile cases where 'squatters' in local government owned houses in central London (the Boroughs of Lambeth, Camden and Southwark) have secured the freehold to valuable properties (one valued at £500,000) through the adverse possession rule.

The doctrine of adverse possession has attracted a number of economic justifications.[33] The immediate and obvious one is that it reduces uncertainty by basing ownership on a possessory right. If a person has lived continuously in one place, acted as the owner, and this has not been effectively disputed, it can be viewed as strong evidence that he or she is the owner and that the 'real' owner is not sufficiently concerned to assert ownership over the property. This seems a sensible rule where there is not a well-developed land title registration system.

On this view, adverse possession reduces the risks and transactions costs of title transfer. A potential purchaser, aware that the current occupier has lived on the property for the statutory period, can be assured that the title he acquires is good. If this were not the case, and ownership uncertain, it would reduce the value of the property by the amount equivalent to the risk and loss of the true owner asserting a claim on the property. Further, this would have the effect of halting the use of land in its higher-valued use and eventually to derelict properties.

Another theory is that adverse possession provides an efficient solution to boundary disputes. The doctrine provides incentives for the occupier to avoid boundary errors prior to investing in the development of land (the first-best solution), and for the 'true' owner to mitigate errors in a timely way after the occupier has commenced any development (the second-best

---

[33] D. G. Baird and T. H. Jackson, 'Information, Uncertainty, and the Transfer of Property', 13 *Journal of Legal Studies*, 299–320 (1984); T. Merrill, 'Property Rules, Liability Rules, and Adverse Possession', 79 *Northwestern University Law Review*, 1122–1154 (1986); T. J. Miceli and C. F. Sirmans, 'An Economic Theory of Adverse Possession', 15 *International Review of Law and Economics*, 162–173 (1995); J. M. Netter, 'Adverse Possession', in P. Newman (ed.), *The New Palgrave Dictionary of Economics and Law*, London: Macmillan, 1998.

solution) to reduce the ability of a true owner to act opportunistically to extract 'rents' from the occupier.[34]

A common adverse possession case concerns boundary disputes. Take a recent newspaper report of the dispute between the Dunne and Kupfer families over a six-inch strip of boundary land. The Dunnes commenced building over a strip of land adjoining their neighbour's (the Kupfers') property. A dispute broke out and moved to the courts. The Dunnes probably placed a higher value on the disputed land then the subjective valuation of the Kupfers. If it was discovered that the piece of land was in fact owned by the Kupfers, there would be room for negotiations. However, if construction of the Dunnes' extension had already started, the maximum amount the Dunnes would be willing to pay would increase because they had already made investment in the extension which had zero scrap or salvage value. The Kupfers in theory might be tempted to allow building to commence and then raise an objection. This action would drive up the stakes and the potential amount the Kupfers could demand. The difference between the value the Dunnes attached to the land prior to the construction and the value after it had commenced would represent what economists refer to as an '**appropriable quasi-rent**', defined as the difference between the initial value of the investment and its salvage value. If the possessor is convinced that the land is his – or, worse has encroached intentionally – the owner should move to correct the error. But since the value of the land to the possessor grows as his investment increases, the 'true' owner will lack an incentive to correct the error in a timely fashion. This is because by waiting he will be able to extract a higher payment. The possibility for the appropriation of quasi-rents by the owner is due to the fact that the owner can eject the possessor from the land at any time if a bargain is not struck. Thus a time-limited property rule, where the owner retains a right to eject a possessor from his land if a bargain is not reached, such as the doctrine of adverse possession, offers a solution to both problems. It provides the possessor with incentives to correct errors in a timely manner and limits bargaining costs between both parties.

The preceding analysis, while plausible, does not fully explain the rule. It does not seem that a twelve-year time limit would create an adequate incentive to avoid boundary disputes. It would, however, act asymmetrically to prevent someone who has not been diligent in monitoring land boundaries

[34] T. J. Miceli, *Economics of the Law: Torts, Contract, Property, Litigation*, Oxford: Oxford University Press, 1997.

for twelve years and one day later seeking to assert their property rights and creating continuing uncertainty over title.

An alternative solution is to use a liability rule to deal with boundary disputes. However a liability rule eliminates the occupier's incentive to discover errors before developing and may encourage him intentionally to encroach on another's land in order to obtain it more cheaply than in a free market transaction with the true owner. Indeed, some recent developments in law have created this perverse incentive.

TRANSFER OF TITLE

Establishing ownership of property is often not straightforward. This is excerbated where there is no title registration system, or where theft is involved. Consider the latter. All purchases of goods are subject to a risk that the seller does not own the good. The risk of stolen goods requires law that determines where the risk is to fall – on the true owner or the purchaser.

The law's treatment of ownership of stolen goods differs.[35] In England the purchaser acquires title if the goods were bought in good faith. This must be a genuine belief, and it should be necessary for the buyer to have taken reasonable steps to verify the true owner. In the USA, the rule is the opposite. A person can obtain good title only from someone who possesses it. These two rules lead to very different allocation of risks. The English (and European) rule places the risk on the original owner, and gives an incentive for the owner to protect his or her property. The US rule places it on the buyer, and gives an incentive for the buyer to verify that the seller is the true owner. The US rule deters theft while the English rule increases trade by increasing the certainty about title passing to the buyer. The economic choice between the two rules depends on whether the costs of the owner protecting his or her goods is higher or lower than the costs of the buyer verifying title.

ECONOMICS OF INCOMPATIBLE PROPERTY USE

Often the uses and activities on adjoining properties are incompatible. *A* wants to have a party on his land every weekend; *B* wants to have a quiet

---

[35] H. R. Weinberg, 'Sales Law, Economics and the Negotiability of Goods', 9 *Journal of Legal Studies*, 569–592 (1980); D. Baird and T. Jackson, 'Information, Uncertainty, and the Transfer of Property', 13 *Journal of Legal Studies*, 299–320 (1984).

day in the garden next door. Both are using their property as they want, but clearly *A*'s use reduces *B*'s enjoyment of his property. The exclusivity of *A*'s and *B*'s property rights will need to be tempered, since to enforce *A*'s right to use his property as he sees fit compromises his neighbour *B*'s enjoyment.

In these cases, the uses are incompatible. The efficiency goal of the law where there is an incompatible land use (principally nuisance) is to maximise the wealth derived from the use of the adjoining properties. In *Bamford* v. *Turnley*, a case involving nuisance caused by brick-making, Bramwell set a legal test in efficiency terms:

> The public consists of all the individuals of it and a thing is only for the public benefit when it is productive good to those individuals on the balance of loss and gain to all. So that if all the loss and all the gain were borne and received by one individual, he on the whole would be the gainer.[36]

Interestingly, this way of expressing the test points to the need to get both parties to take into account the full costs, benefits and alternatives of the different uses. This would be the case if both properties were owned by the same person – in *Bamford* the costs and losses of dust would be internalised and fully taken into account under single ownership.

Bramwell's statement, however, disguises the complex nature of the economic test to decide optimal land use patterns. This requires that the courts make at least two simultaneous cost-benefit calculations:

- **Marginal abatement test** which compares marginal costs and losses of different levels of abatement assuming that the two incompatible activities coexist.
- **Total activity test** which compares the net wealth generated by incompatible land uses when both parties have taken the efficient level of abatement with the net wealth when the two uses are separated.

The abatement decision assumes that the two activities should remain together and the efficient level of nuisance or annoyance has to be determined. This is arrived at by comparing the marginal costs of abatement with the marginal reduction in nuisance losses and selecting a level (and remedy) which brings this about. Where bargaining is costless this will be achieved without the need for legal intervention (Coase Theorem). The law simply has to set out the initial property rights from which the parties can begin their negotiations.

---

[36] (1860) 3 B&S 66; (1862) 122 Eng. Rep. 27. However Bramwell was clearly a Pareto efficiency man: 'law to my mind is a bad one, [which] for the public benefit, inflicts loss on an individual without compensation', 33.

In many cases more abatement is simply not an efficient outcome. This can clearly be seen by planning controls and covenants which prohibit certain activities in some areas and control (some would argue overcontrol) land use. To put it graphically, the central issue may not be whether the defendant operates his dynamite factory with greater care but whether it should be located in a residential area! The efficient solution is the separation of the incompatible uses.

Arguably for many incompatible uses this locational decision – a judicial zoning solution – is key to determining efficient law and understanding the law. It explains, for example, why in nuisance the law treats the defendant's abatement efforts asymmetrically – the failure to abate a nuisance will often suggest an actionable nuisance while abatement itself is not a sufficient defence.

Nuisance bargains

Some of the relevant considerations can be illustrated by *Sturges* v. *Bridgman*.[37] This concerned a dispute between two adjoining landowners in central London in 1879. Mr. Bridgman was a confectioner in Wigmore Street who used two mortars and pestles, one being in operation in the same position for over sixty years. This caused his neighbour Mr Sturges, a doctor in Wimpole Street, no bother for eight years until he built a consulting room at the end of his garden next to the confectioner's kitchen. The noise and vibration from the confectioner's mortar and pestle made it difficult for the doctor to use his consulting room. The doctor sued the confectioner and was awarded an injunction requiring the confectioner to cease making the noise and vibrations.

We know from the Coase Theorem that if transactions costs are zero and bargaining cooperative then the Court's decision will not affect the efficient solution. The parties would bargain until the gains from trade are exhausted. Thus if the loss to the doctor is £3 and the gain to the confectioner of being noisy is £8 then, irrespective of the legal decision in *Sturges* v. *Bridgman* the confectioner would continue in business and be noisy. If the doctor is awarded an injunction, as he was, then the confectioner would have an incentive to negotiate to buy out the injunction by offering to compensate the doctor for his loss. There is a bargaining surplus (£3 and up to £8) which the confectioner would be prepared to pay and a bargain will be reached if the parties act cooperative (that is, there is no strategic

[37] (1879) 11 Ch D. 852, CA. *See* 'Social Costs', 8–10.

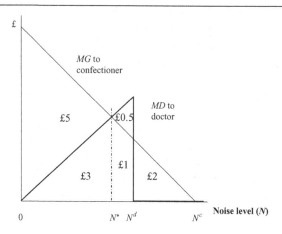

Figure 3.2 Abatement or shut down?

In *Sturges* v. *Bridgman* the court had a choice between abatement or relocation/zoning. The figure above sets out some hypothetical marginal and total cost figures that illustrate the importance of considering both. The figure assumes two possible solutions – optimal abatement and optimal activity level. The downward sloping schedule (MG) is the marginal gain (profitability) to the confectioner of being noisier as his production of sweets increases. The upward sloping schedule (MD) is the marginal damages borne by the doctor. As before, the efficient level of abatement which minimises costs, is the level of noise where the incremental abatement costs (MG) to the confectioner equal the incremental (MD) losses to the doctor, assuming that the two activities are adjoining. This is noise level N^*. This can be seen by tallying up the figures in each segment above (these give the losses or gains for the specific segment). At N^* the profit from making confectionery is £8 (£5 + £3) and the loss to the doctor is £3. Thus there is a 'bargaining surplus' of £5. There is no such surplus for increase in noise greater than N^*. To show that this would not be efficient, look at the effect of an incremental increase in noise from N^* to N^d. The gain to the confectioner is £1.00; however, the loss to the doctor is £1.50 (= £1.00 + £0.50). Thus the confectioner could not offer the doctor a sum sufficient to cover his loss in order to accept the increased noise. The increase is not Pareto efficient. Now look at the shut down option. This requires us to compare total wealth with the confectioner operating at his profitable level ignoring the doctor's losses with the confectioner taking abatement assuming that the doctor's surgery adjoins his property. In the above figure the doctor's *MD* schedule has been drawn assuming that at N^d the level of noise and vibrations is so great that it is no longer practical and profitable for the surgery to continue in operation. As a result, the maximum loss to the doctor is £4.50 – i.e. the total loss up to the point that the doctor is forced to close. However, the total gain to the confectioner of imposing the maximum profitable level of noise is £11.00. The latter is calculated by assuming that, with shut down, the confectioner operates at the profit maximising (equal to the sum of all the figures under the *MG* schedule up to where it intersects the horizontal axis) level. Now compare total wealth with efficient abatement and total wealth with the shut down of the surgery. With efficient abatement wealth is £5 = £8 − £3 compared to the case where the doctor shuts down, which is £11.00 − £4.50 = £6.50. The efficient solution is for the surgery to close down – i.e. a zoning solution.

behaviour). If the doctor is not awarded the injunction then this would be the efficient outcome on the assumed figures. Moreover, the doctor could not bargain to modify the outcome because his loss, and hence his maximum WTP, would only be £3, which is much less than the £8 gain to the confectioner from continuing as before.

If transactions costs are low and bargaining cooperative then the law provides a framework for the parties to resolve the conflicting use. In these circumstances, nuisance law's preference for a property rule (injunction) is consistent with economic precepts – it avoids substituting a costly legal transaction for a cheaper market one. Whether abatement or relocation is wealth maximising, the parties will negotiate the solution irrespective of the legal position.

It would seem that most nuisance claims could be covered by Coasean bargaining. The costs of two adjoining property owners getting together to resolve the conflict will be low. One suspects that many of these disputes are resolved without recourse to law, neighbours inconvenienced by loud music, smells, noise and other disturbances can often gain some accommodation with a polite (or abusive) request to stop. In other cases, the parties can come together to decide on the way they will deal with such difficulties either by formal rules, community norms or consideration for others' welfare.

Bargaining failure

In other cases, the parties cannot resolve their differences even when (physical) transactions costs are negligible. During the period when this book was written, British newspapers reported a number of disputes between neighbours which spilled over into the courts. These were relatively trivial disputes, though no doubt important to the parties. One concerned a disputed boundary which led to legal costs in excess of £150,000.[38] This was topped in early 2004 by a legal action over a boundary hedge brought by, of all persons, a retired lawyer, which generated £350,000 in legal costs and the sale of his property to pay the legal bill.[39] Rational economic man does not pay £350,000 to dispute a hedge worth several hundred pounds! But ordinary men, even lawyers, apparently do.

This type of impasse is as old as the law itself. This was the case in *Sturges* v. *Bridgman*. Sturges and Bridgmen did initially negotiate, albeit without any suggestion of Coasean-type payments changing hands.[40] Before the trial, they talked, and the confectioner took steps to reduce the noise by confining his grinding to certain hours (he abated). However, at some stage relations between the two soured and Sturges sued. If the law was clear to Sturges and Bridgman, there was no need to go to Court – Sturges had the right, and Bridgmen had to come to an arrangement with him. But they could not, and decided to substitute a costly legal transaction for a much cheaper market one.

Such bargaining failure typifies many nuisance cases that come to court. The parties begin by seeking a solution, quickly reach an impasse and resort to law to break the impasse or to vindicate their position.

The reason why this does not go smoothly is straightforward – the transactions costs are not those of getting together but the open-ended bilateral negotiations which lack the constraining influence of substitute performance. This mouthful of jargon can be expressed simply. In a competitive market, or even an uncompetitive one, if you don't like the terms of trade you simply find another buyer or seller. If you dispute the quality of the product, its price, or the terms of the contract, you simply move

---

[38] 'Neighbours' £150,000 fight over six inch strip of land', *Daily Mail*, 1 November 2003.

[39] S. Greenhill, 'A £350,000 bill (and the loss of their home) for couple who cut down neighbours' hedge', *Daily Mail*, 31 March 2004.

[40] This account draws on A. W. B. Simpson, 'Coase v. Pigou Reexamined', 25 *Journal of Legal Studies*, 53–97 (1996). What of Sturges? He became progressively deaf (despite the injunction), and was run over and killed by a Hansom Cab which he did not hear approaching. Ironically the cab was fitted with a noise abatement device – rubberised tyres – although it is not known whether these were responsible for his failure to hear the oncoming danger!

on to the next buyer or seller. Markets offer the possibility of substitute performance: that is what makes them efficient. In a dispute between two adjoining landowners you do not have this option, nor are there external constraints which can cut through the bargaining impasse in the absence of the law or other third-party binding intervention. To be sure, one party can get so fed up that he moves to another location, but this is a costly solution which may not be credible or efficient. To use the distinction made above about markets, the disputants are not price takers since there is no market for nuisance or other incompatible land uses, they are price makers. And it is the indeterminateness of the division of efficiency gains that can result in a failure to reach agreement.

There are significant impediments and frictions involved in a cooperative resolution to land use disputes.

First, the parties may simply not be able to agree on the size of the gains from trade or their division. This can occur because they do not have sufficient information to accurately measure them and disagree on the estimates. In 'loss of enjoyment' cases such as interference caused by smells, noise, or fumes, the losses are often largely subjective. In disputes between neighbours where the losses and gains are not immediately pecuniary but subjective, bargaining is highly personal. The measurement problem is difficult since the injurer will never be sure of the victim's exact pecuniary magnitude of losses which are largely subjective and idiosyncratic. This results in ambiguity over both the efficient solution and the gains from bargaining – if the injurer is liable the victim has an incentive to exaggerate his losses, whereas when not liable the victim will tend to downplay his losses and WTP. In either case there is no cheap method for the injurer to verify the victim's claims. The inability accurately to value either the subjective loss or its pecuniary equivalent will exacerbate the difficulties of reaching a cooperative solution, and the interaction 'tips' into a dispute.

Second, the parties may act in bad faith and opportunistically. In some situations, they may exaggerate the loss/costs. This is an inherent problem when the initial property right is given to the injurer. When the general rule is 'polluter-must-pay' there is a natural starting point from which bargaining can begin – no harm. This is not the case when the victims have no right to be free from harm since the benchmark is some positive but potentially manipulable level of harm which the injurer can use to extort greater payment from the victims. Indeed, one of the early debates among economists over the validity of the Coase Theorem centred on the possibility of extortion and phantom injurers that intentionally caused damage without any otherwise redeeming benefits. This introduces another matter for dispute, and one which the injurer can use to extract a higher payment.[41]

What has just been described economics refers to as **strategic behaviour**. That is, bargaining is possible but inefficient. This, in turn, makes the design of efficient law difficult. For one thing, the dictum that where transactions costs are low the efficient law should simply set out a property rule and let the parties sort it out may not suffice. There is no guarantee that the parties will use the law as a starting point for negotiation. As a result it will leave the dispute festering and the law sticking the parties to a possibly inefficient solution.

In such cases agreement is not likely to be forthcoming, and the law should seek to impose a solution which obviates the need for negotiation. That is, the law in such cases should not be designed to facilitate bargaining, as is commonly suggested, but to reduce transactions costs by making negotiation superfluous.[42]

One hypothesis is that this type of bargaining failure is more pronounced for loss of enjoyment cases than physical damage cases, and that this has influenced (explains) the law. In a loss of enjoyment case the losses are subjective and, as a result, not easy to quantify either in the economists' money terms or in terms of conveying to the other side their severity without appearing unreasonable, intransigent and overemotional.

Further, in loss of enjoyment cases the courts not only see abatement as the critical variable (the 'give and take') but, more importantly the need to cut through the bargaining failure we have identified. Here the law often adopts a standard based on reasonableness which allows some disamenity and inconvenience to a certain level but prohibits what are regarded as excessive levels of disamenity and inconvenience. If the reasonableness standard is based on a comparison of the costs and benefits of different levels of abatement/relocation, then the courts are effectively approximating what they regard as the efficient outcome. Thus it sets down an abatement level and enforces this directly through injunctions which prohibit the harm, rather than indirectly through damage awards.

The reasonableness standard in nuisance is broad enough to deal with the locational decision, since the court can decide that the activity is wholly unreasonable in the locality. But the more important observation is that in setting a reasonableness standard rather than a victim property rule the

---

[41] This is examined in D. H. Regan, 'The Problem of Social Cost Revisited', 15 *Journal of Law & Economics*, 427–437 (1972).

[42] C. G. Veljanovski, 'The Coase Theorem, and the Economic Theory of Markets and Law', 35 *Kyklos*, 53–74 (1982); R. Cooter, 'The Cost of Coase', 11 *Journal of Legal Studies*, 1–34 (1982).

Court is breaking the bargaining impasse of the parties. It is stating that the failure to reach an out-of-court solution will result in a court-imposed solution that is closer to the optimal one and minimises the possibility of post-injunctions bargaining. Under a reasonableness standard, the parties can accept the legal position/court determination, or they can bargain around it. However, a reasonableness standard reduces the scope for further bargaining because there are fewer gains from trade, and less to dispute. Thus a reasonableness standard minimises the prospect of an inefficient outcome, whether or not the parties agree.

The literature has often discussed bargaining in terms of the possibility of post-injunction bargaining.[43] The efficacy of setting legal rules as a framework for post-injunction bargaining as opposed to pre-suit bargaining to avoid a legal dispute is dubious (although the distinction may be largely semantic). It is highly unlikely that the parties who, having worked themselves into such a highly agitated state that one sees litigation as the only solution, would after their day in court, bruised and battered, considerably out of pocket, turn around and return to the negotiating table for round three after one has had their position vindicated by a judge. Obviously while the possibility cannot be ruled out, post-injunction bargaining appears a mirage. But more to the economic point it would be a grossly inefficient mirage if it were a frequent practice – it consumes large initial transactions costs, then a large quantity of legal process costs and then a further dollop of transactions costs: all highly wasteful and avoidable.

Where bargaining is not possible

Where bargaining is not possible the law should assign the right in a way that is most efficient. The efficiency of different responses will depend on the underlying costs and benefits.[44]

Whereas a property rule was efficient when transactions costs were negligible it is not necessarily so when they are prohibitive. A property rule

[43] See B. H. Thompson, 'Injunction Negotiations: An Economic, Moral and Legal Analysis', 27 *Stanford Law Review*, 1563–1595 (1975); W. Farnsworth, 'Do Parties to Nuisance Cases Bargain After Judgment? – A Glimpse inside the Cathedral', 66 *University of Chicago Law Review*, 373–436 (1999), reprinted in C. R. Sunstein, *Behavioral Law & Economics*, Cambridge: Cambridge University Press, 2002, chapter 12.

[44] For theoretical analysis of nuisance remedies, see A. M. Polinsky, 'Resolving Nuisance Disputes: The Simple Economics of Injunctive and Damage Remedies', 32 *Stanford Law Journal*, 1075–1112 (1980); A. M. Polinsky, 'Controlling Externalities and Protecting Entitlements: Property Right, Liability Rule, and Tax-Subsidy Approaches', 8 *Journal of Legal Studies*, 1–48 (1979); A. M. Polinsky, *An Introduction to Law and Economics*, Boston: Little Brown, 1989, chapters 4 and 12.

protecting victims from interference with their property will be efficient only if the victim is not required to take any abatement measures, and the injurer should cease his activities or relocate. For example, if a railway running steam engines[45] is prohibited from emitting sparks, farmers as a group would have little incentive to take appropriate cost minimising actions. Moreover, wheat farmers as a group would disregard the costs that they impose on the railway when they seek an injunction.[46] The wheat farmers would simply treat the cessation of railway transport as having zero opportunity costs. In the long run, such a rule will tend to encourage wheat farming at the expense of railways.

On the other hand a property rule which imposed no liability for the damage caused by spark-emitting trains would be efficient only if farmers are the ones who should relocate or take all the abatement measures. In the more general case where the railway can take action to reduce the emission of sparks, the rule would be inefficient since the costs of the railways would be understated and there would be both inefficient abatement and excessive railway activity.[47]

These potential inefficiencies of absolute property rules can be dealt with if the courts use a judgmental or cost-benefit standard which allows an intermediate solution to trigger culpability. This approach is adopted in loss of amenity cases where the assignment of property rights between the adjoining landowners is based not on full protection but a reasonableness, neighbourhood, or locality test (discussed below). That is, the victim is given judicial protection only from unreasonable loss of amenity and enjoyment, and is therefore expected to put up with those losses or harms which are reasonable. For example, residents may be greatly inconvenienced by noise, vibrations, dust and traffic caused by a building site which occurs day and night. The court could balance the interests of the builder with that of the adjoining residents by regarding not all noisy activity as unreasonable, but only the noise between the hours of 6.00 p.m. and 9.00 a.m. The Courts, in employing the reasonableness standard, define each party's property right in terms of an acceptable level of harmful activity. If a

---

[45] *See* A. C. Pigou, *The Economics of Welfare*, 4th edn., London: Macmillan, 1932, 183; 'Social Costs', 29–35; P. S. Atiyah, 'Liability for Railway Nuisance in the English Common Law: A Historical Footnote', 23 *Journal of Law & Economics*, 191–196 (1980).

[46] In *Vaughan v. The Taff Vale Railway Company* (1860) 5 H.&N. 679, 157. E. R. 1351, Bramwell notes the difficulty of 'holdouts' created by granting the claimant an injunction: 'a man who would not accept a pecuniary compensation might put a stop to works of great value and much more than enough to compensate him.'

[47] T. Merrill, 'Trespass, Nuisance, and the Cost of Determining Property Rights', 14 *Journal of Legal Studies*, 13–48 (1985).

reasonableness test is used by the Courts, and economically based, then it eliminates one alleged inefficiency of injunctions.

Summary

From the above discussion three economic propositions can be derived:
- The law of nuisance defines the components of the bundle of property rights which attach to land. As such they define 'ownership' and influence the value of land. Land with greater protection against interference from incompatible adjoining land uses, or from pollution, will be more valuable than land where the law does not protect land from these disamenities.
- Where transactions costs are low the law should facilitating bargaining by delineating the initial property rights.
- Where negotiations are possible but fraught with strategic bargaining problems the law should seek to limit the scope of negotiations by setting out a judicial solution which eliminates most of the gains from trade. This is done by setting legal standards which approximate the efficient solution.

NUISANCE

Nuisance is a tort covering undue interference with the use and enjoyment of land. It is the area of common law most associated with the protection of the environment, although its role has diminished with the rise of environmental protection legislation, and planning controls.[48] Here we confine our attention to private nuisance involving property disputes.

Legal position

English nuisance law distinguishes between two types of nuisance – those involving physical damage to property and chattels, and those involving loss in enjoyment and use of the property. *St Helen's Smelting Co.* v. *Jipping*[49] is authority for the distinction between 'material injury to property', which is an actionable nuisance, and harms which occasion 'personal discomfort' which must satisfy the reasonableness test. In the former case it will be

---

[48] For an excellent introduction to the English law of nuisance, see R. A. Buckley, *The Law of Nuisance*, London: Butterworths, 2nd edn., 1996.

[49] (1895) 11 HL Cas. J2. N. Morag-Levine, *Chasing Wind – Regulation of Air Pollution in the Common Law State*, Cambridge, MA: Princeton University Press, 2003; A. W. B. Simpson, *Leading Cases in the Common Law*, Oxford: Clarendon Press, 1995.

sufficient if the claimant can show that he has suffered 'sensible material damage' that has resulted in a diminution in the value of the property. The damage must be more than trifling but need not be substantial to establish liability. In cases where there is a loss of enjoyment and amenity courts 'often make ... a comparison between what would be gained and what would be lost'[50] in determining liability.

These features have led to criticisms of the efficiency of nuisance law. In particular, the refusal of the Courts to award damages (liability rule) is seen as inefficient because it does not permit the injurer to decide the appropriate level of abatement, while an injunction is a blunt instrument which does not allow a flexible response, can potentially freeze land use and gives the claimant a powerful weapon with which to hold a defendant to ransom or cease an activity with a considerable economic value. Damages, on the other hand, avoid these inefficiencies. As a result, a number of reformulations of nuisance law have been proposed that place greater reliance on damages as the preferred remedy.[51] This can be termed the 'case for damages'. Further, the greater protection given to physical interference with property rights compared to loss of enjoyment and amenity is seen as anomalous. Indeed, the doctrinal structure of the law of nuisance has been described as an 'impenetrable jungle'[52] and containing limited economic logic.[53] Here we examine the economics of some of the doctrines and remedies of private nuisance law.

Physical vs amenity loss

The law's different treatment of physical and non-physical harm has attracted considerable criticism. It is argued that the common law gives greater protection from physical interference than the loss of enjoyment.

In *St Helens Smelting Co.*, Lord Westbury intimated that the distinction between material damage and discomfort would not apply where the immediate result was 'sensible injury to the value of the property'. We now know enough about the operation of property markets to treat this as a specious qualification since one would expect that all discomforts

---

[50] 'Social Costs', 27–28.

[51] R. C. Ellickson, 'Alternatives to Zoning: Covenants, Nuisance Rules, and Fines as Land Use Controls', 40 *University Chicago Law Review*, 681–781 (1973); E. Rabin, 'Nuisance Law: Rethinking Fundamental Assumptions', 63 *Virginia. Law Review*, 1299–1348 (1977); Note, 'Internalizing Externalities: Nuisance Law and Economic Efficiency', 53 *New York University Law Review*, 219–240 (1978).

[52] W. L. Prosser, *Handbook of Torts*, St Pauls, MN: West Publishing Co., 1971, 516.

[53] A. I. Ogus and G. Richardson, 'Economics and the Environment: A Study of Private Nuisance', 36 *Cambridge Law Journal*, 284–325 (1977).

sufficient to warrant litigation would affect property values – and, indeed, wage rates – in the locality. The price of land will reflect actual and potential residents' valuation of nuisance (and workers required to live and work in areas where there is pollution will, all things equal, demand a wage premium). Hence a reference to diminution in land values involves a circularity. If land values reflect the losses imposed by a nuisance, then using a diminution in the value of land to make the nuisance actionable would either find all significant nuisances actionable or none, but would not support the court's distinction between physical harm and loss of enjoyment cases. The distinction also takes an *ex post* view of the matter. When individuals buy a house they are, in effect, buying a bundle of property rights, including the right to bring a claim if there is an actionable nuisance, and to have covenants and statutory environmental controls enforced. In cases where there is a breach, the offender should be required to comply. If the property market worked perfectly land value would be depressed only by the expected costs of enforcing these various amenity rights.

As suggested above, the distinction may arise more from a belief that where physical damage is involved the parties are more likely to negotiate because the damages are more verifiable.

The reasonableness test

When an action is based on the discomfort or inconvenience of the claimant caused by, for example, noise and smells, the Courts have explicitly recognised the reciprocal character of the dispute, and in deciding liability balance a number of considerations.[54] The factors governing liability, while they do not have a one-to-one correspondence to the economic concepts, seem to have a close affinity.

Substantiality

First, in order for the defendant to be liable the harm must be substantial. This requirement ensures that trivial cases do not come to Court, thus economising on legal costs. Moreover, nuisance disputes involving large losses are also more likely to be those for which some corrective action is warranted. The greater the damage, the larger the cost savings from a reduction in or cessation of the nuisance.

---

[54] For example, Wright L.: 'a balance has to be maintained between the right of the occupier to do what he likes with his own land, and the right of his neighbour not to be interfered with.' *Sedleigh-Denfield* v. *O'Callaghan* [1940] AC 880 at 903.

Locality

Locality is another factor taken into account by the courts to determine whether the defendant's activities are reasonable. This test is captured in the oft-cited dictum in *Sturges* v. *Bridgman* that 'what would be a nuisance in Belgrave Square would not necessarily be so in Bermondsey'. The application of this test appears to be very finely graduated so that what is a nuisance at one end of the street in England, need not be at the other. In *Adams* v. *Ursell*[55] a fried fish and chip shop in a predominantly working-class area was set up near houses of 'a much better character'. The court found Mr Ursell's frying a nuisance but the injunction did not even extend to the whole street. Presumably the defendant was able to move his chippie down the road where the houses were of 'a worse character'.

The locality test makes economic sense. As we have seen in the formal analysis there are two dimensions along which the efficiency calculation must be applied – abatement and locality. The failure of the defendant to take measures to abate the nuisance that are not excessively expensive will usually attract liability, although the converse will not, even if cost-justified, avoid liability. The refusal of the Courts to regard reasonable care/abatement as a complete defence has a clear economic logic. The Courts may decide that, taking everything into account, the level of, say, vibrations is excessive and should be reduced. Alternatively, the Court may decide that no level of vibration is reasonable in the particular locality. In such a situation the cost-benefit calculation takes place not over the actions of the respondent but the activity itself.

Consider the operation of a dynamite factory in an urban area. Applying the reasonableness test to this would require one to compare the marginal costs and marginal benefits of the different ways of safely handling dynamite. Alternatively, one could find that the total gain and losses from handling dynamite in a residential area, even if carried out in the safest possible way, did not warrant the harm that could be inflicted. Nuisance law focuses on this calculation more than negligence-type reasonableness.

Hypersensitivity

A claimant will not usually be entitled to a higher level of protection than others living in the same area. The rule in *Robinson* v. *Kilvert*[56] holds that a person whose activity is abnormally sensitive to interference, either personally or in terms of the activities carried out on the land, may not have a claim if other activities do not suffer a similar loss.

[55] [1913] 1 Ch 269.   [56] [1913] 1 Ch 269, 82 LJ Ch 157.

The Court's refusal to determine liability based on the losses of hyper-sensitive individuals or uses has an economic logic. This is the problem of adverse selection already discussed. The optimal solution requires not only that joint costs be minimised, but that the calculation be based on the damages sustained by only those individuals for which losses are the lowest. For example, the benefits from reducing the noise and vibrations in *Sturges* v. *Bridgman* will, if based on actual damage, depend on the type of patients being treated. To take an extreme example, the losses inflicted on the doctor would be greater if he carried out a psychiatric practice than if he were treating deaf mutes for eye complaints. Basing liability on normal damages deters high-loss individuals from locating near nuisances.

In other cases the claimant may have an exaggerated reaction to the nuisance. Many amenity losses may fall into the category of 'impressions upon the mind rather than facts',[57] and therefore liable to exaggeration and disproportionate attention by the alleged victims. In *Gaunt* v. *Fynney* it was stated that:

a nervous, or anxious or prepossessed listener hears sounds which would otherwise go unnoticed, and magnifies and exaggerates into some new significance, originating within himself, sounds which at other times would be passively heard and not regarded.

Consider a more topical variant of the above. Suppose that the Government announced that it planned to build a new airport in a rural area. The initial effect of the announcement would be to depress land values in the area. Those who live in the countryside do so to escape traffic congestion and aircraft noise, and the land values reflect this. The disamenity to the existing residents caused by the airport would be capitalised in the initial fall in property values. However, over time property values would rise. This is because a different type of resident would move into the area who did not mind traffic and aircraft noise as much.[58]

This example raises two questions. The first is whether as a matter of public policy the initially affected residents who suffer a significant diminution in the value of their properties should be compensated. The second, and more relevant one from a nuisance point of view, is what should be the

---

[57] *Gaunt* v. *Fynney* (1872), 8 Ch App. 8 at 12–13. Street comments that 'physical damage is a more tangible and readily proved loss than personal annoyance; English courts are always chary of protecting personal discomforts', *Street on Torts*, 231.
[58] Some argue that there should be additional compensation for so-called 'irreplaceable consumer surplus' generated by sentimental/emotional attachment to the land. *See* R. C. Ellickson, 'Alternatives to Zoning', 733–737.

correct measure of damages – the diminution in the value of the property of people who intensely dislike aircraft noise or the diminution in value when the land is occupied by people who do not mind it as much. The answer to this question is clear – it is the latter measure.

Social utility

Nuisance law has been criticised for not taking into account the social utility of the defendant's activities. If the defendant's conduct is totally devoid of 'social utility' – where, for instance it is deliberately designed to annoy his neighbour – liability will result.[59] However, in English law the courts will not usually take into account the social utility of the defendant's activity.

Two cases illustrate the problems with the rule. In *Bellew* v. *Cement Co.*[60] the claimant complained about the vibrations brought about by blasting in an adjoining quarry. The claimant had sold the land to the developer, had warned the claimant about the blasting and advised him not to build near the quarry, and prior to the legal action the quarry had considerably reduced the annoyance by changing its blasting techniques. The unusual fact in this case is that the defendant was the only cement producer in Eire and supplied 80 per cent of the country's cement at a time when building was an urgent public necessity. An injunction would have closed down the factory for three – six months. The Court held that the rights of the parties should not be sacrificed to public convenience. This case is criticised for resulting in an alleged cost imposed on the defendant disproportionate to the benefits to the residents.

In contrast, the US case of *Boomer* v. *Atlantic Cement Co.*,[61] based on similar facts, substituted damages for an injunction. In *Boomer* the New York Court compared the costs and benefits to determine the appropriate remedy. A plant costing $45 million to construct and employing 300 workers inflicted a loss on the claimant of $185,000. In view of the disparity between the harm to the defendant if an injunction were granted, and the benefit to the claimant, the court awarded damages.

---

[59] *Christie* v. *Davey* [1893] 1 Ch 316 (where the defendant deliberately hammered and beat trays to interrupt neighbours' music teaching) and *Hollywood Silverfox Farm* v. *Emmett* [1936] 1 All ER 825 (defendant spitefully shot off guns near silver fox farm, frightening foxes and caused them to miscarry).

[60] [1948] Ir. R. 61.

[61] (1970), 257 N.E. 2d 870 (N.Y.S.C.). However, the precedent set by *Boomer* has been diminished by the New York Court of Appeals in the later case of *Coport Industries, Inc.* v. *Consolidated Edison Co.* 41 N.Y. 2d 564.

Two English cases have taken account of public benefits. In *Miller* v. *Jackson*[62] the Court substituted damages for an injunction because of the public benefits from cricket and in *Kennaway* v. *Thomson*[63] the Court of Appeal substituted an injunction on terms which allowed the activities of a speed boat club to continue, but in a restricted way, on the grounds of general public benefit. But the common law rule is that the claimant's rights should not be compromised because it can be shown that the world at large is receiving great benefits.

The refusal of courts to take social utility into account appears inefficient. However, it is not clear why the rights of the residents should be compromised because of wider considerations. If the Court's decision was based on the costs and benefits of further abatement and/or relocation, it would need only to evaluate the costs of reducing the nuisance against the benefits to the residents. The 'social utility' of the defendant's activity would already be incorporated in the loss of profitability to the quarry from complying with the injunction. But perhaps the greatest danger is that the inclusion of the social utility of the defendant's conduct would permit the consideration and argument of a wide range of vague considerations which would reduce the protection afforded to those suffering from otherwise unreasonable interference.[64]

COMING TO THE NUISANCE[65]

Coming to the nuisance is not a defence in England although at one time it was considered that a person who acquired a property near a harmful activity impliedly consented to the nuisance.[66]

Allowing coming to a nuisance as a defence has a certain economic appeal. It establishes a property right in favour of the party first in time at a particular location, and if the damage is fully anticipated it will be capitalised in the value of the adjoining properties. The rule also encourages only those individuals to locate near harmful activities for whom the net benefits

---

[62] [1971] 3 All ER 338 (CA).   [63] [1980] 3 All ER 329.

[64] This appears to have been the position in the USA. J. L. Lewin, 'Compensated Injunctions and the Evolution of Nuisance Law', 71 *Iowa Law Review*, 777–832 (1986).

[65] D. Wittman, 'First Come, First Served: An Economic Analysis of Coming to the Nuisance', 9 *Journal of Legal Studies*, 557–568 (1980); D. Wittman, 'Optimal Pricing of Sequential Inputs: Last Clear Chance, Mitigation of Damages, and Related Doctrines in the Law', 10 *Journal of Legal Studies*, 65–91 (1991).

[66] *Bliss* v. *Hall* (1838) 4 Bing. N.C. 138. English and American nuisance law diverge in this area as coming to a nuisance is a defence in some American states. *See* P. M. Irvine, 'Balancing Pollution and Property Rights: A Comparison of the Development of English and American Nuisance Law', 7 *Anglo–American Law Review*, 31–56 (1978).

(inclusive of harm) outweigh those of alternative locations. However, if it should turn out that the party first in time is the better avoider of the loss, then allowing coming to a nuisance as a defence will be inefficient. Again, we are confronted with the need to provide both parties with the incentive to take efficient action in the way they behave and where they live. But the calculation also involves a tricky decision of the optimal use of land in particular areas, which is a complex inquiry.

Miller v. *Jackson* illustrates some of the competing considerations relevant to coming to the nuisance cases. The case concerned a village cricket field that had previously been surrounded by open fields and upon which cricket had been played for the past seventy years. The adjoining fields were subsequently turned into a housing estate and the evidence shows that some of the houses, including the claimant's, had been built too close to the field. As a result the claimant's property was damaged by the occasional 'six' hit by the better batsmen and while the game was in progress there was the constant fear of balls being hit into the property. The claimant had complained both to the council and the cricket club about the situation and as a result had the council rates reduced, and the cricket club took measures to reduce the risk of balls entering and damaging the property. The cricket club had sufficiently reduced the risk of harm that the rating authority subsequently restored the council rates to their original level.[67] In addition, the cricket club had offered to remedy all damage and pay all expenses.

Lord Denning's judgment implicitly accepts coming to the nuisance as a defence. According to Denning, the task was to 'balance the right of the cricket club to continue to play cricket . . . , as against the right of householders not to be interfered with'. For Denning, the answer was clear: cricket should not be stopped; the claimant was the least-cost avoider. The fact that Mrs Miller was hypersensitive and did not wish to bear the risk of injury resulting from her choice to live near the cricket club was not sufficient to impose liability. As several of the judges pointed out, the claimant's having accepted the benefits of the open spaces they should also accept the disadvantages. If the claimant did not address herself to the latter then she should have, and a rule of law that encourages people to make informed choices is desirable.

---

[67] Some interesting facts emerged in the case. In 1975 there were 13,326 balls bowled of which six struck the Millers' house, and in 1976 there were 15,696 balls bowled of which nine struck the Millers' house. This works out as a 5 in 10,000 chance of a ball striking the house, of which the chance of actually damaging the house was 3 in 10,000. To put this risk in perspective, the chance at the time of actual bodily injury or death in UK manufacturing industry was 68 in 10,000. The Millers were awarded damages of around £174.14 for past loss, which works out to about £30 per year. The cricket club spent £700 taking measures to abate the nuisance.

Denning also implicitly recognised that this involved more than the right of cricket versus freedom from 'sixes'. There was also a question of who should be living in the house. If the Millers had made a 'mistake' of buying the house they should bear the loss or move away, there would be many cricket lovers willing to buy it. To grant an injunction would be to effectively reward the claimant for making a mistake and this would be inefficient if the optimal solution was cricket and adjoining residents who were cricket lovers.

The case also illustrates the actual and prospective incentive effects of nuisance law. The cricket club obviously realised that coming to a nuisance was not a defence and should the case go to Court they would in all likelihood lose. They thus sought to take 'every feasible step to prevent injury' and in addition agreed to compensate the claimant for any residual loss. Had the law been otherwise one conjectures that the willingness of the cricket club to go to such lengths would not have been as strong. It would appear that in *Miller* v. *Jackson*, on a strict market test, the defendants were willing to cover the costs of abatement and damages and that the nuisance should continue.

REMEDIES

Legal position

In English law the injunction – or, more accurately, a 'perpetual prohibitive injunction' – is the usual remedy where the nuisance is of a continuing nature or is likely to be repeated. Damages are confined to valid claims for past losses, or as the sole remedy only where all of the following conditions exist – the damage must be small, capable of monetary estimation and be compensated by a small monetary payment, and it would be oppressive in the circumstances to grant an injunction.[68]

The courts in England are opposed to giving damages as the remedy for a nuisance. The general judicial attitude is that the Courts should not 'allow a wrong to continue simply because the wrongdoer is able and willing to pay for the injury he may inflict'[69] because to do so would 'fix judicially the price that an intending tortfeasor could pay for the licence to commit a wrong'. Damages would in effect give the defendant the right compulsorily to purchase the claimant's property, something which would

---

[68] *Shelfer* v. *City of London Electric Lighting Co.* (1895).
[69] *Leeds Industrial Co-operative Society Ltd* v. *Slack* (1924) AC 851, 315–16.

normally require legislative authority. It is also been argued that damages are hard to measure and would be inadequate because they do not reflect the subjective losses of the claimant, while an injunction gives the claimants 'full' compensation.

Economics of damages

Many commentators have advocated damages as the preferred remedy in nuisance. They give the injurer the freedom to determine whether paying compensation to the victim is cheaper than abatement, and to decide whether an intermediate solution is better. However, the 'case for damages' and strict liability is predicated on two assumptions – that strict liability with compensatory damages is 'efficient' and that the court can measure and monitor losses fairly accurately and cost-effectively. These two (implicit) assumptions can be explored in more detail.

The first objection to strict liability coupled with compensatory damages is that it does not convey the correct incentive to victims to take abatement, or relocate if this is the efficient solution.[70] This can again be illustrated by the spark-emitting steam train which frequently sets fire to wheat fields adjoining the tracks. If the railway is required to compensate the wheat farmers for the lost profits on destroyed crops it might be thought that this is the efficient solution. The railway bears the social costs of running trains; the farmers' losses have been internalised, to use the economists' jargon. This gives the railway an incentive to invest in spark-arresting equipment if this costs less than the damage payments it has to make to the farmers.

This, however, ignores the incentives this conveyed the wheat farmers adjoining the track. If they are compensated for their actual lost profits from destroyed wheat, they will be indifferent between selling their wheat on the market, or having it burned and receiving compensation. While it would be far-fetched to suggest that farmers deliberately want their wheat burned, the receipt of full compensation will make them (marginally) less careful either in planting wheat too close to the track or taking other preventative measures.

To make the example a little more interesting (and perhaps a smidgen far-fetched), suppose that a new variety of spark-resistant wheat is developed which reduces the farmer's losses. If wheat farmers received full compensation for their actual losses they will not be encouraged to plant such

---

[70] E. K. Browning, 'External Economies, Compensation, and the Measure of Damages', 43 *Southern Economic Journal*, 1279–1287 (1977).

fire-resistant wheat. There is a moral hazard problem of the type described above – the compensation payment reduces incentives on the farmers to be careful and thereby increases the risk of an accident/loss occurring.

The cause of this problem is the combination of strict liability and the way damages are calculated. If the actions of farmers can, as assumed above, significantly affect the likelihood and extent of losses, then they should *not* receive compensation for actual losses. Compensation irrespective of the actions of the farmer operates as a perfect insurance scheme, and does not encourage (pay) the farmer to spend any money on abatement, or re-locate if this is the efficient solution. That is, a moral hazard problem is created. Thus compensation based on the actual losses of the victim without any limitation on the circumstances under which it is given is not efficient.[71]

The correct damage measure is the lost profits (or diminution in the value of land) when farmers take the efficient/optimal avoidance measures – i.e. planting fire-resistant wheat or re-locating. This **mitigated damage measure** preserves the incentive on the victims (farmers) to take cost-justified precautions. Viewed by the farmer, his level of compensation is invariant to the actions he takes and therefore he will use the type of wheat that maximise his profits – which with respect to the potential damage is the expected losses plus the compensation received. This rule extends to the trickier question as to whether the two incompatible land uses should be together or separated. If the efficient response is for the two conflicting activities to be in separate locations then the efficient mitigated damage measure will be zero even if the farmer has planted fire-resistant wheat.

This can be illustrated with a few figures. Assume that the loss from destroying standard-variety wheat is £400 while that of fire-resistant variety wheat only £100. The maximum liability of the railway should only be £100 and not £400 whether or not fire-resistant wheat is planted. If the farmer were to receive only £100 in damages every time his standard wheat field burned away he would quickly seek to minimise his losses, and this can be done only by planting fire-resistant wheat. Given this arrangement, the farmers would find that they maximised profits (inclusive of compensation for destroyed crops) by planting fire-resistant wheat. Thus if the spark-resistant wheat rarely ignites or burns only in a small strip before extinguishing itself, then the compensation should be for that level of loss and not for actual losses even if the whole farm, including the farmer's

---

[71] This inefficiency does not result from the economists' (Pigouvian) tax proposal that a tax be imposed equal to the actual damages. This is because the tax is not given as compensation to the victim. Hence a pollution tax effectively confronts both the injurer and the victim with the social costs and so the victim takes the efficient action.

house, burns down. If the latter never ignites then the correct level of (mitigated) damages is zero (as it would be if an efficiency calculation showed that wheat farmers should not be located near railway tracks, even if they plant fire-resistant wheat).

This mitigated damage measure is not used in nuisance cases. This seems sensible for fairly straightforward reasons. In practice, it would be too hard to calculate, it would not be based on compensatory principles but on the hypothetical losses of individuals who should locate near the nuisance with the lowest losses. This is a 'counterfactual' which increases the evidentiary burden on the Court.

There are two other considerations which limit the case for damages in land use cases.

First, there are good reasons to believe that the estimation of the efficient damage measure in nuisance cases would be subject to considerable errors given the complexity of the variables that must be taken into account. This would be the case for physical damage such as described, but particularly where the losses are more subjective, as in loss of enjoyment and amenity nuisance disputes.

Second, damages as a remedy to an ongoing nuisance may not be an adequate response because it would not directly control the level of nuisance. The level of abatement or whether one party should prevail would not be the subject of the court's direct judgment. The court would calculate the appropriate damages, impose these on the injurer and the outcome would depend on the injurer's response. So the remedy would have no certainty and would leave the possibility of post-judgment conflict and rancour.

Third, compensatory damages generate significant error costs because the level of abatement is sensitive to the way that damages are calculated. Assume that damages are awarded for losses on a continuing (annual) basis but that the court makes a mistake. Under a strict liability rule if the court overestimates the losses there will be too much abatement; if it underestimate's the losses there will be two little abatement. This miscalculation will not only affect the level of compensation but also the level of abatement and nuisance. If the damages are too low the level of nuisance will be excessive and if too high the level of nuisance will be too low. Under a strict liability plus compensatory damages rule the level of abatement is highly sensitive (elastic) to the calculation of damages, and this tends to generate significant error costs.

These damage-induced errors costs can be reduced by a judgmental or fault-based standard. To revert to the train/wheat example, although it is not the position in law, the efficient solution could be induced by the award of compensatory damages based on actual losses of the wheat farmers, but denying compensation if there has been insufficient abatement. If the railway company were allowed a defence of, say, 'inadequate abatement' when the 'wrong' type of wheat was planted, then the monetary calculation of the farmer would radically alter. Farmers would receive compensation only if they planted the right type of wheat and not otherwise and therefore they will find it profitable only to plant the right type of wheat or bear the losses themselves. It could also be handled by a fault-type standard imposed on the railway company. The railway would be liable for damages if it failed to take the cost-justified level of care/precaution. This would induce the railway company to avoid liability and as a result wheat farmers would seek to minimise the losses without compensation, thus encouraging them to take efficient abatement. The difference here is that the court can substantially miscalculate the losses and still gain compliance with the judicially determined level of abatement. This is because of the discontinuous nature of the imposition of damages triggered by breaching the judicially determined level. Compliance with the standard results in the party avoiding all damages and incurring only abatement costs. Thus as long as the incorrectly estimated losses exceed the abatement costs there will be compliance. The conclusion is that a reasonableness standard in nuisance when damages are the routine remedy would avoid some of the inefficiency identified above.

Injunctions

As stated above injunctions – what has been termed a 'property rule' – can be grossly inefficient when bargaining is not possible. Take the facts in *Bellew* and *Boomer* where an injunction in the absence of post-injunction bargaining would put a stop to productive activity many times more valuable than the losses that the smoke and dust inflicted on neighbours. In *Boomer* the figures speak for themselves – damages of $185,000 compared to capital investment in the plant of $45 million.

In practice injunctions are, first, not as inefficient or as totally bereft of economic logic as often portrayed. In many cases the potential inefficiency of injunctive relief is reduced by the reasonableness standard in determining whether a nuisance is actionable (as discussed above).

Second, an injunction 'on terms' can be granted. This is where the injunction does not simply ban the defendant's activities but requires a reduction in the level of harm. For example, in the Canadian case of *Huston* v. *Lloyd*

Refineries[72] an oil refinery moved to a predominantly residential area emitting a combination of offensive odours, oily soot and noise. Prior to the hearing the refinery reduced the noise level coming from the cracking unit from what was described as a 'whining and screeching' noise to a 'moaning noise' which could still be heard by the claimant. The defendant argued, and the Court accepted, that further improvement would involve 'an expenditure of money economically beyond the plant size of the defendant and would destroy the Canadian $0.5m' (at 1930 prices). The Court awarded an injunction on terms specifying an acceptable level of harm: the nuisance was not to exceed the level existing during October 1936; the cracking unit was not to be cleaned between 7 p.m. and 7 a.m. and damages were also awarded to the claimant for past and future loss.

This approach has been used in England. In *Halsey* v. *Esso Petroleum Co. Ltd*[73] the defendant's lorries caused a nuisance and their movement and number was restricted during certain hours. In *Kennaway* v. *Thomson* an injunction on terms was awarded. The claimant built a house near a lake used for speedboat racing and water skiing. Over time boating activity on the lake increased. The case was appealed because the judge awarded damages of £1,600 since he concluded that an injunction would be oppressive given the public benefits. The court overturned this but substituted an injunction on terms. It decided that the noise level when the claimant came to the nuisance must have been reasonable and that the problem was the subsequent increase in noise largely due to the use of powerful speedboats. The claimant was awarded an injunction which specified in detail the permissible the level of activity on the lake – no more than one three-day international event; two two-day events separated by at least four weeks; no boat to make a noise greater than 75 decibels except at events; club motor boat racing restricted to six weekends; and no more than six speedboats for water skiing on the lake at any one time.

Economic considerations are taken into account in the implementation of injunctions. The court may award a suspended injunction to allow the defendant a reasonable time to comply, thus economising on abatement costs.

The courts are also aware that the parties may make strategic use of injunctions. Often the claimant will want to stop the defendant's activities immediately. If the delay before the trial is substantial, the defendant may try to steal a march on the claimant. In *Isenberg* v. *East India House Estate Co.*[74] the claimant complained that his right to light had been diminished by

---

[72] [1937] OWN 53 (HC).   [73] [1961] 2 All ER 579.   [74] (1863) 3 de GJ & Sm 263, 3 New rep 345.

the building the defendant was constructing. The defendant, knowing that the claimant was bringing an action, accelerated his work. An interlocutory injunction deals with such a situation by affording the claimant interim relief pending a trial. Obviously the claimant can use this as a way of imposing heavy costs on the defendant. The Courts have wisely dealt with this form of strategic behaviour by normally requiring the claimant to undertake to pay the defendant's losses should his action for a full injunction fail.

TRESPASS

Trespass is an intentional tort which violates an owner's right to the possession and use of his or her property. The adverse possession rule condones one type of trespass. However, more usually the common law provides for absolute protection of property's exclusivity by prohibiting trespass and allows the landowner to eject the trespass and claim damages.

In the general case, such actions take place in situations of low transactions costs and the goal of the law should be to force the trespasser to seek a consensual solution rather than a unilateral 'taking' of the owner's property. Thus economics would support the unconditional deterrence of trespass and protection by a property rule.

The rationale for taking such an approach is to ensure that property rights are protected and the transfer is subject to a market test. If the owner's rights can be 'taken' at will there is no evidence that the trespasser values the use or ownership more than the existing owner. If the trespasser does, then he should pay the owner's asking price and this establishes both that his value is greater than the existing owner's and avoids the disincentive and economic waste of persistent challenges to ownership.

The law allows exceptions to the strict property rule approach of trespass law which are consistent with economic logic. The most obvious is the defence of necessity. If a person is in peril or engaged in some socially useful activity and passes over or uses the land and chattels of another, then he or she will have a defence.

Even where the trespass is inadvertent a market solution is possible provided transactions costs are low. Animal trespass provides one example. Take the example of straying cattle which trample adjoining wheat fields. Given the ability to quantify the losses and gains on both sides and a cooperative demeanour, the optimal solution would be arrived at whether the farmer was held liable or not. This is a simple application of the Coase Theorem. The parties would either agree a level of compensation or payment to reflect the opportunity costs of reducing the number of straying cattle, or build and maintain fences. Who pays for these actions would depend on the initial property rights.

Coase's use of animal trespass to illustrate the Coase Theorem has stimulated empirical research on trespass laws' effects on how ranchers and farmers resolve the problem of animal trespass.

Vogel's study examined animal trespass laws in California between 1850 and 1890.[75] During this period the law favoured ranchers who were not legally liable for the damage caused by trespassing cattle. This apparently hindered the development of agriculture and over the period no less than 150 laws designed to alter the law in favour of farmers were enacted. Vogel's econometric analysis shows that changes in animal trespass laws had a significant effect on crop production and contributed to the growth of agriculture. He suggests that the change in the law had allocative effects because transactions costs were positive but lower under a strict liability rule. Under a no liability rule favouring ranchers, each farmer would have had to negotiate with all ranchers likely to own trespassing cattle to arrive at an *ex ante* contractual solution, whereas under the strict liability rule ranchers had only to negotiate with a more limited number of farmers likely to be affected by his straying cattle. Ellickson's study examined cattle trespass disputes in Shasta County, California. Under open-range laws ranchers were not usually responsible for accidental trespass whereas they were under closed-range laws. Ellickson found that ranchers and their neighbours acted cooperatively to resolve disputes regardless of the legal position based on community norms.[76] He also found that invariably it was the ranchers who erected fences irrespective of the law because both groups believed that straying cattle 'causes' the damage and therefore the rancher should be liable. That is, community norms substituted for the law and the parties were often unaware of the legal position. Interestingly, neighbourliness appears to have fashioned the response, and 'causation' was used as a basis for 'liability'. Hanley and Sumner's study of roaming red deer in the Scottish Highlands reaches similar conclusions to Ellickson.[77]

[75] K. R. Vogel, 'The Coase Theorem and California Animal Trespass Law', 16 *Journal of Legal Studies*, 149–187 (1987).

[76] R. C. Ellickson, *Order without Law: How Neighbours Settle Disputes*, Cambridge, MA: Harvard University Press, 1991 and his earlier articles 'Of Coase and Cattle: Dispute Resolution among Neighbors in Shasta County', 38 *Stanford Law Review*, 623–687 (1986) and 'The Case for Coase and Against "Coaseanism"', 99 *Yale Law Journal*, 611–630 (1989).

[77] N. Hanley and C. Sumner, 'Bargaining Over Common Property Resources: Applying the Coase Theorem to Red Deer in the Scottish Highlands', 43 *Journal of Environmental Management & Economics*, 87–95 (1995).

This empirical research suggests that animal trespass problems may often be resolved without Coasean-type bargaining involving financial payments. This does not refute the Coase Theorem, which the reader should be reminded is a theoretical proposition. While the Coase Theorem, taken literally suggests that a payment system will be used to mediate between the parties, this is only one of a number of possible cooperative outcomes. As Coase stated in an article two decades before 'Social Costs', where the costs of using the price system are high individuals and organisations will use non-market arrangements. Thus, as shown above, they may mutually agree on the efficient outcome without the need for payment and/or compensation arrangements.

RIPARIAN RIGHTS

Under the common law people who own or occupy land beside lakes and rivers have the right to the natural flow of water beside or through their property, unchanged in quantity or quality. These riparian rights evolved from early nuisance cases over water pollution where neighbours would bring actions against those disposing of their wastes in rivers and streams. The industrial revolution caused an unprecedented deterioration of water quality across Britain; those suffering brought a large number of cases which fine-tuned the law to develop a riparian doctrine by 1850.

The common law allows a riparian to use an unlimited amount of water for 'ordinary' purposes. Riparians do *not* have a right to divert water for use of their property, or to abuse it. Extraordinary water users may not interfere with other riparians' property rights: they must return the water to the watercourse substantially undiminished in volume and unaltered in quality. Riparians can sue polluters to protect their rights even if they have suffered no evident harm: their rights to unaltered water exist whether or not they use the water and whether or not its alteration interferes with any of their activities. Moreover, it is not a defence or consideration that polluters' activities promote the greater good – the courts for a long time refused to consider the economic or social costs of prohibiting pollution.

The development of water rights seems to have been influenced by economic factors. One example is the difference in the law on the use of surface water between the eastern states of the USA and those of the west. The eastern states broadly follow the English riparian rights. The western states follow the doctrine of 'prior appropriation', which gives the rights to the first established user of the water resource. The cost of riparian rights is that it inhibits the use of water to its more productive uses. The western states have scarcer water and the law evolved to deal with intense uses of water such as hydraulic mining.

The common law is often regarded as ineffective and inefficient where large-numbers pollution or environmental damage occurs and government regulation is better. The following provides a salutary corrective to the view that the common law is moribund. The activities of the Anglers' Conservation Association (ACA) show that the common law remains a powerful weapon for environmental control while government has not always acted to control pollution. The ACA was formed in 1948 by an English fisherman/barrister, John Eastwood, as a means of sharing the costs of suing those polluting rivers used by anglers. In England and Wales, anglers are able to purchase leases from those with riparian rights possessed by the owners of the land bordering the river to maintain the quality and quantity of water. At a time when the environmental movement was as yet unborn and government agencies were reluctant to stand up to industrial and municipal polluters – and, indeed, did a lot of the polluting – the ACA clarified the law and in some cases won significant damages which were often used to rehabilitate rivers. In *Pride of Derby and Derbyshie Angling Association Ltd* v. *British Celanese Ltd*,[78] the ACA sued a private corporation (British Celanese Ltd), a municipal government (the Corporation of Derby) and a statutory corporation (the British Electricity Authority) for polluting a river. British Celanese withdrew its defence before the trial started and ceased the worst of its pollution fairly quickly.[79] But the two government bodies fought on, insisting that they were not responsible for the effluents, that heated water was good for fish and that in any case they possessed statutory powers giving them immunity from the common law. Having lost the case, they sought repeated suspensions of the injunctions to allow them time to comply. By the end of 1999 the ACA had forty-two legal actions underway. Five actions had been won or settled throughout the year and damages of £366,890 had been recovered. In mid-2000 the ACA settled another case for £415,000, half of which was placed in a trust fund for environmental improvement. Angling clubs and fishing syndicates have been around in England for hundreds of years. Riparian rights date back to medieval law and beyond. These are mature institutions that have enabled use of the common law to protect the environment, often against government as a polluter! Indeed, three times throughout its history

---

[78] [1953] Ch 149, [1953] 1 All ER 179.
[79] R. Bate, *Saving Our Streams*, London: Institute of Economic Affairs, 2001.

the ACA has had to fight attempts by the government to abolish riparian rights.

- The economics of property rights are set out in a number of books and anthologies: Y. Barzel, *Economic Analysis of Property Rights*, 2nd edn., Cambridge: Cambridge University Press, 1997; T. Eggertsson, *Economic Behaviour and Institutions*, Cambridge: Cambridge University Press, 1990 and A. Clarke and P. Kohler, *Property Law – Commentary and Materials*, Cambridge: Cambridge University Press, 2005. There are several useful though dated anthologies: E. Furubotn and S. Pejovich (eds.), *The Economics of Property Rights*, Cambridge, MA: Ballinger, 1974; B. A. Ackerman (ed.), *Economic Foundations of Property Law*, Boston: Little Brown, 1975.
- Although there is a vast literature among economists on property rights there has been relatively little on property law itself. T. W. Merrill and H. E. Smith, 'What Happened to Property in Law and Economics?', 111 *Yale Law Journal*, 357–398 (2001).
- Economists have undertaken empirical analysis of the evolution of different property rights based on anthropological data. Demsetz drew on the work of anthropologists to explain the development of different property rights among Native American Indians (H. Demsetz, 'Toward a Theory of Property Rights', 57 *American Economic Review*, 347–359 (1967); and generally the seminar issue, 'The Evolution of Property Rights', 31 *Journal of Legal Studies* (2002)). Bailey reviews fifty anthropological studies of aboriginal societies and finds that they have property rights arrangements that broadly conform to economic factors. M. J. Bailey, 'Approximate Optimality of Aboriginal Property Rights', 35 *Journal of Law & Economics*, 183–198 (1992). An interesting clash between developed property rights and common law doctrine was played out in Australia with native land rights claims in the Mabo cases. P. L. Williams, 'Mabo and Inalienable Rights to Property', 103 *Australian Economic Review*, 35–38 (1993). Others have applied economics to the historical evidence of different property rights, e.g. D. C. North, *Institution, Institutional Changes, and Economic Performance*, Cambridge: Cambridge University Press, 1990.
- One perplexing aspect of property law is that it often puts a limit on the type of legal rights, thus limiting the divisibility condition discussed above. In the past the law has banned, say, time shares, and a range of other derivative rights. This seems to clash with economic principles, as noted in B. Rudden, 'Economic Theory v. Property Law: The *Numerus Clausus* Problem', in J. Eekelaar and J. Bell (eds.), *Oxford Essays in Jurisprudence*, Oxford: Clarendon Press, 1987. Several economic explanations have been offered for this, related to excessive divisibility and the law's interest in some level of standardisation which facilitates transactions, avoids the need for costly consolidation and transparency. See T. W. Merrill and H. E. Smith, 'Optimal Standardisation in the Law of Property: the *Numerus Clausus* Principle', 110 *Yale Law Journal*, 1–70 (2000); H. Hansmann and

	Property rule	Liability rule
Victim	**I** Injunction	**II** Damages
Injurer	**III** No remedy	**IV** Reverse damages/ Compensated injunction
	Negotiated price	Judicial sanction

Figure 3.3 Nuisance solutions

R. Kraakman, 'Property, Contract, and Verification: The *Numerus Clausus* Problem and the Divisibility of Rights', 31 *Journal of Legal Studies*, S373–S420 (2002).

• The Calabresi–Melamed framework in chapter 2 offers insight into the symmetry of different legal responses to nuisance. Figure 3.3 depicts the entitlement decision on the vertical axis and the remedy or protection of the entitlement on the horizontal axis. This gives four possible outcomes, with corresponding remedies.

The law can either favour the victim (Quadrant I) or the injurer (Quadrant III) if protected by a property rule. Alternatively these entitlements can be protected by a liability rule or damages. This would in English law take the form of the entitlement given to the victim coupled with compensatory damages. The Calabresi–Melamed framework identifies a fourth unusual remedy – the injurer protected by a 'reverse damages' or 'compensated injunction' (Quadrant IV). That is where the victim pays the injurer a sum fixed by the court or some other body to gain a reduction in or a cessation of a harmful activity. This reverse damage remedy (subsidy) mirrors the bargaining outcome where the victim must 'bribe' the injurer. Such a solution is not uncommon in the public law arena where subsidies to install pollution abatement equipment and setoffs to stop planting crops are often used. In English common law there is no example of such a judicial response, suggesting that it is a figment of the economists' imagination, albeit one first identified by lawyers. Fortunately, in 1972 the Arizona Supreme Court in *Spur Industries* v. *Del E. Webb Development Co.*[80] filled this analytical and legal 'gap'. In *Spur Industries* a residential development expanded toward a feedlot operation (cattle fed in pens rather than roaming in fields). The proximity of the two resulted in considerable problems from the nearby cattle. The Court found for the developer but required it pay the feedlot's costs of shutting down and moving to another location if it wanted to enforce the injunction.

[80] (1972), 494 P 2d 700 (Ariz. SC).

- For a useful discussion of English nuisance see I. Ogus and G. Richardson, 'Economics and the Environment: A Study of Private Nuisance', 36 *Cambridge Law Journal*, 284–325 (1977), J. F. Brenner, 'Nuisance Law and the Industrial Revolution', 3 *Journal of Legal Studies*, 403–433 (1974).
- The harms caused by railways played an important role in the development of the common law. The common law was altered by legislation authorising railways, albeit as interpreted by the courts. *Rex* v. *Edward Pease and Others*[81] (highway users complained that the noise and smoke from locomotives on an adjacent railway line alarmed horses and caused accidents) established the defence of 'statutory authorisation'. This meant that because Parliament had authorised the railway it had tacitly authorised nuisances caused by steam locomotives for 'the greater good . . . of the public in the more speedy travelling and conveyance of merchandise along the new railroad'. The courts confirmed the defence of statutory authority in *Vaughan* v. *The Taff Vale Railway* (saparking locomotive which set fire to a woods),[82] and *Brand and Wife* v. *Hammersmith and City Railway Company*[83] (vibrations, noise and smoke from the railway which reduced the value of and rental from property). The judge suggested that to grant an injunction or damages 'might possibly prevent the increase of railways altogether'. The House of Lords confirmed the decision but not without a dissent by Bramwell who did not accept that a company should be allowed to increase its profits by refusing to compensate the victims of its nuisances. He observed that harms created by the railway company could be prevented but if they did not compensate they would simply risk starting fires. In his view there was no reason why the railway – and ultimately fare-paying passengers – should not bear those risks and costs.
- The policy on radio spectrum shows the tensions in the development of property rights, and between statutory intervention and the common law. It is frequently alleged, and forms the basis of radio spectrum policy across the world, that spectrum bandwith is a scarce natural resource and that radio interference makes markets in spectrum unworkable. These arguments are flawed. First, markets deal daily with scarce resources – that is their purpose. A market in spectrum is similar to that for land. Further, radio interference is akin to a trespass or nuisance arising from incompatible uses. It is where adjacent frequencies are too close resulting in signals on one frequency escaping onto another. The Coase Theorem was originally developed to show that a market in spectrum bandwidth was possible and potentially efficient.[84] Coase noted that prior to the effective nationalisation of spectrum resources and the use of regulatory and administrative controls, a property rights approach was being developed based on common law principles of 'priority in use', 'adverse possession' and nuisance law. The 'trespass' arising from radio interference is clearly more difficult to prevent than, say, cattle roaming on to a wheat field. It requires enforceable

[81] (1832) 4 B. &. Ad. 30, 110 E.R. 366.
[82] (1860) 5 H.&N. 679, 157 E.R. 1351 (Ex.).   [83] (1865) 1 L.R. 130 (QB).
[84] R. H. Coase, 'The Federal Communications Commission', 2 *Journal of Law & Economics*, 1–40 (1959).

technical limits on spectrum use which would be difficult to negotiate *ex ante* as part of the property rights system, or *ex post* as interference problems arise by negotiation and litigation using the common law. As far as English common law is concerned a leading case holds that an electricity line's interference with television reception was (at the time) a 'hypersensitive' use.[85] However, the electricity board causing the interference had already taken all possible steps to abate the interference. The decision can be viewed as concluding that the level of interference was reasonable taking account of the total net benefits of electricity supply compared with the loss from poor television reception. A Canadian decision twelve years later came to the opposite conclusion.[86] Perhaps the value of television had increased over the period, or was more important in Canada than England? The English television viewer seems to have fared no better more recently.[87] Since the 1920s the market solution to spectrum allocation has been rejected by Governments, resulting in gross inefficiency and arbitrary allocations. This 'public trustee model' has in recent years been rejected and a move to market and property rights solutions has begun. There has been widespread use of auctions to allocate initial use rights (licences) and growing acceptance that spectrum bandwidth should be traded to ensure its efficient use. However, few countries have gone as far as Guatemala which allocated spectrum bandwith on a 'first-in-time' basis to those who filed claims with the regulatory agency.[88]

---

[85] *Bridlington Relay Ltd* v. *Yorkshire Electricity Board* [1965] Ch 436; [1965] 1 All ER 264.

[86] *Nor-Video Services Ltd* v. *Ontario Hydro* (1978) 84 DLR (3d) 221.

[87] *Hunter* v. *Canary Wharf* [1997] 2 All ER 426.

[88] P. T. Spiller and C. Cardilli, 'Toward a Property Right Approach to Communications Spectrum', 16 *Yale Journal of Regulation*, 75–81 (1999).

CHAPTER 4

Contract

> The duty to keep a contract at common law means a prediction that
> you must pay damages if you do not keep it, and nothing else.
> Oliver Wendell Holmes, 1897

Contract is a subject where the relevance of economics is immediate and
obvious. Firms and individuals draw up contracts in order to produce,
distribute and sell goods and services. Contracts and contract law facilitate
exchange and production, and freedom of contract is a necessary part of
a market economy. It is therefore no surprise to learn that legal concepts
of contract law have their roots in economics and commercial practice.
As Atiyah observes, the classical legal model of contract 'is without doubt,
based on an economic model, that of the free market'.[1] It would seem that,
this being the case, the economist can contribute much to the analysis and
understanding of contracts and contract law.

THE LAW

The central questions in contract law are clear: When is a promise enforceable? What remedy should be given, if any, for breaking a contract? These
questions would seem easy to answer, and suggest a few straightforward
rules – enforce genuine promises, enforce the terms agreed by the parties
and provide remedies that the parties would have agreed had they addressed
the contractual problems which have arisen subject to public policy
considerations.

The reality is more complex and the law less certain. Key aspects of
contract law are confused, unsettled and puzzling. A standard English contract law casebook states 'that the scope, the basis, the function and even
the very existence of the law of contract are the subject of debate and

---

[1] P. S. Atiyah, *The Rise and Fall of Freedom of Contract*, Oxford: Clarendon Press, 1979, M. J. Trebilcock,
The Limits of Freedom of Contract, Cambridge, MA: Harvard University Press, 1993.

controversy among academic lawyers'.[2] There is no code or definitive legal text which sets out the objectives and principles of contract law. The law, remarkably, does not even provide a definition of a contract. The theories on what a contract is differ – is it a bargain, a promise[3] or some form of reliance?[4] Others, such as Ian MacNeil, have lambasted the 'classical model' of contract based on the sale of goods as inadequate and irrelevant.[5] He argues that many contracts are 'relational' and do not fit into the one-off transaction between strangers which seems to guide legal principles and thinking. More recently some lawyers have claimed that there is no such thing as a separate body of contract law, only a general law of obligations which embraces contract, property and tort. In short, to quote Atiyah, contract law is 'in a mess'.

While the theory and principles of contract law may be tangled, the law in most areas is more or less settled. At the risk of gross generalisation the main features of (English) contract law are:

- Strict liability on the contract breaker. This differs from tort law, where fault liability is used based on a reasonableness test.
- No general duty to disclose information, no liability or recession for unilateral mistakes.
- Contracts which are impossible or extremely difficult to perform may be held to be 'frustrated' and performance excused.
- The usual remedy is compensatory damages limited to pecuniary losses, defined as the sum of money that would put the non-breaching party in the same position had the contract been performed (the expectation measure).
- No compensation for 'unforeseeable' and consequential pecuniary and non-pecuniary losses unless specifically provided for in the contract.
- Mitigation of losses.
- Specific performance where goods are non-replicable or 'unique'.

It is these rules on which an economic theory of contract law must shed light.

---

[2] E. McKendrick, *Contract Law*, 5th edn., London: Macmillan, 2003, 1. See also S. A. Smith, *Contract Theory*, Oxford: Oxford University Press, 2004; R. Crasswell, 'Two Economic Theories of Enforcing Promise', in P. Benson (ed.), *The Theory of Contract Law*, Cambridge: Cambridge University Press, 2001, 19–44.

[3] C. Fried, *Contract as Promise – A Theory of Contractual Obligation*, Cambridge, MA: Harvard University Press, 1981.

[4] L. L. Fuller and W. R. Perdue, 'The Reliance Interest in Contract Damages', 46 *Yale Law Journal*, part I, 52–96, part 2, 372–420 (1936).

[5] I. R. MacNeil, 'The Many Futures of Contracts', 47 *Southern California Law Review*, 691–816 (1974).

THE ECONOMIC FRAMEWORK

The economics of contracts

The starting point for the analysis of contracts in both law and economics is the presumption that exchange is *mutually beneficial*. The parties enter into a contract because both gain. At the moment of making the contract, each party can be assumed to value the promise of the other more than (or at least as much as) any alternative. If a Seller (S) is prepared to sell a widget for £1.50, which the Buyer (B) values at £2.00, then both gain from the trade. Both receive a surplus – S a profit, and B a consumers' surplus measured by the difference between the price paid and B's maximum willingness to pay – i.e. £2.00 – £1.50 = 50 pence. This is the case even where there is an inequality of bargaining power or market power/monopoly. A contract signed under these conditions benefits both parties – otherwise it would not have been entered into. This 'bargain theory' underlies and is fundamental to the common law of contract, although its application does not always lead to the correct economic outcome.[6]

Second, the agreed terms of a contract should generally be enforced. Freedom of contract is the basis of a market economy so that individuals and other legal entities must be given the right to determine their own contractual arrangements. In England, the courts are reluctant to upset the express agreement of the parties. This is sensible because there is no reason to suppose that judges are in a better position to decide what would have been best. The economic approach assumes that, generally, the parties are the best judge of their own welfare. This is the presumption in law also; but it is one that in both law and economics can be overturned when one party has been misled, defrauded, or coerced.

Third, markets for goods and services are generally efficient. This is particularly the case where the market is competitive. In a competitive market the terms of trade reflect the scarcity of the resource and ensure that resources and goods and services flow to those who value them most. This is particularly the case where transactions costs are low.

Fourth, contract terms are fashioned by market forces not individual haggling and negotiations. The competitive market does not rely on buyer and seller negotiating every term of every transaction – price and contract terms are the outcome of the interaction of a great many suppliers and buyers for each commodity and resource. That is, they are fashioned by

[6] M. A. Eisenberg, 'The Bargain Principle and its Limits', 95 *Harvard Law Review*, 741–801 (1982).

impersonal market forces. In the competitive marketplace consumers and firms are price and contract term takers not makers or fixers. In such a marketplace the consumer and firm has no economic power, and the identity of buyer and seller has no importance. This is one major difference between economics and the view of contract as a bargain which underlies the common law.

The market has another feature which makes contracts and contract law appear redundant. The typical market consists of relatively homogeneous inputs, goods and services bought and supplied by many buyers and sellers. It is a world of spot transactions where the exchange of obligations and performance are simultaneous – S offers B a widget for £1 – B pays S £1 as S hands over the widget. There is no possibility of default – no widget: no payment! The typical spot contract can be said to be self-enforcing. Moreover, there is no loss if the exchange does not take place. There is perfect substitute performance in terms of an immediate alternative sale: the consumer can enter the market to secure an identical widget at the same price from another seller. The supplier faced with a buyer who has reneged can sell the widget to another buyer at the same price. There is no loss arising either from the seller's or the buyer's breach. In such a world there exists no need for a separate body of law governing contractual relations;[7] Let the buyer beware (*caveat emptor*) is all that is needed. The bulk of contracts – especially consumer contracts such as grocery shopping, buying petrol, clothes, etc. – have this feature. Of course, there may be disputes over the quality of the widget which we will come to later. We can call this, and more sophisticated market responses, *market governance*. That is, market forces themselves provide a solution to potential contractual difficulties and risks.[8] Empirical research indicates that firms often do not rely on the law to resolve their disputes, although it is formally available.[9]

Fifth, the economic approach starts with a (rebuttable) presumption that real-world contracts are generally efficient adaptations to the costs and uncertainties of transacting. Economics views a contract as an institutional arrangement designed to create wealth in a way that deals with the frictions

---

[7] Indeed, these economic models implicitly assume breach without penalty so that the parties can costlessly re-contract until trades are made at market clearing prices. This assumes away costly and sluggish market reactions to exogenous changes.

[8] Bernstein's study of contract disputes between diamond dealers provides an interesting study of contract enforcement without law. L. Bernstein, 'Opting Out of the Legal System: Extralegal Contractual Relations', 21 *Journal of Legal Studies*, 115–157 (1992).

[9] This was the influential findings of Macauley for the USA, later replicated by Beale and Dugdale for the UK. S. Macauley, 'Non-contractual Relations in Business: A Preliminary Study', 25 *American Sociological Review*, 55–69 (1968); H. Beale and T. Dugdale, 'Contracts between Businessmen: Planning and the Use of Contractual Remedies', 2 *British Journal of Law & Society*, 45–60 (1975).

of exchange, production and negotiations. Where the transactions costs associated with simple contracts are pronounced, individuals and firms will adapt by forming more complex contracts which internalise and economise on these costs.[10] Thus many contracts which seem not to be efficient or easily explained often turn out to be efficient adaptations to risk, uncertainty, principal–agent problems and the like. That is, the contracts we see in practice, together with the institutions arising to facilitate economic activity and adjudicate disputes, are influenced by economic factors.

Sixth, and perhaps most radically for lawyers, contract and the firm are part of the same continuum of institutional arrangements designed to deal with contractual problems. Market contracts are largely mediated by the price mechanism augmented by commercial norms and contract law. When transactions become too costly to be handled by the market other arrangements emerge that better maximise wealth. The firm – which is a complex network of property rights and contracts – is explained by economists as a response to the difficulties and inefficiencies of using market contracts to arrange production and distribution.[11] The firm substitutes market governance through arm's-length contracts and prices with internal command-and-control procedures (administrative governance). In some cases the contractual inefficiencies arising from uncertainty, asset specificity, holdups and opportunism can be only resolved by the common ownership of previously separate legal entities (vertical integration). This same idea also helps explain the evolution of law – those exchange relationships which cannot be dealt with exclusively by contract law develop into specialised branches of law dealing with the problems thrown up by transactions costs – thus labour contracts are dealt with by labour law, the firm by company law, financial instruments by financial regulation and so on.

Seventh, where there is a monopoly, and also where there is oligopoly (a few sellers or a few buyers) on either side of the market, contract terms will not be Pareto efficient and will excessively benefit the party with market power. Thus while the terms of the contract will be mutually beneficial, they will not be efficient. The terms will be more onerous on the weaker party and will result in an inefficiently low level of contractual activity, production and sales, and as a result resources will not gravitate to their highest-valued uses. This is another departure between the economic theory of contract and the law's view of contract as a bargain.

---

[10] C. Veljanovski, 'Organised Futures Contracting', 5 *International Review of Law & Economics*, 25–38 (1985).

[11] R. H. Coase, 'The Theory of the Firm', 4 *Economica*, NS, 386–405 (1937), reprinted in R. H. Coase, *The Firm, The Market, and The Law,* Chicago: University of Chicago Press, 1988.

Finally, contract terms, contract law and price are all interrelated and will tend to adjust if one is altered. Just as we saw in the discussion of property contract is a bundle of rights which gives value to the transaction. If a more onerous term is placed on one party then this will result in offsetting adjustment in other terms. For example, if the seller is made liable for a wide range of contractual problems – such as failure to deliver the specified quality or to meet rigid time limits and other performance criteria – he will demand a higher price. As discussed in chapter 2 this will neutralise both any impact of the law on real variables and its (re-)distributive effects. Where these legal protections are not valued by buyers as much as they cost the seller, then the price will rise and demand will fall. The law will have an allocative effect by reducing the level of contractual activity as a subset of buyers (and sellers) drop out of the market. This, oddly, makes the economic analysis of contract terms and laws much more complicated than tort. The ability of the contracting parties to incorporate and adjust their relationship in the light of changes in contract rules and remedies means that it is often uncertain what effect these have in practice.

Types of contract and contract problems

Not all contracts are the same, nor are the factors which give rise to contractual problems. Economists have identified a number of different types of contracts which are useful in developing the economic principles and concepts relevant to analysing contract law.

The first distinction is between contracts to give and those to make or produce. The earlier economics literature focused on contracts to give which involve the exchange of the legal title to mass-produced goods (and then on the assumption of a given price). That is essentially a sale of goods contract. For these the principal economic goal is to ensure that the existing goods end up in the hands of those who value them the most. For contracts to make an additional concern arises – to ensure that contract terms and legal rules and remedies convey the appropriate incentives for future production of goods and assets, and in particular the efficient level of reliance expenditure (see below). Thus the concept of reliance or transactions-specific expenditure is important for contracts to make.

Cutting across these two categorisations are contracts involving easily replicable goods and assets and those where there are transaction-specific investments. The typical sale of goods contract involves goods sold in well-developed markets where substitute performance is readily available.

For such replicable goods contractual problems are minimised by the possibility of substitute performance, as already discussed. The buyer or seller cannot be held to ransom by failure to perform or honour a promise since either can easily deal with someone else on equivalent terms. Goods and assets traded in 'thin' markets (that is, those with few buyers and/or sellers) or those requiring transaction-specific investment, have weaker market sanctions. These may give rise to contractual difficulties particularly for contracts involving specialised assets or those where one party has incurred significant transaction-specific investment or expenditure. A further (and related) matter is that the nature of the relationship between the parties is different – the sale of goods contract is governed by impersonal market forces where the identity of the buyer and seller is not an issue; for contracts with significant transaction-specific reliance one party becomes 'locked-in' and identity is important – i.e. they can be described as (*ex post*) personal or relational transactions or contracts.

These two contracts also 'map' the different sources of contractual difficulties or breaches. The first are most likely to be affected by changes in market values caused by a change in production costs and/or buyer's or seller's valuation. Contracts to make requiring specific investment are likely to be affected by opportunistic, or 'bad-faith' behaviour designed to re-negotiate the terms of the contract in order to get a better deal.

The first source of breach is relatively straightforward – the seller breaches because unit production costs rise above the contract price or a better offer is received which makes honouring the contract less or unprofitable; the buyer breaches because his or her valuation falls below the contract price or because a substitute has been found at a lower price.

Opportunistic breach requires a bit more explanation. This is essentially 'bad-faith' re-negotiations of contractual terms motivated by significant contract-specific investment or expenditure by one party induced by (in reliance on) a contractual promise. From an economic perspective reliance expenditure must be based on a realistic assessment of the likelihood that the contract will be breached and the expenditure wasted (see below). However, there are forms of reliance expenditure that create acute contractual problems. This is where the expenditure is specific to the contract and has a salvage value (opportunity cost) outside the contract substantially less than its purchase price/cost.

To illustrate, suppose S enters into a contract with B and in order to perform S must invest in specialised stamping equipment which can be used only to make component parts for B's new washing machine. The value of the equipment in its next-best alternative use is significantly less than its current use (or purchase price). There is a large sunk cost which S cannot recoup if the contract fails.[12] S is said to be 'locked-in' to the contract since if the contract fails he will lose a significant proportion of his reliance expenditure. It is this that allows the other party to take advantage of the lock-in to re-negotiate the terms of the contract.

The economic motivation for such a holdout is the existence of what economists call rather inelegantly 'appropriable quasi-rent'.[13] This is defined as the difference between the value of an asset in its contractual use and its second-highest alternative use or salvage value Suppose that the machinery acquired by S to fulfil his contractual obligations cost the equivalent (amortised over its life) of £2,000 per day but that in the next-best alternative use its value is only £1,000 per day. At the time the parties negotiated the contract S had a choice – he could choose to deal or not. Thus the terms will reflect the fact that he relies on B's contractual promise to invest the equivalent of £2,000 daily. The parties agree but when the equipment is installed its salvage value is half of the purchase price, i.e. £1,000 a day. There is a sunk cost of £1,000 or a potential appropriable quasi-rent to B of £1,000. It is potentially appropriable by B because he can seek to re-negotiate the terms of the contract to capture the £1,000 and S would still be prepared to supply the component parts. For S to do otherwise would increase his loss. In this situation the entire quasi-rent is at risk and provides an incentive for B to engage in 'post-contractual' opportunistic negotiations to get better terms.

Finally, there are contracts particularly affected by imperfect and asymmetric information. The problems encountered by these contracts are best illustrated by insurance contracts, although many different types of contracts suffer from the same potential for inefficient incentives and breach, such as agency agreements, employment contracts and contracts between suppliers and subcontractors.

The insurance contract provides coverage for uncertain losses. It requires the insurer to evaluate the risks, calculate premia and decide when to pay out on claims. Insurance, by its nature, involves the pooling and spreading of risks. Thus it is particularly susceptible to dampening incentives of those insured from revealing the specific risks they face and taking sufficient care

---

[12] T. Muris, 'Opportunistic Behavior and the Law of Contract', 65 *Minnesota Law Review*, 521–590 (1981).

[13] B. Klein, R. Crawford and A. A. Alchian, 'Vertical Integration, Appropriable Rents, and the Competitive Contracting Process', 21 *Journal of Law & Economics*, 297–376 (1978). See also C. J. Goetz and R. E. Scott, 'Principles of Relational Contracts', 67 *Virginia Law Review*, 1089–1159 (1981).

to avoid the circumstances and losses that arise from insurable events. While insurance companies will have a lot of information about general risks they often lack knowledge about the specific risks and actions of the individuals they insure. The relationship between insurer and those purchasing insurance is therefore characterised by asymmetric information – the insured is often better informed about the factors that influence and determine the specific risks and losses he or she faces than the insurance company. The insurance company can obtain this information only at great cost. These information costs give rise to two types of problems already briefly touched on in chapter 2 (and encountered again in the discussion of nuisance damages and tort) – adverse selection and moral hazard.

Adverse selection arises where an insurance company has insufficient information to distinguish high- from lower-risk individuals and therefore pools different risks and charges them the same price (premium). The premium will reflect the likelihood of a claim from the average individual in the pooled risk group. However, at this price insurance is too expensive for good risks, who do not buy it, and cheap for the bad risks who insure. The result is that a disproportionate number of bad risks are insured so that the average claim rises. The situation is a variant of Groucho Marx's view of club membership – anyone who wants to buy insurance is a person the insurance company should not insure because he or she is more than likely to be a worse-than-average risk.

Moral hazard is where insurance increases risks by reducing the incentive of the insured to take adequate precautions. It is a term that captures both the inadvertent relaxation of precautions, the deliberate (fraudulent and criminal) creation of risks – insured houses are more likely to be burnt down than uninsured ones – and the almost commonplace exaggeration of the costs of insurance repairs, especially to motor vehicles. Moral hazard arises when (a) the insured can influence the level of risk and the extent of the eventual losses and (b) the insured cannot monitor and accurately price changes in the behaviour affecting individual claims – or, indeed control losses and costs *ex post*. For example, individuals can install sprinklers to reduce the likelihood of a fire. Once an accident has occurred, steps can be taken to reduce the magnitude and extent of the losses (say, by speedy repair). Unless the insurance company can monitor the care taken by the individuals they insure, and adjust the premiums to reflect changes in the risk and loss, individuals will relax their level of self-protection. There will thus be an underinvestment in loss-reducing actions and the risks and losses will rise.

The moral hazard problem is also at the heart of the so-called *principal–agent problem*.[14] A principal–agent contract covers a situation where the relationship between the contracting parties is vertical, such as between employer and employee, shareholder and managers, input suppliers and firm and so on. These are often dealt with by contract law and more specialised branches such as agency, employment and company law. For these contracts the principal – an employer, shareholder, or main contractor – delegates to another – employee, manager, or subcontractor, respectively – certain tasks and duties in return for remuneration. The difficulty arises because the principal can only imperfectly monitor the actions of the agent (his or her effort, probity and good faith) and because the incentives of the agent may only imperfectly align with those of the principal.

This can be illustrated by the tensions between a restaurant owner and his manager. Assume that I (the principal) have a restaurant and hire a manager (the agent) to run it. I want to maximise the profits from the restaurant because this will increase my wealth. However, I cannot easily determine whether the manager is using his best efforts to run the restaurant efficiently, offering good service and so on in a way that maximises my profits. Many factors go into achieving a highly profitable restaurant and some of these will be outside the manager's control, such as the weather, the general state of the economy, road works outside the restaurant or because the principal has underinvested, the concept is wrong, or the menu unappealing to potential customers and so on. Other factors will be under the control of the manager. However, my inability adequately to monitor the effort and actions of the manager and link these to the restaurant's profitability or otherwise, means that my control is weakened, and the manager's incentive to act in my best interest also weakened. In addition, the agent's incentives will often differ from those of the principal. The manager may take advantage of the unobservability of his actions to maximise other objectives – coasting along; chatting to mates; not properly supervising staff and so on. To monitor the manager's effort and actions is costly – it generates agency costs defined as the monitoring expenditures of the principal, the bonding expenditures of the agent (expenditures designed to incentivise him) and the lost profits arising from the divergence between the principal and agent's incentives.[15]

---

[14] See generally, P. Milgrom and J. Roberts, *Economics, Organization and Management*, Englewood Cliffs, NJ: Prentice Hall, 1992.

[15] M. C. Jensen and W. H. Meckling, 'The Theory of the Firm: Managerial Behavior, Agency Costs, and Ownership Structure', 3 *Journal of Financial Economics*, 305–360 (1975).

THE ECONOMICS OF CONTRACT LAW

According to the Coase Theorem, the possibility of bargaining at low costs results in an efficient allocation of resources. Indeed it gives the impression that bargaining – that is, contract – provides a complete solution. The discussion in chapter 3 suggested that in nuisance and trespass cases all the parties had to do was come together to negotiate a contract. However, little was said about whether they would honour their agreements, and what would occur if they did not. The law of contract was simply redundant, although the discussion pointed clearly to potentially severe contractual difficulties even where transactions costs were low. The law of contract indicates that even where the parties voluntarily enter into transactions, there is a real likelihood of non-performance.

The basics

Contract law deals in large part with the idea of a contract as an *enforceable promise*. A promise is a commitment to do something in the future. When performance or an obligation is in the future, it can be broken. *S* agrees to supply 100 widgets to *B* in one month's time. *S* requires pre-payment and *B* in reliance on the supply of the widgets makes plans and incurs costs. If *S* breaks his promise then *B* has to make the effort to reclaim his money from *S*, he may have incurred avoidable losses and out-of-pocket expenses (reliance expenditure) and his plans may be disrupted. *S* has imposed losses and costs on *B* which he has not taken into account. That is, promise making and promise breaking can be inefficient

From an economic perspective we do not want the buyer or the seller to be compelled to perform contracts which are not mutually beneficial and result in a misallocation of resources. There is no purpose served by compelling a manufacturer to deliver 100 widgets when the costs of production exceed the price. On the other hand, there is no necessary reason why the buyer, having concluded negotiations and agreed a price in good faith, should suffer a loss simply because the manufacturer's costs have risen or that a seller should be able to get out of the contract simply because he has made a 'bad bargain'. Such breaches would undermine the value of a promise as a signal of a real intention to make binding commitments on which people can plan and ensure that they can acquire goods, services and inputs to undertake productive activity.

This leads naturally to the idea of optimal promise making and promise breaking. Contract terms and contract law should provide incentives for the parties to enter into contracts and to break contracts taking account of the full costs and benefits that these actions impose. The economic goal is to ensure that the rules and remedies of contract law ensure that only contracts are agreed that are expected to be value maximising, and that once formed they are breached only if this is value maximising. This will usually require that the parties take into account the expected losses of their actions, and liability be placed on the party which can best avoid and/or minimise the resulting losses.

Coase's analysis, and the discussion of competitive markets, indicates that contractual problems in contract law are relatively rare. Indeed, Coase's analysis seems to indicate is that all that is necessary is the ability to contract. However, in the real world there are costs in forming contracts and costs in enforcing contracts. These can be called *ex ante* and *ex post* contracting costs. The *ex ante* contracting costs are the costs of search, information and negotiation which we have already identified. These form the heart of the issues surrounding contract formation and the terms which the parties wish to and are able to negotiate.

Many otherwise valid contracts are incomplete because it is too costly for the parties to negotiate a comprehensive set of precisely defined obligations for many situations when they know that most of these situations would rarely occur. This approach implies that there is an efficient level of contractual incompleteness or gaps. Also, it may often be beyond the capacity of the parties to anticipate the less likely contingencies, or they simply decide to leave this to be resolved *ex post*. Usually the parties specify only the main aspects of their relationship and leave unspecified many less important aspects. By doing this, they tacitly agree that if in the course of performance they cannot then agree on how to deal with a matter not covered by the contract, they will rely on the law to resolve the problem. This reduces transaction costs. It avoids the hassle and haggling costs of the parties every time they draw up a contract to negotiate these or a different set of terms. These terms will either be implied into the contract or expressly incorporated by an overarching statement that this contract is to be governed by the laws of England and Wales, or the USA, or some other mutually accepted jurisdiction.

But because contracts are typically executory there are risks that events will change or that the parties will act in bad faith. In the absence of a costless method of enforcement and of not being able to anticipate all the factors and consequences which affect their relationship, they will need to fashion their agreement to take account of *ex ante* and *ex post* transaction costs. That is, the parties may rationally decide to invest in ensuring that they protect themselves before they enter into a contract, or alternatively deal with contractual problems *ex post* on the basis of a rational calculation of the different costs and their effectiveness. The choice between these will be based on the costs of *ex ante* specification and the expected costs of *ex post* resolution having not dealt with by the original contract contract terms.

The economic rationale for this can be easily stated. Setting out terms to cover all eventualities entails a certain cost, whereas waiting for the adverse event to be realised only gives rise to an expected cost at the time the contract is formed which may or may not be realised. For example, if the costs of dealing with a freakish event is £100 in lawyers' fees and the cost of resolving it if it occurs is £20,000 then it would seem that one should spend the money in having the lawyers deal with it. However, if the likelihood of the event ever occurring is 1 in 10,000, then it would not. This is because at the time the contract is formed the expected loss from dealing with the contractual difficulty *ex post* is £2 (1/10,000 × £20,000) compared with the certain lawyer's invoice of £100. It is cost-effective for the parties not to deal with this event/contractual outcome when drafting their contract. This leads to a fairly straightforward rule – if the *ex ante* costs of stipulating a term are less than the expected *ex post* costs then incorporate the term in the contract; otherwise leave a gap and resolve any difficulties when and if the contractual problem arises.[16]

A concomitant of the economic approach is that contracts are generally 'efficiently incomplete' in the sense that the parties have done the best given the transactions costs they face at the time they concluded the contract.

Contract law as gap filling

One way of looking at contract law is as a giant overarching contract, or what economists call a *complete contingent contract* or hypothetical contract. This is a contract which identifies and sets out the terms, and hence the rules and remedies, for every conceivable contractual risk, problem and default. It enumerates an exhaustive list of terms, conditions and remedies which would have been negotiated in the absence of transactions costs. Such a contract may discharge one party from performing the contract where it would be excessively costly and wasteful to perform, or penalise

---

[16] If the the costs of allocating losses *ex ante* as a term of the contract and *ex post* without being expressly covered by a term of the contract are a and b, respectively, and the probability that the loss/event will occur is p, then the efficient rule is: if a is less than pb ($a < pb$) negotiate and incorporate the term into the contract; if a is greater than pb ($a > pb$) then do not incorporate into the contract because it is cheaper to deal with it should the contingency arise.

the breach by imposing damages. However, it would not simply discharge the contract because one party got things wrong and misperceived the benefits. Bad or ignorant bargains themselves cannot excuse performance, or otherwise people would make bad and ignorant bargains. A complete contingent contract would allocate contractual risks to the party who can best avoid (the least cost avoider) or bear them (the superior risk bearer).

On this view, contract law is a device which fills the gaps in negotiated contracts by providing the parties with default or implied terms and remedies. Stated in a slightly different way contract law is seen as reflecting the terms of a complete contingent contract subject to the legal process costs of doing so. The parties can either accept these or contract out of them to substitute alternative terms which better reflect their views of how commercial and other risks are to be allocated between them.

The complete contingent contract is a benchmark, not a solution. Simply setting out what will happen and how the risks will be allocated does not resolve a dispute between two parties to a contract. In practice it encounters two serious obstacles – verification of the relevant facts and the enforcement of promises against an unwilling party.

First, the parties may dispute that the event specified in the contract or governed by contract law has occurred. The complete contingent contract may contain a clause purporting to deal with a particular contingency but one party disputes the facts.

Second, one party may simply refuse to comply even though liable under the contract. Even when the complete contingent contract sets out the penalties for breach one party may simply refuse to pay the damages or accept liability. If this dispute cannot be amicably settled – some third-party resolution by a judge or arbitrator will be needed.

Thus even in a frictionless setting severe contract enforcement problems can arise. This, in turn, reduces the parties' and society's wealth. There will arise what game theorists call an 'assurance game' – each party will honour their contract if they are confident that the other will. If this trust (assurance) were not present, many people and firms would not enter into otherwise wealth maximising contracts, or waste resources in protecting themselves from losses and a high incidence of broken promises.

In the face of positive transaction costs, the law has two important roles:
1. To reduce transactions costs by giving the parties better enforcement mechanisms and enforcing the terms that parties agree so as facilitate exchange, production and distribution, or to refuse to enforce contracts where there has not been a genuine bargain due to common mistake, frustration, fraud, duress and so on.

2. To supply default terms which fill the gaps in the contract (implied terms and conditions) where the parties have not included an express term.

The concept of the complete contingent contact leads naturally to the proposition that contract rules and remedies should be selected to avoid transactions costs, and in particular the necessity for most parties to negotiate around the law. Clearly, if the body of contract law offers legal terms which are not mutually acceptable to a significant number of buyers and sellers the law will increase transactions costs and achieve little as the parties tailor and replace the rules better to suit their needs.

Bad contract law raises transaction costs. For example, if the law prohibits loans, or security or the enforcement of a debt that would otherwise be negotiated by the parties, this will reduce market efficiency. Not only will the law raise transactions costs directly it will give rise to additional transactions costs as the parties' contract around the law by selecting less efficient means of achieving the same purpose. For example, if the law prevents a seller from recovering a debt or enforcing payment this will increase the default risk and losses. The seller's costs will rise and be reflected in a higher price and less will be sold. The seller will also take more costly action to reduce the default losses, such as holding physical security until full payment has been made and refusing to sell goods on credit, hire purchase, deposit, or to those he regards as high-risk individuals or firms. Thus contract law should seek to enforce the terms that the parties agree and, in particular, not to regulate the express terms of the contract.

In the real world those contracting differ, and will fashion rules to deal with their own particular circumstances and requirements. Thus any general rule may be inefficient for some types of contracts and contracting parties. The transaction costs reduction view of 'default terms' sets out a 'majoritarian' set of rules and remedies which tend to minimise the number of times the parties will need to 'contract around' them. In practice, this approach may be difficult since it will not be obvious which default rule minimises contracting around and hence transactions costs (see discussion below on remoteness).

So far, the focus has been on default terms which are implied into a contract. Ayres and Gertner[17] have added a twist by identifying two other default rules – the '**penalty default rule**' and the 'mandatory default rule'.

---

[17] I. Ayres and R. Gertner, 'Filling Gaps in Incomplete Contracts: An Economic Theory of Default Rules', 99 *Yale Law Journal*, 87–103 (1989); I. Ayres, 'Default Rules for Incomplete Contracts', in P. Newman (ed.), *The New Palgrave Dictionary of Economics and the Law*, vol. 1, London: Stockton Press, 1998, 585–590. Cf. C. A. Riley, 'Designing Default Rules in Contract Law – Consent, Conventionalism, and Efficiency', 20 *Oxford Journal of Legal Studies*, 367–390 (2000).

The penalty default rule is described as 'information-forcing'. It is a rule which suits the majority of contracting parties but encourages those it does not suit to reveal this, and negotiate around the law to include an express condition in the contract. It does this by setting a rule which denies liability to parties with superior information which affects the value of the contract. For example, the law may set out a default rule that the breaching party will not be liable for 'unforeseen' and consequential losses. This may suit most. However, if these losses are a significant and important to one party, the rule 'forces' that party to negotiate with the other to accept liability for agreed consequential losses which may arise from the other's breach.

The 'rule' in *Hadley* v. *Baxendale*[18] is given as an example of a 'penalty' or 'information-forcing' default rule. In *Hadley* the owners of a flour mill sent a broken iron shaft to the defendant who were 'common carriers' and informed them that the mill had stopped operation and that the shaft was to be sent immediately as pattern for a new shaft to made. There was an unreasonable delay in sending the shaft and as a result the mill was closed for longer than it would otherwise have been and the claimant sued for their lost profits due to the delay. The *Hadley* rule is that the breaching party is liable only for the *foreseeable* consequences.

The *Hadley* rule states that if the buyer does not inform the seller that timely completion of the contract will result in significant losses then the seller will not be liable. Suppose that *B* orders a piece of machinery from *S* to be delivered on a specific date, and *S* breaches the contract by delivering the machine three months' late. As a direct result, *B* loses the opportunity to enter into a highly profitable contract with a new customer. The rule in *Hadley* allows *B* to recover only if he informs *S* that delay is likely to lead to this type of consequential loss.[19] The *Hadley* rule saves on information costs by providing a standard term imputed into the contract which encourages *B* to inform *S* about the possibility of otherwise unanticipated consequential losses. If the parties do not agree with the allocation of losses implicit in *Hadley* it is open to them to agree to a different allocation. Knowing this rule, the buyer will make it clear to the seller that there are likely to be significant losses if completion exceeds the delivery dates set out in the contract. This forces the buyer, if he is to take advantage of the law, to reveal to the seller the consequences, and for them to negotiate price and other terms in the light of the potential shift in liability.

---

[18] [1854] 9 Exch. 341, 156 Eng. Rep. 145.
[19] R. Danzig, '*Hadley* v. *Baxendale:* A Study in the Industrialization of the Law', 4 *Journal of Legal Studies*, 249–284 (1975).

Contract law, but usually statute law, also imposes 'mandatory default rules' which cannot be modified by the parties. Some of the fundamental terms of contract law – the building blocks – have this mandatory character. They – such as offer, acceptance and consideration – must be present if a contract is to exist and bind the parties. Others may affect the core of the contract and its value. Price controls such as rent control or the minimum wage legislation make it illegal to negotiate higher rents or lower wages, respectively. The UK Unfair Contract Terms Act 1977 prohibits sellers from agreeing (imposing) terms which exclude liability in consumer contracts unless 'reasonable'. It would, however, be a mistake to assume that mandatory terms directly determine the value of the contract to the parties. The parties can implicitly 'contract around' these mandatory rules by varying other unregulated terms.

Economic functions

From an economic viewpoint contract law has a number of efficiency-related functions.[20] It should encourage efficient contract formation, efficient performance and efficient reliance. Specifically, an efficient contract law should:

- **Reduce transactions costs**   We know from the Coase Theorem that in the absence of transactions costs a contract would be Pareto efficient. In practice, most contracts are incomplete and the law can be seen as filling the gaps by supplying terms and conditions which deal with potential contractual problems. A further implication of this approach is that contracts are designed to economise on transactions costs, i.e. they provide an institutional device that enables the parties to reduce transactions costs.
- **Economise on information costs**   Better (although not necessarily more) information enables individuals and organisations to make better choices, but it is costly to produce. Thus the costs of information have to be balanced against the gains. Further, the law must focus both on the way information is disclosed and on the incentive effects that disclosure rules and laws have on the willingness to produce information. Second, it is not imperfect information which is the core problem but the *asymmetry of information* between the contracting parties. That is, one party knows more. Thus the law must decide whether the better-informed

---

[20] S. A. Smith, *Contract Theory*, Oxford: Oxford University Press, 2004; R. Crasswell, 'Two Economic Theories of Enforcing Promise', in P. Benson (ed.), *The Theory of Contract Law*, Cambridge: Cambridge University Press, 2001, 19–44.

party should disclose relevant information to the other or, failing this, be held liable for the losses of the relatively ignorant party. In both these areas the central economic issue is not only to pay attention to the costs and benefits of disclosure but the impact that more or less disclosure has on the incentives to produce and search out relevant information. This may give rise to what can be termed the 'paradox of disclosure' – requiring more disclosure can lead to less available information because it dampens the incentive to produce information.

- **Efficient breach**   Efficient breach is central to the law and economics of contract law. Under contract law the usual rule is that the parties either honour their promises or else pay damages. There is no obligation generally to undertake the literal performance of all contractual terms; it is an obligation only to compensate the non-breaching party for his or her losses arising from the failure to perform. This approach of contract law is viewed favourably by economists. The purpose of contract law is to deter only those potential breaches which are inefficient. It is therefore necessary to balance the costs of inefficient breach against those of excessive performance. In this way, resources are encouraged to flow to their highest valued uses.

- **Efficient reliance**   Promises induce others to make plans, undertake expenditure and enter into arrangements which increase economic value. This is the legal concept of reliance. Reliance (a) involves the use of real resources, and (b) can give rise to post-contractual opportunism. On the first score, expenditure made to enhance the value of performance must be based on a realistic probability that the contract will be honoured (efficient reliance). As regards post-contract opportunism the rules of contract should ensure that this is controlled to prevent one party from re-negotiating more favourable terms which simply re-distributes wealth and is not a response to changes in market and objective economic circumstances.

- **Efficient risk bearing**   Contracts are risk reduction and distribution devices. The parties enter into a contract as a way of reducing the primary risks of the economic activity they are involved in, and the risks of default. Contract law should facilitate risk sharing by upholding the allocation of risks made by the parties to the contract as set down in its terms. In a hypothetical contract the parties would seek to allocate potential losses in a way that (a) provided incentives to each that best avoid the likelihood of losses occurring and (b) where possible place the residual losses on the party best able to insure or bear them. That is, they would simultaneously seek to ensure optimal precautions against poorly structured contracts and to have an efficient level of risk bearing and spreading.

SALE OF GOODS

Basics of market transactions

The sale of goods contract is the archetypal contract in law and economics. It is the most common contract, covering a variety of everyday transactions mainly for mass-produced items sold to consumers and inputs sold to producers. The common law governing the sale of goods evolved by merchants (the Law Merchant) adopted by the common law, and subsequently codified in statute (the Sale of Goods Act).

The typical sale of goods transaction involves the transfer of title in goods already produced. Buyer and seller meet, negotiate terms and there is an exchange of money for goods. The law is seen as enforcing the agreed-to terms or those which can be reasonably inferred.

As stated above, the economist takes a slightly different perspective. Terms are not negotiated in the marketplace as individually crafted bargains but fashioned by impersonal market forces. The sale of goods contract in a competitive market is determined by the interaction of many buyers and sellers and is an iterative process of aggregative adjustments responding to the underlying forces of supply and demand. As a result buyer and seller are contract terms takers rather than makers or fixers. That is, they accept the price and terms on a take-it-or-leave-it basis.

Sale of goods contracts have several features.

First, the price of the good reflects its quality and the contractual protections given to buyer and seller.

Second, acceptable or 'merchantable' quality must be related to the price. It is no good for the buyer to seemingly negotiate for standard-grade wheat and pay the price for standard-grade wheat, and then complain that he meant superior-grade wheat. Acceptable quality must the read in the light of the representations over quality and price. This, not unsurprisingly is the position under the law as clearly set out by Lord Reid in *Hardwick Game Farm* v. *Suffolk Agricultural and Poultry Producers Association Ltd*:

If the object of the disclosure of the particular purpose is, as I think it must be, to give to the seller an opportunity to exercise his skill and judgment in making and selecting appropriate goods, then it is difficult to see how a stated purpose can be a 'particular' purpose if it is stated so widely that it would cover different qualities of goods, because carrying out the purpose in one way would only require a lower quality of goods whereas carrying it out in another way would require higher quality. Different qualities normally sell at different prices. If a customer sought from a manufacturer or dealer cloth for the purpose of making overcoats the dealer could not know what quality was required. A cut-price tailor would not want to pay the price of cloth used in Savile Row, and the tailor in Savile Row would not use the quality which the cut-price tailor wants. Unless the seller knew the nature of the buyer's business his only clue to the quality which the buyer wanted would be the price which the buyer was prepared to pay. If a high price was offered it might no doubt be right to hold that he must supply goods suitable for high quality coats. But it could not be right that if the cloth was sold at a price appropriate for the merchantable quality the dealer would have to supply a higher quality simply because the buyer had stated that his purpose was to make overcoats and the merchantable quality would not always be reasonably fit for making every kind of overcoat.[21]

Third, price will adjust in line with the quality and nature of contractual liabilities. If the law holds the seller to a higher level of quality or merchantability than would be agreed by the parties then the seller's costs will rise and, all things equal, so will the market price. If the buyer does not value the quality or contractual protections as much as they cost, then the law will have misallocative effects – demand will contract and some firms will go out of business if the cost burden is significant. This will be inefficient.

Fourth, in line with the importance of representations as signalling valuable information, where a buyer indicates that he wants goods of a particular specification then the presumption should be that failure to deliver such goods is a breach. If there is a ready market for such goods then the damages payable on breach will be negligible because the buyer's loss is negligible. If the quality cannot be secured readily in the market then the buyer's loss is the price difference between delivered and contracted for quality.

It should be no a surprise to find that the UK Sale of Goods Act 1979, which 'codifies' the common law, reflects these common sense economic propositions. For example, it implies four terms (sections 13–15) which make commercial and economic sense:

1. where goods are sold by description, they must fit the description
2. where the buyer neither knows or has access to information, the goods must be of 'merchantable quality'
3. where the buyer informs the seller of his purpose in buying the goods and there is actual or implied reliance on the seller's expertise, the goods must be fit for that purpose
4. where the buyer and seller agree that a contract is a sale by sample, the goods must not have any defect making them unmerchantable which is not discoverable on the basis of the buyer's access to the sample, the bulk of the goods must correspond with the sample and the buyer must have

---

[21] [1969] 2 All ER 31, HL, 79–80.

a reasonable opportunity to satisfy himself that the bulk of the goods does match the sample.

Market sanctions

There are other reasons to have confidence in market forces. Markets tend to display self-correcting tendencies. The existence of inefficiency in the market, particularly where large losses are involved, frequently brings forth its own solution.

Consider a potential market failure known as the '**lemons problem**', which is an example of adverse selection (discussed briefly in chapter 2) and gain in relation to nuisance.[22] This arises from *asymmetric information* between seller and buyer – when buyers cannot tell good from bad quality. A buyer may, as a result, buy a lemon. This itself will be an unhappy outcome and a source of inefficiency. But the effects of such generalised ignorance among buyers are more systemic. If the problem persists uncorrected not only will some consumers buy lemons but over time only lemons will be supplied by the market! Bad quality will drive out good quality in such ill-informed markets – an example of Gresham's Law.[23]

To explain this, consider the market for second-hand cars. Assume that there are two types of vehicles – good and bad. A prospective buyer cannot tell the difference between a good and a bad car. He would be prepared to pay £1,000 for a good car but only £500 for an inferior one. The only fact he knows is that 50 per cent are good cars but he cannot identify which specific vehicle is good. In the face of this ignorance it becomes rational for a buyer to offer a price that reflects the *average* quality of the cars being sold in the market. Thus, the maximum price a rational buyer would be willing to pay for a second-hand car is £750(= 0.5 × £1,000 + 0.5 × £500), assuming that half the cars are good and half bad. At this price it is not profitable for the seller to offer good cars – as he would be selling a £1,000 car for no more than £750. Thus the presence of bad cars has the effect of driving good cars out of the market. The consumer is harmed by his ignorance in two ways – he may end up with a bad car (a lemon) and, over time, all consumers are denied the option of being able to buy a good car. There is progressive deterioration in quality in such markets unless the seller of

[22] A. Akerlof, 'The Market for Lemons: Qualitative Uncertainty and the Market Mechanism', 84 *Quarterly Journal of Economics*, 488–500 (1970).
[23] 'Gresham's Law' is the proposition that bad money drives out good money when people find it hard to tell the difference.

good cars can find some way of differentiating (signalling) to prospective buyers that his cars are good.

It would be odd, and bizarre, if sellers of good second-hand cars did not set out to deal with the evident loss of business and profits that such consumer ignorance caused. They would attempt to signal the quality of their products to buyers through advertising, reputation, free after-sales service and warranties. Buyers will learn from these devices the quality of the goods and the reliability of the sellers, or they will invest time and effort in finding out the quality of the good, e.g. having a survey carried out on a house or an inspection of a second-hand car before purchase.

Warranties

One device to deal with defective products is the product warranty. Such warranties are often given for durable white goods such as refrigerators, electronic goods, cars and the like. That is, those goods which have a relatively long life. Product warranties deal with the lemons problem by creating a 'signal' of good quality. But they also serve as an insurance policy and, what might strike one as odd at first, as a repair contract designed to prolong the useful life of the product.[24]

First, a product warranty is an insurance policy offering the buyer either a substitute good or compensation for losses arising from faulty or danger-ous products. As an insurance policy, the warranty would be for a defined period (one year or longer) and provide that the manufacturer would com-pensate the buyer for loss by repair, replacement or a refund of the purchase price. This is the way most consumers view warranties. The analysis of war-ranties is very similar to that of product liability where a product sold with insurance coverage enables the manufacturer (and retailer) to sell at a higher price, and where the producer can insure more cheaply this is a profitable action for it to take. In a competitive market where warranties are standardised, market forces would optimise the terms between the parties.

Second, warranties act as a signal to buyers of the manufacturer's own confidence in the quality of his product. A manufacturer who offers a war-ranty on terms which give greater and longer coverage than his competitors signals to potential consumers that the goods are more likely to be of a higher quality and more reliable.

The third, and less evident, function of a warranty is a repair con-tract which allocates responsibility (liability) between manufacturer and

---

[24] G. L. Priest, 'A Theory of the Consumer Product Warranty', 90 *Yale Law Journal*, 1297–1352 (1981).

consumer to undertake investments which prolong the life of the product. As a repair contract, the hypothetical terms of an efficient warranty would assign obligations on the manufacturer for a specified period to undertake repairs to prolong the useful life of the product. It would also impose obligations on the consumer. In many cases manufacturer repair/care is a substitute for consumer care; where the cost of care exercised by the consumer is cheaper than the hypothetical contract would exempt the manufacturer from a repair obligation. Product misuse or minor repairs which can be undertaken by the consumer will not be imposed on the manufacturer. It would not be efficient to do so because this would raise costs more than the value to consumers in general, since the latter are the cheaper cost avoiders.

Disclaimer or exclusions not only allocate risks and losses arising from product defects but provide incentives to take care of the product. The manufacturers' obligations, together with the exclusions and disclaimers, create incentives on the part of both to invest in care and better product design to minimise the costs of product defects and poor quality. Clearly, if the manufacturer can improve product quality at less cost than the anticipated expected claims under the warranty it will be efficient for it to undertake investment to improve the quality. If, on the other hand, it is cheaper for the manufacturer to repair the product – that is, engage in *ex post* treatment of product defects – it will undertake this. The latter can be viewed as the insurance function.

Warranties are not without their difficulties. One problem is that they usually inefficiently pool high- and low-risk/loss individuals and fail to encourage high-risk individuals to take adequate care. However, the nature and intensity of product use will affect the loss and risks. One would expect that the hypothetical warranty would take account of this and different warranties would be offered to control – by exemption and disclaimer – those uses of the product which increase the likelihood or severity of product claims and losses. This may take the form of extended warranties or more liberal coverage, but at a higher price for the product. Thus, those who have minor problems will buy at cut-price stores while others wanting more coverage or who have higher loss from product failure will purchase from stores offering greater consumer protection. Manufacturers will also seek to control claims and thereby provide incentives to consumers for particular uses of the product. For example, vehicles used for commercial purposes are not covered by standard car warranties.[25]

---

[25] B. Klein and A. Leffler, 'The Role of Market Forces in Assuring Contractual Performance', 89 *Journal of Political Economy*, 615–641 (1981).

Warranties give rise to their own contractual difficulties. For example, a recent investigation concluded that many 'extended warranties' – that is, those offered by the retailer which extend the manufacturer's warranty for an additional second and third year or more – do not offer value for money.[26]

Standard form contracts

Standard form contracts have attracted considerable criticism. This has particularly been the case in the USA where legal academics once argued that because many consumer contracts were offered on a 'take-it-or-leave-it' basis without any negotiation between seller and consumers, they overly favoured the seller.[27] That is, the standard form contract is a manifestation of the seller's bargaining, if not market, power over ignorant and weak buyers.

This approach has been discredited as both bad economics and bad legal theory. As already stated, in competitive markets contract terms and prices are not set by individuals directly negotiating over terms but aggregate market forces on a take-it-or-leave-it basis. Each manufacturer in a trial and error process responds to consumer demand and reacts to the business practices of its competitors. Product quality and contract terms are the outcome of this process, which takes into account the demands of consumers. What one must show, for the monopoly interpretation of standard form contracts to be valid, is the existence of seller market power, and not simply dealings based on standard terms.

Standard form contracts may be oppressive and inefficient in the absence of overt market power if buyers lack adequate information to appraise their terms. Many consumers may be relatively ignorant and not good at interpreting complex terms and small print, with the result that the discipline of market forces on sellers is weak. This in turn may give them market power to impose terms which are not value maximising. However, caution should be exercised in leaping from the claim that consumers are ignorant to the conclusion that markets fail. In markets terms are set not by all consumers but by the marginal consumer who is more sensitive to price and the value they get from the bundle of contract terms offered by

---

[26] Office of Fair Trading, *Extended Warranties on Domestic Electrical Goods*, OFT 387, 2002; Competition Commission, *Extended Warranties on Domestic Electrical Goods*, Cm 6089 (I-III), 2003.

[27] F. Kessler, 'Contracts of Adhesion – Some Thoughts about Freedon of Contract, 43 *Columbia Law Review*, 629–642 (1943); W. D. Slawson, 'Standard Form Contracts and Democratic Control of Lawmaking Power', 84 *Harvard Law Review*, 529–566 (1975).

different retailers. The existence of well-informed consumers generates a beneficial externality to those less informed, or those not prepared to make the effort to take care over the contracts into which they enter.

One can go further to suggest that even when a substantial number or proportion of buyers is relatively ignorant that market forces can still generate standard form contracts broadly reflecting the demands of consumers. This can be illustrated by considering a model where a subset of consumers are comparison shoppers.[28] If there is a group of active comparison shoppers they will generate beneficial external effects for less-informed consumers. For example, suppose there are a hundred people interested in buying a television set; eighty of these are willing to go into the first shop, listen to the salesman's patter and buy the set he recommends. The remaining twenty consumers, however, want to get the best deal so they go from shop to shop comparing prices and quality. If retailers cannot distinguish comparison shoppers from other consumers then they will be forced to treat all consumers as if they were informed and price sensitive. Clearly, if shopkeepers can distinguish comparison shoppers from impulse buyers they can offer the former better terms and exploit the latter (which would mean that they are not offering a standard form contract). However, in the real world where we have not a hundred but tens of thousands of shoppers, comparison shopping by some may be sufficient to make sellers price and maintain quality at efficient levels for fear of losing significant sales. Thus not all consumers need be informed for the market outcome to be efficient.

On the other hand, consumers can be duped by contract terms which they do not bother to read, or comprehend, or see the significance of at the time the contract is formed. It is possible that the law can play a role in giving redress by setting out protective terms (mandatory default rules), or reflecting some sense of fairness or distributive justice.[29]

The lost volume 'puzzle'

In markets where there are standardised goods breaching the contract either by refusing to deliver or refusing to accept the good imposes no loss. This is because of the possibility of perfect substitute performance. The seller can make a sale on the same terms and the buyer can purchase the good from another seller on the same terms. Clearly where there is not perfect

---

[28] A. Schwartz and L. L. Wilde, 'Intervening in Markets on the Basis of Imperfect Information: A Legal and Economic Analysis', 127 *University of Pennsylvania Law Review*, 630–682 (1979).

[29] A. T. Kronman, 'Contract and Distributive Justice', 89 *Yale Law Journal*, 472–511 (1980).

substitute performance or there are costs associated with a breach then this is not the case. But in markets with standardised goods the legal and economic presumption is that the default remedy would be no damages for breach of contract.

This is not, however, how the law treats the matter. There have been a number of cases where a buyer reneges on a contract for the sale of goods sold in markets where damages have been awarded – so-called 'lost volume' sales. The leading cases coincidentally involve the purchase of a motor vehicle. The issue is whether the distributor/retailer is entitled to the lost margin or profits on the sale, the price difference, or nothing.

The law takes into account supply and demand conditions through the legal concept of the 'available market'. Put briefly, if demand exceeds supply or is in balance the price difference method is used to calculate damages. However, where the market is sluggish and demand weak (that is, supply exceeds demand) the law has responded by using the sellers' lost margin as a basis for damages.

In *W. L. Thompson* v. *R. Robinson (Gunmakers Ltd)*[30] the defendant repudiated a contract to buy a new Standard Vanguard from the claimant's dealer. The price of the car was fixed and the dealer's profit was £61. In assessing whether there was a loss the Court employed the concept of the 'available market'. It looked at the state of the market and concluded that demand in the area was not so strong as to readily absorb the lost sale. The seller could not obtain substitute performance and the sale was 'lost'. Because of uncertainty as to whether the seller had lost a sale the Court awarded only 50 per cent of the gross profit margin as damages.

In *Lazenby Garages Ltd* v. *Wright*,[31] a later case, the factual situation was more remarkable. Wright went to Lazenby Garages and agreed to buy a second-hand BMW on 19 February 1974 for delivery on 1 March 1974. The next day he went back saying that he did not want the car. The garage offered it for resale. Two months later they sold it for £1,770, £100 more than Mr Wright was going to pay. Notwithstanding the more profitable resale, the garage sued for the lost profit (£345) on the sale to Wright. The Court made a distinction between new and second-hand cars based on the presence or otherwise of an 'available market' – i.e. whether the car could be readily resold.

The legal position appears to be that where there is an available market damages are to be assessed as the difference between the contract price and the resale price; where the good does not have a ready market

---

[30] [1955] 1 All ER 154.   [31] [1976] 2 All ER 770, CA.

(in *Lazenby Garages* the second-hand BMW was described as 'unique') the damage measure is the lost retail margin. Does this make economic sense?

If we think about the situation a bit more we can see that a lost sale can impose a cost on a retailer. This is because there are costs of retailing and these costs are defrayed (recouped) by the sales in any one period. A lost sale can therefore increase retail costs in any period and if significant reduce the retailer's cashflow. If the market has excess supply then buyer's breach does impose a loss equal to the gross margin. If the law shifts liability and both buyers and sellers have a fairly accurate perception of the probability of default and the loss then the law will not have much effect. However, generally the retailer is in a better position to value the likely losses and to take avoidance action. Goldberg[32] has argued that the law is wrong because the seller has an easy solution. The seller is in the best position to tell the buyer of the potential losses if he reneges and can deal with the potential for default by requiring a non-refundable deposit where there is a delay between agreeing the contract and delivery.

CONSIDERATION

In law the formation of a contract requires the observance of certain formalities. These consist of an offer, its acceptance and consideration. These seem fairly straightforward requirements as evidence of a consensual exchange – a genuine bargain – between the parties. Here we consider the legal concept of consideration which, remarkably, has excited considerable controversy among lawyers.

Consideration in law

Consideration is necessary for the formation of a contract. The classic legal definition states that:

A valuable consideration, in the sense of the law, may consist either of some right interest, profit, or benefit accruing to the one party, or some forbearance, detriment, loss, or responsibility, given, suffered or undertaken by the other.[33]

---

[32] V. P. Goldberg, 'An Economic Analysis of Lost-Volume Retail Seller', 57 *Southern California Law Review*, 283–297 (1984); C. J. Goetz and R. E. Scott, 'Measuring Sellers' Damages: The Lost Profits Puzzle', 31 *Stanford Law Review*, 323–379 (1979).
[33] *Currie* v. *Misa* [1875] LR 10 Ex. 153, 162.

In this sense, consideration can be regarded as the price for a promise, although this is not accurate. Atiyah summarises the (English) 'doctrine' of consideration:

The conventional statement of [the] doctrine of consideration is not perhaps as easily reduced to a simple set of rules as it is often assumed, but few would disagree with the following propositions. Firstly, a promise is not enforceable (if not under seal), unless the promisor obtains some benefit or the promisee incurs some detriment in return for the promise. A subsidiary proposition, whose claim to be regarded as a part of the orthodox doctrine is perhaps less certain, is sometimes put forward, namely that consideration must be of economic value. Secondly, in a bilateral contract the consideration for a promise is a counter-promise, and in a unilateral contract consideration is the performance of the act specified by the promisor. Thirdly, the law of contract only enforces bargains; the consideration must, in short, be (and perhaps even be regarded by the parties as) the 'price' of the promise. Fourthly, past consideration is not sufficient consideration. Fifthly, consideration must move from the promisee. Sixthly (and this is regarded as following from the first three propositions), the law does not enforce gratuitous promises. Seventhly, a limited exception to these propositions is recognized by the *High Trees* principle which, however, only enables certain promises without consideration to be set up by way of defence.[34] [See later for a discussion of the *High Trees* case.]

Yet as one reads contract law texts a deep controversy surfaces as to the nature and necessity of consideration in law. The detriment/benefit principle has, apparently, been whittled down by the Courts so that legal consideration is, some argue, a tautologous legal device to enable the Court to find 'a sufficient reason to enforce a contract' rather than an independent requirement. Needless to say this view has been vigorously rejected by others. Nonetheless legal consideration still seems to serve several important functions, as summarised by Posner, by:

• reducing the number of fake claims by requiring that the claimant prove more than just that someone promised to do something in a legal system that enforces oral contracts
• reducing the likelihood of inadvertent contractual commitments from casual or careless use of promissory language
• avoiding legal costs of third parties entangled in disputes over trivial or gratuitous promises
• avoiding cases where the terms of exchange are vague
• preventing opportunistic behaviour.

The concept of 'valuable consideration' is the *quid pro quo* which binds promises. It has an economic meaning as some benefit or detriment which

---

[34] P. Atiyah, *Essays on Contract*, Oxford: Oxford University Press, 1986, 180.

passes from the promissee to the promissor. This may be a money price, or an opportunity cost in the sense of some detrimental 'reliance'.

The English Courts will not look at the adequacy of consideration to see if the price was reasonable, justified, or just. This also makes economic sense. There is no reason to suppose that the Courts are in a better or even a good position to judge what the 'right' price is, and how to determine it. In the cases where this is relatively easy to determine – that is, where there is a well-functioning market – the price is set by market forces and therefore objectively given to the parties and the Court. It is also a situation where the necessity for the law to intervene is low because the disgruntled buyer can easily obtain substitute performance from another supplier.

Economists are not, however, insensitive to the adequacy of consideration, if the term is understood as the adequacy of the price or other terms. In cases where the price charged is considerably above marginal costs such that there is a monopoly profit then 'consideration' is excessive and resources misallocated. Economists would generally argue that such an 'abuse' should be regulated. However, it would be difficult for the Courts to determine the 'correct' price and to, in effect, administer a system of price regulation. This is best left to competition and consumer protection laws.

The pre-existing duty rule

In English law a promise for a promise unsupported by fresh consideration is said to be unenforceable. This is the so-called 'pre-existing duty rule' applied where contractual terms are re-negotiated. However, this area seems to have been thrown into disarray by recent cases which have allowed contractual modification without 'fresh consideration'.

First, let us see whether economics explains (or criticises) the law.[35] The efficiency of the pre-existing duty rule and the exceptions to it can be examined in two different factual settings – where the existing economic factors have not altered and where they have in a way that makes performance more costly or difficult.[36]

The first situation is captured by the concept of opportunistic breach discussed above. The promisee seeks to re-negotiate the terms because after

---

[35] V. A. Aivazian, M. J. Trebilcock and M. Penny, 'The Law of Contract Modifications: The Uncertain Quest for a Benchmark of Enforceability', 22 *Osgoode Hall Law Journal*, 173–212 (1984); R. A. Halston, 'Opportunistic Economic Duress and Contractual Modification', 107 *Law Quarterly Review*, 649–678 (1991); A. W. Dnes, 'The Law and Economics of Contract Modifications: The Case of *Williams v. Roffey*', 15 *International Review of Law & Economics*, 225–240 (1995).

[36] R. A. Posner, 'Gratuitous Promises in Economics and Law', 6 *Journal of Legal Studies*, 411–426 (1977).

the contract has been formed he or she acquires some leverage over the other party which they now attempt to exploit. The subsequent re-negotiations of the terms reflect this new bargaining power which was not present at the contract formation stage. Furthermore, enforcing the re-negotiated terms will have no *ex post* effect on the efficiency with which resources are allocated. One party's gain is the other's loss, with no beneficial incentive effects, although the effect may be detrimental if opportunism is prevalent and unchecked. In this case, the law should not enforce the re-negotiated terms as this would simply encouraged future opportunistic behaviour.

On the other hand, where the contractual modification is due to changes in economic factors there may be justification to legally enforce the new terms. It could be claimed that re-negotiation is economically justified where the cost of performance exceeds the value of performance to the non-breaching party. However, this simply explains why re-negotiation occurs, rather than whether it is efficient. The analysis must examine the reasons why the re-negotiation has occurred, and its incentive effects.

In markets where goods have close substitutes it is reasonable to assume that any re-negotiation has not been the result of bad-faith opportunism and is to the mutual advantage of both parties. This is because the party seeking the new terms does not have market power or can act opportunistically. The implication that he or she accepts the new terms is that re-negotiation is an efficient response to changed economic factors.[37]

In other cases the conclusion is not clear-cut. Consider the case where performance becomes more costly because, say, the price of oil to a heating oil supplier has increased. As a result the supplier refuses to honour the contract to supply fuel oil to a glasshouse during a severe winter at the lower contract price. The market gardener can insist on compliance with the terms of the original contract, with the possibility that he will lose his crop if the supplier refuses. In this case it may be in both parties' interest to re-negotiate the terms even though the market gardener is worse off than had the original contract been honoured but better off than if the supplier had reneged.

This analysis is incomplete because it considers only *ex post* effects. Suppose that the parties knew that the price of heating oil could fluctuate and that both took this into account at the time the contract was signed. The implication is that the supplier for commercial reasons assumed the risk of an adverse price movement and the possibility of a poor(er) bargain. It

---

[37] C. J. Goetz and R. F. Scott, 'The Mitigation Principle: Toward a General Theory of Contractual Obligations', 69 *Virginia Law Review*, 967–1025 (1983).

must be assumed that this was done to secure the contract. If the contract is then re-negotiated, the assignment of risk alters. But, of more significance, buyers will realise that fixed-price contracts have little value since the supplier will simply re-negotiate when the price risk turns against him. In subsequent negotiations they will ensure that either re-negotiation is not possible, or drive a harder bargain. The oil supplier is potentially in a superior position to ensure that at the time he signs the contract he has sufficient oil supplies to meet orders at the contract price, and it is reasonable to assume that this is the allocation of risk contemplated by both at the time the contract was formed. This is especially the case since a rise in oil prices is not an unusual and unanticipated event.

Does the law recognise the above distinctions?

The early case of *Stilk* v. *Myrick*[38] is consistent with the economic distinctions above. Stilk was part of a group of sailors who refused to crew a ship unless they were given a pay rise. When their ship returned to port the captain refused to honour the terms of the re-negotiated contract. At trial the re-negotiated contract was held to be unenforceable. The court stated that to enforce such a modification would encourage sailors to sink ships in order to get better terms. The purpose of this rule, it was and is argued, was to prevent 'extortionate re-negotiation' – i.e. opportunism. This is where one party acquires leverage over the other party to the contract which he or she then exploits by demanding better terms than in the original contract. In *Stilk* it was the prospect of stranding the ship (the contract was renegotiated in a Baltic port and not on the high seas). The re-negotiated terms are purely redistributive and do not increase joint wealth. This case aligns the pre-existing duty rule with the legal notion of 'economic duress'.

Foakes v. *Beer*,[39] which is the leading case in this area, moves the law beyond economic duress by holding that re-negotiated terms in the absence of fresh consideration are unenforceable. Beer had secured a judgment against Foakes for a debt, and the latter then asked for more time to pay the debt. Beer agreed, and also agreed not to take proceedings on the judgment during the repayment period. When the debt was finally paid Beer sued Foakes for interest on the debt. He succeeded on the grounds that the agreement was not binding since Foakes had not given 'fresh consideration'. The facts of the case indicate no opportunism or economic duress and a clear intention of the part of both parties to alter the contract. The case is hard to reconcile with the above considerations.

---

[38] (1809) 2 Camp 317 & 6 Esp 129. See also *Harris* v. *Watson* (1791) Peake 102.
[39] *Foakes* v. *Beer* (1883–84) LR 9 App Cas. 605 HL.

High Trees,[40] a much later case reported in 1947, marks a change in the law. In 1937 the claimant leased a block of flats from the defendant at a fixed rent for ninety-nine years. In 1940 the lessor wrote to the company confirming a variation to the contract that reduced the ground rent. The reason given was the Second World War, which reduced the lessee's ability profitably to let the flats. The reduced rent was paid until early 1945, when the flats were again fully leased. Later in that year the defendant was asked to pay the rent agreed in the original lease, which it refused and was successfully sued for the difference between the initial and reduced rents for the last two quarters of 1945, although the agreement to reduce the rent until early 1945 was found by the Court to be binding on the parties. Thus in *High Trees* the modified agreement was binding without fresh consideration. This seems a sensible approach.

Williams v. *Roffey Bros & Nicholls (Contractors) Ltd*[41] moves the law yet further away from the pre-existing duty rule. There, a builder appears to have severely underestimated the costs of completing building works and was threatened with insolvency if forced to perform the contract on the agreed terms. The defendant agreed to a variation in the terms to secure completion of the building works but later refused to honour the modified terms. The Court enforced the contractual modification on the grounds that the defendant was given some 'practical benefit' – completion of the building works – from the re-negotiated terms.

What is the economics of *Williams* v. *Roffey*? This needs to be considered both at the time the original contract was negotiated and at the time of the re-negotiation. Consider the latter first. The builder was in real financial problems and most certainly had from the reported facts understated the costs of completion in the original contract. At the time of the re-negotiation it is true that the builder was not acting in bad faith or opportunistically – there were objective circumstances which led to the re-negotiation.

On the other hand, he also had the property owner over a barrel by refusing to complete on the agreed terms. There is no doubt that the developer received a 'practical benefit' from the re-negotiated contract by having his apartments partially completed. However, *Williams* v. *Roffey* sets out perverse incentives for contract formation. Its effect is to transform a fixed-price contract into a cost-plus contract contrary to the initial agreement of the parties. It is common practice for builders (in the UK, at least) to underbid in order to secure building contracts, or to undertake costings in such a slipshod manner as frequently to lead to cost overruns which

---

[40] *Central London Property Trust Ltd* v. *High Trees House Ltd* [1947] KB 130.   [41] (1991) 1 QB.

the developer or homeowner is then expected to cover. The decision in *Williams* v. *Roffey* encourages these practices. It also, like the oil supply example above, fundamentally alters the nature of the contractual relationship between the parties. If a fixed-price contract with penalties for failure to complete on time and to specification can be validly re-negotiated in these circumstances it converts it into a cost-plus contract in circumstances when the disadvantaged party has limited options. This undermines the certainty and protections that the 'buyer' has bargained over. Of course, against this, is the reality that the developer is left with a half-built house/flat. But in setting out contract rules the misery of the defendant in *Williams* v. *Roffey* has to be set against the incentive effects that unenforceability of contract modification gives to all future building contracts.

Re-negotiations motivated to take advantage of the promisee's lack of alternatives (substitute performance) will not promote a more efficient allocation of resources. These attempts should clearly not be enforced. However, the attempt by oil supplier and builder unilaterally to pass on risks occasioned by exogenous events not provided for in the contract will also not achieve a superior allocation of resources.

Unilateral promises

There are many types of promises which are unilateral or gratuitous.[42] That is, they emanate from one party and require nothing in return, such as gifts or promises. For these there is no 'bargain' or immediate price for consideration in the common sense usage of the word and hence they are sometimes called 'non-bargained promises'.

To illustrate, consider the oft-cited US case of *Ricketts* v. *Scothorn*.[43] Katie Scothorn's grandfather gave her a promissory note which read: 'May 1st 1891. I promise to pay to Katie Scothorn on demand, $2,000, to be at 6 per cent per annum. J. C. Ricketts.' He further stated: 'I have fixed something that you have not got to work any more. None of my grandchildren work and you don't have to.' She gave up her job but returned later to work with her grandfather's consent. Her grandfather died having not paid all the interest or the capital sum and Katie sued the executors. The Court rejected her claim on the grounds that the money promised was not dependent on her abandonment of her employment. This is the position in English

---

[42] A. Katz, 'When Should an Offer Stick? The Economics of Promissory Estoppel in Preliminary Negotiations', 105 *Yale Law Journal*, 1249–1309 (1996).
[43] 57 Neb 51 77 NW 365 (1998).

law – reliance and forbearance are not treated as consideration unless expressly required by the promissor.[44] The enforceability of a promise depends on a bargain and a price for performance.

Does this make economic sense?.[45] In *Ricketts* the promise was made with the intention that the granddaughter should not as a result work. She acted in reliance of this promise. If the girl knew that the promise would not have been honoured, she would have kept her job and been better off than the outcome with the broken promise. There has been detrimental reliance and an avoidable cost incurred by the granddaughter. Enforcing such a unilateral promise where it is reasonable that the recipient will act on it, or alter their plans and behaviour on it, provides incentives on grandfathers to make realistic promises to their grandchildren. To the economist, detrimental reliance is equivalent to a 'price'; it is a forgone opportunity or action which has an opportunity cost.

English contract law does not recognise the concept of 'detrimental reliance'. This contrasts with the US legal position where detrimental reliance is treated as consideration and the contract enforceable (*Restatement of Contracts*, section 90), although this is usually applied in commercial contracts rather than gifts. Nonetheless, the appropriate economic rule should be to make a 'non-bargain promise' enforceable in the absence of 'consideration', where the promissor should have reasonably expected it to induce detrimental action or forbearance on the part of the promisee or third person, and which does so. The economic justification is to avoid wasteful reliance.[46]

---

[44] *Shadwell* v. *Shadwell* (1860) 9 CBNS 159, 42 ER 62, Common Bench.

[45] R. A. Posner, 'Gratuitous Promises in Economics and Law' 411–426; M. A. Eisenberg, 'Donative Promises', 47 *University of Chicago Law Review*, 1–33 (1979); C. J. Goetz and R. E. Scott, 'Enforcing Promises: An Examination of the Basic Contracts', 89 *Yale Law Journal*, 1261–1322 (1980), reprinted in A. Ogus and C. J. Veljanovski (eds.), *Readings in the Economics of Law and Regulation*, Oxford: Clarendon Press, 1984, 157–172; S. Shavell, 'An Economic Analysis of Altruism and Deferred Gifts', 20 *Journal of Legal Studies*, 401–421 (1991); A. Kull, 'Reconsidering Gratuitous Promises', 21 *Journal of Legal Studies*, 39–65 (1992).

[46] Goetz and Scott develop a general model which allows for enforcement of 'non-reciprocal promises'. They set up a simple equation which sets out the socially optimal damage rule. If p is the promissor's probability of performing the promise given the prospect of damages D, then the efficient damage award is given by the expression $(1 - p) D = (1 - p) R - pB$, where R and B are the values of detrimental and beneficial reliance, respectively. The promissor's decision to honour his promise will be influenced by the expected damage award which is the left-hand term (damages are discounted by $(1 - p)$ because they are paid only when there is a breach). The right-hand side reflects the promisee's expected net detrimental reliance. The optimal damage rule which internalises detrimental reliance is given by the formula $D = R - (p/(1 - p))B$. That is, optimal damages equal the detrimental reliance minus the prospective odds-on that the the promissor will breach multiplied by benefical reliance. The expression $(p/(1 - p))$ is called by Goetz and Scott the 'good faith ratio'. This is a complicated formula which does not have a legal counterpart. Goetz and Scott, 'Enforcing Promises'.

It would be fair to say that there is a reluctance to make a unilateral contract enforceable, even among law and economics commentators. This relates to the evidentiary difficulties of establishing both the nature of the promise (should an impulse offer or promise of a gift be made enforceable?), and whether there was genuine detrimental reliance. It is easy, for example, to envisage situations where accepting detrimental reliance as adequate consideration may generate perverse incentive effects. Suppose the granddaughter knew there was a likelihood that the promise would be broken, then her reliance on it would have been less. She may have taken no detrimental action based on the promise, because say, her grandfather was doddery, forgetful or just an old fool. This would be efficient. However, if the law made unilateral promises enforceable only if there was detrimental reliance, then it might encourage detrimental reliance. The granddaughter, knowing the legal position, might be encouraged to take some actions as a way of making her grandfather's promise enforceable even though on a realistic assessment of the circumstances she did not believe what was said.

DISCLOSURE AND MISTAKE

A major function of contracts and contract law is to deal with contractual problems caused by ignorance, mistakes, misrepresentations and fraud.[47] These are all difficulties which arise because one party has less information than the other, or both have insufficient information. Generally, the law should provide appropriate incentives for the disclosure of relevant information which does not impair incentives for the efficient production and utilisation of information.

Economics of information

In the real world the future is unknown – there are risks; people make mistakes; assessing and verifying facts is costly and difficult; market and other factors change in unanticipated ways; and, of course, some may deliberately, negligently, or inadvertently mislead others. The result is that *ex post* the agreed terms of a contract may not be wealth maximising for one or both parties when the true situation is realised. They have a contract, but not one that is likely to be performed.

---

[47] A. T. Kronman, 'Mistake, Disclosure, Information and the Law of Contract', 7 *Journal of Legal Studies*, 1–34 (1978).

It may seem that the solution to mistakes is straightforward. Ignorant people will not make contracts which are in their best interests and they will be exploited by sellers and buyers who are better informed, unscrupulous and/or dishonest.[48] The solution is more and better information and presumably rules which render void or voidable contracts based on less than perfect information. However, this ignores two considerations – that information is costly to produce and disseminate (and, indeed, interpret), and the way the law affects the incentives of the parties to produce and obtain more information.

The economics of information provides several tenets or principles useful in assessing the impact and remedies for contractual mistake.

First: most useful information is valuable to have but costly to produce.

Second: the incentive to produce information is positively correlated with the anticipated returns. A rational individual will search for more and better information only if the expected returns outweigh the costs. It could be argued that people cannot make such a rational calculation because the value of a piece of information is often not known until after it has been acquired and it is then too late to decide whether it was worth the expense. But lack of information implies uncertainty and risks, and hence probabilistic decision-making. Individuals can form estimates of the probable value of a piece of information and based on this make a choice by balancing the costs against the *expected benefits*.

Third: a rational individual will not seek to be perfectly informed because it is simply too costly. To the economist there is an optimal or efficient level of ignorance – where costs of more information outweigh the expected benefits, ignorance is bliss! Similarly from society's viewpoint the optimal amount of information (or ignorance) is determined by the (social) costs and expected benefits of more information. Thus just as there can be too little information there can be too much information, in the sense that the costs outweigh the expected benefits.

Finally: the extent of market failure is determined by market forces not the knowledge possessed by any one or a subset of individuals. More specifically, markets may work relatively well even though many buyers are ignorant of the quality of goods and services and the contractual terms and liabilities. This is because market forces create a possibly *beneficial externality* on the ignorant generated by informed buyers who invest in information and undertake comparison shopping. Thus an objective test is

---

[48] M. R. Darby and E. Karni, 'Free Competition and the Optimal Amount of Fraud', 16 *Journal of Law & Economics*, 67–88 (1973).

required to determine whether a party lack of information or mistake does in fact lead to an inferior contract or a loss.

What, then, do these admittedly simplified tenets imply about efficient law?

1. Efficient contract law will allocate the risks/loss from imperfect information but preserve incentives for the production of socially beneficial information.

2. Where information is freely available or obtained at no cost or effort by one or both parties then the law des not need to take into account the impact of contractual rules and remedies on the production of information. The laws can be decided on distributive grounds without any loss of efficiency.

3. Where a party makes a representation or statement on which another relies there should be strict liability. If this is not the rule then contracting parties will not be able to rely on the statements of others and hence know whether they are entering into mutually beneficial contracts. Strict liability encourages care and truthfulness in making representations, statements and promises.

Pre-contractual disclosure

English contract law recognises no general obligation to disclose information.

Where information has been conveyed by one party to another which turns out to be wrong, and as a direct result the other party suffers loss, liability will be strict. That is, the party conveying the information will be strictly liable for the loss. This is efficient because it encourages those offering information either to ensure that it is accurate or else to pay the losses.

Where the loss arises from the non-disclosure of information the efficient rule is less obvious. There is no commercial or economic reason why the seller should be obliged to inform the buyer of all he or she knows, or that all the information either party has should be made available to the other. If I know that a parcel of land can be put to a more valuable use it should not be incumbent on me to tell the seller. If the law forced this information to be given to the seller then it would greatly reduce the incentive of individuals and companies to search out more valuable uses of resources. This is because the return to acquiring such information would be reduced and therefore less would be produced. A full disclosure rule would not only reduce the investment in information production but, by implication, lead to the paradox that less not more information is available to the parties!

Mistake

Often one or both parties bases their promise on a mistake, known in law as unilateral and mutual or common mistake, respectively. Again in thinking about the efficient response the impact of the law on the production of (socially) useful information must be assessed.

Kronman suggests that the legal approach to mistake can be explained by distinguishing two types of information – that acquired by investment and that acquired without any investment.[49] Information acquired through deliberate investment should not be grounds for excusing performance if the party who has made the expenditure is better informed and strikes a good bargain. Information which has been casually acquired or which is not socially useful or productive should be such grounds, since to void a contract against the better informed party will not have adverse incentive effects. Such information has been called 'redistributive information', as it merely gives one party a bargaining advantage and redistributes wealth in his or her favour, but little else.[50] The distinction between productive and redistributive information has been put forward as an explanation of the law's treatment of mistake and the different treatment of unilateral mistake (when only one party is mistaken) and common mistake (when both parties are mistaken).

The US decision in *Laidlaw* v. *Organ*[51] illustrates this rule. During the 1812 war between Britain and the USA the British blockaded New Orleans, which depressed the price of export goods such as tobacco. Organ, a buyer of tobacco, received private information that the war had ended by treaty, so he called on a representative of the Laidlaw firm and offered to buy tobacco. The representative of the Laidlaw firm was ignorant about the peace treaty so a contract was concluded between them at the depressed price. The next day public notice was given in New Orleans that peace was concluded and the price of tobacco soared. The mistake in this contract was obviously unilateral, not mutual – Organ knew about the treaty and Laidlaw did not. Even so, the contract was apparently set aside by the Court after a trial. The evidence was that Organ discovered fortuitously that peace was concluded rather than investing time and resources in making the discovery. Furthermore, the contract merely accelerated by one day knowledge of the

---

[49] A. T. Kronman, 'Mistake, Disclosure, Information and the Law of Contract', 1–34; S. Shavell, 'Acquisition and Disclosure of Information Prior to Sale', 25 *RAND Journal of Economics*, 20–36 (1994).
[50] R. Cooter and T. S. Ulen, *Law and Economics*, 4th edn., New York: Pearson Addison Wesley, 2004.
[51] 15 U.S. (2 Wheat.) 178 (1815).

treaty and did not contribute to production of tobacco, or the more efficient allocation of resources. So enforcing the contract did not increase wealth, it merely re-distributed it.

Common mistake

Common or mutual mistake is often grounds for setting aside a contract if it amounts to frustration, Indeed there is a close connection between mutual mistake and the doctrine of frustration in English law.

If a mutual mistake is fundamental then it has the effect of turning contract into an 'involuntary' exchange which can destroy economic value. For example, if at the time the contract was formed, unknown to the parties, the subject matter did not exist, there would be no economic justification for enforcing the contract.

However, in other cases the grounds for not enforcing the contract are less clear. Take the oft-cited US case of *Sherwood* v. *Walker.*[52] Both the seller and buyer believed that a prize cow (called Rose) was barren although there is some evidence that both appreciated that there was a likelihood that this was not the case. In fact she was pregnant, and worth about ten times the selling price. The mistake was discovered before the cow was delivered to the buyer and the seller cancelled the sale. The Court upheld the cancellation.

It could be argued that this was efficient law. There is no presumption that the cow was more valuable in the buyer's possession that in the seller's, or that the seller had not been careless in thinking the cow barren. The mistake was unavoidable.

An alternative and much more convincing way of looking at the case is to ask how the parties would have allocated the risk had they foreseen it. Although the price of a barren cow will be much lower than that of a fertile one it may nonetheless reflect a premium that the cow may have been fertile. Notwithstanding this, in general the owner will have access at lower cost than the buyer to information about the characteristics of his property and can therefore avoid mistakes about these more cheaply than prospective buyers.[53] On this interpretation *Sherwood* was wrongly decided. It is interesting that in English law mistake as to quality, such as in *Sherwood*, does not make a contract unenforceable.

---

[52] 66 Mich. 568, 33 NW 919 [1887].
[53] For a contrary analysis of *Sherwood*, see J. K. Smith and R. L. Smith, 'Contract Law, Mutual Mistake, and Incentives to Produce and Disclose Information', 19 *Journal of Legal Studies*, 467–488, (1990).

Unilateral mistake

Courts usually enforce contracts based on unilateral mistake. Refusing to set aside a contract because one party is mistaken promotes efficiency by rewarding discovery, or encouraging people to acquire information. Where one party has acquired information through costly and deliberate search, effort and actions, then the unilateral mistake by the other should not be grounds for holding a contract void. This is because to do so would reduce to zero the return to deliberate information-gathering and hence there would be less information produced and resources would not be efficiently allocated. The rules of contract must preserve the incentive for the production of information and not always give the misinformed party the benefit of the doubt.

However, the Courts will look at how the mistake occurred, and this is often consistent with a focus on information costs and production incentives. For example, where a buyer seeks to 'snatch a bargain' because the seller has made a mistake in quoting the contract price which is obviously much too low (£2 instead of £20) the contract will be set aside.

REMOTENESS

The concept of remoteness is used in both contract and tort law. In tort, a loss is remote if it has a very low probability and it would not be efficient to impose liability because the avoidance costs exceed the expected loss. In contract, remoteness deals with (non-)liability for consequential losses that it is not reasonable to make the breaching party pay.

Recall that under the *Hadley* rule the non-breaching party is compensated for the average loss rather than the actual loss unless he has revealed his higher valuation to the seller at the time the contract is formed. It is, in effect, a limited liability rule since the mill owner could not recover his full expectation damages from the carrier. This, it is claimed forces those with higher than average expectation losses to reveal this information to carriers. The revelation will, in turn, affect the contract price. If the carrier is informed that there are large losses to be incurrred due to late delivery and he accepts liability, then the carrier will require a higher price for the expanded liability/damages. This would lead to at least two classes of carriage contracts – those covered under the *Hadley* rule, which presumably are cheaper, and those where the buyer has negotiated greater protection at the higher shipping price and additional liability insurance.

Now consider an anti-*Hadley* rule which gives buyers their full expectation losses including consequential losses. Under this rule the mill owner with potentially high consequential losses would have no incentive to reveal information which would enable the carrier to charge a higher price. However, with such unlimited liability on carriers the price of transporting goods would rise significantly. At the relatively higher price mill owners with low consequential losses would have an incentive to reveal this to the carrier in turn for lower freight charges. They simply do not value the implicit insurance reflected in the price premium that they are required to pay for, in effect, someone else's higher losses. The anti-*Hadley* rule would also force information to be revealed, but this time by low-value buyers not high-loss buyers.

Thus both the *Hadley* and anti-*Hadley* rules produce efficient incentives to reveal relevant information. The overall efficiency of these two very different rules depends on the number of individuals in each group, the relative costs of information and negotiations to each group and so on. But, on the face of it, the law does not seem to affect the information-generating process in such a simple model.

FRUSTRATION

The common law often excuses performance when a contract cannot be performed. This is known as the doctrine of frustration in English law, or of impossibility in US law.

Contracts can be rendered difficult or impossible to perform under their original terms for many reasons – the good no longer exists, or has never existed; the goods cannot be delivered by the shipper because the port is blockaded; the costs of performing have become astronomical; and so on. Where performance is impossible or impractical it may not be efficient to insist on performance. By the same token, someone has to bear the loss. Therefore, some criteria must be developed to excuse performance or impose damages.

Where the parties have specified in their contract the way that frustration affects the contract the law should enforce the allocation of risks explicitly agreed to by the parties.[54] This approach can be used, for example, to explain why the law imposes the loss on a party even where the failure to perform was an event beyond the control of the party in breach. It must be assumed that in the usual case the parties will have allocated the risks of anticipated losses caused by non-performance to the party better able to bear it or

---

[54] A. M. Polinsky, 'Risk Sharing Through Breach of Contract Remedies', *Journal of Legal Studies*, 427–444 (1983); A. M. Polinsky, *An Introduction to Law and Economics*, 3rd edn., Gaithersburg, MD: Aspen Publishing, 2003, chapter 8.

to insure against it, who will typically be the party making the promise. The only exception to this approach would be where the event preventing performance was an unusual one, beyond the scope of the normal risks contemplated by the parties, in which case the doctrine of frustration will operate under English law to terminate further performance of the contract (thus making the parties share the risk).

Where the contract is silent, the law must allocate the risks.

Suppose that S contracts to hire a room to B for a wedding reception and before the wedding the room burns down and the parties have not included terms to cover this contingency. Under English contract law, the contract is said to be 'frustrated' – B will not have to pay for the room and will be entitled to the return of any prepayments and S will not be required to provide a substitute. These legal consequences, which the law has imported into the contract, substitutes for the parties' efforts to obtain sufficient information to explicitly agree to an allocation of the risks due to fire.

An alternative theory of how the law should, and does, work where the contract does not cover the event is to impose liability on the superior risk bearer.[55] This is the party in the best position, either because they are less risk averse or better able to diversify and spread the risks and losses. This views the legal rules governing frustration as, in effect, an implicit insurance policy based on the relative risk aversion of the contracting parties. However, these theories do not generate deterministic results and their application to the law would require an assessment of which party was more or less risk averse in each case. This subjective analysis is unsatisfactory.[56]

Other economic explanations have been suggested that do not rely on attitudes to risk.[57] If a supervening event increases the costs of performance while leaving general market conditions unchanged the parties are likely to agree to excuse performance, but they are not if general market conditions change. If the event makes performing the contract impossible then the expected costs of non-performance to the buyer are zero. The benefits of

[55] R. A. Posner and A. M. Rosenfeld, 'Impossibility and Related Doctrines in Contract Law: An Economic Analysis', 6 *Journal of Legal Studies*, 83–118 (1977); P. L Joskow, 'Commercial Impossibility, the Uranium Market and the Westinghouse Case', 6 *Journal of Legal Studies*, 119–176 (1977).

[56] The complications of using risk aversion as an explanation, see A. O. Sykes, 'The Doctrine of Impracticability in a Second-best World', 14 *Journal of Legal Studies*, 43–94 (1990).

[57] V. P. Goldberg, 'Impossibility and Related Excuses', 144 *Journal of Institutional & Theoretical Economics*, 100–116 (1988). The explanation based on risk aversion has been questioned: C. Bruce, 'An Economic Analysis of the Impossibility Doctrine', 11 *Journal of Legal Studies*, 311–332 (1982); Sykes, 'The Doctrine of Commercial Impracticality', 43–94; M. J. White, 'Contract Breach and Contract Discharge Due to Impossibility: A Unified Theory', 17 *Journal of Legal Studies*, 353–376 (1988).

holding the promissor liable are therefore zero. However, if market conditions change then holding the contract frustrated would mean that one party loses the benefit of a good bargain. If one party were able to renege on a contract every time there was an adverse price movement then this would be inefficient. It would greatly increase uncertainty, reduce the propensity to enter into long-term contracts and, at the more extreme end, would cause the destruction of forward and future markets.

This can be illustrated by shipping cases arising from the frequent closure of the Suez Canal in 1956.[58] As a result, ships could not use the Canal and hence the costs of transporting goods rose. Shippers who had signed fixed-price contracts tried to avoid their contractual obligations. The Court held that the closure of the Canal did not excuse performance, the implication being that the goods should be shipped by a more expensive route. This contrasts with the case of the blockade of the port of destination explicitly stated in the shipping contract. In such a situation, the inability of the master of a ship to deliver the good would be a defence because it is specified in the shipping contract as an excuse. The promissor is excused in the blockade case because he cannot physically deliver the goods to the stated port. This is more so if the contract is executory. In the *Suez Canal* cases delivery is possible, but at a higher price; the shipper has a bad bargain!

DURESS

Contracts can be oppressive, unfair, one-sided, or 'unconscionable'.[59] Legal discussions of 'unfairness' appear to cover a wide range of disparate concerns – monopoly, market power, inequality of bargaining power, duress, ignorance, restraint of trade, onerous terms and even standard form contracts. These concepts are vague and fraught with ambiguity, at least as far as the economist is concerned.

Duress and undue influence are perhaps the easiest to deal with. Where one party is mentally infirm, too young, or unable to exercise adequate judgment, and is coerced into contracting with another, then it is unlikely that the contract will be efficient. Little in the way of economics is required

---

[58] E.g. *Ocean Tramp Tankers Corp* v. *V/O Sovfracht, The Eugenia* [1964] 1 All ER 161 (CA).

[59] M. J. Trebilcock, 'The Doctrine of Inequality of Bargaining Power: Post-Benthamite Economics in the House of Lords', 26 *University of Toronto Law Journal*, 359–385 (1976); M. J. Trebilcock, 'An Economic Approach to the Doctrine of Unconscionability', in B. J. Reiter and J. Swan (eds.), *Studies in Contract Law*, Toronto: Butterworths, 1980; B. Klein, 'Transaction Cost Determinants of "Unfair" Contractual Arrangements', 70 *American Economic Review*, 356–362 (1980); V. P. Goldberg, 'Institutional Change, and the Quasi-Invisible Hand?', 17 *Journal of Law & Economics*, 461–492, (1974).

to support the law in this area. However, where the concepts are extended to contracts between parties who lack knowledge or are ignorant, such as when someone dupes another into a bad contract, then the assessment becomes more problematic. The law should not protect parties from 'bad bargains' *per se* except where the information is patently or extremely hard to decipher. This is because a liberal law, while it might deal with an oppressive and unfair situation, will lead to the parties relaxing their precautionary efforts and the risks and losses of 'unfair' bargains will rise. The law should encourage an optimal level of self-protection.

English law has no concept of inequality of bargaining power. This is consistent with economics where the relative bargaining power of the parties, whether due to innate negotiating skills or the desirability of the product, is not treated as market power *per se*.

To the economist a contract is likely to be 'unfair' if either the buyer or seller has market power. In such cases the contract between the two will be mutually advantageous – both gain – but the division of the gains favours the party with market power and these terms have effects in limiting the number of wealth maximising contracts. That is, the concern is not that the terms are 'unfair' but they restrict the volume of similar transactions by setting terms which a number of buyers or sellers would find mutually advantageous but do not do so because the price is too high or too low.

It has been suggested that the English Courts were, at one time, evolving a doctrine of inequality of bargaining power, although this view has subsided. This was said to be the doctrine to emerge from *Schroeder Music Publishing* v. *MacCauley*[60] where a budding young musician signed a long-term contract with a music publisher. The musician became successful and the terms of the contract were regarded as onerous. The case is now treated as a restraint of trade case, although it is not clear that this makes much difference to the issues.

Consider the facts. For budding artists and music publishers, the world is uncertain. The musician wants the opportunity to break into the industry and be successful. Budding musicians begin with this ambition but very few succeed. For the majority who fail the contractual terms are probably favourable both *ex ante* and *ex post*. For those that succeed the terms now seem one-sided in favour of the music publisher.

On the other hand, the music publisher faces considerable uncertainty and risks. It signs up a number of artists, invests to develop and promote

---

[60] [1976] 1 WLR 1308. See Trebilcock, 'The Doctrine of Inequality' and M. J. Trebilcock and D. N. Dewees, 'Judicial Control of Standard Form Contracts', in P. Burrows and C. G. Veljanovski (eds.), *The Economic Approach to Law*, London: Butterworths, 1981, chapter 4.

their talents even though most fail. It is on the few who are successful, and the even fewer able to produce consistent chart hits, that he must earn his return. Clearly the music publisher, faced with the prospect that most musicians will fail, must structure a contract which over the run of all musicians generates positive returns. This necessarily means that the successful musician will have agreed to and will be bound by terms which cover the losses on the musicians who fail.

However, when one musician is successful (becomes a 'star') he or she has greater bargaining power and incentive to re-negotiate more favourable terms. If the bargaining balance, either because the leverage from fame or through legal rules, swings too much in favour of successful musicians then the ability of music publishers to take risks and foster new talent will be reduced.

This example shows that the economic factors surrounding a contract, and the relationship between the parties, alter over the course of its life. At the beginning most musicians are simply grateful that they have been taken on, but as the failures get weeded out the more successful see the contract as unfair. For those who succeed the contractual relationship transforms into what economists calls the 'economics of superstars'. These are the few talented and lucky individuals who can generate potential returns far in excessive of their opportunity costs and where competition does not erode these excess returns (called 'rents'). Successful singers, actors and sports people fall in this category, as do some in the professions (even lawyers). A contractual relationship which was once replicable and where the music publisher may have had some advantages transforms into one where the successful 'superstar' is able to negotiate more favourable terms. Indeed the situation is often *ex post* so one-sided that the music companies and sports clubs find that it is they who cannot generate profits since most of the rents are transferred to the superstars. Thus these types of contracts raise different issues than those involving standardised products or services.

ECONOMICS OF REMEDIES

Efficient contractual remedies should deter breaches of contracts worth performing and avoid excessive performance which generates no net bene-fits.[61] In common law the usual remedy is compensatory damages. In civil law countries it is (in principle) specific performance – i.e. an order that

---

[61] L. A. Kornhauser, 'An Introduction to the Economic Analysis of Contract Remedies', 57 *University of Colorado Law Review*, 683–725 (1986).

requires that the contract be performed. There is considerable debate as to which remedy is more 'efficient' and the extent to which common and civil law systems differ in practice.

The basics

The choice between damages and specific performance in contract law would not in an idealised setting make much difference. We know from the Coase Theorem that damages and specific performance will be equally efficient if the parties and the courts have perfect information and transactions costs are negligible. Indeed, given these assumptions nearly any remedy will be 'efficient' because the parties can contract out of inefficient laws when initially specifying their contract. However, assume that *ex ante* negotiations over specific remedies are not possible. What effect will the two remedies have?.[62]

The answer to this question depends on the type of contract, and the type of breach.[63] Two types of contracts can be distinguished from each other – contracts to give or transfer title, and contracts to make or produce an article or product. The former transfers title to goods already produced – such as a work of art, land, or goods from inventory; the latter are for the production of an article or product after the contract has been formed. For each of these either the seller or the buyer may breach the contract (Table 4.1).

Consider *contracts to give*. The source of the seller's breach is that the seller has been offered a higher price. Often the higher price offer will be available to both buyer and seller, so if the buyer is given specific performance as the remedy he or she can simply sell the good to the higher bidder and there is

Table 4.1 *Contract type and breach*

Contract type	Sellers' breach	Buyers' breach
Give/transfer	Better offer	Value uncertainty
To make	Production cost uncertainty	Value uncertainty

---

[62] 'The number and sophistication of the articles debating the merits of damages and specific performance is matched only by the lack of consensus as to which remedy is more efficient'. Smith, *Contract Theory*, 408.

[63] W. D. Bishop, 'Choice of Remedy for Breach of Contract', 14 *Journal of Legal Studies*, 299–320 (1985).

little danger of excessive performance. If the Court awards damages then there may be a danger of excessive breach if the Court underestimates the buyer's true loss. If the seller and buyer have equal access to third-party offers then specific performance will not create a difficulty. In land transactions this is probably the case, and helps to explain the Courts' preference for specific performance. But for the sale of many goods this will not be the case since the seller is more likely to receive third-party bids than the buyer. Where this is the case, damages are preferred to specific performance.

Buyers will breach contracts if they revise downward the value they place on the good after the contract has been formed. The likelihood is that there is no alternative bid. Moreover, the seller is likely to have lower costs in making a resale, especially where the seller is a retailer. In these cases the seller is probably in the best position to find an alternative buyer and damages would appear the appropriate remedy.

For *contracts to make* (production contracts) the two remedies have different effects. For these contracts the main source of sellers' breach is uncertainty over future production costs. That is, the seller will breach the contract when an increase in production costs makes performance excessively costly. Clearly, forcing the seller to produce the good when production costs exceed the value of the good to the buyer is inefficient. Thus, specific performance would not generally be an efficient rule since it would lead to excessive performance. On the other hand, giving the buyer damages which puts him or her in the position that they would have been had the contract been performed will result in efficient breach and performance. If the breach is by the buyer, this will arise over a lower valuation placed on the value of the good.

The conclusion is that for contracts to give, the optimal remedy is likely to be specific performance since it is unlikely to induce inefficient breach. This is not likely to be the case for contracts to make, since there will be a trade-off between excessive breach and excessive performance.

Specific performance

English law (and most other common law jurisdictions) occasionally award the equitable remedy of specific performance which requires the breaching party to perform the terms of the contract. As already discussed, specific performance is likely to be as efficient as damages when the two parties have equal access to other buyers. In contracts to make specific performance forces the contract to be performed irrespective of whether this is efficient or not. It would therefore neither encourage efficient breach nor discourage inefficient reliance expenditure. This probably explains why in English law specific performance is applied selectively.

Specific performance tends to be confined to contracts to give involving the transfer of a good whose value is particularly hard to determine. In economic terms, these are goods which have no close substitute and may even be unique.[64] Works of art provide a good example. *B* agrees to purchase a Monet from *S*, who then reneges on the contract. Clearly, for the buyer there is no substitute for the Monet and the Court would have extreme difficulty in determining the value of the painting to the buyer. The easiest solution is to enforce the contract, which would give the buyer full compensation and avoid error costs on the part of the Court if it were undertake the difficult task of valuing things which have no close substitute. Expressed in more formal terms, the award of specific performance by the Courts protects the promisee's (*ex post*) consumers' surplus. Further, for these cases it has no adverse incentive effects since if the Monet is worth more to a third party it is a matter of indifference whether he or she deals with the original seller or the new owner.[65] This explains why specific performance is also given in land contract disputes. Land is in relatively fixed supply so there are no adverse production effects and neither the buyer nor seller necessarily has a comparative advantage in selling on the property to the highest-valued user. Awarding specific performance is an adequate substitute remedy for damages and given the differentiated nature of property and houses achieves greater protection of any valuation attached to land transactions.

Types of damages

The common law appears to offer a bewildering array of damage measures. These include:

1. **Expectation measure (lost profits)** gives the non-breaching party compensation that puts him in the same position as if the contract had been performed.

---

[64] A. T. Kronman, 'Specific Performance', 45 *University of Chicago Law Review*, 351–382 (1978); G. T. Schwartz, 'The Case for Specific Performance', 89 *Yale Law Journal*, 271–306 (1979).
[65] W. D. Bishop, 'The Contract–Tort Boundary and the Economics of Insurance', 12 *Journal of Legal Studies*, 241–266 (1983).

2. **Reliance measure** restores the non-breaching party to the position he would have been in had he not entered into the contract.[66]
3. **Restitution measure** returns to the non-breaching party any benefits conferred on the breaching party; this measure includes damages based on the breaching party's gains, referred to as *disgorgement*.
4. **Cost of cure/reinstatement/completion measure** a sum necessary to enable the non-breaching party to complete performance to that agreed under the contract.
5. **Liquidated damages** damages stipulated in the contract which represent a genuine pre-estimate of the likely loss suffered by the non-breaching party.
6. **Non-pecuniary losses** monetary compensation paid for non-monetary losses and subjective value.

In addition, the law will limit or deny recovery for consequential losses, for losses which could have been mitigated and on grounds of remoteness and causation.

The complexity of determining damages in practice is illustrated by the facts in *Ruxley Electronics and Construction Ltd* v. *Forsyth*.[67] The defendant, Mr Forsyth, contracted with the claimant, Mr Ruxley, to build a swimming pool for £17,797.40. In a subsequent discussion the claimant agreed to increase the depth of the pool by 9 inches without additional charge. The pool was constructed by a subcontractor and its bottom cracked. It was then rebuilt free of charge and Mr Forsyth's professional costs reimbursed. When the second pool was completed Mr Forsyth insisted on a £10,000 reduction, which was agreed. He then refused to pay. The claimant sued for the balance and Forsyth counter-claimed. Forsyth did not initially mention the pool's depth but a number of years later as the trial date loomed amended his claim to include the failure to increase the depth of the pool. The trial judge found that the pool was safe for diving, that the shortfall in depth did not diminish the value of the pool or affect diving, that the only way to rectify the depth was to build a third new pool at an estimated cost of £21,560, and that Forsyth had no intention of rebuilding the pool.

The facts in *Ruxley* enable the different measures of damages to be quantified (Table 4.2). The builder had replaced the (first) defective pool, agreed to a discount of £10,000 on the second pool, and the lower Court gave Forsyth £2,500 for 'loss of fun'.

---

[66] L. L. Fuller and W. R. Perdue, 'The Reliance Interest in Contract Damages', 46 *Yale Law Journal*, part I, 52–96, part 2, 372–420 (1936).
[67] (1994) CA; revsd (1996) HL.

Table 4.2 *Different damage measures in Ruxley*

	(£)	
1. Expectation	0	
2. Reliance	0	
3. Restitution	0	(contractor made losses)
4. Cost of completion	21,560	
5. Liquidated damages	10,000	(*ex post* agreed 'discount')
6. Non-pecuniary losses	2,500	

For lawyers, the apparent perversity of *Ruxley* was that the aggrieved party had no remedy, as there was no loss under the expectation measure and reinstatement costs were denied. He did get damages for subjective loss referred to by the judge as damages for 'loss of fun' in the lower Court which was not considered by the House of Lords. It is therefore argued that the decision was inefficient. However, the Court made the right decision since the parties agreed on the remedies – rebuild the pool (specific performance to remedy the cracks) and then liquidated damages of £10,000 agreed by the parties, plus £2,500 for loss of fun which perhaps should not have been awarded.

Efficient breach

English law generally awards damages to protect the expectation interest in a contract. *Robinson* v. *Harman*[68] is authority that the remedy should put an innocent party in the position he would have been had the contract been performed. *Teacher* v. *Calder*[69] is legal authority for the concept of 'efficient breach' – that the non-breaching party cannot claim damages for the breacher's gain only his loss. Viscount Haldane, in a much quoted statement in *British Westinghouse' Electric and Manufacturing Co. Ltd* v. *Underground Electric Rlys Co. of London Ltd*, sets out the expectation damage:

The quantum of damages is a question of fact, and the only guidance which the law can give are general principles . . . . The first is that, as far as possible, he who has proved a breach of a bargain to supply what he contracted to get is to be placed, as far as money can do it, in as good a situation as if the contract had been performed. The fundamental basis is thus compensation for pecuniary loss naturally flowing from the breach; but this first principle is qualified by a second, which imposes on a claimant the duty of taking all reasonable steps to mitigate the loss consequent

---

[68] [1848] 1 Exch. 850, 855.	[69] [1897] SC 661 at 672–3.

on the breach, and debars him from claiming in respect of any part of the damage which is due to his neglect to take such steps.[70]

The concept of efficient breach is central to the law of contract. For most contracts there is no absolute enforcement of a promise, only the payment of expectation damages which gives the non-breaching party the benefit of the contract. In this way expectation damages subject prospective breaches to a type of efficiency test. To force all contracts to be performed according to their literal terms would not be efficient if performance were more costly than the benefits received by the other party. On the other hand, allowing one party to breach a contract without penalty because it is more costly to perform, or the opportunity of a better bargain has arrived, would not necessarily be wealth maximising. Clearly if the breaching party has to pay the other parties' loss then the breach can be subject to a comparison of gains and losses. If the gains from breach plus expectation damages are small or negative then the breach will not occur, and should not occur from an economic viewpoint. However, if there are gains then it would be efficient to release the resources to alternative uses.

The concept of efficient breach can be simply formalised. In the typical contract there are the sellers' costs of performance (c), the price paid for the good (p), the buyers' valuation (v) and potentially a higher price at which the good can be sold (b). All these determinants of a contract can change after the contract has been formed and before full performance. At the time the contract is agreed we can assume that for the seller price exceeds his costs ($p > c$), otherwise he would not have entered into the contract. We can similarly assume that for the buyer his valuation exceeds the price ($v > p$). Thus a mutually advantageous bargain or contract will be concluded only if the buyer's valuation exceeds the price which exceeds the seller's costs ($v > p > c$).

However, at some time before full performance the relationship between these variables may alter for the seller and/or buyer. The seller will be tempted to breach if his or her production (and other) costs rise to exceed the contract price ($c > p$) such that it is unprofitable to honour the contract, or he receives a better price from another buyer ($b > p$). The buyer will breach if his or her valuation falls below the price ($p > v$). If the law were to insist that all contracts were performed according to their terms then we might force sellers to produce goods which cost more than they were valued; and buyer to accept goods which they valued less than the price.

---

[70] [1912] AC 673, 688–9.

Performance would be inefficient if the higher price is less than the original buyer's valuation ($c > b > v$).

In the absence of a penalty for breach there will be an excessive (inefficient) level of non-performance. The seller will breach if costs exceed the price (or a later price offered by another buyer exceeds the contract price), but this is still less than the buyer's valuation of performance ($c < p < b < v$) and so the breach will be inefficient. However, if damages are set at the buyer's expectation interest ($v - p$) then the seller will breach only if the cost of performance (or the second price offer) exceeds the value the buyer places on performance. That is, expectation damages lead to efficient breach.

The relative efficiency of different damage measures can be assessed under some simplifying assumptions. Let us compare the expectation, reliance and restitution damage measures[71] for sellers' breach of a contract to make (production contract) arising from production cost uncertainty.[72] That is, at the time the contract is negotiated and terms agreed the seller has a range of different possible production costs. When it comes to perform, the costs exceed the contract price and the seller breaches.

To give life to the example, let us place figures for the various variables that affect contract performance, profits and efficiency. Assume that the agreed contract price is £75 and it has been paid to the seller. The buyer's valuation is £100 and in reliance on the seller's promise the buyer spends £10 (reliance expenditure). If the contract is breached, then the three damage measures would award the buyer the following compensation:

- The expectation measure seeks to put the party in the same position as if the contract had been performed and is equal to the return to the buyer of the £75 contract price plus £25 in lost profits from the contract, i.e. £100. The buyer bears the £10 reliance expenditure as that would have been incurred had the contract been performed.
- The reliance measure equals the return of the contract price plus the £10 reliance expenditure, i.e. £85.
- The restitution measure is the return of the monies paid to the seller, which is the contract price of £75.

Based on these figures the seller's incentive to breach under the three methods of calculating damages can be evaluated. These are summarised in table 4.3. The expectation measure is the only one that leads to efficient breach. It is the only measure which imposes on the seller the loss inflicted

---

[71] There is a large literature on optimal remedies in contract: S. Shavell, 'Damage Measures for Breach of Contract', 11 *Bell Journal of Economics*, 466–490 (1980); C. J. Goetz and R. E. Scott, 'Enforcing Promises: An Examination of the Basis of Contract', 89 *Yale Law Journal*, 1261–1322 (1980).

[72] Shavell, 'Damage Measures for Breach of Contract', 486–490.

Damage	Amount (£)	Efficient breach	Efficient reliance
Expectation	100	Yes	No
Reliance	85	No	No
Restitution	75	No	Yes

Table 4.3 *Efficiency of different damage measures*

on the buyer and thereby makes the seller compare the buyer's loss against the cost of performance. Reliance damages and restitution damages (as defined above) result in inefficient breach because they allow the possibility that if the seller's costs rise above £75 he will breach the contract even though the buyer values performance at £100.

Efficient reliance

Contract rules also play a role in regulating the level of contract-specific investment or reliance expenditure. Binding promises induce others to make plans, undertake expenditure and enter into other arrangements which increase economic value. Where there is a risk of breach, the rules and remedies of contract law should ensure that only efficient reliance expenditure is encouraged. Reliance expenditure made to enhance the value of performance should be based on a realistic probability that the contract will be honoured. The parties should invest only in reliance on a contractual arrangement based on the *expected* value of that investment. This, in turn, gives rise to the concept of **efficient reliance**. An efficient contract law should provide incentives for the efficient level of reliance investment and avoid creating incentives for overinvestment.

The example so far has assumed fixed reliance expenditure – or, as we have termed it above, contract-specific investment. Assume that the buyer is able to undertake reliance expenditure to enhance the value of performance under the contract. Assume that the non-breaching party spends an additional £10 to increase the value of performance by a further £15 (to £115). It would seem that this additional reliance expenditure is value maximising – by spending £10 the value of performance is increased by £15, a net gain of £5. However, it is also necessary to take into account the probability that the contract will be breached and the increased value of £15 not realised. If the likelihood of breach is 40 per cent, then the *expected* benefit or increase

in the value due to the £10 additional reliance expenditure is only £9 –
i.e. 60 per cent of £15. *Ex ante* it is not value maximising for the buyer to
incur the additional reliance expenditure given that if the seller breaches
the expenditure will have been wasted.

Based on the assumed figures we are now in a position to assess the
impact of the three damage measures (table 4.3). Under the expectation
measure the value of performance is £115 since the buyer will be induced to
spend £10 to enhance the value of the good by an additional £15. Recall that
the expectation measure puts the buyer in the same position he would have
been had the contract been performed. Under this measure the buyer is
induced to make excessive reliance expenditure because he is compensated
for the increased expectation interest arising from the additional reliance
expenditure. Under the reliance measure the contract price is returned to
the buyer plus his reliance expenditure of £20, i.e. he receives £75 plus
£20. The reliance measure also encourages excessive reliance expenditure.
This is because the buyer is fully compensated for his reliance expenditure.
Under the restitution measure the contract price is returned to the buyer.
This damage measure neither gives the buyer the additional gains from his
reliance expenditure nor compensates him for the wasted reliance expenditure. It therefore does not encourage inefficient reliance and is the only
measure to induce an optimal level of reliance.

What emerges from this simplified treatment is that there is no damage
measure which leads to full Pareto efficiency where both breach and reliance
expenditure can vary. The expectation measure achieves efficient breach
but excessive reliance expenditure; the reliance measure encourages neither
efficient breach nor reliance.

It is possible to develop measures of damages which deal with the overre-
liance problem (perhaps a mitigated-reliance measure) which gives expectation damages assuming optimal reliance expenditure rather than actual
reliance investment. However, this would be beyond the Court's compe-
tence to calculate and difficult to verify.

The efficient damages discussion illustrates the important principle that
where there are two or more factors which can be influenced one legal rule
or remedy will not be able to achieve a fully efficient outcome.

This should not come as a surprise, nor does it necessarily lead to the
conclusion that common law damages are inefficient. This is because the
effect of the damage measure will depend on the relative importance of
performance and reliance.

In law the non-breaching party can choose between expectation and
reliance damages. A rational claimant will elect for reliance damages only

when these exceed expectation damages. The exception is that he cannot recover his reliance loss in an attempt to escape the consequences of a bad bargain. On the other hand, a claimant may be confined to the recovery of his reliance loss where he cannot prove his expectation losses. In *McRae* v. *Commonwealth Disposals Commission*,[73] the High Court of Australia confined the claimant to recovery of expenses and return of pre-payments on the grounds that the expectation loss was too speculative. It has been suggested, though, that the award of reliance damages is not a real contractual claim since people do not enter into contracts to recover their detrimental expenditures.

COST OF CURE/COMPLETION

There are many cases where the buyer suffers a loss not reflected in the diminution of the market value of the good. For example, *B* contracts with *S* to convert a garage into a room to specifications set out in the contract. *S* fails to comply with the specifications and the room is unacceptable to *B*. The defective works do not reduce the value of the property but to rectify the deficiencies requires an additional £3,000. In this case expectation damages are zero, cost of cure damages £3,000.[74]

Tito v. *Waddell*[75] is a 'hard case' which illustrates some of the problems of reinstatement damages. Phosphate had been mined in the Ocean Islands since 1913. The mining company agreed with the islanders that the land would be mined and returned to the islanders replanted. In 1942 the island was occupied by the Japanese who killed and deported most of the inhabitants, and after the war the survivors were re-settled on Rabi 1,500 miles away. The islanders brought an action for reinstatement according to the terms of the original agreement. The Court found that the estimated costs of replanting was A$73,140 an acre but that the islanders did not intend to use the compensation to reinstate the land. It denied recovery.

What is the economics of this case? First, as the reinstatement of the land was an express term of the contract it should have been enforced. Second, it is irrelevant what the islanders intended to do with the compensation since it can be assumed that the mining company got the rights to mining more cheaply based on the promise to reinstate the land. Had the original parties to the agreement been aware of the legal outcome, they would

---

[73] (1951) 84 CLR 377.

[74] T. J. Muris, 'Cost of Completion or Diminution of Market Value: The Relevance of Subjective Value', 12 *Journal of Legal Studies*, 379–400 (1983).

[75] (No. 2) [1977] Ch 106.

have demanded a higher price for mining rights or even denied the defendant the right to mine. It may be claimed that reinstatement was a waste of resources and the claimant's intention supported this view. But these arguments ignore the central point that had the claimants known that reinstatement would not be enforced they would have demanded other terms. It would seem that the defendant unjustly benefited from the court's refusal to enforce the original agreement.

LIQUIDATED DAMAGES, PENALTIES AND DEPOSITS

Liquidated damages are those pre-specified in the contract negotiated by the parties. It would seem that such negotiated damage measures, based on the general principle that what the parties agree should be enforced by the law, would cause little concern. However, liquidated damages seem to attract intense scrutiny by the Courts, who have been willing to overturn them. As a general rule the Courts will refuse to enforce clauses where the stipulated amount is in its view a genuine pre-estimate of the loss caused by the breach. In these cases the liquidated damages are termed 'penalty damages'.

Some economists regard the English penalty rule as efficient.[76] One reason draws on the prospect that if the contract stipulated damages that significantly exceeded the actual loss, and where the benefiting party could influence the probability of breach, it might provide the benefiting party with an incentive to induce the other party to breach the contract. While this form of opportunism cannot be ruled out it does not constitute a generalised defence of the penalty damage rule given that both parties have agreed to this allocation of risks. It also presupposes that the party who suffers in this way, will not dispute that the loss was induced by the party benefiting from the penalty clause.[77]

Other economists see the penalty rule as anomalous and inefficient. Two reasons have been given for enforcing 'penalty' damages.[78] The first is that

---

[76] K. W. Clarkson, R. L. Miller and T. J. Muris, Liquidated Damages versus Penalties: Sense or Nonsense?', *Wisconsin Law Review*, 351–390 (1978).

[77] Liquidated damage clauses can be used to close the market to the entry of more efficient firms: P. Aghion and P. Bolton, 'Contacts as a Barrier to Entry', 77 *American Economic Review*, 388–401 (1987).

[78] C. Goetz and R. Scott, 'Liquidated Damages, Penalties and the Just Compensation Principle: Some Notes on the Enforcement Model of Efficient Breach', 77 *Columbia Law Review*, 554–594 (1977); S. A. Rea, 'Efficiency Implications of Penalties and Liquidated Damages', 13 *Journal of Legal Studies*, 147–167 (1984). For an alternative view, see E. L. Talley, 'Contract Renegotiation, Mechanism Design, and the Liquidated Damages Rule', 46 *Stanford Law Review*, 1195–1243 (1995); R. H. Rubin, 'Unenforceable Contracts: Penalty Clauses and Specific Performance', 10 *Journal of Legal Studies*, 237–247 (1981).

a liquidated damage clause that exceeds the compensation that the courts view as a reasonable pre-estimate of the loss reflects the higher subjective valuation that a non-breaching party attaches to performance and the other party's superior risk bearing. The second is that these damages signal the promissor's reliability. A builder who agrees to such a damage clause signals to the buyer that he is reliable and willing to bear the consequences of time overruns and increased costs. A third reason justifying damages in excess of estimated losses is to adjust for less than complete enforcement of contracts, the costs of enforcement, and/or to induce efficient transaction-specific investment.[79]

It is also the case that the parties can deal, or contract around, the penalty damage rule. If supra-compensatory damages clauses are unenforceable the parties can achieve the same result by negotiating bonus payments, deposits and performance bonds to ensure performance according to the contract. Thus instead of a breach leading to pre-stipulated (penalty) damages, the contract is structured with an initial lower contract price but with a bonus paid on satisfactory completion.[80] These should lead to equivalent outcomes.

To illustrate this, consider a contract to build a house. The owner asks for a contractual stipulation that the building be completed on a set date and the builder agrees. Assume that the selection process makes it clear that timely completion of the project is a critical consideration in the award of the building contract. One option is for the owner to include a liquidated damage clause in the contract in the event that the builder fails to meet the timetable. However, the damages that the owner considers appropriate and the builder accepts would not be enforced by the Courts under the penalty damage rule. So instead the owner has a number of options. He can ask that the builder post a performance bond to be forfeited if the builder breaches the contract. The builder may not have the funds to post such a bond. Alternatively, the owner can pay by instalments as the work progresses. This would protect the owner against opportunism and unsatisfactory performance but not really against delayed finalisation of the project. Yet another option is for the owner to negotiate a contract price which is lower than the agreed price for the job but to give a bonus payment on the successful completion of the project.

---

[79] A. S. Edin and A. Schwartz, 'Optimal Penalties in Contracts', Yale Law School, Research Paper 267 (2002). See also D. Harris and C. G. Veljanovski, 'Remedies for Breach of Contract: Designing Rules to Facilitate Out-of-court Settlement', 5 *Law & Policy Quarterly*, 97–127 (1983).

[80] A. Katz, 'The Strategic Structure of Offer and Acceptance: Game Theory and the Law of Contract Formation', 89 *Michigan Law Review*, 215–295 (1990).

All these alternative options are more or less legally enforceable. Further, they tend to have better enforcement features since they give the buyer increased leverage to ensure contractual performance, and some deal with non-performance in an immediate and timely way by simply refusing to pay the builder. They also reduce legal process costs as they are more or less self-enforcing.

These alternatives are not without problems. For a start, they can give rise to buyer breach. The buyer can use his enhanced leverage to avoid paying for minor infringements or to act opportunistically. Thus the project may be completed on time but the buyer uses the performance bond or the last instalment as an opportunity to, in effect, re-negotiate the contract price.

The counteracting forces are nicely illustrated by security deposits under house or apartment tenancy (rental) agreements. These are designed to protect the landlord against damage to the property. In England and Wales they are typically set at six weeks' rent, payable on signing of a tenancy agreement and refundable at the termination of the rental agreement provided that the apartment is handed back in a satisfactory state. In order to avoid disputes the condition of the apartment is often assessed at the commencement and termination of the rental agreement by an independent 'inventory clerk' selected by the landlord at the beginning of the rental period, and the tenant at the end. This resolves the verification problem and minimises disputes over whether or not the property is in an acceptable state. However, this whole process is often defeated by the tenant withholding the last rental instalment to adjust for the initial deposit. Thus, at the termination of the rental agreement there is a deposit but effectively no compensation should the tenant have damaged the property or left it in a dirty and uninhabitable state. On the other hand, landlords often abuse the system by holding onto deposits for excessive periods, refusing to repay the deposit and/or concocting spurious damage to the property to retain all or part of the deposit. These alleged landlord abuses have led to a law requiring the landlord to pass on deposit to a Government body or regulated agent.[81] This involves fees and increases the costs of deposits as a way of controlling contractual abuses.

A solution to this would be a tapered rental schedule, with higher rents in the initial months falling to below-market values towards the end with a performance payment at the expiration of tenancy. This would avoid

---

[81] The Housing Act 2004 created the Tenancy Deposit Scheme (TDSRA) for UK Assured Shorthold Tenancies (tenancy agreements which run for one year less one day designed to open up the rental market by avoiding giving tenants rights over the property).

the problems created by the deposit system and protect landlords. While it allows the landlord to act opportunistically it is no worse in this regard than the current deposit system.

The law's treatment of deposits and monies owed is unsatisfactory. If there has been a failure to pay money then the damage is the amount unpaid without interest. That is, there is a 'no-interest rule' favouring debtors. The debt is discharged by paying the sum owed. This is easily circumvented by the parties expressly agreeing that the debt carry interest. In English law the situation has been remedied by statute.[82]

In some cases where the defaulting party is aware that that the failure of payment will result in additional charges to the creditor then interest may be payable. In *Wadsworth* v. *Lydall*[83] the purchaser of land agreed to pay £10,000 by a fixed date knowing that the vendor was going to use the money as a deposit for land. The purchaser paid only £7,200, necessitating the vendor to borrow £2,800. The Court held that the vendor could recover the £2,800 plus the interest on the loan of £2,800. This was endorsed by the House of Lords in *President of India* v. *La Pintada Cia Navegacion SA*[84] as an application of the *Hadley* rule.

NON-PECUNIARY DAMAGES

Often the loss arising from a breach of contract is partially non-pecuniary. A good example, or at least one on which there is case law, is where exposed film of a marriage, holiday, or birthday is lost or destroyed. Most film manufacturers and processing shops limit their liability to the cost of a replacement roll of film. However, the images on a film roll are irreplaceable and the loss not adequately compensated by another roll of film!

The general rule in English law is that there is no compensation for non-pecuniary loss. There are exceptions. In *Jarvis* v. *Swan Tours*[85] the claimants booked a winter sports holiday which advertised a number if attractions which failed to materialise. One was a 'Yodeller evening' which transpired to be, according to Lord Denning, 'a local man who sang a few songs in his working clothes'. Denning (in 1973) held that the claimant was entitled to damages for 'loss of enjoyment' and awarded £127. In *Farley* v. *Skinner*[86] the claimant was employed to survey a 'gracious country residence' which was fifteen miles from a major airport. The claimant expressly asked the

---

[82] Late Payment of Commercial Debts (Interest) Act 1998.
[83] [1981] 2 All ER 401.   [84] [1984] 2 All ER 773.   [85] [1973] QB 233.
[86] *Farley* v. *Skinner* [2001] UKHL 49; [2001] 3 WLR 899.

surveyor to report if there was any problem with aircraft noise. The surveyor incorrectly advised that aircraft noise was unlikely to be a problem. The claimant was awarded £10,000 for distress and inconvenience even though the aircraft noise did not affect the value of the property.

Some have proposed compensation for such losses based on the concept of consumers' surplus.[87] As discussed above, many consumers will value the good or service above its market price. The consumers' surplus is their WTP above the contract price and provides a measure of the value of the good to them after purchase. Thus, it is argued, compensating on the basis of (the difference in) market prices will undercompensate the buyer for non-performance. Indeed, in *Ruxley* Lord Mustill expressly referred to the economists' concept of 'consumers' surplus' when referring to the damages for 'loss of fun' due to the swimming pool not being deep enough.

While the existence of consumers' surplus cannot be denied, it should also be appreciated that it is an *ex post* concept which, if compensated, has *ex ante* effects. Let us consider several different situations.

First, where there is a competitive market for the good then there is no need to provide for more than nominal or price difference damages. This is because the consumer can get immediate substitute or near-substitute performance which effectively protects any consumers' surplus.

At the other extreme, where the good is unique, the consumers' surplus measure can be fully compensated by specific performance. However, and this is the crucial consideration, the assumption of uniqueness means not only that there is no substitute performance but that damages will not have a supply-side effect on future transactions. That is, the breach and the remedy will not affect the allocation of resources except with respect to the good at the centre of the dispute.

In markets where the good has to be made or the consumers' surplus varies but the transactions are replicable any assessment of damages for non-pecuniary losses will need to take account of the incentive or *ex ante* effects of the law. Where the issue is not of an immediate substitute then the damages for the price difference provides a remedy. If performance is inadequate then the cost of completion may be a way of ensuring compliance and protecting subjective value.

If the damage rule is pecuniary plus subjective losses then this will affect the allocation of resources. This is because the costs of doing business for the seller will increase. He or she is required not only to compensate for

---

[87] D. Harris, A. I. Ogus and J. Phillips, 'Contract Remedies and the Consumer Surplus', 95 *Law Quarterly Review*, 581–610 (1979).

pecuniary losses, but also for the consumers' *ex post* surplus.[88] This will have the effect of raising *ex ante* marginal costs, some of which will be passed on in a higher price for the good, and this will lead to a supply-side response. Further, the increased damages will, where default is influenced by damages, lead to less default. Thus, the result is likely to be a contraction in quantity supplied and overperformance of contracts.

To this must be added two other considerations which point to limited compensation for non-pecuniary losses. The first is that accurately measuring lost consumers' surplus is likely to be impossible. However, where it is evident that there has been an subjective loss the difficulty of quantifying it should not preclude the award of damages under this heading.

The second – and, for the economist, more serious – obstacle to supporting compensation for non-pecuniary loss is that consumers will often not seek to insure such losses. Economics suggests a complex relationship between 'subjective value' and optimal damages. If the consumer is risk neutral then compensation for the financial loss will be adequate;[89] it will satisfy both compensation and deterrence objectives. If he or she is risk averse and it is assumed that insurance is available at an actuarially fair rate,[90] then full coverage for the financial loss will be demanded. But where the loss is of an irreplaceable good, and affects his or her general welfare, then the consumer may not buy coverage for even the financial losses. This suggests that there is not a strong case for compensating non-pecuniary losses.

UNJUST ENRICHMENT

Very occasionally damages are based on the breaching party's gain rather than the non-breaching party's losses. These are called restitutionary, disgorgement, or unjust enrichment damages. Although use of this damage measure is rare in English law it has attracted considerable attention after being awarded in several cases.

---

[88] The effect of compensating consumers' surplus is to effectively implement a system of *ex post* discriminatory prices. The seller will sell the product at one price that reflects the costs of production plus the expected average claim for non-pecuniary losses.

[89] S. A. Rea, 'Non-pecuniary Loss and Breach of Contract', 11 *Journal of Legal Studies*, 35–54 (1982); J. E. Calfee and P. H. Rubin, 'Some Implications of Damage Payments for Nonpecuniary Losses', 21 *Journal of Legal Studies*, 371–412 (1992). See also the discussion of the economics of pain and suffering damages in tort in chapter 5.

[90] That is, a rate which reflects the claims record and risks without any administrative loading to cover the insurer's expenses.

Gain-based damages are generally not consistent with the goal of efficient breach, because they encourage overperformance of contractual obligations. If there is perfect disgorgement of the gains from breach then sellers or buyers will be indifferent between performance and breach irrespective of the value of the good, asset, or resource to the non-breaching party. They will then tend to perform, since there is no gain from breaching even when performance does not result in resources being allocated to their highest-valued uses.

However, several cases paint a more complex picture. The first and most controversial is *Wroxtham Park Estates Co. Ltd* v. *Parkside Homes Ltd.*[91] This concerned a restrictive covenant which required that the use of land in question to conform to a plan approved by the vendor or his successor in title (Wroxtham Park). The purchaser of a parcel of land, built houses on it which did not conform to the plan. The facts showed that the claimant would not have granted/negotiated a relaxation of the covenant. The difficulty was that the breach did not result in a diminution in the value of the property, so expectation damages would have been nominal. The Court was faced with a possibility of imposing a mandatory injunction which, if enforced by the claimant, would have forced the defendant to demolish the houses. The Court refused to give this remedy on the grounds that it would be 'economic waste'. Brightman J concluded that 'a just substitute for a mandatory injunction would be such a sum of money as might reasonably have been demanded by the plaintiffs from [the defendants] as a *quid pro quo* for relaxing the covenant'. In fixing this reasonable price, it was found that the defendant had made £50,000 profit from the development and damages were assessed at 5 per cent of that profit. The damages were thus a proportion of the defendant's gain. In a subsequent case with similar facts, the court declined to follow this approach and awarded nominal damages.[92]

A contrasting position was taken in *A-G* v. *Blake*,[93] where the Court awarded the entire gain to the claimant. The defendant Blake was an employee of the British security service who turned out to be a double agent for the Soviet Union. As a condition of his employment he signed the Official Secrets Act which created a contractual undertaking not to divulge information. In 1961 he was imprisoned in England for espionage but escaped in 1966 to Moscow. In 1989 he signed a contract with a UK publisher to publish his autobiography for an advance of £150,000. The

---

[91] [1974] 1 WLR 798.
[92] *Surrey County Council* v. *Bredero Homes Ltd* [1993] 1 WLR 1361 CA.   [93] [2001] 1 AC 268.

UK Government did not seek an injunction preventing publication of the book, but damages equivalent to the outstanding advance that Blake was to receive. The damage claim was the prospective remaining gain (Blake had already been paid part of the advance which presumably the authorities felt they could not recover) of the breaching party rather than a proportion of the gain, as in *Wroxtham*.

What is the economics of these cases? In both cases there was a breach of an express term of the contract and in both the defendant appropriated rights/assets owned by the claimant – the right to develop land and the right to use information acquired in the course of employment. The transactions costs of negotiating a modification of these contractual terms at the time of the breach were low. In these cases an injunction (property rule) would have been economically correct. The substitution of damages resulted in the legally enforced exchange based on a judicially determined price (damages). But there is a difference between the two cases!

Wroxtham is wrong in both *ex ante* and *ex post* terms. Consider the *ex ante* effects of the case. If a restrictive covenant can simply be ignored based on a small percentage of the gain being paid to the freeholders, then this will encourage such action in the future. Substituting a judicially determined price in *Wroxtham* makes little sense. It converts a market transaction into a far more costly legal transaction which is in effect determined by the defendant and the Courts against the interests of the property owner. This amounts to an expropriation or forced sale of the claimant's property rights. *Ex post* the Court was also not correct. First, while it would have been an economic waste to pull down the buildings this is a transitional cost to ensure that in future restrictive covenants are enforced. The decision encourages developers to jump the gun and build as fast as possible so they can use the investment they have made as a way of precluding enforcement of the covenant, and then to use their inefficient expenditure to acquire judicial approval. Second, even if a mandatory injunction had been granted in *Wroxtham* this would not necessarily have been the end of the matter. The parties could then have negotiated a release from the injunction if this were value maximising.

Blake makes more sense. In theory, an injunction would deny Blake all the gains from his anticipated breach. A damage claim equal to Blake's monetary gain would have a similar effect to a property rule since it would have the effect of completely blocking the transaction and thereby deterring such breaches by making the breach unprofitable to the defendant. In the normal course of events an injunction would have been the efficient response, and where the defendant is seeking to gain from his notoriety but offers no security threat, damages would suffice to make the act of publishing unprofitable. (It must be assumed that Blake's book really did not reveal any state secrets as the loss to the UK Government would have been many multiples of Blake's royalties.)

MITIGATION

In many cases the losses from a breach can be reduced or avoided by timely action by the non-breaching party. The doctrine of mitigation can be seen as a way of encouraging joint precautions where it is efficient for the non-breaching party to take avoidance action.[94]

The parties to a contract would seek to allocate losses arising from a breach to the party who can best avoid them.[95] This requires not only deterring inefficient breaches but also minimising the losses arising from the breach. In many cases the non-breaching party may be in a good (and even the best) position to minimise the losses. In these cases, the parties would specify a term in the contact requiring the non-breaching party to mitigate the losses if he could do so cost-effectively.

For example, a builder walks off the job leaving the building half complete and the drains blocked by rubble. There is heavy rain, causing substantial flooding and damage to the site. This could have been avoided by the owner who was aware of the blocked drains and was on site at the time of the downpour. The result is that a £100 loss is turned into a £220 loss. The property owner could have unblocked the drains at a cost of £20. In this case the property owner should have mitigated since he would have avoided a loss of £120 at a cost of only £20. To award compensation for the additional damages would be to reward inaction by the land owner. It is therefore not surprising that contract law does not offer full compensation in these circumstances; the property owner would be entitled only to damages net of the avoidable consequential losses that his inaction allowed – i.e. the £100 loss plus £20 in mitigation expenses. A rule which requires mitigation of damages once the breach has occurred makes economic sense. It provides incentives on the non-breaching party to take loss avoidance actions where this is efficient.

The doctrine of mitigation appears to have this economic logic at its heart. The law provides that the non-breaching party can claim damages

[94] *British Westinghouse Electric and Manufacturing Co. Ltd* v. *Underground Electric Rlys Co. of London Ltd.* [1912] AC 673.
[95] C. J. Goetz and R. E. Scott, 'The Mitigation Principle: Toward a General Theory of Contractual Obligations', 69 *Virginia Law Review*, 967–1025 (1983).

for the non-avoidable loss only if he has not mitigated – or, if he has expended money, time and trouble, the reasonable costs of these efforts to reduce avoidable losses. This effectively places the liability for the loss on the party best able to avoid it. If, however, the non-breaching party goes to excessive lengths to avoid the loss he will be compensated only for the costs of taking reasonable mitigation, not for his actual costs. This appears on the face unfair because, by making these efforts, he has benefited the breaching party. However, the purpose of the law is not and should not be to encourage excessive avoidance expenditure and while the promise breaker benefits the incentive effect of the rule is to encourage only efficient not excessive mitigation.

RELATIONAL CONTRACTS

Many contracts are complex and long-term. Some argue that these are fundamentally different types of contract than those that underpin contract law, and that the law's approach should be modified. Their duration, uncertainties and transaction-specific investment mean that they may be more incomplete and rely more on future modification, renegotiation and adjustment to unforeseen physical, market and contractual changes. This, it is argued, destroys the elegance of the economists' market model and the classical model of contract and leads to different contract design and 'governance'.[96] The emphasis is not on a pre-determined set of economising default rules but a mechanism for gaining acceptable adjustments and adaptations to changing circumstances which maintains the ongoing contractual relations against the risks of opportunism:

The longer the anticipated relation and more complexity and uncertainty entailed in that relation, the less significance will be placed upon the price and quantity variables at the formation stage. The emphasis instead will be upon establishing (explicitly or by the incorporation of tacit assumption), rules to govern the relationship: rules determining the adjustment to factors that will rise in the course of the relationship and rules concerning termination of that relationship.[97]

---

[96] I. R. MacNeil, 'A Primer of Contract Planning', 48 *Southern California Law Review*, 627–704 (1975), 632–3. See also I. R. MacNeil, 'The Many Futures of Contracts', 47 *Southern California Law Review*, 691–816 (1974); I. R. MacNeil, *The New Social Contract: An Inquiry into Modern Contractual Relations*, New Haven: Yale University Press, 1980.

[97] V. P. Goldberg, 'Toward an Expanded Economic Theory of Contract', 10 *Journal of Economic Issues*, 45–61 (1976) 49–50. See also V. P. Goldberg, 'Relational Exchange: Economics and Complex Contracts', 23 *American Behavioral Scientist*, 337–352 (1980).

This has led to the development of relational contract theory,[98] and in economics the transactions costs approach (or the New Institutional Economics, NIE)[99] most associated with Williamson's work. These develop descriptive models of the contracting process drawing on insights from Institutional economics, Coase's work on transactions costs and behavioural science (the latter suggesting that individuals are have limited or bounded rationality which prevents them from taking account of all the information that is available to them). In Williamson's framework the critical factors are not long-term contracts *per se*, reputation,[100] or personality, but asset specificity, which results in 'large switching costs', 'lock-in' and *ex post* opportunism, concepts we have defined and examined above.

There is no doubt that the relational contract approach has generated considerable insights into the contracting process. However, it is doubtful whether relational contracts are a distinct legal class of contracts, or give rise to contractual difficulties which cannot be analysed using standard economic theory. Many features of 'relational contracts' are shared by more mundane contracts, or do not necessarily give rise to special contractual difficulties. Further, the concept has not yet found favour in English law. In *Total Gas Marketing Ltd* v. *Arco British Ltd* the court concluded:

the central question is whether on a correct construction of a long-term contract for the sale of gas it was discharged by reason of the non-occurrence of a condition. It is a contract of a type which is sometimes called a relational contract. But there are no special rules on interpretation applicable to such contracts . . . that is not to say that in an appropriate case a court may not take into account that, by reason of the changing conditions affecting such a contract, a flexible approach may best match the reasonable expectations of the parties. But, as in the case of all contracts, loyalty to the contractual text viewed against its relevant contextual background is the first principle of construction.[101]

---

[98] M. A. Eisenberg, 'Contracts and Relationships', in P. Newman (ed.), *The New Palgrave Dictionary of Economics and the Law*, vol. 1, London: Stockton Press, 1998, 445–449. See also C. J. Goetz and R. E. Scott, 'Principles of Relational Contracts', 67 *Virginia Law Review*, 1089–1150 (1981).

[99] O. E Williamson, 'Contract Analysis: The Transaction Cost Approach', in Burrows and Veljanovski, *The Economic Approach to Law*, chapter 2; O. E. Williamson, *Markets and Hierarchies: Analysis and Antitrust Implications*, New York: Free Press, 1975; O. E. Williamson, *The Economic Institutions of Capitalism*, New York: Free Press, 1985; O. E. Williamson, 'Transaction Cost Economics: The Governance of Contractual Relations', 22 *Journal of Law & Economics*, 233–261 (1979).

[100] Indeed, reputation can generate high returns to *ex post* opportunisim. As Telser stresses in an early article, it is the desire to maintain an on-going relationship that serves to control *ex post* opportunism. L. Telser, 'A Theory of Self-enforcing Agreements', 53 *Journal of Business*, 27–44 (1980).

[101] (1998) 2 Lloyds Reports 209, 218 (Lord Steyn). For an analysis in support of acceptance of the relational contract notion in law, see D. Campbell, 'Relational Constitution of the Discrete Contract', in D. Campbell and P. Vincent-Jones (eds.), *Contract and Economic Organisation*, Aldershot: Dartmouth, 1996. Not all lawyers are convinced – see E. McKendrick, 'The Regulation of Long-term

Moreover, to suggest that the law has not evolved to take account of the particular problems associated with many types of 'relational' contracts is misleading. Contract law can be likened to a melting iceberg. When an area of contractual activity becomes too complex and specialised, it is transmuted into a separate body of law. Thus instead of all contracts being governed by contract law they fall into other areas such as employment law, company law, intellectual property law and so on. Indeed, perhaps the most relational contract of all, marriage, is governed by different rules and has increasingly been modified to take account of transaction-specific investment by wives.[102] However, as some commentators have pointed out, even here the theory of relational contracts generates few straightforward insights into the optimal rules of divorce.

CONTRACTS AND COMPETITION

The economists' model of efficient contracts draws predominantly on the existence of competitive markets. The corollary is that while a contract signed under non-competitive conditions benefits both parties – otherwise it would not have been entered into – it may nonetheless not be an efficient contract. This is because the contract contains terms that do not ensure that resources are allocated to their highest-valued uses.

Traditionally, contract law has provided weak protection against monopoly abuse, excessive prices and exclusionary practices. For example, the expectation damage measure will not be efficient if a price of the good includes a monopoly mark-up since it will encourage excessive performance and reinforce the misallocation of resources due to monopoly. Some monopoly and market power problems are dealt with by the common law crime of restraint of trade, but inadequately.[103] Generally contract law ignores market power and monopoly abuses unless they amount to duress and extortion, and perhaps rightly so because it would quickly involve itself in many contract disputes in a full-scale market analysis and in assessing the adequacy of consideration. That is why other laws intervene in cases where there is monopoly and anti-competitive 'abuses'.

Contracts in English Law', in J. Beatson and D. Friedmann (eds.), *Good Faith and Fault in Contract Law*, Oxford: Clarendon Press, 1995.

[102] L. R. Cohen, 'Marriage: The Long-term Contract', in A. W. Dnes and R. Rowthorn, *The Law and Economics of Marriage and Divorce*, Cambridge: Cambridge University Press, 2002, chapter 2 and the references cited therein.

[103] M. J. Trebilcock, *The Common Law of Restraint of Trade – A Legal and Economic Analysis*, London: Sweet & Maxwell, 1986.

As if to underlie the problem of inefficient yet mutually beneficial contracts, a large part of competition (or anti-trust) laws deals with contractual restrictions designed to abuse market power and foreclose markets to competitors.[104] Most antitrust laws have extensive rules regulating contracts and restrictive practices, the infringement of which render such contracts void. Much of the economics and concept which evolved in this area of law would be entirely alien to the contract lawyer.

Under EC competition law, which applies to the twenty-seven countries of the enlarged European Community and is part also of their national laws, it is an infringement for a firm to abuse its dominance (Article 82 of the EC Treaty) and for firms to enter into any agreements or understanding 'which have as their object or effect the prevention, restriction or distortion of competition within the common market' (Article 81(1) of the EC Treaty). The latter applies to both horizontal and vertical agreements which affect firms in the same market or those downstream or upstream, respectively, and a range of practices such as exclusive dealing, tie-in sales and excessive contract duration.[105]

Competition laws have been used in two ways to regulate contracts. They have been used as a 'weapon' to attack directly a monopoly abuse or anti-competitive restriction. This allows public enforcement agencies to investigate the infringement and apply sanctions and, as stated above, any contracts which are part of the infringement are void. In addition, firms and individuals can bring private actions in the Courts to claim damages where competition rules have been infringed. The second use of anti-trust in contract disputes is as a defence (frequently called the 'Euro defence'). This uses the antitrust rules not to challenge a monopoly or restrictive practice but as part of an attack on the validity of the contract in a separate contractual dispute.

Contractual restrictions have been the subject some of the most expensive antitrust cases (e.g. Kodak and Microsoft). Most of these are not concerned with the traditional exploitative abuses of monopoly (high prices and poor

---

[104] See C. G. Veljanovski, *The Economics of Law*, London: Institute of Economic Affairs (1999); 2nd edn., 2006, chapter 4 for a brief introduction to the economics of competition law. See also K. N. Hylton, *Antitrust Law – Economic Theory and Common Law Evolution*, Cambridge: Cambridge University Press, 2003.

[105] EC Commission, *Notice Guidelines on Vertical Restraints*, 2000/C 291/01; EC *Guidelines on the Applicability of Article 81 of the EC Treaty to Horizontal Cooperation Agreements*, 2001/C 3/02; EC *Guidelines on the Application of Article 81(3) of the Treaty*, 2004/C 101/08; and UK Office of Fair Trading (OFT), *The Chapter I Prohibition*, OFT 401 (1999; rev. 2004) and OFT, *Assessment of Individual Agreements and Conduct*, OFT 415 (1999; rev. 2004). See also P. W. Dobson and M. Waterson, *Vertical Restraints and Competition Policy*, OFT Research Paper 12 (1996). Case C-234/89 *Stergios Delimitis* v. *Henninger Brau AG* [1991] ECR I-935.

terms) but exclusionary abuses designed to foreclose the market to competitors and thereby reduce competition. For example, the new antitrust economics has focused on more subtle forms of contractual abuse designed to raise rivals' costs. This literature often finds competitive problems with contractual practices which had not been previously regarded as abusive, or would in any way be regulated by contract law.

One example of the way contract can be used to inhibit competition, and the complexity of the analysis required, can be illustrated by the so-called 'aftermarket problem'.[106] This is the commonly observed problem of buying a proprietary good and finding that the prices of branded spare parts and consumables are considerably higher than non-branded ones available in the marketplace.

Aftermarket problems have been the subject of considerable antitrust litigation and competition law investigation and indicate both the subtlety of contractual problems and the potential differences in interpretation.

Consider a contract for the sale of a durable asset such as a computer or photocopier which requires the buyer to purchase on-going peripherals, maintenance and other complementary services. This gives rise to a tension between *ex ante* and *ex post* competition.[107] When a firm is deciding which computer system to purchase it has a choice and there will be aggressive competition for what might be a lucrative contract. However, once the computer system is purchased, and requires a host of ancillary services, the buyer may be locked-in and subject to high aftermarket prices.

Clearly this problem does not occur where buyers are relatively informed and the seller cannot discriminate between existing and new customers. In this case the buyer will evaluate the so-called 'life-cycle costs' of different computer systems and base his purchase decision on these. This will be reinforced by the competitive pressures in the computer market when new customers base their purchase on life cycle costs, thus protecting existing customers. This is because higher maintenance prices will reduce computer sales and the lost sales will deter excessive pricing of aftermarket services and products. If, on the other hand, the competitive constraints are weak, because buyers do not have adequate information, anti-competitive practices in the aftermarket may be profitable.

Economic theory suggests that high aftermarket prices may be a method of metering and hence a form of price discrimination used to identify

---

[106] C. Shapiro, 'Aftermarkets and Consumer Welfare: Making Sense of Kodak', 63 *Antitrust Law Journal*, 483–511 (1995).

[107] C. G. Veljanovski, 'Competition Law Issues in the Computer Industry – An Economic Perspective', 3 *Queensland University of Technology Law & Justice Journal*, 3–27 (2003).

consumers with intense demand. The implication is that high aftermarket prices are counterbalanced by low(er) hardware prices. This, argue some economists, is not anti-competitive in the same sense that a restaurant 'overcharges' for wine or a pub 'undercharges' for food in order to maximise profits.[108] What is at issue is whether the total price of the hardware and maintenance package is set at near-competitive levels, not individual prices. Others argue that the practice is inefficient in the broader sense by (a) creating excessive hardware purchases and therefore encouraging buyers to economise on 'overpriced' aftermarket services and (b) leading to excess potential entry of independent service providers and obviously a spate of antitrust actions.

Yet another source of contractual problems is where an essential input is supplied to firms by a vertically integrated rival who also competes downstream. This often occurs in network industries where a the gas, telephone and electricity network operator supplies access and carriage to its network to those it competes with in selling gas, phone calls and electricity at the retail level. Here it is argued that the vertically integrated network operator can price squeeze its rivals by raising the access charge to a level which makes competition unprofitable, or adopt other practices which impose onerous and ultimately fatal conditions on its downstream competitors. In this case the contractual problem arises because the buyer is captive and the seller has an incentive to leverage its (upstream) market power.[109] Again, this type of contractual practice would not be treated as giving rise to a cause of action in contract law even though the foreclosure effects on downstream competitors can be severe and ultimately harm consumers.

FURTHER TOPICS AND READING

- Examples of the literature on the economics of contract and contract law can be found in A. T. Kronman and R. A. Posner (eds.), *The Economics of Contract Law*, Boston: Little Brown, 1979; V. P. Goldberg (ed.), *Readings in the Economics of Contract Law*, Cambridge: Cambridge University Press, 1989; P. Burrows and C. G. Veljanovski, *The Economic Approach to Law*, London: Butterworths, 1981, chapter 4. See also the review article C. G. Veljanovski and D. Harris, 'The Use of Economics to Elucidate Legal Concepts – The Law of Contract', in T. Daintith and H. Teubner (eds.), *Contract and Organisation: Legal Analysis in the Light of Economic and Social Theory*, Berlin: Walter de Gruyter, 1986.

---

[108] B. Klein, 'Market Power in Aftermarkets', in F. S. McChesney (ed.), *Economic Inputs; Legal Outputs – The Role of Economists in Modern Antitrust*, New York: Wiley, 1998.

[109] P. Crocioni and C. G. Veljanovski, 'Price Squeezes, Foreclosure and Competition Law – Principles and Guidelines', 4 *Journal of Network Industries*, 28–60 (2003).

- For a less sympathetic view that 'economics fails to explain contract law', see E. A. Posner, 'Economic Analysis of Contract Law after Three Decades: Success or Failure?', 112 *Yale Law Journal*, 829–880 (2003) and the responses of Ayres and Craswell in the same issue.

- Beale *et al.* (see chapter 1, n. 3) note that there are only about twenty empirical studies of the way that contract law operates in practice. The two classic articles, which find that business people rarely resort to contract law to resolve their disputes, are S. Macauley, 'Non-contractual Relations in Business: A Preliminary Study', 25 *American Sociological Review*, 55–69 (1968) and H. Beale and T. Dugdale, 'Contracts between Businessmen: Planning and the Use of Contractual Remedies', 2 *British Journal of Law & Society*, 45–60 (1975). There is, however, a very large empirical literature by economists on contracts. One survey concludes, in relation to the transaction costs approach, that: 'Progress in the application and testing of transaction cost economics can only be described as phenomenal' (S. E. Masten, 'Transaction Cost Economics', in O. E. Williamson and S. E. Masten (eds.), *Transaction Cost Economics – Volume 2: Policy and Applications*, Cheltenham: Edward Elgar, 1995, xi) and 'an empirical success story' (O. E. Williamson, 'Empirical Microeconomics: Another Perspective', Working Paper, 2000). Examples and surveys of this empirical work are J. A. Wilson, 'Adaptation to Uncertainty and Small Numbers Exchange: The New England Fresh Fish Market', 11 *Bell Journal of Economics*, 491–504 (1980); B. Lyons, 'Empirical Relevance of Efficient Contract Theory: Inter-firm Contracts', 12 *Oxford Review of Economic Policy*, 27–52 (1996); K. Crocker and S. Masten, 'Regulation and Administered Contracts Revisited: Lessons from Transaction Cost Economics for Public Utility Regulation', 9 *Journal of Regulatory Economics*, 5–39 (1996); A. Rindfleisch and J. Heide, 'Transaction Cost Analysis: Past, Present and Future Applications', 61 *Journal of Marketing*, 30–54 (1997); H. Shelanski and P. Klein, 'Empirical Research in Transaction Cost Economics: A Review and Assessment', 11 *Journal of Law Economics and Organization*, 335–361 (1995); C. Boerner and J. Macher, 'Transaction Cost Economics: A Review and Assessment of the Empirical Literature', unpublished manuscript, 2000; S. Masten and S. Saussier, 'Econometrics of Contracts: An Assessment of Developments in the Empirical Literature on Contracting', 92 *Revue d'Economie Industrielle*, 215–236 (2000), reprinted in E. Brousseau and J. M. Glachant (eds.), *The Economics of Contracts – Theories and Applications*, Cambridge: Cambridge University Press, 2002.

- Contracts can be fairly complex, especially where risk and uncertainty are central. Surprisingly, the media throws up the most complex contracts, given the risks and uncertainty associated with many media products and the creative forces involved. For a stimulating analysis of the Hollywood film industry, see A. De Vany, *Hollywood Economics – How Extreme Uncertainty Shapes the Film Industry*, London: Routledge, 2004. Franchise contracts have also grown in importance and give rise to principal – agent problems and risk management. R. D. Blair and F. Lafontaine, *The Economics of Franchising*, Cambridge: Cambridge University Press, 2005.

- Relational contract theory has been applied to the real-world contractual and regulatory problems and increasingly in antitrust and regulatory law. However, the relational contract label does not necessarily lead to the right interpretation of observed behaviour. This is illustrated by the controversy surrounding the so-called 'Fisher Body story' frequently used to illustrate how severe contractual opportunism led the parties to substitute ownership (vertical integration) for contract (e.g. O. E. Williamson, *The Economic Institutions of Capitalism*, New York: Free Press, 1985; O. Hart, *Firms, Contracts and Financial Structure*, Oxford: Clarendon Press, 1995). This concerned a ten-year contract which General Motors (GM) signed with Fisher Body to purchase closed car bodies, and who also acquired a 60 per cent interest in Fisher Body in 1919. The contracts contained a price clause designed to protect Fisher Body from a holdout arising from the need to commit significant asset-specific investment to fulfil the contract in the form of presses, dies and stamps. In the 1920s the demand for closed bodies increased and Fisher Body allegedly took advantage of this to charge high prices which it was said made GM uncompetitive. By 1926, the situation was described as intolerable and GM acquired Fisher Body. The contractual problems arising from asset specificity were argued to have been eventually resolved by GM in this acquisition. That is, ownership was used a means of dealing with contractual inefficiency arising from opportunism. Others argue that this analysis misrepresents the facts. Contrary to the version above, there was close collaboration between the two companies, the initial acquisition in 1919 was accompanied by substantial investment by GM in Fisher Body, there was equal representation on the Board by GM and Fisher Body, Fisher Body did not price opportunistically, many Fisher Body plants were located near GM plants and, perhaps most damaging of all, there was no large transaction-specific investment in metal presses and dies because the technology was wood-based and labour-intensive. The full acquisition of Fisher Body had little to do with contract failure. The alternative explanation for the merger was that the growth in the car market, and the increasingly-complex technology, made close coordination necessary and vertical integration efficient. See R. H. Coase, 'The Acquisition of Fisher Body by General Motors', 43 *Journal of Law & Economics*, 15–31 (2000); R. Casadues-Masanell and D. F. Spulber, 'The Fable of Fisher Body', 43 *Journal of Law & Economics*, 67–104 (2000), both reprinted in D. F. Spulber (ed.), *Famous Fables of Economics: Myths of Market Failures*, Malden, MA: Blackwells, 2002.

CHAPTER 5

Tort

liability depends upon whether B is less than L multiplied by P
Judge Learned Hand

Tort law determines whether or not the victim of a road accident or medical mishap should be compensated by those who injure him; whether an employer is liable for the injury costs of his workers; or whether a lawyer should be held liable for the losses because of incorrect advice. It is, in short, concerned with accidental losses, and the economics of care, safety and precautions.

The economic approach views tort law as a set of loss (cost) allocation rules that shift (internalise) accident losses selectively with the implied objective of efficiently deterring wrongs. It is an *ex post* method of creating an accident contract which draws on the fact that the legal process costs are cheaper than market transactions costs.

Economics has had a long and prominent role in the development of tort and its analysis. There is little doubt that in England in the nineteenth century judges adopted the prevailing political economy of Adam Smith in developing significant parts of the common law (e.g. contract and employers' liability). In the twentieth century welfare economics was frequently used as a basis for normative theories of tort, such as enterprise liability and the notion of the superior risk bearer, used to attack tort law.[1] Beginning with workers' compensation legislation there was a drive to abolish tort liability completely in the 1960s, 1970s and 1980s with no-fault compensation schemes.[2] The law was seen as an inefficient and costly

---

[1] H. C. Klemme, 'The Enterprise Liability Theory of Tort', 47 *University of Chicago Law Review*, 153–232 (1976). See generally, I. Ezlard, 'The System Builders: A Critical Appraisal of Modern American Tort Theory', 9 *Journal of Legal Studies*, 27–69 (1980).

[2] In the UK, the Pearson Report provided the focus for these efforts in the 1970s and 1980s. *Royal Commission on Civil Liability and Compensation for Personal Injury* (Chairman: Lord Pearson), London: HMSO, 1978. See also D. R. Harris, *et al.*, *Compensation and Support for Illness and Injury*, Oxford: Oxford University Press, 1984.

lottery for victim compensation, with no evidence that it deterred accidents. Yet apart from these efforts and the growth of social security schemes tort has survived. Today it remains the principal source of claims for third-party injury and its scope has widened to cover more harms (economic loss, emotional loss); tort principles are also used in damage claims for breach of statute, most recently under European competition laws.

OBJECTIVES

The objectives of tort liability are a mystery. Holmes, one of the few judges to venture a positive theory of the common law, argued that tort law and society had no interest in shifting the loss from the victim of an accident to others unless this served some social objective.[3] Shifting losses is costly and it follows, at least to an economist, that it should be undertaken only if it achieves some beneficial outcome.

The legal literature suggests at least three possible objectives relevant today – corrective justice, compensation and deterrence.[4] Again there is no consensus as to which of these is the dominant goal of tort liability and whether the law can be explained as pursuing any one or a combination of these. Indeed, the search for the overarching goal of tort law has been described as a 'pursuit of futility'.[5]

As already discussed, corrective justice – returning those wronged to the position they were prior to the wrong – is self-evidently a goal of tort. But it is tautological, leaving unanswered the question how tort law determines whether there has been an actionable wrong.

Many legal scholars have evaluated tort in terms of its ability to compensate accident victims. This is surprising because it is self-evidently a poor method of achieving victim compensation and makes no pretence that this is something it values highly. This literature labours under an obvious misconception that because the function of the usual remedy in tort – damages – is full compensation, the goal of tort itself is compensation. This logic does not follow. Further, a compensation theory of tort doctrine would support strict liability and not the predominant basis for liability, which is fault. Thus at a bare minimum the existing law shares with the economic approach little immediate concern over whether accident victims

[3] O. W. Holmes, Jr, *The Common Law*, New York: Macmillan, 1881.
[4] G. Williams, 'The Aims of the Law of Torts', 4 *Current Legal Problems*, 137–176 (1951).
[5] F. James, Jr, 'Tort Law in Mid-stream: Its Challenge to the Judicial Process', 8 *Buffalo Law Review*, 315–344 (1959) 315.

are compensated or not; it links compensation to some actionable wrong which leaves many victims bearing their own losses!

Another objective of tort is deterrence. This suggests that the doctrines are fashioned to deter wrongdoing, and encourage individuals and firms to avoid negligent and costly acts. Thus the law should shift losses only when this encourages those involved to take greater precautions. *Salmond on the Law of Torts* is unequivocal – 'pecuniary compensation is not the aim of tort' it 'exists for the purpose of preventing men from hurting one another'.[6] This view of tort has fallen into disregard among most lawyers. They will argue that the cumbersome nature of the law and the impact of injurer ignorance about the law, insurance and the high costs and delays of litigation make it implausible that tort deters wrongful behaviour – and more to the point, there is little evidence that it does. Moreover, as an explanation of the law, while it had some merit in the nineteenth century, today judges do not advance deterrence as a goal. Thus it is implausible that this objective is overriding.

The economic approach has led to a renaissance of the deterrence explanation and analysis of tort doctrines and remedies. It examines tort law in terms of its ability to minimise and internalise costs. A tort or wrong is defined as an accident or harm which could have been avoided cost-effectively and hence was preventable by the injurer or victim taking greater care and precautions, or stopping the activity altogether as already analysed for nuisance. This economic interpretation elegantly combines deterrence and efficiency considerations by making the economic avoidability of accidents the social justification for loss shifting.

TORT AS CONTRACT

A tort committed between strangers is an example of an external cost. Motorist *A* crashes into *B*'s vehicle and causes substantial damage. There is no market for crashing vehicles. In the absence of a liability rule which assigns the losses to those who can avoid driving badly, there would be an excessive number of accidents and poor driving would be subsidised by those injured. These costs must be internalised to generate an efficient level of safe driving.

Although torts frequently occur in such non-contractual settings they can be dealt with in contractual terms. As the Coase Theorem tells us, if bargaining between injurer and victim is informed and costless the

---

[6] R. F. V. Heuston, *Salmond on the Law of Torts*, 17th edn., London: Sweet & Maxwell, 1977, 13.

cost-justified level of accidents will result without the need for judicial intervention. All that is required is for the law to set out a general victim or injurer entitlement as a starting point for negotiation. The gains from trade inherent in an inefficient level of safety will encourage the parties voluntarily to negotiate a mutually advantageous accident bargain that minimises their joint costs/losses. The resulting 'accident contract' would have four main features:

1. It would allocate the losses to the party who can most cheaply reduce them.
2. Where the optimal solution is for both parties to take avoidance measures (**joint care**), it would structure responsibility for taking accident prevention in such a way that both are given an incentive to take optimal precautions.
3. Where the accidents are unavoidable, the losses would be allocated to the party best able to spread or insure the risks and consequent losses.
4. There will be other provisions to deal with the myriad situations which may arise when there are costly interactions between the parties.

For many types of accidents classed as 'torts', bargaining and contractual solutions are feasible and do take place. Indeed, it strikes the economist as odd why these are not treated as a matter of contract, rather than tort. This is certainly the case for industrial accidents and product liability (barring those accidents/defects which harm third parties not in the contractual chain from the manufacturer to the ultimate consumers) where markets exist for workplace conditions and product quality, respectively, and which take into account accident costs and liability. In these cases the transactions costs of negotiating additional terms which reflect the 'accident bargain' are low. Workers in risky jobs subject to industrial accidents and diseases can negotiate wage premia or explicit liability and compensation arrangements that protect them (see below). Their employers, faced with a higher wage and insurance costs, will be encouraged to provide greater workplace safety. However, if consumers and workers are ill informed or cannot calculate risks then wage and price premia will not provide the corrective signals to employers and manufacturers, and the market solution will be less than efficient.

For accidents between strangers the rationale for tort liability is more straightforward. There is no pre-existing contractual relationship which can take into account accident costs and care levels. The transactions costs of direct negotiations over an 'accident contract' would be prohibitive. Road accidents are the most prevalent tort claim. These are accidents between strangers whose only contact is the accident and the legal action that may follow. The physical transactions cost of a motorist likely to injure others in contacting and negotiating a binding contract with those they are likely to injure would be prohibitively costly, and impractical. The identity of the likely victims would not be known, nor would the movement of the parties – How would a London driver negotiate a contract with a Glasgow or Scunthorpe pedestrian on the offchance of a visit to either town which might involve a risk of an accident? Thus while there might exist some statistical information on the likelihood and type of injury that can be sustained in different localities there would be no way to negotiate agreements with all potential victims to agree on the care to be taken and the uniqueness of an accident. A contractual solution with the world at large is simply infeasible.

NEGLIGENCE PRINCIPLES

The main basis for liability for accidental loss under the common law is fault or negligence. Under a fault-based law a defendant will usually be held liable – at fault – if his conduct falls short of that which the court regards as reasonable. In *Blyth* v. *Birmingham Waterworks*, Alderson B. stated that:

Negligence is the omission to do something which a reasonable man, guided upon those considerations which ordinarily regulate the conduct of human affairs, would do, or do something which a prudent and reasonable man would not do.[7]

The most famous statement of negligence in English (and Scottish) law is by Lord Atkin in the 'snail-in-the-bottle' case, *Donoghue* v. *Stevenson*. There the Court held that if one finds a half-decomposed snail in one's ginger beer the legal test for the manufacturer's liability requires answers to the following questions:

You must not injure your neighbour, and the lawyers' question: Who is my neighbour? receives a restricted reply. You must take reasonable care to avoid acts or omissions which you can reasonably foresee would injure your neighbour. Who then, in law, is my neighbour? The answer seems to be persons who are so closely and directly affected by my act that I ought reasonably to have them in contemplation as being so affected when I am directing my mind to the acts and omissions.[8]

---

[7] (1856) Eng. Rep. 1047, 1049.

[8] (1932) AC 562. Note that the 'external cost' of nausea and vomiting was caused by Minchella Donoghue discovering that she had drunk ginger beer containing the decomposed snail. This could have been dealt with as a matter of contract and the fiction of implied term discussed later in contract law. However, because of the then requirement of privity – i.e. a direct contractual relationship between the parties – Minchella was barred from bringing an action in contract because she had had no direct contractual relationship with the manufacturer, only the retailer. Hence the action was brought in tort.

The constituent parts of the 'neighbour principle' – reasonable care, reasonable foreseeability and proximity – are supplied by the decisions of judges in specific cases. These terms, unfortunately, are often vague, frequently used interchangeably and do not provide specific guidance to the way the courts assign liability.

To deal with this, legal academics and textbook writers break down the determination of the defendant's liability into four sequential questions which have all to be answered in the affirmative:

1. Does the defendant owe the claimant a duty of care?
2. Has this duty been breached?
3. Is there a causal relation between the breach and the harm?
4. Has the harm resulted in compensable losses?

If the answer to all four questions is 'Yes', then the defendant is found negligent. In addition, the defendant has available a number of defences – the contributory negligence of the claimant, the loss or harm was too remote, etc. – which may negate or limit the damages awarded to his victim or victims.

The economic analysis of negligence does not mirror this categorisation, nor should it. Moreover, while the lawyer spends considerable time on whether there is a duty of care the economic approach invariably collapses the four questions into what lawyers would see as the breach of duty. This is partly presentational since both approaches are artificial representations of the way Courts deal with negligence.

Hand test

A springboard for an economic formulation for liability at common law is the so-called '**Hand Test**' set out in *United Slates* v. *Carroll Towing Co.* There, Judge Learned Hand formulated the defendant's duty of care in economic-like terms.[9]

The question before Hand in *Carroll Towing* was whether it was negligent for the Conners Company, the owner of a barge, to leave it unattended for several hours in a busy harbour when it broke away from its moorings and collided with another ship:

there is no general rule to determine when the absence of a bargee or other attendant will make the owner of the barge liable for injuries to other vessels if the she breaks away from her moorings . . . It becomes apparent why there can be no such general rule, when we consider the grounds for such a liability. Since there are occasions when every vessel will break from her moorings, and since, if she does, she becomes

---

[9] 159 F. 2d. 169, 173 (2d Cir.) 1947.

a menace to those about her, the owner's duty, as in other similar situations, to provide against resulting injuries is a function of three variables: (1) The probability that she will break away; (2) the gravity of the resulting injury, if she does; (3) the burden of adequate precautions. Possibly it serves to bring this notion into relief to state it in algebraic terms: if the probability be called P; the injury L; and the burden B; liability depends upon whether B is less than L multiplied by P: i.e., whether B < PL . . . In the case at bar the bargee left at five o'clock on the afternoon of January 3rd, and the flotilla broke away at about two o'clock in the afternoon of the following day, twenty-one hours afterwards. The bargee had been away all the time, and we hold that his fabricated story was affirmative evidence that he had no excuse for his absence. At the locus in quo – especially during the short January days and in the full tide of war activity – barges were being constantly 'drilled' in and out. Certainly it was not beyond reasonable expectation that, with the inevitable haste and bustle, the work might not be done with adequate care. In such circumstances we hold – and it is all that we do hold – that it was a fair requirement that the Conners Company should have a bargee aboard (unless he had some excuse for his absence), during the working hours of daylight.

According to the 'Hand Test', the defendant's liability is determined by the 'BPL formula' which balances 'the burden of adequate precautions' (B) against 'the likelihood of an accident' (P) multiplied by the 'gravity of the harm should the accident occur' (L). The defendant is at fault only if accident avoidance is the cheapest solution. More specifically, a defendant is liable if B is less that PL, and not liable (at fault) if B is greater than or equal to PL. This formulation mirrors the economics of safety discussed above.

While judges rarely base liability on the monetary quantification of safety costs, probabilities and losses, the Hand Test focuses on the three principal factors (risk, precautions and gravity) used by the Courts in all common law countries.[10] Indeed, a very similar formulation to *Carroll Towing* can be found in Lord Reid's dicta in *Morris* v. *West Hartlepool Steam Navigation Co. Ltd*:

It is the duty of an employer, in considering whether some precaution should be taken against a foreseeable risk, to weigh, on the one hand, the magnitude of the risk, the likelihood of an accident happening and the possible seriousness of the consequences if an accident does happen, and on the other hand, the difficulty and expense and any other disadvantage of taking precautions![11]

[10] Many standard casebooks and texts in the main common law countries organise their discussion of negligence around Hand Test factors: B. Hepple and M. Matthews, *Tort – Cases and Materials*, 2nd edn., London: Butterworths, 1980, chapter 4; R. A. Posner, *Tort Law – Cases and Economic Analysis*, Boston: Little Brown, 1982; A. M. Linden, *Canadian Tort Law*, Toronto: Caswell, 1977, 80–90; H. Luntz *et al.*, *Torts: Cases and Commentary*, Sydney: Law Book Co., 1980, chapter 3.

[11] [1959] AC 522. Hand-like statements can also be found in *Mackintosh* v. *Mackintosh* (1864) 2 M. 1357; *Ryan* v. *Fisher* (1976) 51 ALJ 125.

A similar though not identical test has been a feature of English industrial safety legislation. Under the Factory Acts, which are as old as the common law of employers' liability, an employer's culpability is governed by the standard of 'reasonably practicable'.[12] In the leading modern case *Edwards* v. *The National Coal Board*, the Court of Appeal held that:

reasonably practicable' ... seems to me to imply that a computation must be made by the owner in which the quantum of risk is placed on one scale and the sacrifice involved in the measures necessary for averting the risk (whether in money, time or trouble) is placed in the other, and that, if it be shown that there is a gross disproportion between them – the risk being insignificant in relation to the sacrifice – the defendants discharge the onus on them.[13]

The 'reasonably practicable' test differs from the Hand Test by appearing to set out a cost-effectiveness standard which looks only at the reductions in risks rather than the expected loss – i.e. it is a 'BP formula' rather than a 'Hand-type' BPL formula.

The Hand Test sets out the basic ingredients of negligence in both law and economics, or rather the factors relevant to setting the standard of care.[14]

Under the Hand (and Reid) Tests, the defendant is more likely to be found in breach of his duty if the costs of care are low, the risks of injury high and the severity of the injuries, should an accident occur, high. It is the interplay of these three factors that is important to the decision whether the defendant has breached his duty of care. As we shall see, all these factors are important in law.

The likelihood of injury (P) is a relevant factor in determining whether the risk created by the defendant is unreasonable. In *Fardon* v. *Harcourt-Rivington*[15] Lord Dunedin stated that 'people must guard against reasonable probabilities, but they are not bound to guard against fantastic possibilities'. In *Bolton* v. *Stone*,[16] a batsman hit a ball over a fence onto an adjoining highway, injuring the claimant. In the ninety-year period over

---

[12] C. Veljanovski, 'Regulatory Enforcement – An Economic Case Study of the British Factory Inspectorate', 5 *Law and Policy Quarterly*, 75–96 (1983).

[13] [1949] 1 KB 704; [1949] 1 All ER 743. See Health and Safety Executive, 'Principles and Guidelines to Assist HSE in its Judgments that Duty Holders have Reduced Risk as Low as Reasonably Practicable', www.hse.govuk/risk/theory/a;arp1.htm.

[14] R. A. Posner, 'A Theory of Negligence', 1 *Journal of Legal Studies*, 29–96 (1972). Posner's study is based on analysis of 1,500 US appellate decisions over the period 1875–1905. Wright has analysed the tort judgments of Posner and Easterbrook, concluding that they have been unable to employ the Hand Test. R. W. Wright, 'Hand, Posner, and the Myth of the "Hand Formula"', 4 *Theoretical Inquiries in Law*, 1–132 (2003).

[15] [1951] 1 All ER 1078.   [16] [1964] 3 All ER 185.

which cricket had been played on the field no-one had ever been injured, and in the previous thirty years the ball had been hit over the fence only six times. The House of Lords found the defendant not liable because the chance of injury 'was very small'. Lord Reid applied the following test:

whether the risk of damage to a person on the road was so small that a reasonable man . . ., considering the matter from the view of safety, would have thought it right to refrain from taking steps to prevent the danger.

In economic terms, the risk of injury was very small so that the damage was discounted very heavily (i.e. $P \times L$ is very low). Also, the facts in the case show that the fence was already 29 ft high (it was a 12-ft fence built on a 17-ft rise) so that the costs of avoiding such an accident were bound to be very high (hence B is considerably greater than $P \times L$).

On the other hand, if an action which can avoid an accident is relatively cheap, this would tend to attract liability even if the risk was low, provided that the gravity of harm was high. In *The Wagon Mound (No. 2)*[17] Lord Reid stated that a 'real risk' which is 'remote' is not for that reason alone 'not reasonably foreseeable' 'when it is easy to prevent'.

In *Haley* v. *London Electricity Board*[18] the Hand factors are discussed more fully. The defendant (the London Electricity Board) was excavating a pavement and as a precaution placed a punner (a tool for ramming earth around a post to make it firm) at one end of the excavation on the completion of the day's work. This was because the safety fence arrived after the workers had decided to go home. The claimant, who was blind and could avoid ordinary obstacles only with the aid of a white stick, missed the punner and tripped. As a result he hit his head and became deaf. In this case the defendant alleged that the chance of a blind man coming along the road that day was small and that therefore it was not reasonable to expect him to take precautions. Lord Reid did not agree. Evidence was presented that one in 500 people in London at the time were blind. He went on to consider the costs of taking adequate precautions. Padded lamp-posts, for example, were not justified in view of the risks. But he continued:

A moment's reflection . . . shows that a low obstacle in an unusual place is a grave danger: on the other hand, it is clear that quite a light fence some two feet high is adequate warning. There would be no difficulty in providing such a fence here.

---

[17] *Overseas Tankships (UK) Ltd* v. *Miller Steamships Co. Pty Ltd (The Wagon Mound) (No. 2)* [1967] 1 AC 617.
[18] [1965] AC 778; [1964] 3 All ER 185.

The standard of care required of the defendant will tend to rise with the magnitude of the harm. In *Paris* v. *Stepney Borough Council*[19] a one-eyed man was blinded when a chip of metal lodged in his good eye. The claimant argued that his employer was negligent in failing to supply him with goggles even though these were not usually provided to employees. The Court held that, although it would not have been negligent not to provide full-sighted employees with goggles it was in this case because the consequences were more serious. In Lord Morton's judgment he stated that 'the more serious the damage which will happen if an accident occurs, the more thorough are the precautions which employers must take'. He also made it clear that the right-hand side of the Hand Test ($P \times L$) is relevant:

In considering generally the precautions that the employer ought to take for the protection of his workmen it must, in my view, be right to take into account both elements, the likelihood of an accident happening and the gravity of the consequences.

The cost of reducing risk is explicitly referred to in other cases. In *Watt* v. *Hertfordshire County Council*[20] Lord Denning stated that in determining due care one must balance the risk against the measures necessary to eliminate it. If the costs of precautions are low, liability is more likely to follow. In the Australian case *Mercer* v. *Commissioner for Road Transport and Tramways*,[21] the driver of a tram collapsed at the controls and, despite the efforts of the conductor to stop it with the hand brakes, a collision resulted. The claimant alleged that a 'dead man's handle' which automatically stops a tram if released would have avoided the accident. The Court held that, in terms of the risk that would be avoided, the costs would be disproportionate.

ECONOMICS OF LIABILITY

Having established that the Hand Test (or BPL formula) is not a selective piece of law, it can now be given a more rigorous economic formulation and extended.

The economic approach to tort assumes that individuals and companies respond on average to an increase in expected costs by substituting lower (net) cost alternatives. Thus, if the costs of accidents go up, say, because common law damages have increased, the cost bearer is assumed to increase his level of care where this leads to a net cost saving. This assumes that there is an inverse relationship between greater safety or care and the frequency and severity of accidents – more care: less accident losses!

[19] [1951] 1 All ER 42.   [20] [1954] 1 2 All ER 368, 371.   [21] [1937] 56 CLR 580.

Secondly, greater care does not eliminate all accident or accident costs, it often only reduces the risk. The level of risk reduction depends on the amount of care and they way that the risk of an accident responds to greater care. As already stated, the optimal amount of care balances the marginal costs of greater care with the expected reduction in accident losses.

The preceding economic proposition provides guidance to a modification of the Hand Test to encourage optimal care.[22] As stated in *Carroll Towing*, the Hand Test suggests that the due care standard is set by balancing the total costs of care against the total expected accident losses, with the implication that there has been complete avoidance of the accident. However, this is not the case in both economics and in law. For most unintentional torts care is not an on/off situation but a continuum of more or less care or actions which reduces the likelihood (the risk) of an accident. Most unintentional torts arise from inadvertence, lack of forethought, failure to take adequate precautions and so on. That is, there is less than certainty that the act or lack of act will cause an adverse outcome or event. In more technical parlance, the harm is *probabilistic* and occurs generally with a low probability. Clearly, the higher the probability of an accident the less likely that the harm is caused unintentionally. However low probability or not, greater care only reduces the likelihood of the accident or loss and hence there will always be residual risks and uncompensated losses arising from hazardous activities governed by tort liability.

Under an economic version of the *marginal* Hand Test, the defendant is liable for the loss only if at the level of care exercised, the marginal cost of greater care is less than marginal expected damages.[23] Care should be increased so long as £1 spent on greater safety avoids expected accident losses of more than £1. When the additional £1 cost of safety reduces expected accident losses by £1, it is the optimal or cost-justified level of safety. Thus if incremental care would have cost £10, and reduced the risk of £10,000 loss to the victim by 1 in 500 then the defendant would be held liable since the additional cost of £10 saves £20 in expected losses ($P = 1/500$ and $L = £10,000$, therefore $PL = £20$). A rational defendant who knows that he will bear the victim's loss in these circumstances will take greater care because it is the cheaper alternative. Thus, basing liability on the efficiency criterion encourages the defendant to avoid all accidents deemed negligent by the Courts.

---

[22] J. Brown, 'Toward an Economic Theory of Liability', 2 *Journal of Legal Studies*, 323–349 (1973).
[23] Brown, 'Toward an Economic Theory', 331–335.

Further, making the defendant liable for all losses, whether negligently caused or not, would not encourage him to take more than the efficient level of care. For accidents not efficient to prevent, and hence not negligently caused, the defendant will find paying damages cheaper than taking greater care. Thus the selectivity of liability under fault which denies accident victims compensation when the defendant is not at fault, is given an economic (and social) justification – imposing all the losses does not encourage the injurer to take greater care.

In practice, the Courts decide tort cases in this way, albeit less formally and rigorously. The adversarial nature of common law adjudication forces the lawyer and judge to think not in terms of absolutes but of incremental changes. Even though the judge makes binary choices (guilty/not guilty) the grounds upon which judges decide negligence are incremental. The assignment of liability is conduct-based. That is, the Courts look at the conduct of the defendant and the claimant relative to the norm of the 'reasonable man' to determine whether the defendant should bear the loss. The loss allocation process fixes on the behaviour of the parties, as does the economic approach. To establish fault, the claimant has to persuade the judge that on the balance of probabilities the defendant did not act with reasonable care. The claimant will enumerate actions which, had the defendant taken them, would have avoided the accident. The defendant will counter with reasons why this would not have reduced the likelihood of harm or would have been impractical, too expensive and unreasonable. The basis on which the judge decides, and the process by which he arrives at this decision, are very similar to the way in which an economist would approach the problem (see figure 5.1).

A judicial example of the marginal Hand Test can be found in *Latimer* v. *AEC Ltd.*[24] The respondent's factory was flooded by an unusually heavy thunderstorm and water and oil collected on the floor. Sawdust was spread on the floor but this was insufficient to deal with the large quantity of water. The appellant, who was working on the night shift, was injured while loading a barrel onto a trolley when he slipped on a wet, oily patch, crushing his leg. This case nicely illustrates that the Courts take into account the costs of additional care and balance them against the incremental reduction in risks. The issue before the Court was whether a 'reasonably prudent employer would have closed down the factory rather than allow his employees to run the risks involved in continuing work'. Lord Tucker decided the danger was not such as to require the factory to close. The Court held that there was

[24] [1953] 2 All ER 449.

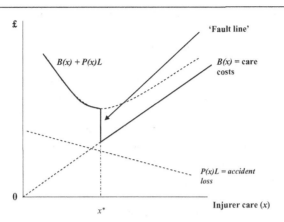

Figure 5.1 Defendant's care under negligence standard

The efficient level of care, the due care standard and the way fault liability induces optimal care in joint care cases can be illustrated using the above diagram. Denote the total expected accident costs as (C) which, according to the Hand Test, comprises, B, L and P. Denote the level of care exercised by the injurer as x, and assume that the total costs of care are $B(x)$ which increase as more care is exercised, and the risk as $P(x)$, which is assumed to fall as more care is exercised. Hence expected total accident costs are $C = B(x) + P(x)L$.

From this simple model, the following can be derived:

- First, the level of care which minimises expected total accident costs C is x^* as shown by the curve which is the sum of care costs and expected losses. It has this shape because as one moves from no care expected losses decrease more than care costs increase until x^*. After x^* expect care costs rise more than expected injury costs fall. As this diagram indicates, from an efficiency viewpoint there can be too much safety, as there can be too little safety.

- Second, the optimal level of care is determined by a comparison of the marginal costs of care and the reduction of marginal expected losses. The optimal level of care is where the last £1 spent on avoidance equals a £1 reduction in the expected losses. If the symbol Δ (called delta and used often to denote a 'change in') is used to represent the marginal losses/gains for any given act of care, and assuming that care affects only the likelihood of an accident (rather than the size of the loss), the marginal expected accident costs for any level of care is $\Delta C = \Delta B(x) + \Delta P(x)L$. The costs of an increase in care

are justified only if the reduction in the expected loss is greater, i.e. $\Delta PL > \Delta AB$.

• Third, a defendant should be held at fault or negligent when at the level of care he or she exercised at the time of accident the additional costs of care were less (that is, cheaper) than the reduction in expected loss, i.e. $\Delta B(x) < \Delta P(x)L$; and not at fault if more care was not cheaper that the avoided expected losses $\Delta B(x) \geq \Delta P(x)L$. In the above diagram this means that the judicial standard of care is set at x^* (the efficient level), and the bold unbroken line traces out the total costs of fault liability for each level of care.

To show that fault liability provides optimal deterrence in joint care situations assume that the judicial standard of care is set at the efficient level. That is, the threshold between reasonable and unreasonable care, is set at x^*. If the due care standard is set at x^* the bold unbroken line gives the injurer's *total* costs as more care is taken. At x^*, the defendant faces a kinked or disjointed damage schedule. For care levels below x^*, the defendant will be found negligent and required to pay compensation to the claimant and thus bears total care and damage costs. If the defendant exercises care x^* or greater, his total costs fall to the costs of taking greater care only. Thus a potential defendant faces costs $B(x) + P(x)L$ for care below that held negligent and only $B(x)$ for levels of care equal to and in excess of x^*. As can be seen, total expected accident costs are lowest when the defendant complies with the legal standard. Thus the injurer minimises his costs at the judicially set standard of care, does not compensate the victim but at the margin faces the victim's loss. Under the negligence standard, injurers will take reasonable care, and therefore are never found negligent. As a result, victims bear their own losses and thus face the correct incentives to take preventative actions. Thus a negligence standard without a contributory negligence defence is efficient in joint care situations.

adequate sawdust to meet any situation that could have been foreseen. In economic terms, Lord Tucker was comparing the additional costs of shut-down against the incremental reduction of the risks of injury to workers. He found that shutting down the factory would have imposed a cost burden on the employer not fully offset by the gain to workers.[25]

---

[25] In terms of the symbols used in figure 5.1 the Court felt that the employer was at x^* – the economically efficient level of care – and that under the marginal Hand Test the additional effort was not cost-justified – i.e. $\Delta B(x) > p(x)L$.

Joint care

In joint care situations the law must provide incentives on both injurer and victim to take efficient care.

Joint care is where both parties can influence the accident rate by taking greater care. It usually also implies that the care exercised by the parties are (economic) substitutes. That is, as one party increases his or her level of care and thereby reduces the risk, the other party will adjust by reducing his or her precautions. This simple relationship arises from the economists' notion of substitutability at the margin, and underpins the analysis of liability.[26] This phenomenon is widely known and manifests itself in a number of areas. For example there is research which indicates that smoke alarms increase deaths due to smoke inhalation. This is because smoke detection and fire prevention is a combination of a number of different actions. A smoke alarm increases the level of protection to a householder but at the same time reduces other inputs into fire prevention such as vigilance and taking other precautions. The fire alarm may then give a false sense of security. Another example from recent research found that cyclists wearing helmets were more likely to be hit by a vehicle. It appears that motorists drove closer to cyclists wearing helmets than to those without a helmet when overtaking.[27] This was attributed to a perception that cyclists wearing helmets were more experienced, and their behaviour more predictable.

It would appear impossible for a liability rule constrained to shifting one loss between several parties to encourage two or more parties to all adopt the efficient level of care. Any permutation would result in inadequate cost internalisation of one or both parties – if the law shifts the loss to the injurer (strict liability) the victim would take too little care; if it is left with the victim (no liability) the injurer takes too little care; if the loss is split between the parties (shared liability) each bears only a fraction of the loss and both have insufficient incentives to avoid the harm. Thus it would appear that a liability rule restricted to shifting the loss between the victim and the injurer is not efficient.

This is not the case, and it is one of the main contributions of the economic approach to show that the common law has a solution to the

---

[26] The reason is that as one party increases care the marginal return to care alters for the other party because the situation is now safer. As a result, he or she finds that they are exercising too much care because the greater care exercised by the other reduces the marginal expected benefit of the last unit of care below its costs. The rational response is to reduce the level of care to the now new lower cost-effective level.

[27] 'Cyclists with helmets "more likely to be hit"', *Daily Mail*, 12 September 2006, 29.

joint care problem. It works this way. Under fault liability the injurer is liable to compensate the victim of a careless act only if the level of care he or she exercises falls below the legally determined 'due care' level. If the due care threshold is set at the efficient level of care for the injurer then the injurer will have to pay damages only if his or her care falls below the level of care deemed appropriate by the Court. This threat of paying damages for negligent actions induces the injurer to take the efficient level of care. If the injurer responds in this way, then he or she is not found negligent. As a result the victim bears the loss and takes the level of care which minimises his or her losses. Thus fault-based liability, even though it shifts the one loss, encourages both injurer and victim to take the efficient level of care – the injurer because he or she is threatened with having to pay damages if at fault; and the victim because he or she bears the cost-justified losses that remain when the defendant acts non-negligently. Thus liability rules which base damages/compensation on satisfying a judicially determined level of acceptable care induce both parties to take the efficient level of care, even though the law shifts one loss and holds out the prospect of full compensation to the victim. It should be noted that if fault liability worked as just described it would be rare both for anyone to be found negligent and for victims to receive tort compensation.

The activity test

The problem of controlling activity levels has already been addressed in chapter 3 on nuisance. This is more problematic in a fault-based regime and points to a weakness or flaw in the marginal Hand Test. This is because the test, even if applied correctly in the sense that it induces all the parties to exercise the efficient level of care, may nonetheless result in an inefficiently high number of accidents and injurer activity and an inefficiently low level of victim activity. This is so for the simple reason that under a fault-based liability regime the costs of non-negligent accidents are left with the victims and hence the injurer's cost structure does not reflect the full external costs of risk taking activity.

This can be explained better using traffic accidents as an example. The total number of road accidents is determined by the care exercised by each motorist, and the total number of motorists – or, more accurately, the amount of driving (miles, journeys, etc.). Thus for a given likelihood of collision the aggregate accident rate will be higher the more driving and the more motorists. Shifting the loss will affect both the level of care and the level of an activity for each group. For example, fault liability relative to a strict liability will result in injurers as a group paying less in damages and victims left with the remaining non-negligently caused losses. Thus the returns to activities generating accidents will be higher and those associated with victims lower, so that the former will expand and the latter contract. This will not be efficient because injury-generating activity will not bear the full costs it generates.

For full economic efficiency the outcome must satisfy two tests:

1. **Marginal Hand test** that for each party the marginal costs of safety equal the marginal expected losses, and hence each party is exercising efficient care
2. **Activity test** that each party bear the total expected losses to ensure that the benefits of the activity cover the total costs, and the level of activity maximises net benefits.

Liability rules, whether fault or strict liability, violate the Activity Test and are therefore generally not efficient. This is because they fail to impose the total costs of accidents on each party and therefore generate either excessive levels of accidents or too few accidents.

The care activity distinction provides some insight into one persistent debate among legal historians. Some have argued that the apparent shift from strict to fault liability at the beginning of the industrial revolution was an attempt to give industry a 'judicial subsidy'.[28] If this was in fact the case then the claim is correct, since fault liability relieves industry and railways of all the costs of accidents and pollution even if it satisfies the care test. Posner, while agreeing that negligence relative to the strict liability leads to higher profits for railways and more railway activity and accidents, argues that it was and is not a subsidy. The basis for his view is that it is not a subsidy 'unless it is proper usage to say that an industry is being subsidised whenever a tax levied upon it is reduced or removed'.[29] This is not correct since industry or the railway is being relieved not of a 'tax' but real external losses and hence are being 'subsidised'.

The care/activity distinction points to an inherent limitation of tort liability in achieving full efficiency. It arises because the judge has only one legal instrument – shifting the victim's loss – to control two variables – care and activity levels.[30] The economic theory of policy states where a policy-maker (judge or legislator) has two or more policy objectives then he must

[28] M. J. Horowitz, *The Transformation of American Law, 1780–1860*, Cambridge, MA: Harvard University Press, 1977.

[29] Posner, 'A Theory of Negligence', 30.

[30] R. A. Posner, 'Strict Liability: A Comment', 2 *Journal of Legal Studies*, 205–221 (1973); C. G. Veljanovski, 'The Economics of Job Safety Regulation: Theory and Evidence', paper to ESRC Research Seminar in Law & Economics, Oxford, 1978; S. Shavell, 'Strict Liability versus Negligence', 9 *Journal of Legal Studies*, 1–25 (1980); A. M. Polinsky, 'Strict Liability vs. Negligence in a Market Setting', 70 *American Economic Review (Papers & Proceedings)*, 363–367 (1980).

have at least the same number of instruments if all objectives are to be fully achieved.[31] This means that if a liability rule has to achieve changes in two or more variables (such as care, activity levels and full compensation), it requires at least two policy instruments.[32]

In English law there is some recognition of the impact of liability on activity levels, although hardly in a systematic or routine way. One notable example is *Daborn* v. *Bath Tramways* Motor Co. Ltd,[33] which gives a key to how the care/activity distinction can be used. The claimant was driving a left-hand-drive ambulance which collided with a bus. Although the claimant gave a signal this was ineffective because of the left-hand-drive position of the driver. The defendant's lawyer argued that 'the driver of such a car should, before executing a turn, stop his car, move to the right-hand seat and look backwards to see if another car was attempting to overtake him and then start up again': in economic terms, exercise much more care. Lord Asquith concluded that this procedure might be ineffective and involve delay. While the risk could be eliminated by banning such vehicles the resultant cost must be weighed against the reduction in risk. The Court considered another cost. It was a time of national emergency requiring all transport resources to be employed. Banning such ambulances or requiring them to take the suggested measures would have repercussions. *Daborn* is seen as a case in which 'social utility is taken into account'. In economic terms, it is a case in which the Court was looking both at the care and activity level issues and implicitly maximising some net wealth calculation, looking at where (a) greater care was efficient and (b) whether controlling the activity satisfied a cost-benefit test.

This type of comparison, while not routinely reflected in negligence cases, is a feature of tort liability. Judges have in the past often expressed concern that to impose liability would impose an excessive burden on industry using coded phrases such as 'the floodgates of litigation' or the fear of 'crushing liability'. This can be seen in a judicial weighing of the

---

[31] L. Johansen, *Public Economics*, Amsterdam: North-Holland, 1965, chapter 2. This was first applied to tort law in R. L. Birmingham, 'The Theory of Economic Policy and the Law of Torts', 55 *Minnesota Law Review*, 1–13 (1970–1).

[32] It should be noted that the economist's traditional approach to external costs does not suffer from this potential inefficiency. Economists normally propose non-compensatory taxes (or fines) to control external costs. If these are calculated correctly, which in most tort situations is a big 'if', they create the correct marginal and total cost incentives on both injurers and victims. This is because the victim bears his or her own losses and the injurer the tax (assumed to be equivalent to the victim's loss). Thus at the margin both bear the loss and decide on the optimal level of care, and because each bears the full residual fine/losses of accidents once the optimal care level is decided the total costs of each activity takes into account the social costs of accidental activities.

[33] [1946] 2 All ER 33.

total economic benefits of a hazardous activity and a 'policy' decision not to impose liability because this would not be efficient.

This claim amounts to little more than a technical way of re-expressing judicial support for industrial development over the plight of victims of the industrial revolution. The fact remains, support for industry or economics or not, tort liability is inefficient because it does not control activity levels properly. But there is another way of looking at the structure of tort based on the care/activity distinction which indicates that this concern may be overblown.

Often, victim and injurer do not form distinct classes. This is certainly the case for the largest source of tort actions – road traffic accidents. Over time, a motorist is likely to be both victim and injurer and this may even be the case for other road users such as cyclists and pedestrians. Thus it is unlikely that the liability rule will have a major impact on the level of driving and a fault liability rule will not lead to inefficiency due to excessive activity levels.

For the second largest source of tort actions – industrial accidents – a market already exists which will minimise the impact on actual levels. Many industrial injuries and deaths occur between victim and injurer who have an exchange relationship. As discussed below, the reassignment of liability in contract situations is likely to have very little affect on industry costs and workers' overall compensation levels because wage rates adjust to offset or neutralise the legal reallocation of costs.

REASONABLE MAN STANDARD

In practice, the Courts determine fault by comparing the defendant's actions against the conduct of the 'reasonable man'. This is an objective judicial standard. To quote *Glasgow Corp.* v. *Muir*: 'The standard of foresight of the reasonable man . . . eliminates the personal equation and is independent of the idiosyncrasies of the particular person whose conduct is in question'.[34] This standard is not an immutable one since the actions of the reasonable man are governed by the circumstances of each case.

There is a good reason why the courts use an objective standard of care. An individual or subjective standard would be excessively costly to administer and not be an effective deterrent. If personal circumstances were allowed to excuse the defendant as a matter of course there would be no end of excuses. The defendant would always be able to raise some reason

---

[34] Per MacMillan L., *Glasgow Corp.* v. *Muir* [1943] 2 All ER 44.

(I was distracted, stupid, in a rush) that impeded him or her from taking due care. But, more importantly, it would act as a positive disincentive for defendants to raise their level of care by remedying inadequacies in their present safety practices. An objective standard seeks to raise conduct to one which reflects the care that that should have been taken.

Of course the 'reasonable man' standard does not achieve this without some inefficiency since those with particularly low prevention costs are not encouraged to take more care than the 'reasonable man'. Some people can avoid accidents more cheaply than others. This gives rise to some problems if we interpret the reasonable man standard as the level of care that the average person in a group would have taken. Suppose that the costs of avoiding an accident for the average man are £30, and that the expected accident loss is £35. For a subset of potential defendants the costs of avoiding the accident is £45. For such a group the negligence test has been converted into strict liability. This is because they will always be found negligent given their higher costs of care; and paying compensation is cheaper than prevention. At the other extreme, some people may be able to prevent accidents more cheaply than the average person but they would only be induced to exercise a lower judicially set level of care.

From the preceding discussion it can be concluded that a tort system influenced by economic considerations would tend to vary the 'reasonable man' standard where (a) the law has no deterrent effect; (b) the costs of care to the group in question are excessively high or low relative to the average; and (c) the law would allow personal circumstances to exclude liability where there is little scope for defendants to concoct excuses. The law recognises some of these considerations.

Custom

The Courts will take customary practice into account as a 'weighty circumstance' in deciding where the standard of care has been breached. In *Stokes* v. *Guest, Keen and Nettlefold (Boltes and Nuts)*[35] Snick J. deduced the following from cases on the employer's duty to workmen. An employer is entitled to follow common practice unless in the light of common sense or newer knowledge it is clearly bad. Where there is developing knowledge the employer must keep reasonably abreast of it and not be too slow to apply it, and where there is in fact greater than average knowledge of the risks he may be obliged to take more than the average or standard precautions.

---

[35] [1969] WLR 1776.

This shows that the law is conscious of deficiency of custom alone as the litmus test of liability. As the cases state, the ultimate test is still whether the defendant exercised reasonable care. Custom is only one element of the equation that determines this and operates asymmetrically – failure to follow custom attracts liability whereas conforming to custom does not necessarily make a defendant immune from liability.

What economic factors are relevant to the use of custom or common practice in determining liability? First, common practice has considerable evidentiary value since it provides a benchmark for what might be reasonable (efficient) behaviour. It is correct for the Courts not to regard it as an absolute benchmark. This is because it involves a circular logic. In cases where injurer and victim are complete strangers, common practice in the absence of fault liability would be for the injurer to exercise too little care.

In contractual situations, common practice has greater evidentiary value because of the ability of parties to bargain (implicitly) for lower and higher levels of care, and have this reflected in the price of the good or service. Thus common practice in professional services markets (lawyers, doctors, surveyors) would be a relevant consideration since it will be determined in part by the wishes of the potential victims. However the evidentiary value of custom depends on how well the market is working. In many professional service markets concerns have been expressed by competition and consumer protection bodies about the adequacy of professional standards. For example, the UK Office of Fair Trading (OFT) has taken action against restrictive practices among lawyers, dentists and other professional groups which have resulted in poor-quality service and practice. In imperfect markets, professional standards may fall far short of the efficient ones and these (do not) and cannot serve as a complete defence.

Special skill

In situations where the defendant belongs to a class of persons who has specialised knowledge or skills, the standard of care is higher. This makes sense since the costs of taking adequate precautions is arguably lower for specialists than for members of the general public. In *Phillips* v. *William Whitely Ltd*[36] the claimant had her ears pierced by the employee of a jeweller. Several days later an abscess appeared. The Court held that the standard of care required was that of 'ordinary cleanliness' not 'surgical cleanliness'. How is this case to be analysed? If one goes to a less expert

---

[36] (1938) 1 All ER 566.

person then the quality of the service offered is lower and this is reflected in the price charged. To demand that the jeweller carry out the piercing of ears under surgical conditions will raise his charges. It will also reduce the welfare of society as people can no longer assume higher risks in return for a lower price. One could argue that rigid application of the 'reasonable man' standard would have little effect because jewellers henceforth would merely contract out of liability. If this is permitted, then the argument is correct but it raises process costs.

On the other hand, the decision in *Nettleship* v. *Weston*[37] is harder to rationalise. There, the claimant was teaching the defendant to drive when an accident broke his knee cap. The defendant argued that as a learner driver she owed the claimant a lower standard of care. Since the claimant was aware of this fact and the driver was under his instruction and control it would seem that the defendant's position should have been accepted by the Court. The Court held that that the standard of care was that of a 'the competent and experienced driver'. It is possible because of the contractual nature of the relationship between the parties that the existence of insurance had an influence on the Court. The claimant had been told by the defendant's husband that he was covered as a passenger by the fully comprehensive insurance policy in the event of an accident. However, it is rare for the Court to take the existence of insurance into account when determining liability.

Minors

The law makes an exception for minors and treats them as a separate category.[38] This rule makes a certain amount of sense in isolation as it can be argued that (a) the ability of minors to take care and respond to incentives is low and (b) that they are usually judgment-proof. But this latter consideration gives a clue to the likely inefficiency of the exception. If the standard of care for minors takes into account what the average minor would have done, then this may raise the level of care. But the incentives generated by legal responsibility are more likely to bear on the parents and those in charge of the minors. They are in a better position to control behaviour and to take into account the risks. Thus the relevant costs are not those affecting minors but those related to the supervision of minors where this is a feasible arrangement.

---

[37] [1971] 3 All ER 581.   [38] *McHale* v. *Watson* [1969] ALR 513.

Errors and compliance

Fault liability and the 'reasonable man' standard has another attraction, especially where damages are hard to estimate. It is simply this. As noted above fault liability is a discontinuous standard – for levels of care which comply with the standard of care set by the Court the injurer bears only his care costs; for care falling short of the legal standard care costs and damage payments. Thus the prospect of paying much higher costs for breaching the legal standard acts as a powerful incentive to comply. Now take a situation where the legal standard is set at some level treated as 'reasonable' by the Court but not necessarily at the efficient level and the courts have difficulty accurately estimating losses. Compliance with the legal standard is not conditional on accurate estimation of damages. Injurers will be induced to take the legally determined level of care by the threat that if they breach the due care level set by the courts their costs jump from the costs of care to the significantly higher costs of care plus damages. Thus a fault standard is able to gain compliance with a legal due care standard even where there is judicial error in calculating damages. The discontinuous nature of costs facing injurers under negligence means that errors in estimation of damages do not directly translate into higher or lower care. Thus error costs pose less of a problem under a reasonableness standard.

This contrasts with strict liability. The elasticity (the responsiveness) of injurer care is higher under strict liability because damages are awarded for all levels of care.[39] Thus, all things equal, if damages overestimate or underestimate the true losses then the level of care will be below or above their efficient level, respectively, and because there is no judicially set level of due care strict liability does not necessarily generate a specific level of care.

CONTRIBUTORY NEGLIGENCE

Most liability systems give the defendant a number of defences. The contributory negligence of the claimant is one. In England prior to 1945 contributory negligence was a complete defence. If the victim failed to take reasonable care even though the injurer had also failed to do so, then he or she would get no compensation. The Law Reform (Contributory Negligence) Act 1945 altered the defence so that 'the damages recoverable shall be reduced to such an extent as the court thinks just and equitable

---

[39] R. Cooter, 'Prices and Sanctions', 84 *Columbia Law Review*, 1523–1560 (1984).

having regard to the claimant's share in the responsibility for the damage'. This new defence of contributory negligence with apportionment – or comparative negligence as it is called in the USA – reduces the victims' compensation based on the relative fault of the parties. Consider both defences.

The contributory negligence defence would seem an efficient rule in joint care cases since it provides the victim with an incentive to take care where it is efficient for him or her to do so. The logic is the mirror image of that already discussed for fault liability. The claimant/victim will compare total costs (care plus losses plus compensation payments/damages) for different levels of his or her care. If the claimant's due care standard under an absolute defence of contributory negligence is set at the efficient level of victim care, then the claimant will avoid being found contributory negligent.

However, as shown above, there is no need for an absolute (or any) defence of contributory negligence when there is fault liability. Fault liability deals efficiently with situations where both parties can (efficiently) avoid accidents (joint care). The logic is as follows. The threat of being required to pay damages is sufficient incentive for the defendant to take the cost-justified level of care. He thereby avoids paying damages and minimises costs. As a consequence, the claimant (victim) bears his own loss for the remaining (cost-justified) accidents. Since the claimant will bear the full loss he or she minimise his or her loss by taking the cost-justified level of self-protection. Thus fault liability induces both parties to take the efficient level of care even though it is based on shifting a single loss and compensatory damages. The defence is, however, needed under a strict liability rule (see below). Nonetheless contributory negligence would add to the incentives for victims to take care independent of the principles governing injurer liability, and thereby provide an additional incentive for victim to act with reasonable care.

It is often claimed that the US comparative negligence/English contributory negligence defence is inefficient. This is based on the argument that by apportioning damages on the basis of relative fault, inadequate pressure is placed on both injurer and victim to take efficient care. The defence has the effect of splitting the damages between injurer and victim so that neither party faces the full losses! However, this is incorrect because it ignores the fact that any loss-splitting is still dependent on fault and as a result both parties can avoid completely the loss by acting non-negligently.

A relative fault-based apportionment of damages does not operate as a simple loss-splitting rule because the parties can always fully avoid the loss if they are not at fault. Thus if the due care standard for each is set at the efficient level then an inefficient outcome is not a stable solution.[40] For example, if the defendant's standard of care is set at the efficient level he will not act negligently and, irrespective of whether there is a contributory negligence defence, the claimant will take the efficient level of care. Where the defendant is not (initially) exercising the appropriate level of care he will, however, realise that for a small increase in avoidance costs he can completely avoid liability. This will encourage the defendant to take the appropriate level of care.

In practice comparative negligence may not be fashioned with such an acute eye to the efficient due care standards. If so it may dampen incentives for accident avoidance and increase the accident rate compared to a fault or fault plus absolute contributory defence liability regime.

STRICT LIABILITY

Strict liability is usually confined to property torts, ultra-hazardous activities and no-fault reforms of the tort system. Nonetheless a positive theory of tort must be able to explain the pockets of strict liability and why negligence is used rather than strict liability. Here we explore some aspects of strict liability using both the care and activity-level concepts.

Much of the economic literature gives the impression that strict liability is inefficient. This is not correct. The usual economists' analysis of externalities is based on strict liability, albeit with fiscal fines rather than compensatory damages. Calabresi, using broadly the same economics as Posner, plumps for strict liability as the efficient liability rule.

We know from previous analysis that strict liability can achieve deterrence efficiency under the same (idealised) assumptions that enable fault liability to be an efficient legal standard. In the formal model of liability rules there is symmetry between negligence (with or without a contributory negligence defence) and strict liability with a contributory negligence.[41] However, unlike negligence in joint care situations, the efficiency of strict liability depends critically on a contributory negligence defence. This is so for the following reason. Under a strict liability the injurer faces the victim's losses at all levels of care. Thus the costs of accidents are reflected in the injurer's actions and he will take the efficient level of care. The victim has no incentive to act with due care since the victim is fully compensated

---

[40] D. Haddock and C. Curran, 'An Economic Theory of Comparative Negligence', 14 *Journal of Legal Studies*, 49–72 (1985).
[41] G. Calabresi and J. T. Hirschoff, 'Toward a Test for Strict Liability in Torts', 81 *Yale Law Journal*, 1054–1085 (1972).

for all losses regardless of his or her actions. Thus a contributory negligence defence is necessary to provide appropriate incentives on the victim to take reasonable care. For the same reason that the negligence standard results in efficient care, a contributory negligence defence which leaves the entire loss with the claimant if he or she fails to act non-negligently is necessary. Thus, in theory, negligence and strict liability with a contributory negligence defence are symmetrical liability rules and equally efficient.

The major difference between fault and strict liability is who bears the remaining losses when the cost-justified level of care is taken – under negligence, it is the victim; under strict liability, it is the injurer. Thus a choice between the two can be made without adversely affecting the incentives for optimal deterrence.

Application of the Hand Test can also at times point to strict liability. The so-called *Rylands* v. *Fletcher*[42] rule imposes 'strict' liability for (loosely speaking) ultra-hazardous activities such as flooding reservoirs. The rule makes sense since for those activities – leaking dams and munitions factories – the injurer is likely to be best able to evaluate the risks and take avoidance actions. Expressed in terms of the marginal Hand Test, ultrahazardous activities have a very high P and a high L. The rule in *Rylands* can be viewed not as strict liability as such but a presumption that in those cases the injurer is the least cost avoider. But it is also the case that *Rylands* is concerned with controlling activity levels in the same sense as nuisance law generally. The strict liability is simply based on a decision not about care but that the hazardous activity bear the costs, leading to less such hazardous activity irrespective of whether the optimal level of care is taken.

DUTY REVISITED

Generally the economics of tort treats the duty question as an irrelevance. All questions of liability are reduced effectively to an application of the marginal Hand Test. However, one hypothesis is that law's focus on the defendant's duty and the pockets of no liability may be explained by the care/activity distinction discussed above.

The twist in the analysis comes from the need to take account of both the external costs and external benefits of hazardous activities. If an activity imposes external costs it will be overexpanded when there is no liability. However, this claim cannot be made if at the same time it generates external

[42] [1861–73] All ER Rep. 1.

benefits. If the external benefits exceed the external costs, then the activity is not overexpanded; if external costs exceed external benefits then it is; if they cancel each other out to zero the activity level is efficient. Indeed, a workable rule is that in the absence of liability a hazardous activity is overexpanded, underexpanded, or optimal depending on whether the ratio of external costs to benefits is greater, less than, or equal to one, respectively.

This simple set of 'rules' can now be applied to a range of tort situations. The law's focus on injurer's care – and hence fault liability – is appropriate where total costs and external benefits more or less net out. This is the case for the major classes of torts – workplace and traffic accidents – the external cost-benefit ratio is likely to be around one and hence fault liability is unlikely to generate excessive and inefficient activity levels.

Trespass and other intentional torts fit the framework. The intentional infliction of harm implies that external costs greatly exceed benefits (a ratio greater than one) and therefore the overriding presumption is to deter all types of trespass by imposing strict liability.

Negligence misrepresentation also fits this theory. Information has public good aspects and is often used by individuals who have not paid for it. Publicly available information can both benefit and harm those who use it. If a producer of information were forced to pay the costs of those harmed by the use of the information they have freely acquired, but reaps no return for the benefits it generates to the same class of people, then clearly this would result in an inefficiently low level of resources devoted to information production. Thus, the external cost-benefit ratio of professional information given outside an exchange relationship is likely to be is less than one and suggests that the provider should not be under a duty of care. This supports the law's reluctance to impose liability for every misstatement and confines it to those in a 'special relationship'. The special relationship can be treated as covering situations where the maker of misstatements is likely directly or indirectly to benefit from reliance on these and liability should therefore attach to those made negligently using the Hand Test.

This can be illustrated using the leading case on negligent misrepresentation, *Hedley Byrne & Co. Ltd* v. *Heller & Partners Ltd* (1964),[43] which expanded liability for negligent misstatement to parties in a special relationship. Prior to that there was no liability. The economic grounds for liability and its limitations related to whether the information imparted is valuable, the impact that a liability rule makes in generating more informed representations and the asymmetry in the treatment of the loss and gains

[43] AC 465.

from information production and dissemination. There are, however, many externalities which are beneficial to third parties. A new *invention* has many spillover effects which provide profitable opportunities to other individuals but in respect of which the inventor does not receive a reward. If we have a legal regime which only penalises inventors for errors causing harms but imperfectly compensates them for the benefits they confer on society, there will be an inefficient level of inventive activity.[44] This asymmetry provides an additional ground for limiting liability when it would lead to crushing liability. Misinformation can cause loss, some of which could be avoided cost-effectively if the party who provided the information took greater care. But there are some forms of information which have public good features and which create severe non-appropriability problems. A news service reports widely on world affairs by publishing a news bulletin. This information is valuable and widely distributed; many businesses gain from it. Occasionally it gets things wrong and individuals suffer losses as a result of acting on the information. But it would not be economically desirable to impose liability for such a loss because this would inhibit news services from carrying on an activity which (overall) benefits society.

The simple analysis appears even to explain some of the prominent areas of statutory modification of tort. Take the case of railway liability. The benefits generated by railways in the nineteenth century were significant. The steam engine brought immense direct economic and social benefits to the local community, including farmers. Indeed, in some countries the farms would not have been there but for the expansion of the railways to bring people to the frontier and carry their produce to markets. However, the benefits which railways generated could not be appropriated by the railway company; therefore there were large uncompensated external benefits. Thus the external cost-benefit ratio of railway activity was likely at its formative stages to have fallen well below one and hence may explain why railways were immune from liability for spark damage in the nineteenth century, albeit by statute and provided that they took adequate abatement measures.

CAUSATION, FORESEEABILITY AND REMOTENESS

Tort liability is also based on the concepts of causation, foreseeability and remoteness. These are confused areas of the law which have little to do with

---

[44] W. Bishop, 'Negligent Misrepresentation: An Economic Reformulation', in P. Burrows and C. G. Veljanovski, *The Economic Approach to Law*, London: Butterworths, 1981, chapter 7.

how accidents are caused and a lot to do with limiting the scope and extent of liability. The confusion is heightened because the terms have a chameleon-like quality and are used interchangeably. As Bob Hepple observes: 'The confusion between the concepts of fault, factual causation, remoteness, and the notional duty of care lie[s] at the heart of the formal incoherence of negligence law'.[45] Here some considerations raised by this aspect of negligence are discussed, with no pretence at an adequate resolution.[46]

Lawyers distinguish between *physical* causation and *legal* causation. The former is a factual matter and the latter a legal concept often (it seems) reflecting 'policy judgments' by the Courts designed to restrict liability or the extent of damages (remoteness). From an economic perspective the complexity of the law seems unnecessary because:

1. Physical causation is not sufficient to determine liability – every accident or harm is jointly or severally caused. This applies even when the victim is passive and has no ability to avoid the accident by his conduct.
2. Duty, breach and causation can all be covered by the application of the marginal Hand Test, albeit to more complex factors which involve many parties, intervening events and different types of damages.
3. Causation, foreseeability and remoteness are *ex ante* (probabilistic) notions. However, a number of legal causation tests, such as the 'but for' test, are *ex post* concepts and therefore not economically correct.

In the run-of-the-mill tort case, determining the physical causation (or what in US law is called 'proximate cause') is not difficult. It is only where there are a number of parties, or there has been some latent or supervening event, that the issue becomes complicated.

Foreseeability and Remoteness

Let us deal with remoteness and foreseeability first.

Remoteness has a common sense meaning of something very unlikely. In economic terms, it is an event with a very low probability of occurrence. However, a low-probability event is not itself sufficient to avoid taking care, or being liable. The costs of precautions must be compared to the risks and

---

[45] B. Hepple, 'Negligence: The Search for Coherence', 50 *Current Legal Problems*, 69–94 (1997) 82.

[46] G. Calabresi, 'Concerning Cause and the Law of Torts: An Essay for Harry Kalven, Jr.', 43 *University of Chicago Law Review*, 69–108 (1975); M. Grady, 'Proximate Cause and the Law of Negligence', 69 *Iowa Law Review*, 363–449 (1984); S. Shavell, *The Economic Analysis of Accident Law*, Cambridge, MA: Harvard University Press, 1987, chapter 5; W. M. Landes and R. A. Posner, *The Economic Structure of Tort Law*, Cambridge, MA: Harvard University Press, 1987, chapter 8. Cf. R. W. Wright, 'Actual Causation vs Probabilistic Linkage: The Bane of Economic Analysis', 14 *Journal of Legal Studies*, 435–456 (1985).

the losses. If the change in the likelihood of something occurring is very small, it may not be efficient to hold the defendant liable if the costs of an increase in precautions are positive, albeit low. This will be the case if the increase in care is more costly than the reduction in the expected losses.

An economic version of remoteness can be firmed up. Suppose there are two potential types of losses – Loss 1 (L_1) and Loss 2 (L_2) which are the same at, say, £200 ($L_1 = L_2 = £200$). Further, assume that both have the same initial probability of happening of 50 per cent – i.e. $P_1 = P_2 = 0.5$. However, the impact of additional precautions in reducing the likelihood of these two losses occurring is very different. The defendant could reduce the risk of the first loss by 0.25 (ΔP_1) by taking care that costs £20 (ΔB). The same £20 (ΔB) spent on increased care in the second case will reduce the probability of the second loss only by (ΔP_2) 0.02. Thus for the same loss and the same increased cost of care the expected reduction in the probability of occurrence – and, hence, the expected loss – are radically different. In the first case it is 0.25 × £200 ($\Delta P_1 L_1$) equal to a reduction in expected loss of £50. In the second case it is 0.02 × £200 ($\Delta P_2 L_2$) giving a reduction in expected loss of only £4. Plugging these figures into the marginal Hand Test generates the following impact on total costs of taking greater care:

Loss 1: £20 − £50 = −£30

Loss 2: £20 − £4 = £16

Thus for Loss 1, the impact on total costs is that the £20 leads to a £50 reduction in expected losses and hence an overall total cost saving of £30. The loss in economic terms is not 'remote'. However, for Loss 2 the £20 safety expenditure has a very small effect on expected losses – the expense of £20 in greater care reduces expected loss by only £4, so that total costs increase by £16 by taking the greater precaution. It is not efficient for the defendant to take greater care to avoid the loss since it costs more than it saves. Loss 2 can be considered 'too remote'. Thus avoiding the first loss is efficient but the second not. Translated into legal terms, the first loss is foreseeable while the second is 'too remote'.

In other cases the actions of the defendant, even if negligent, might not have avoided the harm either because it had a zero impact on the likelihood of the accident happening (no link between the carelessness and the loss), or the loss would not have been avoided even if the defendant had not been negligent.

Table 5.1 *Conditional probabilities and losses*		
Successive accidents	Conditional probability	Expected loss (£)
First collision	0.5	50.00
Second collision	0.25	25.00
Third collision	0.125	12.50

In other cases it is the actual loss that is so freakish and unusual that had liability been imposed the defendant would not have taken additional care. In order to deal with these cases we need to introduce a new concept – the **conditional probability**. A conditional probability is the likelihood of an adverse event happening, given the risk of an initial or prior adverse event occurring. Suppose that driving carelessly has a 0.5 probability of a head-on collision. Conditional on this event the car may career across the road hitting and damaging a second vehicle which then knocks down an electricity pylon, blacking out the city for several hours. These losses are all the result of the one negligent act and *ex post* all are real and some of the successive losses quite large. Thus looking at them *ex post* suggests that they would inevitably feature prominently in the decision as to liability and damages. But from an *ex ante* perspective the effects of these successive losses are, again, radically different.

To illustrate and simplify, assume that each successive loss occurs with a 50:50 chance and each imposes the same monetary loss of £100. The effect is that each successive loss occurs with a lower conditional probability because it is less likely than the previous one. As a result of its lower conditional probability the expected value of successive losses progressively declines and carries less weight in the marginal Hand Test.

This is illustrated in table 5.1, which calculates the conditional probabilities and expected loss for an identical £100 loss for each successive accident. The immediate loss is multiplied by the 50:50 chance, the next consequential collision by 50:50 times 50:50, giving a conditional probability of 0.25, and so on. It can be seen from this way of looking at the problem that the successive losses, although equally real and with the same *ex post* magnitude and probabilities, are in *ex ante* terms much smaller. Based on the assumption of each having a 50:50 chance the conditional probabilities halve and the expected losses arising from each successive £100 loss also halve. Clearly, if these probabilities are very low then this will mean that the expected losses of successive sequential accidents will have a very small impact on the standard of care – and, correspondingly, on the actions of potential tortfeasors.

In applying some versions of the foreseeability principle the courts will inquire into the *ex post* link between the negligent act of the defendant and the harm. This is cast in terms of whether 'but for' the defendant's negligent act the accident would on the balance of probabilities have occurred. For example, in *Barnett* v. *Chelsea and Kensington Hospital*[47] a doctor was accused of being negligent in failing to diagnose that a patient was suffering from acute arsenic poisoning. The doctor was found not to be liable because the court held that even if the doctor had made a correct diagnosis the poisoning was so advanced that the patient's life would not have been saved. The decision has an economic rationale based on the previous logic. The incremental probability of saving the patient by the doctor exercising greater care – or, indeed, any care – at the time the patient was admitted was zero. Therefore, the incremental reduction in the likelihood of avoiding death was zero. Applying the marginal Hand Test would have raised not lowered total costs.[48]

The legal concept of 'remoteness' also seeks to place limits on the type of consequences and the extent of the damages that a negligent act inflicts. Remoteness often restricts recovery for certain types of damage. For example, the courts have traditionally been reluctant to allow recovery for pure economic loss even if caused by a negligent act (see below). This contrasts with personal injury cases where the general rule is that the defendant takes his victim as he finds him, and is liable for all the resulting losses no matter how 'remote'. Thus if a hammer is negligently dropped on a passer-by, whether it bounces off his head or staves it in, the defendant is liable for the full loss to each victim. In such 'eggshell skull cases' the court does not regard injury to an especially vulnerable victim as 'too remote'.

In other areas, the law is more confusing. In *Wagon Mound (No. 1)*[49] the defendant's employee negligently discharged furnace oil into Sydney Harbour, fouling the claimant's wharf and halting repairs on two ships. After the claimant was advised that the oil would not ignite he resumed welding. A piece of molten metal ignited the oil and the fire destroyed the two ships. The Court held that while damage by pollution was foreseeable, damage by fire was not. The wharf owner could not claim damages. In

---

[47] [1969] 1 QB 428.
[48] This analysis may not be correct if doctor care is not a divisible activity in the sense that two types of patients cannot be distinguished.
[49] [1961] AC 388.

the simple framework developed above, the conditional probability of fire given the oil spill was very low so that imposing liability was not likely to encourage greater care.

This contrasts with earlier ruling in *Re Polemis and Furness, Withy & Co.*,[50] which had almost identical facts. A stevedore employed by the defendant dropped a plank into the hold of the claimant's ship which contained petrol vapours. The falling plank caused a spark and the resulting fire destroyed the ship. The court rejected the argument that the defendant should not be liable for a loss which was not 'foreseeable'. Here the Court imposed a direct physical causation approach. *Wagon Mound (No.1)* overturns this to limit liability to 'directly' caused injuries which are 'foreseeable'. In economics it would seem that given the factual finding that a falling plank would not result in igniting petrol vapours *Re Polemis* was wrongly decided, since there was no way that a defendant would have been induced to take preventative measures.

In *Hughes* v. *Lord Advocate*[51] the Court required that the source of the danger be foreseeable although not the actual details of how it came about. In this case, Post Office workers (during this period the Post Office ran the telephone network in the UK) uncovered a manhole in the road, covered it with a temporary shelter and went for a tea break. Four paraffin lanterns were placed around the area to warn off people. Two boys carried one of the lamps into the shelter to explore, one tripped and the lamp spilled paraffin which vaporised and exploded, burning a boy. The workmen were found negligent for leaving the manhole unattended. The court found that the lamp was a foreseeable source of danger even though the type of accident (an exploding lamp) was not. The distinction between burning and explosion was presumably a fine one.

Simultaneous joint torts

The position where the victim is injured at the same time by two negligent acts is settled in law – both are liable. If two hunters negligently discharge their shotguns injuring the same victim but it cannot be determined which hit first, both parties will be held liable.[52] Or, if a pedestrian is hit on a Pelican crossing (cross walk) first by a negligently driven car travelling in one direction and then, while injured on the ground, by a vehicle travelling too fast in the other direction, both drivers would be jointly and severally liable for the full damages.[53]

---

[50] [1921] 2 KB 560. [51] [1963] AC 837.
[52] The US case of *Summers* v. *Rice* 119 P 2d (1948). [53] *Fitzgerald* v. *Lane* [1987] QB 781.

The law's approach is efficient. If the law makes each party liable if they fail to act non-negligently, and the negligence standard is set at the efficient level of care, then each will act non-negligently to avoid being found liable.

However, under the 'but for' causation test used by the courts neither would be liable. In the double shooting case, the first defendant could validly argue that 'but for' his negligence the victim would have been killed by the other shooter; while the second defendant could with equal validity make the same claim. Therefore neither 'caused' the harm.[54]

Successive torts

In cases involving sequential harm or successive 'joint' torts, English law adopts an incremental damage rule. In *Performance Cars Ltd* v. *Abraham*,[55] a car had been negligently damaged, requiring a repaint, when it was later negligently hit by the second defendant. The Court held that the second defendant was liable only for the incremental loss caused by hitting the damaged car. In probabilistic terms this seems correct and a generalisation of two principles which are partially applied – that the injurer takes his victim as he finds him and cannot be liable for greater losses than he inflicts. From an economic perspective making the second tortfeasor liable for the full loss would not increase the level of precaution or alter his or her behaviour.

ECONOMIC LOSS

Many negligent acts cause financial losses – a worker digs up a power cable which blacks out a city; a bank manager makes a statement which he has not properly checked, causing losses to a customer who has relied on it; a contractor is careless in requiring others to undertake remedial work, raising the costs of a whole project. Historically the Courts have been reluctant to provide compensation for purely financial losses and have

---

[54] Interestingly, the economist David Friedman argues provocatively that the 'but for' test provides the correct economic outcome that neither party is liable. He states that to hold otherwise is to fail to recognise the difference between marginal and average costs. He illustrates this by pointing out that the total value of water is very high but its price is low because it is determined by the marginal costs of an additional litre of water. Intellectual provocation aside, the legal solution is correct. This is because the loss is a legitimate cost of each party's activity. Thus if this is a recurring situation the damage payment may not directly affect care while shooting, but would affect the level of participation in shooting where multiple shooters are present (that is, our care/activity distinction). D. D. Friedman, *Law's Order: What Economics Has to do with the Law and Why it Matters*, Princeton: Princeton University Press, 2000.

[55] [1961] 1 QB 33.

searched for 'control mechanisms' to limit liability. More recently, liability for economic loss has expanded but the rules and exceptions are confusing, leaving lawyers (and economists) scrambling to explain the law.[56] Here some of the issues raised by economic loss cases are examined for accidents between strangers.[57]

Not all uncompensated third-party losses are real social costs. As the courts have observed, 'the philosophy of the marketplace presumes that it is lawful to gain profit by causing others economic loss'.[58] This was discussed in chapter 2 where a distinction was drawn with pure offsetting wealth transfers or pecuniary externalities where one party's loss is offset by another's gain. They involve wealth transfers which cancel out and do not increase the costs faced by society. If someone builds a better mousetrap other mousetrap producers will be injured and resources will be rechannelled to higher-valued uses. Some resources will decline in value, firms producing old mousetraps may go bankrupt and real distress may be caused to workers and owners of these firms. But these losses are a direct result of resources being shifted to higher-valued uses and are taken into account by the producer of new mousetraps in the price he pays for inputs previously used by the old mousetrap producers. The losses are, in effect, a signal to the old mousetrap makers that their products are no longer in demand and that the resources they are using should be released to the rest of the economy. To award compensation for such losses would clearly be inefficient since it would (a) create incentives for the perpetuation of obsolete industries and production processes; and (b) stifle innovation and market efficiency if all new industries had to pay compensation to those producers they displaced (even though they could in principle, otherwise the new mousetraps would not be Kaldor–Hicks efficient).

Weller & Co. v. *Foot-and-Mouth Disease Research Institute*[59] provides a good example of the pecuniary externality distinction. An infection of foot-and-mouth disease escaped from the research institute as the result of their negligence. Cattle in the surrounding areas were affected and the Minister of Agriculture, acting under statutory powers, closed the local cattle markets in which the claimants carried on business as cattle auctioneers. Since the claimants owned no cattle or other property at risk it was held that no duty of care was owed to them in respect of their loss of business profits.

---

[56] W. Bishop, 'Economic Loss in Tort', *Oxford Journal of Legal Studies*, 1–33 (1982).
[57] The discussion here is based on D. Harris and C. G. Veljanovski, 'Liability for Economic Loss in Tort', in M. Furmston (ed.), *The Law of Tort*, London: Duckworth, 1986.
[58] Goff L., *Leigh and Sullivan Ltd* v. *Aliakmon Shipping Co. Ltd* [1986] AC 785.
[59] [1966] 1 QB 569.

The loss was a pecuniary externality. The negligent act of the defendant did not directly affect Weller's production activities, but only led to a change in the market for their services – a fall in demand, which was similar to falls caused by other fluctuations in the market resulting from non-negligent factors. The social cost was the technological externality of harm suffered by the farmers, whose loss in physical production would be met by the undisputed liability of the defendant towards them. The compensation paid to the farmers preserved their incentive to raise cattle in the future, and the Institute's liability to them provides incentives to similar research institutes to take care. Since the farmers' real rate of return was unaffected the auctioneers suffered no permanent or long-run diminution in the demand for their services or their productive capacity.

A more difficult case is *Spartan Steel and Alloys Ltd* v. *Martin Co. (Contractors) Ltd.*[60] In the course of excavating a road with a power shovel the defendant's employees damaged a cable that carried electricity to the claimant's factory, with the result that the electricity supply was cut off for fourteen hours. The factory worked continuously so the deprivation of power caused serious loss of output. Molten metal in the furnace at the time of the cut-off was damaged, leading to a loss of profit (the first loss); a further loss of profit resulted from the loss of four further melts which could have been carried out during the period of the cut-off (the second loss). The Court of Appeal awarded damages for first loss since it arose from physical damage to the metal; but by a majority denied damages for the second loss.

Spartan Steel involves a technological externality (a social loss) in respect of all the losses suffered by the claimant. Electricity is an input into the production of steel; the negligent disruption of electricity involves a loss to society because electricity is a non-storable commodity not available for productive use during the period of power failure. Moreover, the second loss was a real loss since the facts indicated that the foundry had no spare capacity to make up lost production. If, on the other hand, the foundry could have made up the lost production then there were grounds for ignoring the loss as being *de minimis*.

The denial of recovery for pure economic loss may have been based on other considerations. It could be that the factory was the least cost avoider of the second loss, and that a non-recovery rule gives the claimant an incentive to take avoidance measures. The only precaution which the claimant could realistically have taken was to install a back-up generator.

---

[60] [1973] QB 27.

This is a 'lumpy' investment; one either has a generator or not, especially given the requirements of steel production. The decision whether to invest in a back-up generator will be governed by the full risk of power failure from any cause and not merely that caused through a third person's negligence. Since negligently caused power failure is only a small part of the total risks faced by the manufacturer non-recovery will provide only a small incremental incentive for greater precautions to be taken. The defendant, on the other hand, is clearly the cheapest cost avoider. Not only are the costs of care low – checking plans or maps and digging more carefully – but the level of care can be varied in relatively fine graduations. Thus, imposing liability on the defendant would provide an incremental incentive for him to take greater avoidance measures.

Excluding recovery may have some logic on the grounds of marginal deterrence. In cases where negligence can give rise to mass claims for pure economic loss, making the defendant liable for all losses would not encourage **marginal deterrence** but would impose a crushing liability. In *Spartan Steel* the cut power line provided electricity to the claimant's factory, but should a contractor be liable for all losses if the power line supplies 1,000 factories, or an entire city? In network or public utility industries such as gas, water, telephone and electricity, a moment's inadvertence can impose large aggregate losses on masses of people. Consider the following example. A worker negligently cuts a power cable to an industrial estate. His employer will be vicariously liable for any loss imposed by the courts. Assume that the cost to the employer of taking greater care was £10 in checking plans and giving his employee explicit instructions. The loss to the electricity company is £2,000 in repair costs and the lost profits to business from not being able to continue production are £60,000. Assume further that if the employer had taken the extra care costing £10, the risk of cutting the power cable would have been dramatically reduced from 1 in 50 to 1 in 1,000, and that further reductions in the risk were not practical (either for the builder or for the electricity supplier): that is, for an expenditure of £10 the expected losses to the power company would have been reduced from £40 ($= 0.02 \times £2,000$) to £2 ($= 0.001 \times £2,000$), a saving of £38 at a cost of £10. Clearly, if the employer is burdened with the loss to the electricity company he would take the efficient level of care since *ex ante* prevention is cheaper than paying compensation (£10 is less than £38). In this example, the efficient level of care can be achieved by imposing liability for only a fraction of the losses. This type of situation seems to arise in many 'public utility' cases: the (marginal) costs of avoiding the accident are insignificant in relation to the anticipated losses. Where this is the case the increase in deterrence achieved by burdening the defendant with more of the losses is insignificant.

This proposition is reinforced by uncertainty as to the magnitude of harm caused by a single negligent act. The likelihood of cutting a power cable and the damage this may cause to the cable will be fairly predictable. But the extent and nature of the losses to industry as a result of the power disruption may not. Moreover, the conditional probability that the negligent act will result in a mass of claims will generally be low. Take an example. Suppose, as before, that the probability of damaging the cable is 1 in 50 and that the conditional probability (if the cable is damaged) of causing a £2,000 loss of profits to three firms is another 1 in 50. If the injurer is potentially liable for the latter loss he will discount it more heavily in his calculations because it is more unlikely or 'remote'. The probability of actually inflicting the loss is 1 in 2,500 and the expected loss only 80 pence (1/2,500 × £2,000 = 80 pence). The same £2,000 loss to the power company is, however, valued at fifty times this amount because it is 50 times as certain to occur – i.e. a 1 in 50 chance rather than a 1 in 2,500 chance. Thus the more probable the anticipated loss the greater the impact it will have on the amount of care exercised by the potential injurer and the more likely that it will be cost-effective for him to avoid causing the loss.

This can be worked into a general proposition. Under the negligence rule the care required of the defendant increases with the number of people potentially affected, the magnitude of their anticipated losses and the like-lihood that they will occur. It also depends on the way the risk decreases with additional care and on the costs of care. If a negligent act can be avoided at modest cost then efficient deterrence can generally be achieved by limited liability – imposing liability for all the losses does not achieve greater safety but consumes resources in shifting the loss and processing claims. This will typically be true where the costs of care are low and the conditional probability of widespread liability is also low, which is precisely the situation which judges have in mind when fearing the consequences of relaxing the exclusionary rule in cases of pure economic losses.

The prospect of crushing liability itself may also affect the incentive for deterrence. This claim has several components. First, the marginal deterrence effect will be affected if the defendant is judgment-proof or protected by limited liability. If a company anticipates the risk of paying for astronomical damage it will take into account the fact that its liability is limited by the company's assets. It will therefore discount the possibil-ity that it might have to pay large compensation, and may not take any more care than it would if its liability were more limited. That is, potential defendants will discount anticipated damages not only by the probability of an accident occurring but also by the probability that they will actually have to pay the amount claimed. Thus, burdening the defendant with all losses will not achieve additional deterrence.

Further the prospect of very large claims may have another perverse incentive effect. Firms threatened with mass-liability claims may deliberately underinsure in order to discourage litigation, since the likelihood of being sued depends on the claimant's estimate of the defendant's solvency and insurance coverage. Unless the law compels potential defendants to carry liability insurance for unlimited amounts, rules on insolvency may undermine the deterrent effect of liability rules.

Finally, tort liability is expensive to operate and one of the goals is to balance deterrence against the legal costs – to the parties and of the courts. The judicial fear of a multiplicity of claims provides one express policy justification for denying recovery of economic loss, although this argument alone is not convincing.[61]

PRODUCT LIABILITY

Liability rules in exchange relationships have different effects because negotiations over liability and compensation are possible. This implies, first, that the accident and compensation levels are more likely to be efficient; and, second, that the impact of any change in the law is likely to be minimised by offsetting adjustments in market prices.

Consider the choice between *caveat emptor* ('let the buyer beware'), and *caveat venditor* ('let the seller beware') or manufacturers' liability.[62] It is frequently argued in the legal literature that strict manufacturers' liability is efficient because the costs of product defects are reflected in the price of the product and this gives the producer a direct incentive to avoid selling defective products. In the absence of liability, consumers bear the costs, and the producer has no incentive to improve the quality of his product. This analysis is wrong, as we would suspect from the Coase Theorem.

---

[61] An interesting though not persuasive explanation for the exclusionary rule is that it minimises wasteful litigation by encouraging 'channelling contracts' which allocate liability beforehand. M. J. Rizzo, 'A Theory of Economic Loss in Torts', 11 *Journal of Legal Studies*, 281–310 (1982).

[62] R. McKean, 'Products Liability: Implications of Some Changing Property Rights', 84 *Quarterly Journal of Economics*, 611–626 (1970); H. Demsetz, 'Wealth Ownership and the Ownership of Rights', 1 *Journal of Legal Studies*, 223–232 (1972); W. Y. Oi, 'The Economics of Product Safety', 4 *Bell Journal of Economics*, 2–28 (1973); K. Hamada, 'Liability Rules and Income Distribution in Product Liability', 66 *American Economic Review*, 228–234 (1976).

In product liability cases the direct or indirect contractual relationships between manufacturer and consumer/victim allow the existing price to adjust in light of the legal position, and to reflect the victims' demand for greater product quality and safety. This creates an implicit market for product quality which, when transactions costs are negligible, neutralises the effects of changes in the legal rule affecting quality,[63] even though the price of the product differs under the two liability rules.

The neutrality of product liability law can be illustrated using some figures. Assume that one-third of products are defective and as a result there is an expected loss of £2 per unit sold. The retail price of the product is £6. The value of a non-defective unit of the product to the consumer is therefore £4(= £6 − £2). If the manufacturer is held fully liable for product defects the consumer pays the £6 which consists of £4 for the non-defective good and £2 for the warranty to cover the costs of the defective units. The net price to both sides is £4 – the manufacturer gets £6 but has to pay out on average £2 compensation; the buyer pays £6 but effectively gets only £4 worth of the good.

Suppose now the law changes to *caveat emptor*, so that the manufacturer is no longer legally liable for the defects. Does this change the outcome? In this case the buyer is prepared to pay the manufacturer only £4 because he or she now has to cover (self-insure) the £2 expected costs of the defective units. The price of the product falls from £6 to £4. This decline in the observed retail price does not mean that the costs of defective products are no longer taken into account by the manufacturer. The full price (equal to retail price plus expected losses due to defective units) is still influenced by demand, supply and the actions/choices of the parties. The seller will be as well off as before the change in the rule, and no better. This is because although he no longer has to compensate for the defective products, consumers are no longer prepared to pay £6 but only £4. The buyer is as well off as with manufacturers' liability because while he gets the product cheaper he must either bear the loss or insure against defects. The expected costs or (actuarially fair) insurance premium would be £2. Thus while the change in the law has altered the price of the good, it has not altered much else – the *ex ante* distribution of income between manufacturer and buyer, the quantity of the good bought and the incentives on the part of the manufacturer to improve the safety of the product all remain the same.

---

[63] For a comprehensive but critical discussion of the economics of product liability, see J. Stapleton, *Product Liability*, London: Butterworths, 1994.

There are number of qualifications to this analysis. First, the regimes differ in terms of the compensatory arrangements. Under a no-liability regime there will be uncompensated harm to consumers, especially if they fail to insure against product losses. Thus *ex post* the wealth position of consumers will differ. Second, *caveat emptor* may not be efficient if consumers do not accurately perceive the likely risks and losses. This will mean that (a) consumers buy inadequate insurance, (b) the producer does not bear the full costs of its defective products and (c) consumers make the wrong purchase decisions. However, in these cases, a move to manufacturers' liability will not fully deal with all the consequences of market failure. This is because where information is imperfect and losses differ, consumers will still base their purchases on incorrect information about product quality.[64]

Another relevant factor in evaluating product liability laws is consumer misuse. It would be reckless for the producer or the law to offer compensation regardless of the circumstances or the behaviour of the consumer. A law which made the seller responsible for every error, mistake and deficiency in his product regardless of its use by the consumer would not only drive up the price and perhaps put the seller out of the market but would also reduce the incentive of consumers to make better-informed decisions and to take care in the use of the product. The solution could in fact be worse than the disease, resulting in fewer products because manufacturers' costs have risen, and more damage because consumers are less careful in their use of the product (see chapter 4 on warranties).

EMPLOYERS' LIABILITY

Next to traffic accidents, the largest category of tort claims are from work accidents. Workplace accidents also have a special role in the history of the common law and its reform. They have given rise to a considerable amount of legal doctrine, and the alleged inadequacy of tort has led to successful lobbying to replace the complex rules governing liability for workplace injuries with compulsory workers and more generally no-fault liability compensation schemes.[65]

---

[64] M. Spence, 'Consumer Misperception, Product Failure and Product Liability', 44 *Review of Economic Studies*, 561–572 (1977).

[65] There have been a number of previous attempts to examine the economic structure of employers' liability: L. M. Friedman and J. Ladinsky, 'Social Change and the Law of Industrial Accidents', 76 *Columbia Law Review*, 50–82 (1967); G. T. Schwartz, 'Tort Law and the Economy in Nineteenth Century America: A Reinterpretation', 90 *Yale Law Journal*, 1717–1775 (1981); R. A. Epstein, 'The Historical Origins and Economic Structure of Workers' Compensational Law', 16 *Georgia Law Review*, 775–819 (1982).

Employers' liability law prior to 1880

The first recorded case in England of a worker suing his employer for personal injury was *Priestly* v. *Fowler* in 1837.[66] From that date to about 1880 the courts developed an elaborate doctrinal structure governing the eligibility of injured workers to sue their employers for damages. An employer had a general duty to take reasonable care to select competent employees and not to expose his workers to unreasonable risks. This duty was qualified by three defences available to the employer. First, under the doctrine of common employment the employer was not liable if the injury was caused by the act or negligence of another worker. Secondly, an employer could avoid liability if it could be shown that the injury arose from a risk that was incidental and 'ordinary' to the job and that the employee was, or should have been, aware of the risk. This was known as the doctrine of *volenti non fit injuria* (voluntary assumption of risk). Finally, where the injury was the proximate or direct consequence of the action of the injured worker he was barred from recovering damages from his employer. That is, the contributory negligence of the injured worker acted as a complete defence. The employer was liable only for his personal negligence in such matters as directing the use of a dangerous machine,[67] or setting out safety regulations that did not protect his workers.[68] But if he hired a competent worker who subsequently acted in a careless and negligent way, he could not be successfully sued by the injured worker.

Risk, negligence and common employment

The analysis of employers' liability is similar to product liability, which we discussed above. To summarise, in the job market the wage rate will reflect the marginal value productivity of the labour and the conditions on the job. Where there are risks of an industrial accident (or disease), workers will demand a wage premium for the hazards. In a competitive labour market this compensating wage differential will reflect the expected injury costs of workers. Where the employer offers no accident compensation, the worker will demand a higher wage.[69] The higher wage bill will, as in the product

---

[66] (1837) 1 M&W. 1 (Ex Ch).   [67] *Roberts* v. *Smith* (1857) 26 L.J. Ex. 319.

[68] *Vase* v. *Lancashire & Yorkshire Rly Co.* (1858) 27 LJ.

[69] Useful evidence from the English coal mining during the heyday of the common law can be gleaned from evidence given to the House of Commons *Select Committee on Employers' Liability*, 1877. Briggs, a colliery owner, stated that in West Yorkshire miners received, as a result of the efforts of their labour union, 1 penny to 2 pence extra in wages per tonne of working coal in districts where it was deemed

liability case, consist of a premium to compensate for the risk of industrial injury and death. The premium will also give the employer an incentive to improve workplace safety because a reduction in the likelihood of an accident will reduce his wage bill. If the law makes the employer liable for all his workers' injury costs then his wage bill will fall but his labour costs will be unaffected because what he was previously paying as a risk premium in the form of higher wages is now an explicit insurance premium to cover workers' compensation. Thus changes in the liability rules will not have an impact on total compensation levels, safety levels and labour costs.

This theory of accident-related wage rates and the neutrality of the law was known to English and US common law judges, and shaped employers' liability law. For example, Bramwell LJ., foreshadowing the Coase Theorem, pointed out in his extra-judicial writings that making employers' liable for injuries to workers would not have any effect:

Every prudent employer of labour will immediately draw up a form to be signed by his workmen that the master shall not be liable for his fellow-servant's negligence. Or he will hire men somewhat on these terms: – 5s. a day, and no liability; 4s. 6d., and liability; and I will either compensate you myself or apply 6d. to insurance for you.[70]

This model of the labour underpinned tort liability for industrial accidents in the nineteenth century. English judges adhered to the view that workers were compensated for the hazards of the job, and therefore it was not necessary to make the employer liable. The worker was deemed at law to have agreed to run all the ordinary and incidental risks of his employment, including the negligence of fellow workers.[71] In *Farwell* v. *Boston & Worcester Rail Corp*, the leading US case on common employment this is clearly stated:

he who engages in the employment of another for the performance of such specified duties and services, for compensation, takes upon himself the natural and ordinary risks and perils incident to the performance of such services, and in legal presumption, the compensation is adjusted accordingly.[72]

---

prudent to work with a safety lamp. This increased his wage bill by £2,000, to £3,000 per annum. Wages were also higher for men who worked underground than for those who worked on the surface (6 shillings 4 pence compared to 3 shillings 6 pence per day) for shorter hours (eight hours compared to ten hours). C. G. Veljanovski, 'The Impact of the Employers' Liability Act 1880', paper to the inaugural meeting of European Association of Law and Economics, Lund, March 1984.

[70] Cited in T. Beven, *The Law of Employers' Liability*, London: Waterlow Bros. & Layton, 1881, 124. Bramwell is reacting to the Employers' Liability Bill which modified the common law.

[71] *Hutchinson* v. *York, Newcastle and Berwick Rail Co.* (1850) 5 Exch. 343; *Bartonshill Coal Co.* v. *Ried* (1858) 3 Macq. (H.L. Sac) 266. Bramwell rejected this fiction of implied contract terms stating that 'it should be expressed thus: that he [the worker] had not contracted to be indemnified'. *Select Committee on Employers' Liability*, para. 1127 (1861).

[72] (1842) 45 Mass. (4 Met) 49.

These 'natural and ordinary risks' included the negligence of fellow workers. Again *Farwell* makes the point:

Where several persons are employed in the conduct of one common enterprise or undertaking, and the safety of each depends much on the care and skill with which each one shall perform his appropriate duty, each is an observer of the conduct of the others, can give notice of any misconduct, incapacity or neglect of duty, and leave the service if the common employer will not take such precautions and employ such agents as the safety of the whole party may require. By these means the safety of each will be much more effectively secured than could be done by the resort to the common employer for indemnity in case of loss by the negligence of each other.[73]

Thus the common employment defence was absolute. The worker could complain but if he did not like the risky behaviour, he should leave. If he complained and was injured before he left then he could not claim because in law he was presumed to have agreed to the risk.[74] That is, the law read into his employment contract an implied term that he would indemnify his employer against work-related accidents, including those caused by fellow workers.

Posner has suggested that the doctrine of common employment provided 'a powerful incentive for industrial safety' because it gave the worker a 'strong incentive to report careless workers to their supervisors'. However the market sanctions that judges had in mind were far less direct – excessive labour turnover combined with an accident-related wage premium were the financial incentives that led employers to improve safety levels[75]. Moreover, in England the scope of the defence was very wide so as to make it impossible for workers to effectively monitor the care exercised by fellow workers. The common employment defence successfully defeated claims involving workers on separate trains employed by the same company,[76] a worker employed to secure barges injured while passing through his employer's warehouse,[77] a labourer pushing a tram,[78] a guard on a train injured by a

---

[73] *Farwell* v. *Boston & Worcester Rail Corp* 59. This reason was not, however, the basis for Judge Shaw's decision in *Farwell*. At a later point in the judgment Shaw states: 'The master . . . is not exempt from liability because the servant has better means of providing for his safety . . . but because the implied contract of the master does not extend to indemnify the servant against the negligence of anyone but himself.'

[74] *Assop* v. *Yates* (1858) 27 L.J. Ex. 156; *Gallagher* v. *Pipes* (1864) L.T. 718.

[75] Posner, 'A Theory of Negligence', 44–45. See also W. M. Landes and R. A. Posner, 'The Positive Economic Theory of Tort Law', 15 *Georgia Law Review*, 851–894 (1981).

[76] *Hutchinson* v. *York, Newcastle and Berwick Rail Co.* (1850) 5 Exch. 343.

[77] *Lovell* v. *Howell* (1876) 34 L.T. 183.   [78] *Lovegrave* v. *London R.R.* (1864) 10 L.TI 718.

derailment caused by the negligence of a worker maintaining the tracks[79] and a labourer injured while climbing defective scaffolding constructed by another worker.[80] In all these cases there was no practical opportunity for the injured worker to have observed the conduct of the person who injured him, let alone monitor that behaviour. In England the scope of the doctrine was determined not by the worker's opportunity to monitor but the nature of the risk. Guards on trains could anticipate derailments caused by the careless and negligent laying of tracks and demand a compensating wage premium. The English courts also applied the defence to the negligence of workers in supervisory positions. In many US States a distinction was made between servants exercising no supervision and those 'clothed with control and management'. Under the so-called Vice-Principal rule the employer was vicariously liable for the negligence of the latter. This distinction was not followed in England.[81]

Some further theory

The economics of workplace safety is more complicated than the 'judicial economics' of Bramwell would indicate. This is because it involves at least three parties – employer, fellow workers and supervisors. Thus in the workplace incentives have to be given to all three. This is an additional complication of the hierarchical nature of the firm. Superior employees – managers, safety officers, foreman – have a responsibility delegated by the employer to take care of the workers under their control and ensure a safe working environment. This gives rise to a principal–agent problem.

This complex 'triangle' could in principle be dealt with by a perfectly operating labour market. If bargaining were costless, workers could bribe one another to take reasonable care and the employer could 'pay' supervisory employees to ensure that the implicit safety arrangements are enforced. But such a system of bargains would tend to break down because of free rider problems. The payment by one worker to another to exercise greater care would tend to benefit all workers with whom the latter came into contact.

---

[79] *Waller* v. *South Eastern R.R. Co.* (1863) 8 L.T. 325. See also *Tunney* v. *Midland and R. R. Co.* (1868) L.R. 1.

[80] *Assop* v. *Yates* (1858) 27 L.J. Ex. 156.

[81] Firmly established in *Wilson* v. *Merry* (1868) L.R. 1 (HL Sc) 326. The English Employers' Liability Act 1880 altered the doctrine of common employment by imposing on the employer limited liability for the negligence of foremen and superintendents to workers under their control, thus effectively reversing the rule in *Wilson* v. *Merry*. The Act, with modifications, remained in force until 1948 when the doctrine of common employment was finally abolished.

As a consequence each worker would be undermotivated to monitor and pay for greater care and the level of worker safety would thus be inefficiently low.

Liability rules could substitute for such *ex ante* payments. This was the legal position. An injured worker had a right of action against a negligent worker. Yet there is no reported case of a worker being sued by a fellow worker for negligence. The generally accepted reason was that workers as a class were impecunious, lacking sufficient funds to pay reasonable compensation. Obviously if the defendant was judgment-proof the threat of liability would not deter him from being negligent. The common law simply ignored these free rider and enforcement difficulties.

There is another aspect of the economics of employers' liability law. The worker's employment contract is with the employer and only indirectly through its terms with other workers. Indeed, the firm (and employer) can be viewed as an institution designed to facilitate 'team production' and the employer as receiving profits for ensuring that the team works efficiently.[82] In property rights terms the employer is the residual claimant who maximises profits by ensuring that all inputs are coordinated and operate efficiently together. Applying this to common employment, it is the employer who should resolve the free rider problem by acting as an intermediary between workers in the collection of bribes and enforcement of the implicit safety contract between the employer and all workers. If workers are aware that a substantial proportion of accidents are the result of fellow workers' carelessness they will demand a wage premium. Thus the costs of these accidents will be reflected in the employer's wage bill. If the risks are reduced, the employer benefits because his wage bill is lower. Thus he will have a direct pecuniary incentive to control the care exercised by workers. The lower wage bill is in fact the payment by workers to the employer to enforce the implicit terms of the safety contract which workers would have entered into with one another had free rider and transactions costs difficulties been insignificant. The employer enforces the implicit safety contract by monitoring the actions of his workers, employing supervisors to direct their work and sacking or disciplining workers who have been careless.

Applying this to accidents caused by fellow and superior workers would result in a different view of the law. It would not imply a term of a worker's

[82] A. Alcian & H. Demsetz, 'Production, Information Costs, and Economic Organization', 62 *American Economic Review*, 777–795 (1972).

employment contract indemnifying the employer from a fellow worker's negligence. The implied term is more likely to be that the employee does not agree to the negligence of his fellow workers or to an employer not properly acting to monitor, control, and take action when given notice of an employee's risky behaviour would be in breach of the implied term. Further, an employee would not agree to the risk of negligence inflicted by supervisors. Thus an efficient law would not apply the common employment defence to negligence by fellow workers or superior employees.

Volenti *and deterrence*

Prior to the 1880s it was assumed by the courts, that workers agreed to run all the risks, including negligence. *Smith* v. *Baker*[83] altered the law in 1881. In order for the defence of *volenti* to be successful it was necessary to show that the worker knew of, and comprehended, the *risk*.

The defence of voluntary assumption of risk makes economic sense in a properly functioning labour market. It allows workers to accept employment in risky jobs and the assumption is that they receive compensation in the form of a higher wage, all things equal. The pre-1880 rules went further. The employer was liable only if he knew of the danger and the employee was totally ignorant. If both were unaware of the danger, the worker was held to have consented to bear the risk.[84] As one judge observed, these rules have a perverse incentive effect on care: 'if . . . personal knowledge . . . be necessary . . . the more a master neglects his business and abandons it to others, the less he will be liable.'[85]

It is clear that where workers are ill informed or ignorant of the risks, the market solution will not be efficient. The risk-related wage premium will be insufficient and therefore labour costs and the pressure for more safety understated. However, while employers' liability more accurately imposes costs and risks on the employer, it does not correct workers' misperceptions. Thus irrespective of the law, workers will still make the wrong employment decisions based on inaccurate risk assessments. The only way this can be corrected is by directly informing workers of the correct risks. However, if the employer is made liable and it is assumed that he can make a better assessment of the risks, then employers' liability will lead to a more efficient level of workplace safety, all things equal. This may not always be the case.

---

[83] (1891) AC 325.   [84] *Hall* v. *Johnson* (1865) 34 L.J. Ex. 22; *Allen* v. *New Gas Co.* (1876) 1 Ex. D. 251.
[85] *Clark* v. *Holmes* (1862) 7 H.N. 937.

Indeed, there are cases where employers' liability can reduce workplace safety.[86]

DEATH AND PERSONAL INJURY DAMAGES

Under common law the award of damages seeks to give the wronged victim a sum of money that restores him or her to the position before the accident. It is often said that damages seek to make the victim 'whole'. Damages are given for all related past losses (such as medical and hospital expenses, the adaptation of equipment, possessions and the home), future net losses (of earnings, wages, profits) incurred as a result of an injury and for pain and suffering and loss of amenity (non-pecuniary losses).

Meaning of 'full compensation'

The term 'full compensation' has a number of possible meanings when examined more rigorously. At least three different notions can be considered.

The first is to take a literal view of full compensation as a monetary sum that reimburses all financial losses and a further sum which literally returns the victim to the same total utility level as he or she had prior to the injury. For minor injuries this may be possible but where limb and life are involved it is not. Restoring a person's pre-accident utility for a severely disabling injury through monetary compensation may simply be impossible, and where possible may involve astronomical sums. Further, if the victim is killed there is no sum that can return him or her to life.

Second, full compensation can be interpreted as the insurance coverage an individual would have purchased had he or she been fully aware of the risks and losses of an injury. This measure of full compensation in theory would demand knowledge of the claimants' attitudes to risk and preferences. If he or she is risk neutral or risk averse they would take out full coverage (if at actuarially fair premia), and if risk preferring underinsure the loss. The courts do not take the risk preferences of the claimants into

---

[86] This 'perverse outcome' may arise because of the difference between marginal and average worker injury costs. Under no employer liability the wage rate is set by the marginal worker, who will be the one with the highest injury costs. Under employers' liability, the employer responds to the way his compensation payment schedule alters with the claims' record of the firm. Since the firm's compensation bill or insurance premium is determined by the average compensation paid to injured employees, it follows that the average injury costs will be below the marginal injury costs. The move from no liability to full employers' liability may thus result in a higher injury rate, and more not fewer accidents. See further C. G. Veljanovski, 'The Employment and Safety Effects of Employers' Liability', 29 *Scottish Journal of Political Economy*, 256–271 (1982).

account nor, with some notable exceptions, whether they are insured or not – or, indeed, whether the defendant is insured. Further where non-pecuniary losses are involved, the insurance coverage purchased by victims may fall far short of even full monetary compensation (see the discussion of pain and suffering on p. 233).

The final measure of damages is that required to achieve appropriate deterrence. This requires that the full social costs of the negligent act be internalised. Often *ex post* compensation measures and deterrence damages will be similar and there is no trade-off or compromise. However, in other areas the differences are marked. The clearest cases are between the damages for wrongful death and pain and suffering. In the former case the court use a net loss to survivors' measure which is inadequate.

Optimal deterrence damages

From a deterrence viewpoint the economic measure of damages will in general consist of three components:
1. **Past monetary losses**   Covering out-of-pocket expenses resulting from the accident, such as medical expenses
2. **Future earnings/income**   The lost value of the output as conventionally measured by the net present discounted value of the stream of income
3. **Economic loss**   The WTP for greater safety, which measures the monetary value of statistical life (VSL) or a statistical injury (VSI).

The courts take into account 1, partially 2, but ignore 3, the most important component from the economists' deterrence perspective.

Future income losses

Common law damages covering 2 reflect the net loss to those injured, and in death cases to survivors, thus underestimating the full economic losses. If restricted to these amounts, as victims are, they effectively treat the victims of negligence in the same manner as slaves valued only for their net contribution to output. If used in cost-benefit assessments it would show that projects that caused the death of pensioners and dependents were Kaldor–Hicks efficient.

Further, the English courts have in the past severely undercompensated injured victims because of the use of high discount rates.[87] Following,

---

[87] For an assessment of this head of damages from an human capital perspective, see N. K. Komesar, 'Toward a General Theory of Personal Injury Loss', 2 *Journal of Legal Studies*, 457–486 (1973).

several Law Commission reports, the courts have abandoned their hostility to actuarial principles and adopted a more economically sound approach to discounting future losses to reflect the time value of money.

Many accident victims suffer continuing losses which impair their ability to work full time or as productively as before the accident. In such cases the judge must estimate the future lost stream of income and then discount this by some interest rate to arrive at a fixed sum to award the victim 'full' compensation. Instead of using economic and actuarial evidence the English courts use a *multiplier/multiplicand* approach. This has two parts. First, the judge determines the victim's annual loss arising from the accident. This is a question of fact. The court must then convert this annual sum into the present value (PV) of the claimant's prospective loss. The judge does this by first determining a multiplier which he uses to multiply the victim's annual loss. The implied multiplier takes into account two factors – discounting to reflect the time value of money and an allowance for what lawyers refer to as the 'vicissitudes of life'. Discounting is required to adjust for the fact that the victim is in early receipt of his compensation and can invest it over the remaining period of his life to earn an annuity. The courts also adjust future losses downwards to take account of contingencies that would reduce the loss attributable to the accident – such as remarriage, the prospect of unemployment and the likelihood of illnesses that could shorten life. These factors are not explicitly taken into account in any principled arithmetic fashion. Rather, the judge (juries no longer sit in civil trials in England and Wales with the exception of libel actions) arrives at a figure that in his judgment provides 'full' compensation.

Before recent reforms of the law in this area, the courts used multipliers between 5 to 18, with 15 often the maximum. These were low, and led to severe undercompensation of injured victims. Indeed, most legal practitioners and judges remained ignorant of the discount rate implied by multipliers until Lord Diplock revealed in 1979 that it was around 4–5 per cent.[88] Kemp and others have argued both for the increased use of actuarial evidence and for a discount rate of around 1.5–2.3 per cent per annum.[89]

To illustrate the impact of the court's choice of multiplier (and implicitly discount rate), consider the facts in *Mitchell* v. *Mulholland*[90] (incidentally a case in which Lord Justice Edmund Davies ruled that the expert evidence of economists was inadmissible). Using the 'multiplier' approach, the Court

[88] *Cookson* v. *Knowles* (1979) AC 556 (H.L.).
[89] D. Kemp, 'The Assessment of Damages for Future Pecuniary Loss in Personal Injury Claims', *Civil Justice Quarterly*, 120–132 (1984).
[90] [1971] 2 All ER 1205 CA.

of Appeal multiplied the claimant's net pre-trial loss of annual earnings by 14 to arrive at total damages of £20,833.

If an economist had been asked to compensate the claimant in *Mitchell* v. *Mulholland*, he would have ended up much better off.[91] Using the claimant's annual net earnings at the time of injury (£1,255), and assuming that he worked until retirement at 65, that productivity grew at 1 per cent per year and using a discount rate of 2 per cent, the estimated loss to the injured victim at the date of the injury would have been £36,438. If interest were added the figure would have increased to £48,262 at the time of the trial in 1969, and to £54,243 at the time of the Court of Appeal decision in 1971. The final sum calculated using these reasonable assumptions is more than two-and-a-half times that awarded to the claimant by the court. This area of undercompensation has now been recognised as inappropriate and recent reforms have resulted in personal injury damages in the UK being placed on sounder actuarial principles using the so-called 'Ogden Tables'.[92]

Nonetheless, in the estimation of losses there is still a way to go to achieve full compensation through the English courts. Recent research based on compensation for personal injury in 100 court cases found that if better account had been taken of labour market information, as used by US courts, there would have been an increase of 25 per cent on average in the compensation payments, although in one-quarter of cases the award would have been lower.[93] The research found that compared to the US method of calculating future personal injury losses, the UK courts:

- consistently under-compensate men
- underestimate the impact of disability on post-injury earnings potential, and therefore undercompensated on this account
- may undercompensate people from ethnic minorities for future loss of earnings
- do not always determine the 'multiplier' accurately.

---

[91] A. M. Parkman, 'The Multiplier in English Fatal Accident Cases: What Happens when Judges Teach Economics?', 5 *International Review of Law and Economics*, 187–197 (1985).

[92] Government Actuary's Department, *Actuarial Tables for Use in Personal Injury and Fatal Accident Cases* (the Ogden tables), 5th edn., London: Stationery Office, 2004. Named after the first chairman of a multi-disciplinary working party, Sir Michael Ogden, QC, which advised the UK Government Actuary's Department in the preparation of actuarial tables. The tables provide an aid for those assessing the lump sum appropriate as compensation for a continuing future pecuniary loss and consequential expense.

[93] R. McNabb, R. Lewis, H. Robinson and V. Wass, 'Court Awards for Damages for Loss of Future Earnings: An Empirical Study and an Alternative Method of Calculation', 29 *Journal of Law and Society*, 406–435 (2002); R. McNabb, R. Lewis and V. Wass, 'Methods for Calculating Damages for Loss of Future Earnings', *Journal of Personal Injury Law*, 151–165 (2002).

The judicial calculation of damages also falls down in providing adequate incentives for injurer care. This is because netting out tax payments and other avoided expenditure by victims externalises a considerable amount of losses which should be borne by the injurer. For example, in death cases the loss-to-survivor measure nets out tax payments and expenditure by the deceased because these are items which are not incurred by the victim as a result of the accident. However, these are nonetheless losses generated by the costly interaction which should be borne by the injurer.

Death and WTP

The common law ignores the WTP of the victims to avoid a statistical injury or death. In chapter 2 we saw that the economist values life and limb by the WTP of potential victims for greater safety.[94] Thus, if potential victims are more or less identical and each willing to pay £20 to reduce the probability of death by 1 in 1,000, the WTP to avoid a statistical death would be £200,000 = £200/0.001.

Estimates of the value of a statistical life and injury (VSL and VSI, respectively) have come from studies of risk premia in wage rates for hazardous jobs and occupations,[95] survey methods[96] and other risk taking behaviour of individuals. For example, empirical studies of the wage/risk trade-off using US labour market data have estimated VSLs of between US $1 million and $6 million.[97] It has proved harder to obtain estimates of VSIs because of the variety of such injuries and the fact that injury risks tend to be highly correlated, making it difficult to identify the risk premia associated with each individual type of injury.[98]

There have been several studies using UK data estimating the VSL which have used labour market data (table 5.2). The studies by Marin

---

[94] T. Schelling, 'The Life You Save May be Your Own', in S. Chase (ed.), *Problems in Public Expenditure Analysis*, Washington, DC: Brookings Institution, 1968, 127–162; E. J. Mishan, 'Evaluation of Life and Limb: A Theoretical Approach', 79 *Journal of Political Economy*, 687–705 (1971).

[95] W. K. Viscusi, *Employment Hazards: An Investigation of Market Performance*, Cambridge, MA: Harvard University Press, 1979. It is interesting that in the USA this approach to damage valuation, known as 'hedonic demage' estimation, has been used in trial proceedings: J. O. Ward and T. R. Ireland (eds.), *The New Hedonics Primer for Economists and Attorneys*, Tucson, AZ: Lawyers & Judges Publishing Co., 1996.

[96] M. W. Jones-Lee, *The Economics of Safety and Physical Risk*, Oxford: Blackwell, 1989.

[97] W. K. Viscusi, J. M. Vernon and J. E. Harrington, *Economics of Regulation and Antitrust*, 2nd edn., Cambridge, MA: MIT Press, 1995, chapter 20; K. W. Viscusi and W. J. Eldy, 'The Value of a Statistical Life: A Critical Review of Market Estimates throughout the World', New York: National Bureau of Economic Research Working Paper 9487, February 2003.

[98] W. K. Viscusi and M. Moore, 'Workers' Compensation: Wage Effects, Benefit Inadequacies and the Value of Health Loss', 49 *Review of Economics & Statistics*, 249–261 (1988).

Table 5.2 *Estimates of value of statistical life*

Study	Probability of death (mean)	Pre-tax WTP in 1979 prices (£000)
Marin and Psacharopolous (1982)	na	£1,079–£3,735
Veljanovski (1981)	221.3 × 10⁻⁵ (man years)	£2,352–£3,186
Needleman (1980)	4.5 × 10⁻⁵	£87–£502

Sources: A. Marin and G. Psacharopolous, 'The Reward to Risk in the Labour Market: Evidence from the United Kingdom and a Reconciliation with other Studies', 90 *Journal of Political Economy*, 827–853 (1982); C. G. Veljanovski, *Regulating Industrial Accidents – An Economic Analysis of Market and Legal Responses*, University of York, D.Phil. thesis, 1981; L. Needleman, 'Valuation of Changes in the Risk of Death by Those at Risk', 48 *Manchester School*, 229–254 (1980).

and Psacharopolous and Veljanovski (see table 5.2) are based on econometric analysis of wage data to disentangle the implicit risk premium paid for hazardous jobs in the UK manufacturing sector. These have generated implicit VSL estimates of between about £1–£3.7 million at 1979 prices, or £3.4 – £12.6 in 2005. Needleman's study (see table 5.2) uses 'condition money' and risk data for a sample of construction workers during a week in July 1968. He derives a lower post-tax estimate of the VSL of £73,533 (at 1979 prices). Needleman's estimate gives a VSL twenty times that of the undiscounted earnings of the workers at risk in his sample. This suggests that the law seriously underestimates the VSL.

Pain and suffering

The common law compensates victims for non-pecuniary losses. Compensation is given for pain and suffering which includes both the physical pain of injury and the mental element of anxiety, fear, embarrassment and distress surrounding injury and loss of amenity, which is anything which reduces the claimant's enjoyment of life – the artist who cannot see; the jogger who cannot walk. Since the Administration of Justice Act 1982 the courts also award damages for 'suffering caused by injuries or likely to be caused by awareness that the expectation of life has been . . . reduced'. In Britain over half of the value of tort compensation is for non-pecuniary losses and the proportion is relatively higher for smaller claims.

In the legal literature, there are sharply contrasting views on the legitimacy of damages for pain and suffering. Some say that being a purely subjective loss, it is beyond economic valuation. Atiyah argues that 'economists normally value things by looking for the market price but there is no "market" for pain',[99] continuing that '[T]here appears to be simply no way of working out any relationship between the value of money and damages awarded for pain and suffering'.[100] Calabresi, on the other hand, emphasises administrative costs and deterrence. He accepts that in principle these damages are susceptible to valuation, but that their idiosyncratic nature makes individual determinations expensive and where these losses are great: 'the victim is the cheapest cost avoider, if for no other reason than that he is more likely to be aware of the risk than anyone else'.[101] Others have argued that the real purpose of damages for pain and suffering is to defray part of the claimant's legal fees or as the 'price of settlement'.

Some simple economics can shed light on optimal damages and compensation for pain and suffering. Assume that the financial loss is £20,000 inflicted on a risk averse person – i.e. one that attaches a disutility to variations in his or her wealth. Such an individual will fully insure his or her loss if offered insurance at an actuarially fair premium. Now assume that in addition the prospective injury will be permanently incapacitating or grossly disfiguring, so that it has significant long-term psychological effects. One formal way of modelling this is to assume that the accident will reduce both the victims' wealth *and* the utility he derives from any given level of wealth.[102] More specifically, the injury causes a fall in the marginal utility of money at each level of wealth.[103] What insurance coverage would this prospective victim buy? Intuitively one would say more than £20,000 to cover the financial loss plus the additional utility loss. However this is incorrect. Such an individual offered insurance at an actuarially fair premium would not buy insurance to cover the full financial loss. This

---

[99] P. S. Atiyah, *Accidents, Compensation and the Law*, London: Weidenfeld & Nicolson, 1977, 188.

[100] Atiyah, *Accidents*, 187.

[101] Calabresi, *The Costs of Accidents: A Legal and Economic Analysis*, New Haven: Yale University Press, 1970, 215–225.

[102] R. Zeckhauser, 'Coverage for Catastrophic Illness', 21 *Public Policy*, 149–72 (1973); P. Cook and D. Graham, 'The Demand for Insurance and Protection: The Case of Irreplaceable Commodities', 91 *Quarterly Journal of Economics*, 143–200 (1977); S. Shavell, 'Theoretical Issues in Medical Malpractice', in S. Rottenberg (ed.), *The Economics of Medical Malpractice*, Washington, DC: American Enterprise Institute, 1978, 35–64.

[103] Assume that we are considering an individual's welfare (utility) in two different states – utility when healthy, $U(w, p)$ and utility when injured $V(w, p)$, where w represents the victim's financial wealth and p the risk of injury. The condition for optimal insurance coverage, assuming an actuarially fair premium at a rate of $p/(1-p)$, is $\Delta U = \Delta V$, where ΔU and ΔV are the marginal utility of wealth when uninjured and injured, respectively.

is because such a person values the compensation payment when injured at less than the same £20,000 when healthy. This implies that 'full compensation' under the law, if interpreted as equivalent to optimal insurance coverage, would not pay out a separate sum for pain and suffering[104] and be less than the financial loss suffered.

This is a dramatic and counterintuitive conclusion. There are two possible resolutions. The first is the full compensation means exactly that – restoring the person to the *ex ante* total utility in so far as money can. In economic terms, this would mean giving the individual more than his financial losses to raise the post-injury utility to the level enjoyed before the injury. The second interpretation is that pain and suffering damages are designed to provide additional deterrence to avoid permanently disabling accidents. This has an economic justification. Using the same model which showed that the individual would underinsure it can be shown that the WTP to avoid an accident inflicting significant psychological losses would be higher, all things equal. The reason is simple – since there is a larger (uncompensated) utility loss, such an individual is prepared to pay more to reduce the likelihood of an injury.[105] Interestingly recent empirical work indicates that in the USA pain and suffering damage awards in physical assaults and consumer product-related injuries provide an implicit WTP to avoid a statistical death of between $1.4 and $3.8 million (in 1995 dollars), which is similar to estimates of the value of statistical life derived in the US labour market and other studies.[106]

There are several implications arising from this, admittedly simplified, treatment of pain and suffering damages. The first is the reiteration of the point made above: that the same measure of damages cannot simultaneously

---

[104] This discussion assumes in addition that $\Delta U > \Delta V$ for any given w – i.e. the marginal utility attached to the same pound – is less when injured than when healthy. The 'underinsurance' result arises because, in buying optimal coverage, the individual equalises the marginal utility of different states by transferring income between them. Since the marginal utility in the insured state is lower for each level of wealth, less income is transferred from the healthy to the injured state. There could be situations where injury increases the marginal utility of money – perhaps the art collector who finds hours of quiet contemplation enjoyable, and the injury affords him the time to do this. If injury has this effect then the prospective victim would insure for a sum greater that the economic loss.

[105] The WTP for reductions in the probability of injury is given by the expression $U - V/[(1 - p) \Delta U + p\Delta V]$ – i.e. it is determined by the ratio of the *ex post* loss of utility from injury $(U - V)$ divided by the expected marginal utility of income $((1 - p)(\Delta U + p\Delta V))$. Since the utility loss with state-dependent utility functions is larger than when utility is unaffected by injury, and the expected marginal utility lower, the WTP is greater than in the absence of pain and suffering. See C. G. Veljanovski, *Regulating Industrial Accidents – An Economic Analysis of Market and Legal Responses*, University of York, D Phil Thesis, 1981, 42–43.

[106] M. A. Cohen and T. R. Miller, ' "Willingness to Award" Nonmonetary Damages and the Implied Value of Life from Jury Awards', 23 *International Review of Law & Economics*, 165–181 (2003).

satisfy the two or more goals, whether they be full compensation, optimal insurance coverage, or deterrence. Second, although the common law purports to be a compensatory mechanism, the award of pain and suffering is more consistent with deterrence – i.e. WTP to avoid one statistical permanently disabling injury. Having said this, the magnitude of pain and suffering payments, coupled with evidence that they tend to be more prominent for smaller awards, is not easily rationalised.

EXEMPLARY DAMAGES

The general rule is that damages are compensatory. In some very limited cases supra-compensatory damages, known as exemplary damages (or in the USA punitive damages), can be imposed. *Rookes* v. *Barnard* held that they may be awarded for:

wrongful conduct which has been calculated by the defendant to make a profit for himself which may exceed the compensation payable . . . To mark their disapproval of such conduct and to deter him from repeating it, then it [the jury] can award some larger sum.[107]

The award of exemplary damages in English law is rare and deeply controversial.[108] The latter is so because the overt purpose of damages in tort is to compensate, not to penalise.

Perhaps the most well-publicised award of punitive damages is the 'The Ford Pinto case' in the USA.[109] The car maker Ford became aware of a design fault in the fuel system which increased the risk of an explosion if the Pinto model was involved in an accident. Ford decided not to alter the design because it would cost $11 per vehicle even though it would save 180 lives. The aggregate cost of the modification was $137 million but avoided a much lower sum of $49.5 million in damage and related claims.

For an economist, penalising those who compare the costs of safety with those of liability is the core logic of the ability of tort to deter. This judicial justification for exemplary damages makes little sense since this is what tort law is designed to encourage. Clearly, though, US juries saw the matter in a very different light.[110]

---

[107] [1964] AC 1129, 1127–1128, per Lord Devlin.
[108] For a historical account of the development of punitive damages in England, see T. B. Colby, 'Beyond the Multiple Punishment Problem: Punitive Damages as Punishment for Individual, Private Wrongs', 87 *Minnesota Law Review*, 583–678 (2003).
[109] *Grimshaw* v. *Ford Motor* Co. 19 Cal App 3d (1981); G. T. Schwartz, 'The Myth of the Ford Pinto Case', 43 *Rutgers Law Review* 1013–1068 (1991).
[110] C. R. Sunstein *et al.*, *Punitive Damages – How Juries Decide*, Chicago: University of Chicago Press, 2002.

Notwithstanding this, there are two cases where supra-compensatory damages are economically warranted.

The first is where the tort is intentional in situations with low transactions costs. That is where the tortfeasor seeks deliberately to inflict loss and bypass the market mechanism. In these cases the gain to the tortfeasor may exceed the loss of the victim and purely compensatory damages would be insufficient. To deter such intentional acts, an additional sum must be imposed. This is examined in more detail in the analysis of crime in chapter 6.

The second justification is where the litigation rate or the probability of damages being imposed on a tortfeasor is less than certain. If the litigation rate is less than one, then the *ex ante* damage (the expected damages) which influence the actions of the parties is less than the *ex post* damages and there will be underdeterrence. In order to boost *ex ante* damages to take account of the fact that many actions are not pursued or are too costly to pursue through the courts or even an out-of-court settlement, the actual damages must be some multiple of those required to compensate the victim fully. For example, if only 50 per cent of tort cases are brought to court then deterrence efficiency requires that damages be multiplied by the reciprocal of the conviction rate c – i.e. $1/c = 2$ or a double damage rule.[III] This follows from the economics of optimal deterrence.

The '$1/c$ multiplier rule' is not straightforward in cases of private enforcement and tort litigation. This is because the likelihood of litigating a claim is a function of the likely damage award. Thus, for example, if the initial litigation rate is 10 per cent and the optimal damage multiplier is set at 10, the prospect of getting ten times your losses will result in more victims suing and the litigation rate rising dramatically. This would mean that there would be overdeterrence and excessive litigation costs. Thus the level of exemplary damages in tort would have to be calculated taking account of the impact on the litigation rate, and would result in a much lower optimal multiplier.

[III] A. M. Polinsky and S. Shavell, 'Punitive Damages: An Economic Analysis', 111 *Harvard Law Review*, 869–962 (1998); R. Crasswell, 'Deterrence and Damages: The Multiplier Principle and its Alternatives', 97 *Michigan Law Review*, 2185–2238 (1999). *Cf.* C. R. Sunstein, D. Schkade and D. Kahneman, 'Do People want Optimal Deterrence?', 29 *Journal of Legal Studies*, 237–253 (2000). See also A. Duggan, 'Exemplary Damages in Equity', 26 *Oxford Journal of Legal Studies*, 303–326 (2006); K. N. Hylton, 'Punitive Damages and the Economic Theory of Penalties', 86 *Georgia Law Journal*, 421–472 (1998). For an interesting discussion, see G. Calabresi, 'The Complexity of Torts – The Case of Punitive Damages', in M. S. Madden (ed.), *Exploring Tort Law*, Cambridge: Cambridge University Press, 2005, chapter 10.

Hylton and Miceli[112] have examined this feedback effect to show that the necessity for a large damage multiplier in tort may not be necessary. They distinguish between the optimally deterring multiplier which internalises the sum of accident and litigation costs and the socially optimal multiplier, which minimises the sum of injuries, injury avoidance and litigation costs.[113] These multipliers move in the opposite directions. The deterrence multiplier which was discussed above (and in chapter 2 and will be further in chapter 6) increases as litigation costs increase because the litigation rate declines. The socially optimal multiplier decreases as litigation becomes more expensive because the marginal deterrent effect of increased litigation falls when the costs of litigation are taken into account. That is, where litigation is costly, less should take place. Thus what Hylton and Miceli call the socially optimal multiplier takes into account that supra-compensatory damages increase the litigation rate and hence litigation and enforcement costs. Hylton and Miceli suggest that given that supra-compensatory damages raise the litigation rate, the deterrence multiplier using US data is about 1.6 whereas the socially optimal multiplier is lower at around one, i.e. single damages. Thus paradoxically, and somewhat counterintuitively, the presence of significant litigation costs leads to single or compensatory damages being approximately efficient.

FURTHER TOPICS AND READING

• The first formal analysis of liability rules was by Brown, using a game theoretic approach (J. Brown, 'Toward an Economic Theory of Liability', 2 *Journal of Legal Studies*, 323–349 (1973)). The now vast literature is reviewed in S. Shavell, *The Economic Analysis of Accident Law*, Cambridge, MA: Harvard University Press, 1987; W. M. Landes and R. A. Posner, *The Economic Structure of Tort Law*, Cambridge, MA: Harvard University Press, 1987; R. Cooter, 'Economic Theories of Legal Liability', 5 *Journal of Economic Perspectives*, 11–30 (1991). See also the earlier works by R. A. Posner, *Tort Law – Cases and Economic Analysis*, Boston: Little Brown, 1982; R. L. Rabin (ed.), *Perspectives on Tort Law*, 2nd edn., Boston: Little Brown, 1983. See also C. G. Veljanovski, 'Legal Theory, Economic Analysis and the Law of Torts', in W. Twining (ed.), *Legal Theory and Common Law*, Oxford: Blackwell, 1986, chapter 12.

---

[112] K. N. Hylton and T. J. Miceli, 'Should Tort Damages be Multiplied?', 21 *Journal of Law, Economics & Organisation*, 388–416 (2005).

[113] There is a vast literature on the economics of legal conflict and settlement, starting with J. P. Gould, 'The Economics of Legal Conflict', 2 *Journal of Legal Studies*, 279–300 (1973). For a survey, see R. D. Cooter and D. L. Rubinfeld, 'Economic Analysis of Legal Disputes and Their Resolution', 27 *Journal of Economic Literature*, 1067–1097 (1988).

- Paralleling the development of the common law was a growing body of statutory law regulating the conditions of employment and industrial safety, beginning with the Factory Act 1844. Unlike the common law, the Factory Acts and similar legislation in other industries relied on criminal prosecutions and financial penalties to induce employers to comply with their provisions. However, although to all outward appearances the common law and statute law differed there were nonetheless similarities – e.g. fines paid as compensation to injured workers, private enforcement through the use of informers rather than government inspectors, a tendency to use fault-type standards to determine whether an offence should be prosecuted and a preference for negotiating compliance rather than prosecuting. Modern safety legislation has moved away from this approach to rely on public enforcement and criminal prosecution.
- The striking example of adaptive behaviour is the response of drivers to compulsory seat belt legislation. There is now strong evidence that seat belt laws have not had a significant impact on road safety. This is not because they are ineffective in protecting vehicle occupants, but because they encourage risk taking and accidents by drivers. Seat belts reduce driver risks and injuries, causing them to adjust their behaviour by driving faster and with less care. This causes fewer driver fatalities and more pedestrian fatalities and injuries and damage to vehicles, thus increasing accident costs. The economics of the drivers' decision is simple to explain. Compulsory seat belt laws decrease the expected loss to those wearing belts and lead to driving more aggressively. Empirical analysis of compulsory seat belt legislation in the USA[114] and other countries[115] confirms that occupant deaths per accident fell substantially as expected, but that this reduction was entirely offset by more accidents to those not protected by seatbelts – i.e. pedestrians and cyclists.
- Shavell lists four principal considerations in the choice between tort and safety regulation: (1) asymmetric information of risks; (2) capacity of the injurer to pay (i.e. judgment proofness); (3) probability of private suit; and (4) relative magnitude of legal and regulatory costs. Liability rules are attractive if the victim is better informed, potential defendants can afford to pay claims, there is a high probability of suit should there be an actionable wrong and legal process costs are low. Where these factors are weak, then public law techniques become more attractive either as a replacement for the common law or as a complement to it. S. Shavell, 'Liability for Harm versus Regulation of Safety', 13 *Journal of Legal Studies*, 357–374 (1984).
- Liability at common law is usually personal liability. That is, the person committing the act causing the injury is the one to pay damages. There are pockets of vicarious liability (or *respondeat superior*) where an employer is strictly liable for the torts of his servants and employees in the course of their employment. This has been justified on the grounds that employers have 'deep' pockets and

---

[114] S. Peltzman, 'The Effects of Automobile Safety Regulation', 83 *Journal of Political Economy*, 83 677–725 (1975).
[115] J. Adams, *Risk*, London: Routledge, 2005. Safety researchers call this 'risk compensation'.

employees are judgment proof and hard to sue. However, the economic rationale for vicarious liability relates to the hierarchical nature of the firm and the role that employers play in controlling their employees to act in a safe manner. L. A. Kornhauser, 'An Economic Analysis of the Choice between Enterprise and Personal Liability for Accidents', 70 *California Law Review*, 1345–1392 (1982); A. O. Sykes, 'The Economics of Vicarious Liability, 93 *Yale Law Journal*, 1231–1280 (1984).

- Some have argued that it is not necessary to discount future income losses in personal injury claims. This is called the *offset rule*. The proposition is based on the claim that labour productivity, and hence future income, equals the discount (interest) rate and hence both cancel out (offset) one another. If correct, this would greatly simplify damage calculations. For analyses and evidence supporting the offset rule, see R. A. L. Carter and J. P. Palmer, 'Real Rates, Expected Rates, and Damage Awards', 20 *Journal of Legal Studies*, 439–462; 'Simple Calculations to Reduce Litigation Costs in Personal Injury Cases: Additional Support for the Offset Rule', 32 *Osgoode Hall Law Journal*, 197–223 (1994).

- There has been limited empirical research on whether tort laws deter accidents. For a comprehensive though dated review of empirical evidence, see D. Dewees and M. Trebilcock, *The Domain of Tort Law: Taking the Facts Seriously*, Toronto: Oxford University Press, 1997; P. Cane, *Atiyah's Accidents, Compensation and the Law*, 6th edn., Cambridge: Cambridge University Press, 2002; D. Harris, D. Campbell and R. Halston, *Remedies in Contract and Tort*, 2nd edn., Cambridge: Cambridge University Press, 2002. For a more recent empirical analysis which concludes that tort does not deter, see P. H. Rubin and J. M. Shepherd, 'Tort Reform and Accidental Deaths', Emory University, 2006.

CHAPTER 6

Crime

Men are not hanged for stealing horses, but that horses may not be stolen.

Marquis of Halifax, 1750

The basis of criminal law is the common law – the intentional torts of assault and battery, conversion, (theft) and fraud. These remain torts but have been embodied in statute and are publicly enforced by the state – the police, public prosecutors and the courts. Here the nature of crime and criminal penalties are explored.

FEATURES OF CRIMINAL LAW

The basic features of the criminal law can be set down rather crudely as acts which are:
1. intentional
2. prosecuted by the state
3. based on a higher standard of proof than civil law – beyond reasonable doubt rather than the lower civil standard of 'on the balance of probabilities'
4. attract sanctions designed to punish offenders and which are not paid to their victims – i.e. criminal sanctions are 'decoupled' from victim compensation
5. attract both monetary, and non-monetary sanctions such as imprisonment.

These basic features of the criminal law suggest that there is something different about a crime which makes victim enforcement and compensatory damages inadequate. In law sanctions imposed under criminal law expressly seek to punish offenders rather than compensate victims. This is clearly not the focus of tort law. Indeed, in Anglo-American legal systems the victim of a crime also has an action in tort for damages. This suggests that the law recognises that compensation of victims is an inadequate sanction where there is an intention to inflict harm. The criminal law can be seen as a complementary penalty system to deal with the difficulties created by acts where the offender's gain exceeds the victim's loss.

CONCEPT OF CRIME

How are crimes to be treated from an economic perspective? There are several approaches.

One view is that a crime is simply another species of the economists' concept of an external cost. This is the position taken by Gary Becker in his seminal article on crime.[1] Crime is essentially a tort, and the economic goal of criminal law is to impose the external costs inflicted by the perpetrator. *A* steals *B*'s vehicle and is caught, and *A* should either return it or pay its market value as compensation plus the costs incurred in detecting and prosecuting the offence. That is, a fine equal to the victim's loss plus enforcement costs is seen as sufficient punishment. Further, it suggests a morally neutral position, as Becker's analysis takes into account the utility that the thief (or murderer or rapist) derives from his coercive and possibly violent act. Becker takes the offender's gain into account and thus takes no moral position on act of crime.

A moment's reflection suggests that this view of crime cannot be correct. If the only penalty associated with a theft is to pay the profit the buyer would have made from selling the vehicle then there would be little reason to purchase goods. Thieves would not necessarily be deterred from committing crimes because there is no reason to believe that their gain from the coercive act does not exceed the victim's loss. Compensatory damages are insufficient. Crimes such as murder, rape and assault which are intentionally committed and reflect a decision by the criminal to by-pass the market and consensual arrangements in situations of low transactions costs. The utility the offender receives from these coercive acts may well outweigh the damage done to the victim and the costs of catching and convicting him. If a criminal is required only to compensate his victim he will be indifferent between criminal coercion and consensual exchange. Such a penalty would not convey the right incentives because it would not induce the prospective criminal to substitute the voluntary transaction for a coercive one.

[1] G. S. Becker, 'Crime and Punishment: An Economic Approach', 76 *Journal of Political Economy*, 167–217 (1968).

On the other hand, it is clear that some actions labelled as 'criminal' do have social value and generate benefits to those committing them which society regards as legitimate.

One approach is to distinguish 'crimes' on the basis of whether they are associated with unproductive and productive activities, the former implying unconditional deterrence and the latter conditional deterrence and the idea of an 'efficient offence'.

'Unproductive' crimes can be defined as those solely motivated by the criminal's desire to circumvent the market and consensual exchange in order to redistribute wealth coercively, or injure property or person, in situations of low transactions costs. They are not associated with otherwise productive activity, and therefore do not have offsetting social or wealth-creating benefits. In these cases, two things follow:

1. the utility or gain to the offender should not be taken into account when assessing the efficiency of the act and the appropriate response; and
2. the act should be unconditionally deterred so as to force the 'transaction' from a coercive to a voluntary consensual exchange.

This is the position taken by Posner, who proposes that there should be unconditional deterrence of intentional coercive acts which substitute for market – i.e. consensual, transactions.[2] The purpose of criminal sanctions – which must exceed the offender's gain – is to force criminals not to commit the crime and substitute a market transaction. This goes some way to explaining why some acts are labelled as 'criminal'. They are ones where it would be relatively easy for there to be substitute voluntary transactions, and their commission indicates that *ex post* compensatory damages would be an insufficient deterrent. This, in turn, implies the need for additional sanctions and different penalty structures.

On the other hand, there are many actions and harms labelled as 'criminal' that are associated with productive and otherwise legitimate activities. Such crimes are incidental by-products of otherwise socially useful or wealth-creating activities, where the gain to the offender is regarded as legitimate, or there are reasons which mitigate the offence. The speeding father-to-be, or the theft driven by necessity, such as the lost hungry stranger who breaks into a house to get food, are examples. Breaches of many statute laws are crimes but are associated with productive activity where an economist would balance the offender's gains against the external costs. Here the concept of an efficient offence and optimal level of

---

[2] Posner, *Economic Analysis of Law*, 6th edn., Gaithersburg, MD: Aspen Publishers, 2003, chapter 7. Posner's view of unconditional deterrence of attempts to circumvent the market is equivalent to ignoring the criminal's utility.

lawbreaking are appropriate notions, as they are in tort. This implies that for these offences the penalty should be related to the victim's loss, and deterrence should not be unconditional. For example, price fixing in the UK, USA and many other jurisdictions is a criminal offence. It is a crime which takes place in settings of low transactions costs but it is one where the sanction proposed by Posner and others is conditional deterrence, with the optimal fine set at the consumer's loss (adjusted upwards by a damage multiplier to take into account the less than certain detection).[3]

There is another set of crimes which runs against the grain of economic considerations. In the past and present many types of market activity have been criminalised – such as speculation, gambling, futures trading, touting, black marketeering, insider trading, prostitution and selling body parts, blood and babies. These generate economic and social benefits (and no doubt some costs) and are often victimless crimes. Take insider trading, which is somewhat of a cause *célèbre* among economists. Insider trading, the use of non-public price sensitive information, is a criminal offence in many countries. Many economists disagree, seeing it as (a) efficiency enhancing and (b) a crime with no real victims. However, it is nonetheless an (efficient) crime.

It would seem that in practice the label 'criminal' is applied to a diversity of acts which have different economic features, some of which justify the label and others not. It is clear that society does take a normative view of crime based on 'ethical' judgments about what are legitimate sources of utility, gain, or happiness and those that are not. On this interpretation the label 'crime' can be seen to attach to those actions which society or the law regard as illegitimate sources of utility or gain. However, this is not an entirely satisfactory explanatory theory of the criminal law, since many 'crimes' *do* generate valuable and legitimate offsetting gains and many market transactions which are efficient and generate little adverse external costs are criminalised. And, for the economist, such an ethical approach makes a positive theory of crime impossible, because it simply defines away the problem.

Fortunately, the above does not exhaust the factors relevant to explaining why some acts are treated as criminal and others not. Several other reasons have been and can be advanced.

[3] W. M. Landes, 'Optimal Sanctions for Antitrust', 50 *University of Chicago Law Review*, 652–678 (1983); K. N. Hylton, *Antitrust Law – Economic Theory and Common Law Evolution*, Cambridge: Cambridge University Press, 2003 chapter 2 provides an excellent description of the economics of optimal enforcement. Indeed, Posner has talked about efficient cartels and therefore the need for conditional deterrence. R. A. Posner, *Antitrust Law*, 2nd edn., Chicago: University of Chicago Press, chapter 10.

The first is enforcement costs. The view that many crimes should be unconditionally deterred ignores the costs of deterring them. Positive and rising marginal enforcement costs would put a break on unconditional deterrence, even if this were the correct goal.

Some mileage in distinguishing torts from crime can be had by focusing not on offender gains and utility but on the way the law is enforced. The common law is privately enforced by victims of torts who bring and finance a claim against the tortfeasor. This is often straightforward since the person inflicting the loss is easy to identify. However, for most criminal acts the identity of the offender is not obvious and most criminals intentionally conceal their identity. Thus the cost of identifying the criminal tends to be high whereas for torts, whether unintentional or intentional ones such as nuisance, the costs of detecting the injurer are low. A system totally reliant on victim enforcement would therefore struggle to detect the offender whose identity is not initially known and bring him or her before the courts. The costs of private enforcement will thus be much higher than for many torts, and the effectiveness of the law in deterring concealable acts much lower, because many crimes will go unpunished.

Under this approach the concealability of the criminal's identity makes public enforcement more efficient than victim enforcement. Put more technically, there are economies of scale in law enforcement which make public (monopoly) enforcement more cost-effective. Ball and Friedman have made this argument.[4] According to them, an act is classed as 'criminal' because public enforcement is more cost-effective than victim enforcement. A major implication of this hypothesis is that one would expect to see private enforcement where the identity of the offender was easily determined by the victim. Thus contract and tort law are victim enforced because the injurer is known. Murder is a crime because victim enforcement is inefficient.

Concealability has another implication. It means that the optimal penalty must generally be some multiple of the harm to the victim. However, as we shall see, if multiple damages are imposed and paid to victims there will be overenforcement of the law and excessive litigation. Criminal law 'decouples' the penalty from victim compensation, and avoids this inefficiency.

Another possible and related reason is that criminal law allows for non-monetary sanctions which are necessary to deal with the insolvency of criminals. Many crimes are committed by the poor, less well off, or are of

4 H. V. Ball and L. M. Friedman, 'The Use of Criminal Sanctions in the Enforcement of Economic Legislation: A Sociological View', 17 *Stanford Law Review*, 197–223 (1965).

such a character that the perpetrator could not compensate his victim if caught. For such individuals the threat of compensatory damages – and, indeed, fines – would not provide a sufficient deterrent since they know that they will not have to pay. Criminals tend to be judgment proof. The criminal law allows the courts to impose non-financial penalties to deal with the judgment proof criminals. Criminals face the prospect of custodial or supervisory sanctions which are not available as a remedy to the successful claimant in a civil action, and for those who are solvent the possibility of what are exemplary (punitive) damages, which are rarely available in civil actions.

DETERRENCE

As one would expect, the economic approach to crime is based on the assumption that criminals and other actors in the criminal justice system are rational and respond in predictable ways to changes in costs and benefits. The decision to engage in crime is seen as no different in character from that of choosing a job. An individual participates in criminal activity because it offers a stream of net benefits greater than that of legitimate uses of his time and effort. 'Persons become "criminals"', states Becker, 'not because their basic motivations differ from that of other persons, but because their benefits and costs differ'.[5]

A corollary to this economic view of criminal behaviour is that any factor which reduce the expected returns to criminal activity will, other things equal, reduce the criminal's level of participation in illegitimate activities. The punishment meted out by the criminal justice system is viewed as 'tax' or 'price'. Just as a tax or increase in the price of a good tends to decrease the quantity consumed of that good, so an increase in the penalties imposed by the law will decrease the level of crime.

The economic approach to crime differs from the applications elsewhere in this book because it is largely empirical and concerned with the effects of the law rather than its rules and remedies. Its principal use has been to derive testable predictions about the response of criminals to various forms of punishment and to organise data for statistical testing of the deterrence hypothesis.[6] This has generated a large body of literature and empirical evidence on questions of deterrence, the operation of the criminal justice system, police effectiveness and the costs and benefits of

[5] Becker, 'Crime and Punishment', 167–217.
[6] L. Ehrlich and R. A. Posner, 'An Economic Analysis of Rulemaking', 3 *Journal of Legal Studies*, 257–286 (1984).

crime control. Beginning with the work of Isaac Ehrlich[7] in the USA, there have been literally hundreds of statistical studies broadly confirming the economists' deterrence model.[8] Moreover, these studies have often provided estimates of the impact on crime of changes in enforcement activity and penalties.[9]

For example, David Pyle's statistical study of property crime in Britain finds that criminal sanctions deter.[10] Within an explicitly formulated economic model of crime, Pyle examined the impact on the incidence of property crime of changes in key enforcement variables (the number of police, conviction rate and length of imprisonment), the economic gains from illegal activity and the unemployment rate. The results supported the predictions of the economic model; those variables which increased the expected penalty tended to reduce the incidence of property crimes, while those which increased the gains to illegal activity or decreased the gains to legitimate activity had the opposite effect. Pyle's statistical findings are reproduced in figure 6.1. They indicate the impact of a 10 per cent increase in each enforcement variable on the rate of property crime.

Results such as those calculated by Pyle are valuable inputs into evaluating the cost-effectiveness of different policies to reduce crime. Table 6.1 matches Pyle's statistical findings with the costs of each enforcement activity in achieving a 1 per cent reduction in the incidence of property crime. They show clearly that reducing crime by employing more police is not cost-effective. To achieve a 1 per cent reduction in property crime by greater policing would require an annual expenditure of over £51 million. This is ten times the cost of achieving the same reduction through an increase in the imprisonment rate or the length of imprisonment.

This type of research has extended to the 'death penalty' to resolve the thorny question of whether there is statistical evidence that capital punishment has a deterrent effect. The first such statistical study, by Isaac Ehrlich,[11] estimated that one extra execution annually led to eight fewer murders. This attracted considerable notoriety and deep controversy because Ehrlich's

---

[7] I. Ehrlich, 'Participation in Illegitimate Activities: A Theoretical and Empirical Investigation', 81 *Journal of Political Economy*, 521–564 (1973).

[8] S. Cameron, 'The Economics of Crime and Deterrence: A Survey of Theory and Evidence', 41 *Kyklos*, 301–323 (1988).

[9] D. J. Pyle, *The Economics of Criminal Law and Law Enforcement*, London: Macmillan, 1983.

[10] R. A. Cart-Hill and N. B. Stern, *Crime, The Police and Criminal Statistics*, London: Academic Press, 1979; D. J. Pyle, 'An Economic Model of Recorded Property Crimes in England and Wales', University of Leicester, PhD thesis, 1984; D. J. Pyle, 'The Economics of Crime in Britain', 9 *Economic Affairs*, 6–9, December 1988–January 1989.

[11] I. Ehrlich, 'The Deterrent Effect of Capital Punishment: A Question of Life and Death', 65 *American Economic Review*, 397–417 (1975).

Table 6.1 *Estimated costs of reducing property crimes by 1 per cent*

	Policy option	Cost (£ million)
Either	Increase number of police officers[a]	51.2
or	Increase number of people sentenced to imprisonment[b]	4.9
or	Increase average length of imprisonment[b]	3.6

Notes: [a] The costs of employing an additional police officer is estimated as £16,000 per annum
[b] The costs of keeping someone in prison is estimated to be £15,000 per annum.
Source: D. J. Pyle 'The Economics of Crime in Britain', *Economic Affairs* 9, December 1988–January 1989, 6–9.

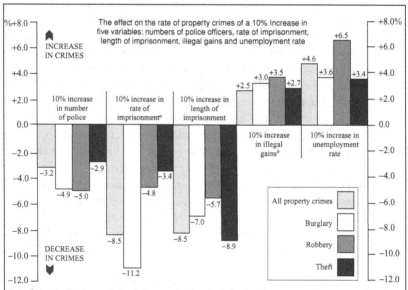

Notes: [a] The rate of imprisonment refers to the proportion of convicted offenders who are sentenced to immediate imprisonment.
[b] An increase in illegal gains or profits from crime, is measured by the rateable value per head.
Source: D. J. Pyle, 'The Economics of Crime in Britain', 9 *Economic Affairs*, December 1988–January 1989, 6–9.

Figure 6.1 Elasticity of property crime

research was cited in the US Supreme Court in *Gregg* v. *Georgia*[12] which re-introduced the death penalty in the USA. Wolpin's study of crime rates in England and Wales from 1928 to 1968 similarly showed that when the death penalty existed (it has since been abolished), one execution prevented four murders on average.[13] More recent research using better data and controlling for other factors[14] – such as distinguishing premeditated murder and crimes of passion – finds that in the USA one execution deterred an estimated eighteen murders, with a 10 per cent margin of error – i.e. between a minimum of ten and a maximum of twenty-eight avoided homicides. It should be noted that this does not mean that the death penalty is the most effective or cost-effective deterrent, or the principal explanation of the murder rate. Often the statistical analysis shows that other factors are equally or more important (such as labour market conditions) and that imposing the death penalty is often expensive.

EFFICENT PENALITIES

If criminals are deterred by the penalties meted out by the law, then society must decide on the type of penalties and the levels at which they should be set. For the economist, this will be determined by the extent to which different penalties – fines, imprisonment, community service, etc. – deter crime, and the costs of these sanctions.

Optimal deterrence

The concept of optimal deterrence has already been explained. The expected penalty influences a criminal's actions and is the product of two elements: the severity of the sanction and the frequency with which it is imposed. By multiplying these two we get the *expected* penalty. Thus if the penalty is a fine of £200 and only 50 per cent of offenders are apprehended and convicted, then the expected penalty is £100 ($0.5 \times £200 = £100$). If criminals are risk neutral, the same level of deterrence can be achieved by reducing either the level of the fine or its certainty, provided that there is a compensating increase in the other. Thus a 50 per cent chance of a

---

[12] *Gregg* v. *Georgia* (1976) 428 U.S. 153, Supreme Court.
[13] K. I. Wolpin, 'An Economic Analysis of Crime and Punishment in England and Wales, 1894–1967', 86 *Journal of Political Economy*, 815–840 (1978).
[14] H. Dezhbakhsh, P. H. Rubin and J. M. Shephard, 'Does Capital Punishment Have a Deterrent Effect? New Evidence from Postmoratorium Panel Data', 5 *American Law & Economics Review*, 344–376 (2003).

£200 fine brings about the same level of deterrence as a 25 per cent chance of a £400 fine (assuming that criminals are risk neutral). In each case the expected fine is £100. The proposition can be stated in a slightly different way: the heavier the penalty, the lower the level of enforcement necessary to achieve the same level of deterrence.

This proposition can be pushed further by taking into account the costs of detecting, apprehending and prosecuting offenders. The optimal combination of apprehension/conviction rate and the severity of the penalty are, in the economic model, solely determined by the costs to society of using them. Apprehending and convicting offenders are very costly, whereas a fine or other penalty deters by the threat that it will occasionally be imposed. Thus the costs of enforcing the criminal law and deterring crime can be lowered by increasing the penalty and reducing the detection/conviction rate.

Cost considerations also suggest the best type of punishment. It is always cheaper to use monetary fines rather than imprisonment or other custodial sanctions. Fines are easy to calculate and involve a simple transfer payment from the offender to the state which can be used to compensate the victim and defray the costs of the police and courts. Imprisonment incurs additional avoidable costs, such as the investment in prisons, the wages of warders and probationary officers and the value of the offender's lost production in legitimate activities. Society gains nothing from this form of punishment when the alternative of costless effective monetary fines is available.[15]

What has been outlined is Becker's so-called 'case for fines'. Namely, the costs of achieving a given level of deterrence can be reduced by lowering the level of enforcement activity and raising the severity of the punishment. Further, the punishment should take the form, where possible, of high monetary fines because they deter crime costlessly. This leads to the policy prescription of very high penalties many multiples of the harm inflicted and a relatively low detection/conviction rate. That is, a public enforcement agency which has optimal deterrence as a primary goal will be guided to conserve enforcement costs by adopting a penal enforcement strategy – a 'boil them in oil' approach – which rarely prosecutes offenders but when it does imposes a draconian penalty. For example, if the conviction rate is 1 per cent, then a fine 100 times the damages inflicted would be required to achieve optimal deterrence.

---

[15] A. M. Polinsky and S. Shavell, 'The Economic Theory of Public Enforcement of the Law', 38 *Journal of Economic Literature*, 45–76 (2000).

The above 'case for fines' can be summarised as follows:

- the same level of deterrence can be achieved with a reduction in enforcement activity (policing, apprehension and prosecution) provided there is a compensating increase in the severity of punishment
- punishment should take the form, where possible, of high monetary fines because they deter crime costlessly
- for crimes which have no redeeming features the economic goal should be unconditional deterrence
- for any given level of enforcement activity, the optimal sanction should be increased by the reciprocal of the detection/conviction rate, what in the previous discussion has been termed the 'damage multiplier' – e.g. if 1 in 10 criminals are caught, and the losses inflicted are £100, then the optimal sanction is £1,000 (= £100/0.1).

So why aren't punishments draconian?

It is true that in less developed countries penalties were and are often draconian, and in England during the eighteenth century the death penalty was routinely meted out for offences which today would not be regarded as serious. However, in most industrialised societies the trend has been for the severity of the penalties to decrease, as policing and the Court system have developed in sophistication. This is not to say that penalties exceeding the gravity of the offence cannot be found. An obvious example is the award of triple damages in private actions under US antitrust law and the occasional use of exemplary sentences in English criminal law.

If high penalties deter relatively costlessly, why are they not routinely used? Economic theory suggests some reasons why there is in practice a limit on the severity of fines.

One factor is the criminal's lack of assets and income. This places an upper limit on the effective fine. Many criminals are poor and therefore do not have the money to compensate their victims, let alone the costs that society expends in apprehending them. Where the offender is a corporation, the protection of limited liability places a limit on the penalty that the company is legally forced to pay. Therefore very high penalties will not have a deterrent effect because those likely to commit the crime know that they will never have to pay them. These solvency problems also give rise to collection costs where, for example, bankruptcy or insolvency proceedings must be instigated. Severe sanctions will also have the effect of impoverishing criminals and their families, which in turn may require costly social welfare programmes. In order to deal with these solvency problems non-monetary penalties will be used to deter offences where the appropriate penalty is very high. Since imprisonment and other custodial sentences are costly, it may be cheaper to deter crime by increasing the detection rate and reducing the severity of the fine.

Second, harsh penalties may be nullified by juries and judges. When minor crimes attract stiff penalties, juries may refuse to convict the accused. One argument often made against the death penalty is that juries are more likely to find the guilty innocent because they do not want to inflict such a draconian penalty or for fear that they will erroneously convict an innocent person. Thus instead of having the hypothesised deterrent effect, the high penalty is nullified by those who determine guilt.

Third, severe penalties give rise to increased litigation and other legal costs. The earlier discussion implicitly assumed that proving guilt and sentencing was a costless process. In the real world to establish whether the defendant committed the crime is never an easy matter and, in any case, a system which imposed severe penalties for all crimes would encourage innocent and guilty defendants to invest considerable resources in establishing their innocence: the harsher the penalty, the greater the incentive of the accused has to fight the charge. Since the probability of conviction will in part be related to the quality of counsel and expenditure on the case, a system of high fines will increase the costs of a trial.

Fourth, uniformly high fines will lead to perverse incentives. If all fines (or any sanction) are draconian, prospective criminals will not be deterred from committing more heinous crimes. If stealing a loaf of bread and shooting the baker while stealing the bread both attract the same penalty, the law does little to discourage the more serious crime. Differential fines must, therefore, be built into the criminal penalty system to create incentives to deter the more serious crimes, i.e. to create **marginal deterrence effects**.[16]

Fifth, high fines and onerous prison terms increase crime and enforcement costs. First, draconian penalties for minor crimes will be viewed as unjust and may bring the law into disrepute. The law may in fact encourage crime, since disobedience will be seen as a legitimate response to an unacceptable regime of penalties.

The concealability of crime may be another factor why draconian penalties are not used. Unfortunately, public institutions are not perfect nor do they have perfect information. Establishing the facts and the guilt of the offender is generally a costly matter and inevitably leads to uncertainty as

---

[16] G. J. Stigler, 'The Optimum Enforcement of Laws', 28 *Journal of Political Economy*, 526–536 (1970); M. K. Block and J. G. Sidak, 'The Costs of Antitrust Deterrence: Why Not Hang a Price Fixer Now and Again?', 68 *Georgetown Law Journal*, 1131–1139 (1980).

to whether a guilty person will in fact be tried and convicted. There is also the danger that an innocent person will be convicted, and this may dilute the deterrent effect of high penalties. This is because it reduces the expected benefits of being innocent.[17] However, society may want to deal with the risk of convicting the innocent person differently from the danger of acquitting someone who is guilty.

The arguments made so far indicate that the costs of collecting fines rise with their severity. This suggests that:

- non-monetary sanctions will have to be used where the accused is insolvent;
- a positive detection rate will be optimal to avoid excessive solvency problems resulting from high monetary fines and the costs of custodial sentences;
- lower fines (and other sanctions) with higher detection rates will be required to counteract the tendency of courts and juries to nullify excessive penalties and to deal with doubt about the accused's guilt
- the structure of fines must preserve incentives for marginal deterrence.

These factors apply with equal force to all types of crimes. Two additional considerations limiting the use of severe penalties apply where offences give rise to social benefits.

Many laws are overinclusive, by prohibiting conduct that is socially beneficial. For example, a motorist can be prosecuted for speeding regardless of the reason. But, as we have suggested, the reason is important from an economic perspective. Speeding because one is fleeing a crime is very different from speeding in order to rush one's wife to a hospital or come to the assistance of a friend in distress. If society relied only on high monetary fines it could deter speeding but in the process also deter many forms of socially valuable activity. In practice the police and enforcement officials are given discretion to deal with this problem. Empirical research indicates that this discretion is often exercised to alleviate the undesirable effects of such overinclusive laws. The implication of this observation is much wider than supporting the case for less severe but more certain penalties. Laws become obsolete and prohibit activities that give rise to no harm or to harm that cannot be reduced at reasonable expense. This is particularly true for statutes that regulate industry. Where this is the case the optimal level of enforcement and deterrence is zero. Or, expressed more forcefully, there is a socially optimal level of lawbreaking that results from the imperfections of the law in accurately identifying harmful activities.

---

[17] J. R. Harris, 'On the Economics of Law and Order', 78 *Journal of Political Economy*, 165–174 (1970); D. Wittman, 'Two Views of Procedure', 3 *Journal of Legal Studies*, 249–256 (1974).

Polinsky and Shavell point to another cost which may result from high penalties.[18] So far, it has been assumed that potential violators are risk neutral. This, however, is unlikely to be the case when very large changes in wealth are considered. If individuals are risk averse then a high penalty imposes an additional cost which could overdeter offences which involve some gain to society. For example, consider a motoring violation which inflicts a cost of £10. If the offender is risk neutral then the optimal sanction should have an expected value of £10. To reduce enforcement costs the optimal combination will be a high fine and low detection rate, say a 1 in 10,000 chance of a fine of £100,000. A risk averse person will value this uncertain penalty at more than £10 because he or she attaches disutility to uncertain variations in his or her wealth. Consequently, a penalty with an expected value of £10 may be subjectively valued by a risk averse person at £11 or more, and hence deter some socially beneficial offences. These risk bearing costs can be reduced by lowering the fine and increasing the detection/conviction rate. This, however, increases enforcement costs requiring a balance to be struck between risk bearing and enforcement costs.

These considerations lead to an extended cost-benefit assessment of fines and other penalties, which waters down the 'boil them in oil' prescription of the simpler model. Nonetheless the basic propositions remain – the choice of enforcement activity and penalties is to be determined by their incentive effects and relative costs.

Actual criminal sanctions

While the operation of the criminal justice system has some economic features optimal deterrence, even taking into account the above modifications, does not seem an overriding one. Indeed, one can confidently say that the criminal justice system of most Western democratic countries falls far short of the type of sanctions suggested by economic theory, implying that there are excessive levels of crime.

One reason is the *ex post* focus of the criminal law. A general principle of the Anglo-American system of criminal sentencing is that the punishment should fit the crime. This is an *ex post* view which fails to take account of the need for the sanctions to deter others from committing crimes and to deal with their concealability. While the courts may sometimes impose a heavy sentence to deter others, the general rule is that the penalty must

---

[18] A. M. Polinsky and S. Shavell, 'The Optimal Tradeoff between the Probability and Magnitude of Fines', 69 *American Economic Review*, 880–891 (1979).

fit – that is, be proportionate – to the crime and not designed to achieve some utilitarian objective such as general deterrence in which the offender is penalised out of proportion to the gravity of the criminal harm he or she has inflicted. This means that, unlike the economic model, penalties are geared to *ex post* notions of severity and 'just deserts', and not *ex ante* adjustments to ensure that expected gains and costs reflect *ex post* ones.

English sentencing practice pays little attention to the uncertainty and costs of conviction. It is concerned with the actual treatment of offenders. The Court of Appeal has confirmed that the prevalence of crime in an area is a proper consideration 'so long as it does not result in a convicted man being made the scapegoat of other people who have committed similar crimes but have not been caught and convicted'.[19] This is in direct opposition to the economic approach, which requires the criminal unfortunate enough to be caught to be a 'scapegoat' to minimise the costs to society of enforcing the law. As is readily apparent, the individual in this schema counts for little; he is valued only to the extent that he is instrumental in achieving the goal of cost-effective deterrence.

There appears to be a clear tension between, the economics of optimal sanctions and the principles of criminal law. This is not to say that deterrence does not play a role in the criminal law, nor that it has no ethical appeal. The economists' prescription that fines be set to unconditionally deter offences may seem unpalatable but it has at least two possibly appealing moral justifications. The first is the old adage that prevention is better than cure. If severe criminal sanctions deter most crimes then society is better off, even though the unlucky criminal who has been caught suffers mightily. Second, the efficient economic penalty structure is equitable or just in an *ex ante* sense. Each prospective criminal knows that if he or she is caught, he or she will suffer a high penalty. *Ex ante* the penalty is fair since all prospective criminals face the same expected punishment and presumably an identical likelihood of being the unlucky one caught if he or she is misguided enough to commit the crime.[20] Nonetheless, justice in criminal law is clearly an *ex post* concept. It must be assumed that society is willing to sacrifice efficiency for these other goals: a trade-off which means that society prefers lower penalties, higher detection rates and more crime than is economically ideal!

---

[19] *Withers* (1935) 25 Cr App. Rep. 54.
[20] For an interesting discussion of the interrelation between efficient and just penalities, see J. Waldfogel, 'Criminal Sentences as Endogenous Taxes: Are They "Just" or "Efficient"?', 36 *Journal of Law & Economics*, 139–151 (1993).

Notwithstanding this, criminal sanctions conform to some aspects of the economic model. First, the fine is by far the most widely used penal measure and has been described as 'the cornerstone of the British penal system'.[21]

The increased used of fines and reduced severity of penalties, such as hanging, transportation and long prison terms since the industrial revolution is consistent with the economic model. In a pre-industrial society it is frequently not possible to fine people because they simply do not have surplus cash. The economic model predicts that as the cost of an enforcement instrument decreases relative to others there will be a tendency to use it more intensively. In England, the conviction rate has increased over time while the duration of sentences has fallen. Although there are a multitude of factors influencing these variables, such as the level of unemployment, one can argue that as the courts have become more sophisticated and the law more developed, the relative costs of deterring crime by conviction have fallen and hence society has substituted a higher conviction rate for lower and more costly custodial sentences.

It is interesting to note that these trends are not as evident in the USA, where penalties tend to be more severe than in the UK and Europe.[22] A possible explanation for this difference is that in the USA the accused has a higher degree of protection afforded by the Constitution and hence the more stringent exclusionary rules governing the admissibility of evidence in criminal trials make conviction and trial more costly to the prosecution. In order to compensate for the lower deterrent effects, penalties must be higher.

MENS REA AND ATTEMPTS

Two other features of criminal law distinguish it from a tort – the much greater focus on intention and a guilty mind (*mens rea*), and the punishment of attempts which do not lead to the successful commission of an offence

Consider attempts. In tort law there is no such wrong as an 'attempted tort', or legal action for near misses in accident cases. It is a system that punishes outcomes where there has been a loss causally related to the failure to act in a non-negligent manner. The criminal law, however, punishes attempted crimes which have failed, been thwarted by the intervention of others, or are simply in the planning stages. That is, it focuses on the act itself and the intention to commit a wrong.

---

[21] *Fine Default*, London: NACRO, 1981, 1.
[22] R. Gillespie, 'Sanctioning Traditional Crimes with Fines: A Comparative Analysis', 5 *International Journal of Comparative & Applied Criminal Justice*, 197–204 (1981).

There is merit in this approach. Punishing both an attempt and an unsuccessful commission of a crime increases the penalty facing the potential offender. The criminal will know that whether or not the crime is successful, there is likelihood that he will be punished and therefore the law deters the act irrespective of the consequences.

Further, in law attempts are not punished as severely as successful crimes. This also has an economic justification in providing appropriate incentives for marginal deterrence. The lesser penalty for an attempt encourages the criminal to have second thoughts and not to seek to blast his way out of a failed robbery. If the penalty were the same, the criminal would not be deterred, in the course of robbery where a shot has been fired, from shooting again and killing someone.[23]

Mens rea is another feature of the criminal law. In the usual tort case, liability is not dependent on whether the injurer intended to cause the accident. In criminal law, it is. Further, the state of mind of the injurer plays little role unless it is shown that he intended to commit the tort, or his actions were so dangerous as to border on a wilful effort to inflict harm. It has been suggested that in criminal law *mens rea* is an indirect measure of the 'elasticity of the response' of the criminal to sanctions. Where the offender did not intend to commit the crime, he or she is not likely be sensitive to sanctions – i.e. punishing crimes which are mistakes or unintended will not generate marginal deterrence. However, where they are intended then the elasticity of the response to sanctions can be expected to be greater, and therefore punishing the offender will generate greater marginal deterrence.

PUBLIC VS PRIVATE ENFORCEMENT

As noted already, a major difference between tort, contract and property law, and criminal law is the method of enforcement. The former are victim enforced while the latter are publicly enforced. Indeed, the relative efficiency of public enforcement is one reason for labelling certain wrongs 'criminal'. The privatisation of law enforcement based on giving those who apprehend criminals a bounty would seem to have all the advantages of the competitive provision of a service – assiduous and cost-effective enforcement. However, the inefficiency of private enforcement is more general, with economic theory suggesting that privatising enforcement is also inefficient.

---

[23] S. Shavell, *Foundations of the Economic Analysis of Law*, Cambridge, MA: Harvard University Press, 2004, chapter 24.

Private enforcement was common in the past. In the nineteenth century individuals who apprehended criminals received bounties or a proportion of the fine, and many statutes were enforced by common informers. Today there is a substantial industry in crime prevention. Individuals and firms often offer rewards for information leading to the conviction of murderers and robbers and it is in general open to any individual to bring a criminal prosecution in England and Wales. The latter is mainly confined to prosecutions brought by shopkeepers against shoplifters. In addition, many breaches of statute which cause injury to individuals often give rise to a civil action for damages and this can be an indirect way of enforcing the law by private means. In the USA, private bounty hunters are still used.

Under common law individuals can bring private actions but there are many practical obstacles. First, the issue of a warrant or summons is a judicial act and the Court may refuse to issue either. Secondly, the private prosecutor must finance the prosecution, may be liable for the costs of the accused if he is acquitted and if the prosecution was irresponsible will expose him to a civil action for damages for malicious prosecution. These cost factors, plus the fact that the individual obtains no remuneration for his services, probably explains why the great majority of prosecutions are brought by the Director of Public Prosecutions (DPP), government departments and local authorities.

However, a more careful analysis of the question reveals that the private law enforcement may lead to inefficient overenforcement of the law.[24] This relates back to the case for fines and the role that a higher fine plays in economising on the resources needed to deter crime. As we saw above, there is a trade-off between apprehending and convicting criminals and the level of fine. Increasing the fine reduces the resources needed to apprehend and convict a criminal to achieve the same level of deterrence. However, if the law was privately enforced an increase in the fine would encourage bounty hunters and private companies to devote more resources to catching criminals not less, because the returns have increased. In short, private enforcement would lead to overenforcement relative to the cost-effective solution.

PLEA BARGAINING

Economic considerations also have an impact on pre-trial and trial procedures. One striking example is the plea bargain. This is the practice whereby the accused enters a plea of guilty in return for a sentence discount. In the

---

[24] W. M. Landes and R. A. Posner, 'Private Enforcement of Law', 4 *Journal of Legal Studies*, 1–46 (1975); A. M. Polinsky, 'Private versus Public Enforcement of Fines', 9 *Journal of Legal Studies*, 105–127 (1980).

USA, plea bargaining is openly practised, it has been estimated that in 90 per cent of criminal cases a guilty plea is entered and it is believed that about 50 per cent of these involve a bargain between accused and prosecutor. In England and Wales, figures are not available because the legal profession and judges have been reluctant to admit that the practice exists.

The plea bargain has a straightforward reason: it is a cheaper way to gain a conviction. The prosecutor, in effect, faces an economic problem: how to allocate his limited resources to dispose of the maximum number of cases weighted by the sentence.[25] A rational prosecutor, given discretion, will set about his job in the most cost-effective manner. Plea bargaining facilitates the disposition of cases. The prosecutor trades a lower sentence for the certainty of conviction and also saves the costs of proving guilt. The accused, on the other hand, is encouraged to plead guilty by comparing the uncertainty of a trial which may impose a more severe sentence if he insists on pleading not guilty with the certainty of a lower sentence if he pleads guilty. If the prosecutor's maximum offer (sentence discount) exceeds the defendant's minimum sentence discount then a guilty plea will be entered. Cost factors drive both parties to seek a compromise through pre-trial settlement.

This explanation for the practice of plea bargaining is not a unique insight gained from economics. Glanville Williams, for example, offers a normative (economic) justification for the practice:

> offenders who have no defence must be persuaded not to waste the time of the court and public money; pleas of guilty save the distress of witnesses in having to give evidence, as well as inconvenience and loss of time and in the present conditions such pleas are essential to prevent serious congestion of the courts.[26]

The value of the economic approach is the additional insights it generates into the effects and factors influencing plea bargains. Specifically, the likelihood of going to trial will increase with: (1) the greater the disagreement over the trial outcome between defendant and prosecutor; (2) the severity of the crime as measured by the potential sentence; (3) the level and availability of legal aid to the defendant; it is (4) inversely related to the length and unpleasantness of pre-trial detention.

The rules of evidence will also affect both the level and sentence discounts of plea bargains. In England, the exclusionary rules of evidence are much weaker than in the USA. All other things equal, this will lead to a

---

[25] W. M. Landes, 'An Economic Analysis of the Courts', 14 *Journal of Law & Economics*, 61–108 (1970); R. P. Adelstein, 'The Plea Bargain in England and America: A Comparative Institutional View', in P. Burrows and C. G. Veljanovski, *The Economic Approach to Law*, London: Butterworths, 1981, chapter 10.

[26] G. Williams, 'Questioning by Police: Some Practical Considerations', *Criminal Law Review*, 325–346 (1960).

higher probability of conviction of defendants in England and, in turn, a lower sentence discount. Thus the disparity between the sentences imposed on those who plead guilty in England to those who insist on a trial will be less than in a jurisdiction with strong exclusionary rules. Also, if criminal investigation and prosecution are integrated into one law enforcement agency, there will be a predictable impact on the number of cases disposed by trial. All other things being equal, the cost saving of a pre-trial settlement is higher for an agency which must bear the costs of both investigation and prosecution. However, once the case goes to trial such an agency will be more reluctant to dismiss the case.

Cost savings are not the only factor explaining the practice of plea bargaining. If both the accused and the prosecutor are risk averse they may agree to exchange a lighter sentence for a plea of guilty to avoid the uncertainty of trial. Plea bargaining is here being used as an insurance device.[27] Plea bargaining can also be used by the prosecutor to screen the guilty from the non-guilty. A guilty person is much more likely to plead guilty in return for a lighter sentence, all other things equal. Thus the practice can be seen as an efficient way of sorting the guilty from the non-guilty. However, this is the case only if all the accused are equally risk averse. If those accused of crimes but who are innocent are on average more risk averse, they may plead guilty simply to avoid the uncertain prospect of a heavier penalty if their case goes to trial. Moreover, prosecutors may engage in overcharging as a way of encouraging defendants to plead guilty. They may bring a number of unjustified charges in order to encourage the accused to believe that the sentence discount that is being offered is large and generous. This effectively imposes a surcharge on going to Court and may result in those preferring a trial to get a stiffer sentence to deter trials rather than crimes; that is, the innocent 'crowd out' the guilty in criminal proceedings and more resources are spent on trying innocent people.[28]

Widespread plea bargaining has another effect on the procedures of criminal law. It is a principle that in criminal cases the guilt of the defendant must be proved beyond a reasonable doubt. It is, however, a mistake to treat the burden of proof in practice as identical to that laid down by law. Plea bargaining has the effect of reducing the standard of proof required to gain a conviction. This is because the prosecutor is able to trade doubt (and poor evidence) about the accused's guilt for a lower sentence.

---

[27] G. M. Grossman and M. L. Katz, *Plea Bargaining and Social Welfare*, 73 *American Economic Review*, 749–757 (1983).
[28] E. M. Noam, 'Blindfolded Justice led by the Invisible Hand', 3 *Law & Policy*, 490–501 (1981).

FURTHER TOPICS AND READING

- The economics of crime has a well-developed theoretical and empirical literature: I. Ehrlich, 'Crime, Punishment, and the Market for Offenses', *Journal of Economic Perspectives*, 43–67 (1986); D. J. Pyle, 'The Economic Approach to Crime and Punishment', 6 *Journal of Interdisciplinary Studies*, 1–22 (1995); G. S. Becker and W. M. Landes (eds.), *Essays in the Economics of Crime and Punishment*, New York: Columbia University Press, 1974; W. Anderson, *The Economics of Crime*, London: Macmillan, 1976; D. J. Pyle, *Cutting the Costs of Crime*, Institute for Economic Affairs, 1995; A. M. Polinsky and S. Shavell, 'The Public Enforcement of Law', 38 *Journal of Economic Literature*, 45–76 (2000).

- The economics of crime differs from that of the rest of the common law, as it tends to focus on deterrence and the empirical testing of deterrence models rather than the principles of criminal law. Paradoxically, the economic analysis of criminal law has remained relatively underdeveloped: C. G. Veljanovski, 'Economics of Criminal Law and Procedure', 23 *Coexistence*, 137–153 (1986); F. H. Easterbrook, 'Criminal Procedure as a Market System', 12 *Journal of Legal Studies*, 289–332 (1983); R. A. Posner, 'An Economic Theory of Criminal Law', 85 *Columbia Law Review*, 1193–1231 (1985); K. N. Hylton, The 'Theory of Penalties and the Economics of Criminal Law', 1 *Review of Law & Economics*, 173–175 (2005); J. Parker. 'Economics of *Mens Rea*', 79 *Virginia Law Review*, 741–811 (1993).

- The law's distinction between tort and crime has been investigated by a number of authors. A. Dnes and J. Seaton, 'An Economic Exploration of the Tort–Criminal Boundary using Manslaughter and Negligence Cases', 17 *International Review of Law & Economics*, 537–551 (1997); D. D. Friedman, *Law's Order: What Economics has to do with the Law and Why of Matters*, Princeton: Princeton University Press, 2000, chapter 18; S. Shavell, *Foundations of the Economic Analysis of Law*, Cambridge, MA: Harvard University Press, 2004, chapter 24.

- Unlike France, England during the nineteenth century relied on the private enforcement of criminal law. Whether this reflected exclusively a revulsion against the highly interventionist French system of state control or the economics of law enforcement is an interesting issue.

- Organised crime can act as a mechanism for reducing crime levels. There will generally be less crime if it is run by the mob or the Kray brothers than if it is 'disorganised'. This prediction is a simple application of the economist's monopoly model. If crime is 'disorganised', or competitively supplied, we have the commons problem – victims are like fish and criminal activity will increase until the expected returns to criminal activity equal the expected costs. If, however, criminals are organised and controlled by one organisation they will restrict the level of crime to maximise the returns. That is, the monopoly supply of an economic and social bad is preferred for the same reason that it is made illegal for economic goods – it restricts output. J. M. Buchanan, 'A Defense of Organized Crime?', in S. Rottenberg (ed.), *The Economics of Crime and Punishment*, Washington, DC: American Enterprise Institute, 1975.

- A law student's view of optimal sanctions! 'Regardless of the several drawbacks, economics is very useful in analysis and formulation of criminal law. Indeed as far back as 1489, when Old Hall (an institution in west central London for training barristers) was built, the Benchers of this Inn of Court took into account the economic principle of expected penalty for crimes. The fine for being caught fornicating in this Inn's courtyard was twenty shillings and the fine for being caught for the same act in one's room was five times as great. These men were compensating for the decreased detection rates in rooms thus making the expected penalty for copulating equal both in and out of doors'. Essay answer from law student at UCL (early 1980s).

- One area where economics has had an impact is leniency or immunity programmes for price fixers under competition (antitrust) laws. Pricing fixing is a secret activity whose detection is difficult. A leniency or immunity programme encourages price fixers to report the illegal cartel by granting immunity to the whistleblower. This alters significantly the payoff matrix to individual price fixers who compare the gains from overcharging customers by restricting the total and their individual output (market sharing) with the expected costs of being caught. Clearly, if they believe that all fellow price fixers will stick together then they will not react. However, if they cannot trust their fellow price fixers then they may be driven to 'squeal' to beat others to the competition authority. The Prisoners' dilemma game is often used to illustrate the basis of such devices. It depicts the choices confronting two suspected criminals who are being interrogated in separate rooms. The police know that they have committed a crime (say, armed robbery) but cannot prove it. So they offer each the following options. If neither confesses to armed robbery they will both be charged with a relatively minor offence. If both confess, they will be charged and convicted of armed robbery but with a recommendation to leniency. If only one confesses while the other does not the 'squealer' will receive a suspended sentence while the other will be convicted and receive the full sentence. Hence the dilemma – if they trust each other to remain silent they both get off lightly; but if they don't trust each other the best each can do is minimise the worst outcome by each confessing. The action that is individually (and socially) rational is collectively irrational.

- Another topical issue is whether the illegal gains from criminal activity should be confiscated to increase the deterrent effect of the law. R. Bowles, M. Faure and N. Garoupa, 'Economic Analysis of the Removal of Illegal Gains', 20 *International Review of Law & Economics*, 537–549 (2000).

Economic glossary

activity levels Activity giving rise to risk or loss imposing harm. This may be the amount of driving for traffic accidents or the number of firms for pollution and torts.

adverse selection Where an insurance company has insufficient information to distinguish high-risk from low-risk individuals and is therefore required to pool different risks and charge them the same price. This result arises from asymmetric information and creates inefficiency because the price of insurance is too low for high-risk individuals and therefore encourages more high-risk individuals into the risk pool. The problem of adverse selection arises outside the insurance industry.

alternative care Where only one party can influence the risk of an accident or harm.

anti-commons problem Arises where there are a large number of 'owners' who each have the right to exclude and permission obtained to use or exploit the resource. This generates wasteful expenditure in asserting property rights claims and the underexploitation of a resource.

appropriable quasi-rent The difference between the value of an asset in its contractual use and its second-highest alternative use or 'salvage value'.

asymmetric information Where one party to a contract, transaction or interaction is better informed than the other party or parties.

cheapest cost avoider The party who can avoid the costs of an accident or harm most cheaply.

Coase Theorem Proposition that in a world of zero transactions costs the initial assignment of property rights does not affect the efficient allocation of resources.

common property problem Where property is unowned or collectively owned with no restraint on its use it will be overexploited because the resource or asset is unpriced.

competition Where firms and buyers in the market do not have the ability to influence the terms of trade and thus act as price takers.

complete contingent contract   An exhaustive contract which sets out terms, and hence rules and remedies, for every conceivable contractual risk, problem and default. It contains the terms, conditions and remedies which would have been negotiated by the parties. It provides the basis of an efficient contract law.

conditional probability   The likelihood of an uncertain event happening, given the risk of an initial or prior uncertain event occurring.

consumers' surplus   The difference between the maximum **willingness to pay** (**WTP**) and the price actually paid for a good or service.

corrective justice   Rendering to each person whatever redress is required because of the violation of his or her rights by others.

cost-benefit criterion   *see* **economic efficiency**

damage multiplier   A factor by which damages or losses are multiplied to take account of the fact that they are imposed with less than certainty. Generally the optimal multiplier is the reciprocal of the conviction or litigation rate, or $1/c$, where $c =$ the litigation/conviction rate. Thus if 50 per cent of cases are prosecuted/litigated successfully, the damage multiplier will be $1/0.5 = 2$, i.e. a double damage rule.

default rule   Term implied into a contract by the law.

distributive justice   Principles determining the fair distribution of wealth and income in society.

dynamic efficiency   **Economic efficiency** criterion which incorporates investment in new technology and R&D which increases the country's productivity.

economic efficiency   Maximising the difference between economic gains and costs or losses.

economic rationality   An assumption that individuals and organisations prefer, more to less, and maximise net benefits, whether utility, wealth, or profits, as perceived by them.

efficient breach   A breach where the (social) benefits of breach exceed the social costs.

efficient reliance   The level of reliance expenditure or transaction-specific investment which balances the initial costs against the expected return taking account of the probability of breach.

elasticity   A measure of the proportionate responsiveness in one variable to a proportionate change in another. For example, the price elasticity of demand gives the proportionate change in the quantity of a good demanded for a proportionate reduction in the price of the good. Thus if the price falls by 1 per cent and the quantity demanded increases by 2 per cent, the (inverse) price elasticity of demand is 2 and demand is said to be 'elastic'.

endowment effect   Where the initial assignment of rights or entitlements affects the victims' valuation of a tradeable right. This can be based on changes in wealth or different perception of real and opportunity costs (the framing effect)

expected cost/benefit   The *ex ante* value of a cost or benefit where there are risks. It is the product of two elements – the (*ex post*) cost/benefit and the likelihood that it will be realised. By multiplying these two, we get the *expected* penalty.

expected utility   *see* **expected cost/benefit.**

expected value   *see* **expected cost/benefit.**

externality (also **technological spillover, third-party effect, external cost/ benefit** and **divergence between private and social costs**)   Where the action of one person (or persons) affects the production function or individual utility imposing either a benefit or cost on another for which no payment or compensation is made.

free rider   A person who fails to contribute, share, or reveal true **willingness to pay** because they cannot easily be excluded from consuming the good or service in question.

Hand Test or **BPL formula**   Test that determines the defendant's liability based on whether 'the burden of adequate precautions' (B) is less than 'the likelihood of an accident' (P) multiplied by the 'gravity of the harm should the accident occur (L)'. Under the marginal Hand test the defendant's liability is determined when the marginal costs of adequate precaution are less than the marginal expected losses.

holdout problem   Where one party in an existing contractual relation threatens breach solely to obtain better terms.

joint care   Situation where the actions of injurer(s) and victims(s) both influence the level of risk.

Kaldor–Hicks efficiency (also **potential Pareto improvement, hypothetical compensation test, cost-benefit test, wealth maximisation, allocative efficiency, maximisation of joint (producers' and consumers') surplus,** or simply **efficiency**)   Where those that gain can in principle compensate those that have been 'harmed' and still be better off. That is, where the economic benefits exceed the costs, and are maximized. Unlike **Pareto efficiency**, there is no need for the gainers to compensate the losers.

lemons problem   Problem of **adverse selection** arising when the buyers cannot tell good from bad quality. As a result they are willing only to pay for average-quality goods so that the price is too high for bad-quality goods and too low for higher-quality goods. At the average price sellers are prepared only to offer bad-quality goods.

liability Rule   A legal remedy which imposes damages on an actionable wrong.

marginal deterrence   The incremental deterrent effect of an additional sanction, damage, or fine.

marginal analysis   In any activity, to obtain the maximum utility or profit from the available resources they must be allocated so that the marginal benefit from the last unit of a resource devoted to each use is equal to its marginal costs. Thus the maximisation principle not only requires that benefits exceed costs for each activity but that the level of each activity be at a point where the marginal costs of expanding the activity are equal to the marginal benefits. The latter determines the *optimal* level of the activity which yields maximum net benefits.

market failure   Any departure from the perfectly competitive market outcome. The main sources of market failure are **market power**, imperfect information, **externalities** and **public goods.**

market power   Where a seller has the ability to profitably raise price (or other contractual terms) above the competitive level.

mitigated damage measure   Damages calculated as the lost profits when the victim takes the efficient/optimal avoidance measures.

moral hazard   Where (a) the insured can influence the level of risk and the extent of the eventual losses; and (b) the insurer cannot monitor and accurately price changes in this behaviour. Moral hazard arises from **asymmetric information.**

net present value   Present value of a future stream of income discounted by a suitable interest rate.

normative theory of law   An ethical theory of law which identifies just laws.

opportunism   Post-contractual opportunism is where one party seeks to re-negotiate the terms of a contract simply to get a better deal based solely on the sunk costs or lock-in of the other party. Opportunism is most pronounced where one party has made a significant transaction-specific investment or reliance expenditure.

opportunity cost   The value of a resource, asset, or good in its next-best alternative use.

optimal care/deterrence   The level of care which minimises the costs of care and of expected losses. The optimal level of care (and associated risk and deterrence) is given by the condition that the marginal costs of care equal the marginal reduction in expected losses.

Pareto efficiency   A situation where all parties benefit or none is harmed by a reallocation of resources, goods or assets, or a change in the law.

pecuniary externalities   A pure **wealth transfer** which results from price changes rather than real harmful effects reducing the economy's productiveness or individuals' utility.

penalty default rule   Default rule designed to force a party with better information about adverse contractual outcomes to reveal this to the other party. Also described as an 'information-forcing' default rule.

positive theory of law   Theory which explains the law as it exists. This may be either a descriptive theory which explains the legal doctrines and remedies, or an effects theory which predicts and tests for the impact of the law on extra-legal variables, e.g. does negligence reduce the accident rate?

principal–agent problem   Inefficiency arising from misalignment of incentives between a *principal* – such as an employer, shareholder, or main contractor – who delegates to an *agent* – an employee, manager, or sub-contractor, respectively – certain responsibilities and duties in return for remuneration. The inefficiency arises because it is costly for the principal to monitor and verify the actions of the agent (his effort, probity and good faith) and to devise methods of aligning the agent's incentives with maximising the profits to the principal.

property rule   Absolute protection of rights which allows the transfer upon payment only to the holder of his asking price in a voluntary consensual transaction.

public good   A good where consumption by one individual does not detract from that of any other individual – i.e. there is non-rivalrous consumption. The classic example is defence – a standing army provides national defence to all a country's citizens.

rent   A return to an asset, resource, or skill above the competitive level which is not competed away.

rent dissipation   Effect of common property problem as overuse leads to the extraction by users of the rents attributable to the unpriced natural resource or asset. The overuse is attracted by the capture of these rents by users and continues to attract entry and usage until all the rents have been captured by users.

rent-seeking   Socially unproductive efforts to alter laws or public policy motivated by distributive gains.

residual claimant   Entity which receives the difference between the cost of an asset, resource, or business activity and its revenues.

risk aversion   Where a lesser certain sum is preferred to an uncertain sum with a higher **expected value.**

risk neutral   Where one is indifferent between a certain sum and an uncertain sum with the same expected value. *See* **expected cost/benefit.**

static efficiency   *see* **economic efficiency.**

statistical life/injury/deterrence damages   The **willingness to pay** (WTP) of those at risk to reduce the risk sufficient to avoid one future death/injury.

strategic behaviour   Interaction between two or more individuals or groups where there is a recognised interdependence between the two. This leads to actions based on the likely actions of the other party or parties and in strategies to gain an advantage or minimise losses from the interaction.

technological externalities   *see* **externality.**

tragedy of the commons   *see* **common property problem**

transactions costs   The costs of search and trading, and designing, policing and enforcing contracts. There are two broad types of transactions costs – the physical costs of organising trades and those arising from **strategic behaviour**.

wealth effect   Where the level of wealth affects the **willingness to pay (WTP)** or accept payment for a reduction in harm.

wealth transfer   Where a loss to one entity is offset by an equivalent gain to another. Also a **pecuniary externality.**

willingness to pay (WTP)   The maximum amount a consumer or buyer is willing to pay for a good or service.

Select bibliography

The Select bibliography is organised alphabetically in reverse chronological order, so that students may access the most recent material before titles of more historical interest.

TEXTS

Bottomley, S. and S. Bronitt, *Law in Context*, Sydney: The Federation Press (1991); 3rd edn., 2006

Ogus, A., *Costs and Cautionary Tales – Economic Insights for the Law*, Oxford: Hart Publishing, 2006

Mercuro, N. and S. G. Medema, *Economics and the Law: From Posner to Post-Modernism and Beyond*, Princeton: Princeton University Press (1997); 2nd edn., 2006

Spurr, S., *Economic Foundations of Law*, Mason, OH: Thompson-South Western, 2006

Veljanovski, C. G., *The Economics of Law*, London: Institute of Economic Affairs (1999); 2nd edn., 2006

Wittman, D., *Economic Foundations of Law and Organization*, Cambridge: Cambridge University Press, 2006

Dnes, A. W., *The Economics of Law*, Mason, OH: Thompson-South Western, (1996); 2nd edn., 2005

Ippolito, R. A., *Economics for Lawyers*, Princeton: Princeton University Press, 2005

Cole, D. and P. Grossman, *Principles of Law and Economics*, New York: Pearson, 2004

Cooter, R. and T. S. Ulen, *Law and Economics* (1998); 4th edn., New York: Pearson Addison Wesley, 2004

Dixit, A. K., *Lawlessness and Economics – Alternative Modes of Governance*, Princeton: Princeton University Press, 2004

Miceli, T. J., *The Economic Approach to Law*, Palo Alto, CA: Stanford University Press, 2004

Shavell, S., *Foundations of the Economic Analysis of Law*, Cambridge, MA: Harvard University Press, 2004

Landes, W. M. and R. A. Posner, *The Economic Structure of Intellectual Property Law*, Cambridge, MA: Harvard University Press, 2003

Polinsky, A. M., *An Introduction to the Economics of Law*, Gaithersburg, MD: Aspen Publishers (1989); 3rd edn., 2003

Posner, R. A., *Economic Analysis of Law*, Boston: Little Brown (1973); 6th edn., Gaithersburg, MD: Aspen Publishers, 2003

Harrison, J. L., *Law and Economics: Cases, Materials and Behavioral Perspectives*, St Pauls, MN: West Publishing Co., 2002

Komesar, N. K., *Law's Limits – The Rule of Law and the Supply and Demand of Rights*, Cambridge: Cambridge University Press, 2001

Friedman, D. D., *Law's Order: What Economics Has to do with the Law and Why it Matters*, Princeton: Princeton University Press, 2000

Harrison, J. L., *Law and Economics*, St Pauls, MN: West Publishing Co. (1995); 2nd edn., 2000

Malloy, R. P., *Law and the Market Economy: Reinterpreting the Values of Law and Economics*, Cambridge: Cambridge University Press, 2000

Hirsch, W. A., *Law and Economics – An Introductory Analysis,* New York: Academic Press (1979); 3rd edn., 1999

Butler, H., *Economic Analysis for Lawyers*, New York: Academic Press, 1998

Barzel, Y., *Economic Analysis of Property Rights*, Cambridge: Cambridge University Press (1989); 2nd edn., 1997

Drobak, J. N. and J. V. C. Nye, *The Frontiers of the New Institutional Economics*, New York: Academic Press, 1997

Mattei, U., *Comparative Law and Economics*, Ann Arbor: University of Michigan Press, 1997

Miceli, T. J., *Economics of the Law: Torts, Contracts, Property, Litigation*, Oxford: Oxford University Press, 1997

Pearson, H., *Origins of Law and Economics: The Economists' New Science of Law*, 1830–1930, Cambridge: Cambridge University Press, 1997

Tullock, G., *The Case Against the Common Law*, Fairfax, VA: Locke Institute, 1997

Dewees, D., D. Duff and M. Trebilcock, *Exploring the Domain of Accident Law: Taking the Facts Seriously*, Toronto: Oxford University Press, 1996

Harrison, J. L., *Law and Economics*, St Pauls, MN: West Publishing Co., 1995

Malloy R. P. and C. K. Braun, *Law and Economics: New and Critical Perspectives*, New York: Peter Lang Publishers, 1995

Benson, B. L., *The Enterprise of Law: Justice Without the State*, San Franciso, CA: Pacific Research Institute, 1990

Eggertsson, T., *Economic Behaviour and Institutions,* Cambridge: Cambridge University Press, 1990

Malloy, R. P., *Law and Economics: A Comparative Approach to Theory and Practice*, St Pauls, MN: West Publishing Co., 1990

Spulber, D. F., *Regulation and Markets*, Cambridge, MA: MIT Press, 1989

Coase, R. H., *The Firm, the Market, and the Law*, Chicago: University of Chicago Press, 1988

Coleman, J. L., *Markets, Morals and the Law,* Cambridge: Cambridge University Press, 1988

Stephen, F. H., *The Economics of Law*, Oxford: Harvester Wheatsheaf, 1988

Landes, W. M. and R. A. Posner, *The Economic Structure of Tort Law*, Cambridge, MA: Harvard University Press, 1987

Shavell, S., *The Economic Analysis of Accident Law*, Cambridge, MA: Harvard University Press, 1987

Trebilcock, M. J., *The Common Law of Restraint of Trade – A Legal and Economic Analysis*, London: Sweet & Maxwell, 1986

Buchanan, A., *Ethics, Efficiency, and the Market*, Totowa, NJ: Rowman & Allanheld, 1985

Williamson, O. E., *The Economic Institutions of Capitalism*, New York: Free Press, 1985

Ackerman, B., *Reconstructing American Law*, Cambridge, MA: Harvard University Press, 1984

Mercuro, N. and T. Ryan, *Law, Economics and Public Policy*, New York: JAI Press, 1984

Bowles, R., *Law and the Economy*, Oxford: Martin Robertson, 1982

Mackaay, E., *Economics of Information and Law*, New York: Kluwer Nijhoff, 1982

Veljanovski, C. G., *The New Law-and-Economics – A Research Review*, Oxford: Oxford Centre for Socio-Legal Studies, 1982

Posner, R. A., *The Economics of Justice*, Cambridge, MA: Harvard University Press, 1981

Samuels, W. J. and A. A. Schmid, *Law and Economics: An Institutional Perspective*, Boston: Martinus Nijhoff, 1981

Tullock, G., *Trials on Trial – The Pure Theory of Procedure*, New York: Columbia University Press, 1980

Williamson, O. E., *Markets and Hierarchies: Analysis and Antitrust Implications*, New York: Free Press, 1975

Calabresi, G., *The Costs of Accidents: A Legal and Economic Analysis*, New Haven: Yale University Press, 1970

Tullock, G., *The Logic of Law*, New York: Basic Books, 1970

ANTHOLOGIES

Backhaus J. G. (ed.), *The Elgar Companion to Law and Economics*, Cheltenham: Edward Elgar (1999); 2nd edn., 2005

Clarke, A. and P. Kohler, *Property Law – Commentary and Materials*, Cambridge: Cambridge University Press, 2005

Parisi, F. and V. L. Smith (eds.), *The Law and Economics of Irrational Behavior*, Palo Alto, CA: Stanford University Press, 2005

Polinsky, A. M. and S. Shavell (eds)., *Handbook of Law and Economics*, Amsterdam: North-Holland, 2005

Menard, C. and M. Shirley (eds.), *Handbook of New Institutional Economics*, New York: Kluwer, 2004

De Serpa, A., *Economics and the Common Law – Cases and Analysis*, Mason, OH: Thompson–South Western, 2004

Brousseau, E. amd J.-M. Glachant (eds.), *The Economics of Contracts – Theories and Applications*, Cambridge: Cambridge University Press, 2002

Dau-Schmidt, K. G. and T. S. Ulen (eds.), *A Law and Economics Anthology*, Cincinnati, OH: Anderson Publishing Co. (1998); 2nd edn., 2002

Parker, J. (ed.), *Fundamentals of Law and Economics*, Cheltenham: Edward Elgar, 2002

Wittman, D. (ed.), *Readings in the Economic Analysis of the Law*, Oxford: Blackwells, 2002

Ogus, A. I. (ed.), *Regulation, Economics and the Law*, Cheltenham: Edward Elgar, 2001

Parisi, F. (ed.), *The Economics of Public Law*, Cheltenham: Edward Elgar, 2001

Zerbe, R. O. (ed.), *Economic Efficiency in Law and Economics*, Cheltenham: Edward Elgar, 2001

Bouckaert, B. and G. De Geest (eds.), *Encyclopaedia of Law and Economics*, Cheltenham: Edward Elgar, 2000, http://encyclo.findlaw.com/index.html

Sunstein, C. R. (ed.), *Behavioral Law and Economics*, Cambridge: Cambridge University Press, 2000

Mercuro, N. and W. J. Samuels (eds.), *Fundamental Interrelationships between Government and Property*, New York: JAI Press, 1999

Posner, E. A. (ed.), *Chicago Lectures in Law and Economics*, New York: Foundation Press, 1999

Richardson, M. and G. Hadfield (eds.), *The Second Wave of Law and Economics*, Sydney: Federation Press, 1999

Katz, A. W. (ed.), *Foundations of the Economic Approach to Law*, Oxford: Oxford University Press, 1998

Medema, S. G. (ed.), *Coasean Economics: Law and Economics and the New Institutional Economics*, Boston: Kluwer Academic Publishers, 1998

Newman, P. (ed.), *The New Palgrave Dictionary of Economics and the Law* (3 vols.), London: Stockton Press, 1998

Posner R. A. and F. Parisi (eds.), *Law and Economics* (3 vols.), Cheltenham: Edward Elgar, 1998

Pejovich, S. (ed.), *The Economic Foundations of Property Rights: Selected Readings*, Cheltenham: Edward Elgar, 1997

Bouckaert, B. and G. De Geest (eds.), *Bibliography of Law and Economics*, Dordrecht: Kluwer Academic Publishers, 1993

Barnes D. W. and L. A. Stout, *Cases and Materials on Law and Economics*, St Pauls, MN: West Publishing Co., 1992

Werin, L. and H. Wijkander (eds.), *Contract Economics*, Oxford: Blackwells, 1992

Goldberg, V. P. (ed.), *Readings in the Economics of Contract Law*, Cambridge: Cambridge University Press, 1989

Mercuro, N. (ed.), *Law and Economics*, Boston: Kluwer Academic Publishers, 1989

Ogus, A. I. and C. G. Veljanovski (eds.), *Readings in the Economics of Law and Regulation*, Oxford: Clarendon Press, 1984

Kuperberg, M. and C. Beitz (eds.), *Law, Economics and Philosophy – A Critical Introduction: with Applications to the Law of Torts,* Totowa, NJ: Rowman and Allanheld, 1983

Rabin, R. L. (ed.), *Perspectives on Tort Law,* Boston: Little Brown (1976); 2nd edn., 1983

Rubin, P. H., *Business Firms and the Common Law: The Evolution of Efficient Rules,* New York: Praeger, 1983

Cranston, R. and A. Schick (eds.), *Law and Economics,* Canberra: Australian National University Press, 1982

Pennock, J. R. and J. W. Chapman (eds.), *Ethics, Economics, and the Law,* New York: New York University Press, 1982

Posner, R. A., *Tort Law Cases and Economic Analysis,* Boston: Little Brown, 1982

Burrows, P. and C. G. Veljanovski (eds.), *The Economic Approach to Law,* London: Butterworths, 1981

Kronman, A. T. and R. A. Posner (eds.), *The Economics of Contract,* New York: Little Brown, 1979

Siegan, B. H. (ed.), *The Interaction of Economics and The Law,* Lexington, MA: Lexington Books, 1977

Ackerman, B. A. (ed.), *Economic Foundations of Property Law,* Boston: Little Brown, 1975

Manne, H. G. (ed.), *The Economics of Legal Relationships,* St Pauls, MN: West Publishing Co., 1975

Furubotn, E. and S. Pejovich (eds.), *The Economics of Property Rights,* Cambridge, MA: Ballinger, 1974

SURVEY ARTICLES

Katz, A. W., B. E. Hermalin and R. Craswell, 'The Law and Economics of Contracts', in A. M. Polinsky and S. Shavell (eds.), *Handbook of Law and Economics,* Amsterdam: North-Holland, 2005

Kaplow, L. and S. Shavell, 'Economic Analysis of Law', in A. J. Auerback and M. Feldstein (eds.), *Handbook of Public Economics,* vol. 3, New York: Elsevier, 2002, chapter 25.

Cooter, R. D. and D. L. Rubinfeld, 'Economic Analysis of Legal Disputes and Their Resolution', 27 *Journal of Economic Literature,* 1067–1097 (1988)

Cooter, R. D., 'Economic Theories of Legal Liability', 5 *Journal of Economic Perspectives,* 11–30 (1991)

Shelanski, H. A. and P. Klein, 'Empirical Research on Transactions Cost Economics: A Review and Assessment', 11 *Journal of Law, Economics & Organization,* 335–361 (1995)

Polinsky, A. M. and S. Shavell, 'The Public Enforcement of Law', 38 *Journal of Economic Literature,* 45–76 (2000)

Williamson, O. E., 'The New Institutional Economics: Taking Stock, Looking Forward', 38 *Journal of Economic Literature,* 595–613 (2000)

SPECIALIST LAW AND ECONOMICS JOURNALS

American Law & Economics Review
Asia Pacific Review of Law & Economics
Erasmus Journal of Law & Economics
European Journal of Law & Economics
International Review of Law & Economics
Journal of Law & Economics
Journal of Law, Economics & Organization
Journal of Law, Economics and Policy
Journal of Legal Studies
RAND Journal of Economics
Research in Law & Economics
Review of Law & Economics
Supreme Court Economic Review

Index